ASIAN SOCIALISM & LEGAL CHANGE

THE DYNAMICS OF VIETNAMESE AND CHINESE REFORM

ASIAN SOCIALISM & LEGAL CHANGE

THE DYNAMICS OF VIETNAMESE AND CHINESE REFORM

John Gillespie & Pip Nicholson (eds)

THE AUSTRALIAN NATIONAL UNIVERSITY

E PRESS

Asia Pacific Press at
The Australian National University

ANU

E PRESS

Co-published by ANU E Press and Asia Pacific Press
The Australian National University
Canberra ACT 0200, Australia

National Library of Australia Cataloguing-in-Publication entry

Asian socialism and legal change: the dynamics of Vietnamese and Chinese reform.

Bibliography
ISBN 0 7315 3715 7
ISBN 1 9209 4227 0 (Online)

1. Law and socialism. 2. Socialism - China. 3. Socialism - Vietnam. 4. Law reform - China. 5. Law reform - Vietnam. I. Gillespie, John. II. Nicholson, Pip.

340.115

Editor: Matthew May
Design: Annie di Nallo

First edition © 2005 ANU E Press and Asia Pacific Press

Contents

THE DIVERSITY AND DYNAMISM OF LEGAL CHANGE IN SOCIALIST CHINA AND VIETNAM

ENDURING SOCIALIST IDEOLOGY AND PRACTICE

ABBREVIATIONS

ADB	Asian Development Bank
AFP	Agence-France Presse
ALL	Administrative Litigation Law
ASEAN	Association of Southeast Asian Nations
BTA	bilateral trade agreement
CIEM	Central Institute for Economics and Management
CPL	Criminal Procedure Law
CPC	Communist Party of China
CPV	Communist Party of Vietnam
DRVN	Democratic Republic of Vietnam
HCMCLU	Ho Chi Minh City Law University
HEI	Higher education institutions
IT	information technology
JICA	Japan International Cooperation Agency
LNA	Legal Needs Assessment
MITI	Ministry for International Trade and Industry
MOET	Ministry of Education and Training
MOJ	Ministry of Justice
MPS	Ministry of Public Security
NGO	non-governmental organisation
NPC	National People's Congress
ODA	official development assistance
OECD	Organisation for Economic Cooperation and Development
PAR	public administration reform
PRC	People's Republic of China
RETL	re-education through labour
SOE	state-owned enterprises
SAPR	Security Administrative Punishment Regulations
SRVN	Socialist Republic of Vietnam
UK	United Kingdom
UNDP	United Nations Development Programme
USSR	Union of Soviet Socialist Republics
WTO	World Trade Organisation

Contributors

Bui Thi Bich Lien was a Lecturer at Hanoi Law University from 1993 until 2003. She is now practising law at the Vietnam International Law Firm (VILAF—Hong Duc).

Sarah Biddulph is Associate Director (China) of the Asian Law Centre at the University of Melbourne. She is a graduate of Sydney University in Law and Chinese Studies. Her research and teaching interests are Chinese law and society and administrative law.

Yet Bryant is a Senior Lecturer in the Faculty of Law at Monash University. Her research interests include environmental law, international law, planning law and civil procedure. She has a particular interest in Vietnamese environmental law and building and construction law.

Michael Dowdle is from the Regulatory Institutions Network of the Research School of Social Sciences at the Australian National University. Michael works on issues of Chinese and comparative constitutional and public law development. He has taught at Columbia University, New York University, and Beijing University; and for the summer of 2002 was appointed to the Qinghua (Tsinghua) University Law Faculty as the Himalayas Foundation Distinguished Visiting Professor in comparative constitutional law.

Adam Fforde is Principal Fellow of the Melbourne Institute of Asian Languages and Societies at the University of Melbourne. He has spent over two decades researching Vietnam and the Vietnamese economy. He has combined this with a range of consultancy and humanitarian activities. He is interested in a wide range of matters related to contemporary issues of development and development policy, and also modern Vietnam studies.

John Gillespie is Associate Professor of the School of Law at Deakin University. He is a graduate in Science and has a Master of Laws from Monash University. He is the editor of *Commercial Legal Developments in Vietnam: Vietnamese and Foreign Commentaries* (Butterworths Asia, 1997) and has written numerous articles on commercial law and law reform in Vietnam.

Peter Hansen lectures in the History of Asian Christianity at the Catholic Theological College, Melbourne. He graduated in Law from the University of Melbourne in 1978. He practised in Sydney and Melbourne until the end of 1988, thereafter studying for the Catholic priesthood, and was ordained a priest of the Archdiocese of Melbourne in 1996. From 1990-1993, he worked in refugee camps in Hong Kong and the Philippines, providing legal advice to Vietnamese Asylum Seekers. He has since been an annual visitor to Vietnam, and in 2000 completed an M.A. at Monash

University on aspects of the history of Vietnamese Church-State relations. He is the Executive Director of the Mary of the Cross Centre in Fitzroy, a drug and alcohol treatment Centre providing services particularly to members of Melbourne's Vietnamese community.

Brad Jessup graduated from Monash University in 2001 with Honours degrees in Law and Science. Brad complements his research interest in the development and implementation of international environmental law working as a lawyer in private practice with a leading Australian commercial law firm. He specialises in international and Australian environmental law and Australian planning law.

Nguyen Hung Quang is Director of NH Quang and Associates, Vietnam, based in Hanoi. A graduate of the Hanoi Law University, Quang is a member of the Vietnam Lawyers Association and the Hanoi Bar Association. His interests include advocacy generally and commercial law, civil law, taxation and labour law.

Pip Nicholson is Associate Director (Vietnam) of the Asian Law Centre at the University of Melbourne. A graduate in Law and Arts from the University of Melbourne with a Masters in Public Policy from the Australian National University, Pip teaches on the Vietnamese legal system, comparative law and Australian pulic law. Pip's doctoral research focused on the Vietnamese court system between 1945 and 1976, in the course of an analysis of the extent to which the Vietnamese legal system mirrored or diverged from its Soviet parent. Her recent research interests include Vietnamese court reform, legal reform, comparative legal theory and legal consciousness in Vietnam.

Pham Duy Nghia graduated from the University of Leipzig, Germany in 1988 (magna cumlaude) and earned his PhD degree from that School in 1991. He is Head of the Business Law Department at the Vietnam National University, Hanoi. He was visiting scholar at the Japan Institute for Invention and Innovation (1997), Stanford Law School (1998), Max Planck Institute for Foreign and International Private Law (Hamburg, 2001) and was most recently a scholar at Harvard Law School (2002-2003). He is a member of the Vietnam Bar Association and arbitrator of the Vietnam International Arbitration Centre (VIAC).

Elizabeth St George recently completed her doctoral dissertation on education and policy implementation in Vietnam, with the Australian National University. Between 1999 and 2003 she worked with the government of the Lao PDR on public administration reform and development policy. She currently works in similar fields in Hanoi.

Kerstin Steiner is a Doctoral candidate at the Asian Law Centre, Faculty of Law, The University of Melbourne. She completed her undergraduate law degree in Germany before coming to Australia and pursuing her interest in international law, comparative law and Asian law. She holds a Master of Laws from the University of Melbourne.

Chao Xi is a doctoral candidate at the School of Oriental and African Studies (SOAS), University of London. He is also a part-time lecturer of the University of London LLM program and research assistant of the Centre of East Asian Law (CEAL), SOAS. He now serves as the vice-president of the United Kingdom Chinese Law Association (UCKLA).

Martin Painter is Associate Professor of the Department of Public and Social Administration at the City University of Hong Kong. He previously worked at the University of Sydney, where he was Head of the Department of Government and Public Administration from 1996 to 2000. He studied for his undergraduate and postgraduate degrees at the University of Sussex and the Australian National University. He has held visiting positions at the University of Oxford, the Australian National University and Queen's University Canada. In 2000 he took on the role of Principal Researcher, Building Institutional Capacity in Asia Project at the Research Institute for Asia and the Pacific at the University of Sydney.

Preface

Vietnam and China have occupied an important place in Australia's history. The Chinese came very early to the nascent colonies and the Vietnamese came in increasing numbers, particularly over the last three decades. They have formed large and vibrant communities in Melbourne, greatly enriching the life of the city. It is not surprising that Melbourne is also home to some of Australia's, indeed the world's, leading specialists in the field of Vietnamese and Chinese law. This book is the welcome product of a conference organised by two of the Vietnam specialists. Using the pooled resources of Deakin Law School and the University of Melbourne Law School, a conference about 'Law and Governance: Socialist Transforming Vietnam' was held during 11–13 June 2003. Vietnam experts joined leading Chinese law scholars to debate the many meanings of socialism and its dynamic transformations within Asia. This book, which evolved from those conference discussions, will be essential reading for legal specialists and policymakers interested in the development of law and governance in Asian Socialist states.

I had worked with Associate Professor John Gillespie of Deakin Law School on an earlier project with the Australian International Legal Cooperation Committee (AILEC), which focused its attention on developing links with Vietnam, Cambodia and Laos between 1993 and 1997. John was the driving intellectual force behind a Conference in Hanoi that resulted in the publication *Commercial Legal Development in Vietnam: Vietnamese and foreign commentaries* in 1997.[1] Pip Nicholson was also at that Hanoi Conference, in the early stages of her research program on the role of the courts in Vietnam. Later she would join the Asian Law Centre at the University of Melbourne, adding a formidable expertise on Vietnam to the Centre's program, which already was a strong base for teaching and research on China. The value of their contribution to academic life in Melbourne is borne out by the quality of the papers delivered at the conference and reworked for publication here. There had not been much collaborative scholarship produced on Vietnamese law between the Hanoi and Melbourne Conferences, although individuals have produced key analyses of specific areas. This book will fill a void. The publication also debates how to compare and contrast Chinese and Vietnamese legal change.

The joint editors have written a lengthy introductory chapter outlining the themes of the publication and the key arguments of each contributor. I will not try to précis their work. What stands out, however, is the range of inputs into the process of law-making in Vietnam and China, the complexity of Vietnamese and Chinese society and politics, and the importance of a historical perspective when analysing both states. It also brings out the Vietnamese government's persistent endeavours to maintain its independence in charting the future role of law in their country, and the folly of those who conflate Vietnamese and Chinese approaches to law and governance. This volume brings together experts from Australia and overseas to present a range of very interesting interpretations of a complex phenomenon.

The conference was the third in a series of international conferences in which the Asian Law Centre has played a key role. The first, in 2001, was held in Mongolia, opening that hitherto closed system to scrutiny. The second, in 2002, took up the theme of Islamic Law and its impact on the West. The fourth, in 2005, evaluated legal education reforms in Japan at the end of their first year of operation. Each conference has focused the Australian expertise in the relevant area and so far has produced lively exchanges and valuable published proceedings. The Asian Law Centre under Tim Lindsey's leadership is to be congratulated on its choice of strategic themes, its role in bringing diverse expertise together, and its openness to cooperative academic ventures.

China and Vietnam are now the world's first and second largest socialist states. This volume provides the first sustained account of how socialism influences legal development in these countries, by drawing on Confucianism, religion, education, public administration and international treaty practice. The book also provides comparative insights into the similarities and differences in legal development in these countries.

Those who attended the conference will welcome the chance to read the polished versions of the papers. Those who did not attend are about to be rewarded with a rich offering of views on Socialism and governance in two of the world's oldest and most unique civilizations.

Malcolm Smith
Chuo Law School
(former Director of the Asian Law Centre and member of AILEC)
April 2005

NOTES

[1]   Gillespie (ed.), J., 1997. *Commercial Legal Development in Vietnam: Vietnamese and foreign commentaries*, Butterworths, Sydney.

Acknowledgments

On 12–13 June 2003 about 60 scholars, practitioners and 'legal experts' gathered at the University of Melbourne to debate the many meanings and manifestations of Asian transitional socialism. The conference was enabled by the generous funding provided by the Australian Agency for International Development (AusAID), Deakin University and the Asian Law Centre at the University of Melbourne. Deakin University and the Asian Law Centre also supported this subsequent publication.

The discussion was much enriched by the presence of our Vietnamese and Chinese colleagues. AusAID is to be congratulated for bringing Vietnamese academics and scholars to the Conference under the International Seminar Support Scheme. Their support enabled constructive and focused discussions across complex issues, giving participants new ways of understanding governance and legal reform.

The seamless organisation of the conference was a credit to Kathryn Taylor, Manager of the Asian Law Centre. In her inimitably low-key style Kathryn led a team of doctoral candidates, namely Nguyen Hien Quan and Kerstin Steiner, who together looked after speakers and attendees at the conference. Subsequently, this team took on the first edit of the manuscript. We enjoyed working with these keen scholars. Thank you.

We have enjoyed the support and excellent editing of Matthew May at Asia Pacific Press, who, together with Maree Tait, has produced this publication with a minimum of fuss and a great deal of charm.

We wish to thank our families for the many evenings spent discussing Vietnam. In addition, Pip thanks her young children for their many questions and her partner, Stephen McLeish, for continuing to support her absences and idiosyncracies.

Finally, these papers offer diverse views on various contentious subjects. The views expressed are those of the authors and the editors and those thanked are not responsible for them.

John Gillespie and Pip Nicholson
Melbourne
June 2005

1

The diversity and dynamism of legal change in socialist China and Vietnam

John Gillespie and Pip Nicholson

Asian socialist legal transformation is most often considered from a Chinese perspective.[1] Occasionally analysis of Vietnamese socialist legal change is also undertaken.[2] The unique feature of this book is that the contributors seek to tease out the significance of Asian socialist transformation comparatively, looking to the experience of legal change in both China and Vietnam.[3]

Further, this investigation of socialist legal transformation proceeds from diverse perspectives. Many of those investigating how the laws and legal institutions of both China and Vietnam have been reshaped in the recent past write as 'foreign commentators' on legal change. But their investigations sit beside analyses of legal change by both Chinese and Vietnamese scholars. In the case of Vietnam, 'insider' scholarship written and published in English remains relatively rare (Gillespie 1997). The result is a rigorous comparative analysis of Asian legal transformation from indigenous and foreign perspectives.

The studies presented in this book complement the existing comparative literature on legal transformation in Eastern Europe.[4] They focus on the extent to which 'Asian' legal culture, or more specifically the legal cultures of China and Vietnam, reshape or alter the legal changes introduced to enable a market economy and improve governance structures. The studies engage with two core concerns: how to analyse legal change in Asian transitional socialist states, and the comparative transformative experience of particular institutions and laws in China and Vietnam.

The studies chronicle theoretical and practical responses to legal reform as these countries change from planned economies to socialist-oriented economies. In addition to analysing 'legal change', each author engages either expressly or implicitly with meanings of socialism and their implication for legal reform. The studies address how 'socialism' shapes, constrains, enables or is irrelevant to reform in twenty-first century Asian states.

These issues were initially canvassed at the 'Law and Governance: socialist transforming Vietnam and China' conference in Melbourne on 12–13 June 2003. But as Nguyen Chi Dung of the Vietnamese Office of the National Assembly ironically noted there, Chinese and Vietnamese commentators 'travel to the West to discuss socialism. In Vietnam', he noted, 'these issues are not debated. Instead, we look to practical solutions'.[5]

SOCIALISM VARIOUSLY CONFIGURED

The diversity of opinions about socialism presented here mirrors the many ways it is debated and understood in the twenty-first century, both by comparative scholars and those living within socialist systems. Some authors adopt working definitions of socialism that reflect Soviet Marxist-Leninist doctrine, which they argue was adopted into China and Vietnam during the early days of their revolutions (Gillespie, Chapter 3; Nghia, Chapter 4; Chao Xi, Chapter 5; St.George, Chapter 6; Bui, Chapter 7; Nicholson, Chapter 8; Nguyen and Steiner, Chapter 9; and Biddulph, Chapter 10). Others leave issues of doctrine to one side and frame their discussion in terms of power (Painter, Chapter 12; and Hansen, Chapter 14). One contributor attributes legal change to 'palace wars' between competing Party and state factions in which socialist norms have little impact on legal outcomes (Dowdle, Chapter 2). Still other authors adopt an essentially non-socialist perspective, framing the analysis in terms of economic policy change—the shift from planned to mixed-market economies (Fforde, Chapter 11; Bryant and Jessup, Chapter 13).

Authors differ not only in the way they conceptualised socialism (theoretically, power relations or economic change), but also in whether they think socialism is adapting to social change. There is a point when the meaning ascribed to socialist values changes so much from the Marxist-Leninist canon that they can no longer be considered socialist. But ascertaining when this point is reached depends much on the observer's judgment about the characteristics and utility of socialism.

Although few authors attempt normatively to define socialism, every author employs implicit understandings about its ongoing social relevance. The mixed views about the dynamism and contemporary relevance of socialism contrast with a general Western perception that capitalism adapts to new conditions. Few would argue, for example, that Western welfare states are no longer capitalist because they have abandoned Adam Smith's *laissez faire* prescriptions. Yet many assert that socialist states are no longer socialist because mixed-market reforms have overtaken planned economies.

The way authors conceptualise socialism, at least in part, influences their conclusions about its ongoing relevance. For example, Dowdle (Chapter 2) uses a static, or epistemologically closed, definition of socialism that leaves little space for change and adaptation. On the other hand, authors examining legal and state institutions (St. George, Chapter 6; Bui, Chapter 7; Nicholson, Chapter 8; Nguyen and Steiner, Chapter 9; Bryant and Jessup, Chapter 13) found that certain core socialist ideas about Party leadership, democratic centralism and state economic management remained deeply entrenched even though socialist legality is becoming more law-oriented. Biddulph (Chapter10), Gillespie (Chapter 3) and Nghia (Chapter 4) emphasise the fragmented nature of both Chinese and Vietnamese legal reforms and stress that rights-based economic reforms did not necessarily flow into other social spheres, while Chao Xi (Chapter 5), who focuses on market reforms, argues that socialist theory has pragmatically adapted to new economic conditions without necessarily losing sight of socialist values, such as Party leadership and state economic ownership.

Other authors (Fforde, Chapter 11; Painter, Chapter 12; Hansen, Chapter 14) argue that socialist ideas influenced legal and administrative reforms only marginally (if at all). Overall, however, most authors conclude that core socialist values are contextually adapting to new social conditions.

LAW AND MARKETS IN TRANSITION

The authors accept that China and Vietnam have largely changed from planned economies to mixed-market economies where private enterprise is allowed, even fostered, but the state retains a strong management and ownership role. But an economic definition of transition does not necessarily explain legal changes evident in Vietnam and China. While most contributors agree that China and Vietnam have provided a clear vision for economic reform, they believe that sociopolitical reform has either been largely left implicit (Vietnam) or recast rhetorically as a transition to a rule of law (China). They suggest that change is more experimental than visionary and that legal transition remains opaque, sometimes unstated, contested, dynamic and unresolved.

Authors adopt three approaches to the core question of whether socioeconomic and legal reforms are interrelated, unrelated or even mutually constituted. There is not complete coherence within each approach and most authors argue elements from more than one approach. But the threefold classification is nevertheless useful for illustrative purposes. Fforde and de Vylder (1996) have influentially argued in relation to Vietnam that economic reforms were a gradual, pragmatic response to existing social conditions. In other words, the state has struggled to maintain relevance by legitimising 'bottom-up' economic reforms with *post factum* economic policies and laws. Chao Xi (Chapter 5) makes a similar observation regarding commercial legal development in China, with the proviso that legal reforms aiming to unleash private sector development are not permitted to compromise the Party's leadership and the 'socialist road' to economic development. According to this position, laws respond to social pressure for economic reform, but certain state organisational arrangements are shielded from 'bottom-up' reforms.

Occupying a middle position, Gillespie (Chapter 3), Nghia (Chapter 4) and Biddulph (Chapter 10) agree that much legal development responds to a dialogical exchange between the state and society. But Gillespie and Nghia also stress that

Vietnam is proactively seeking access to international capital and markets and has imported commercial laws and practices to secure these advantages. International trade treaties have flattened regional differences between élite-level lawmakers, creating an international legal dialogue that remains remote from, and frequently incomprehensible to, local political and economic ideas. Because imported legal reforms are not linked to underlying social processes, they are unlikely to engage with, and significantly alter, core socialist precepts like party leadership, democratic centralism and collective mastery.

Gillespie and Nghia share this middle position with many other authors who implicitly see market changes as significant, if not catalysts, for change without specifically engaging in the details of market change and its implications for legal reform discourse (St. George, Chapter 6; Bui, Chapter 7; Nicholson, Chapter 8; Nguyen and Steiner, Chapter 9; and Bryant and Jessup, Chapter 13).

The third position does not specifically attribute any great importance to the influence of economic change on legal change (Hansen, Chapter 14). This chapter examines changes in the Vietnamese treatment of religion without situating these changes in an economic context or without seeing them as affected by economic changes.

METHODOLOGIES AND THEIR IMPACTS

The utility of the chapters lie not only in their stories of change and their conceptions of socialism, but also in the diversity of analytical tools used. It is a feature of the chapters that the different analytical approaches generate varying conclusions about the role of socialism in contemporary China and Vietnam. As a result, they not only offer a diverse range of understandings about socialism and its transformation in China and Vietnam, but also display a range of possible analytical approaches.

Dowdle (Chapter 2), Gillespie (Chapter 3) and Nghia (Chapter 4) use variations of discourse analysis to explore undercurrents in socialist thinking. As most legal thought is communicated, discourse analysis captures conflict and change in legal ideas. It shows how long-standing socialist ideas have alternatively resisted and accommodated new concepts. Both Gillespie and Nghia draw ideas from outside legal thinking, such as economic, cultural and Confucian notions, to assess changes in socialist thinking.

Discourse analysis also offers insight into the potential for change. Discursive groups or communities use epistemologies to determine which ideas are acceptable. If the epistemologies governing 'discursive groups' (like the central Communist Parties of Vietnam and China) are inclusive, these authors argue that there is potential for legal change.

Others, such as Chao Xi (Chapter 5), St. George (Chapter 6), Bui (Chapter 7), Nicholson (Chapter 8), and Nguyen and Steiner (Chapter 9), examine disparities between socialist ideology and theory as it is announced and practised. This analytical tool opens the discussion to interactions between officially promoted ideals and governance practices in legal institutions. The 'gap' between law (or policy/ideology) and practice, as identified by these chapters, raises speculation about reform trends. Nicholson, for example, shows that despite rhetorical movement toward judicial independence, the Party retains a tight control over the ideas circulating within the courts and recruitment of judges. She speculates that the state may face agitation for change from the private legal profession. Nguyen and Steiner (Chapter 9), through their analysis of defence counsel, confirm this. They bring the concept of human agency back into the discussion, demonstrating that individuals opposing orthodox socialist ideals (such as democratic centralism) can alter the administration of justice.

Still others, such as Biddulph (Chapter 10), Fforde (Chapter 11) and Painter (Chapter 12), locate change in particular institutional and social struggles. Biddulph, for example, uses Bourdieu's concept of the 'legal field' to argue that local understandings transformed central 'rule of law' rhetoric into state management. In a similar vein, Fforde suggests that reform of state-owned enterprises has been shaped by local struggles between ministries and directors of state-owned enterprises, more than high-level socialist or capitalist ideals.

Finally, Bryant and Jessup (Chapter 13) and Hansen (Chapter 14) use legal doctrine to search for legal change. Bryant, for example, explores the internationalisation of the Vietnamese legal system by examining doctrinal approaches to the 'incorporation' doctrine in international law. For Hansen, the treatment of the Catholic Church in Vietnam can be explained, in part, through a reading of legal texts and through historical analysis of state–church relations. He finds little evidence that socialist thinking in or outside legal doctrines influences freedom of worship.

TRANSFORMING SOCIALISM: CONSTITUTIONALISM, LEGALISM AND CONFUCIANISM

Turning to the first of the chapters that draws on discourse theory, Dowdle (Chapter 2) employs an epistemological study of socialism to ask what is socialist about law in China and Vietnam. He makes the semantic point that every country is entitled to describe their policies as socialist, but questions whether this makes their policies socialist 'in fact'. Dowdle uses the example of constitutional transformation in China and Vietnam to demonstrate that the major legal changes taking place are largely untouched by socialist values.

Dowdle's main contention is that socialist precepts in these countries are discussed in closed epistemological frameworks and, as a consequence, have not significantly engaged and shaped the emergence of constitutionalism. Put differently, discussion about how socialism should transform state institutions is conducted within élite circles that are largely closed to external ideas. Institutions, he argues, have their own epistemologies that determine which criteria to take into account when assessing ideas. Constitutionalism emerged in the United States, Dowdle explains, because the revolutionary drafters favoured the Enlightenment ideal of political knowledge being open to every citizen. They drafted a constitution that made political institutions accountable to public debate.

Though acknowledging their very different political and economic foundations, Dowdle draws parallels between the rise of constitutionalism in the West and in China. Rather than Enlightenment ideals, he argues that political expediency is propelling constitutionalism in China. According to this account, Deng Xiaoping banished his main rivals to political oblivion in the moribund National Congress. But his rivals reclaimed power by bringing the National Congress into the political mainstream. They achieved this objective by convincing the ruling élite that the Communist Party would not have embarked on the disastrous Cultural Revolution and made other grave errors if the National Congress had performed its constitutional function of representing the views of the masses to political decision-makers. The Party made mistakes because, as a closed epistemic community, it lacked access to the wide range of views required to maintain legitimacy and govern a complex society.

Dowdle further posits that socialist ideals are conspicuously absent from the processes shaping constitutionalism in China. He attributes this to the Party's closed epistemological framework and its reluctance to apply socialist ideas meaningfully to contemporary political problems. Dowdle convincingly argues that although constitutional reforms in China were motivated by power politics, rather than the Enlightenment values underpinning Western reforms, once in place, policymaking based on popular representation may create its own momentum. He calls this process 'runaway legitimisation'.

Where he differs from other contributors is in his assertion that socialist ideas have played a minor role in institutional change. Biddulph (Chapter10) and Chao Xi (Chapter 5), on the contrary, argue that, rather than operating like a closed epistemic community, the Chinese Communist Party has flexibly adapted socialist ideology to accommodate new institutional settings such as private enterprises and to vary institutionalised practices, such as those within the Chinese police. That socialist values are still guiding legal reforms is shown in the way that lawmakers have preserved Party leadership and state ownership.

Consistent with Dowdle's proposition that power politics can induce constitutional reforms, there is compelling evidence that Party politics is exciting representative reforms in the Vietnamese National Assembly. Certain Party leaders believe that some policymaking power should be transferred to the National Assembly, since only a broadly constituted representative body has access to the range of social views needed to resolve complex problems like corruption and land distribution. In tandem with political pressures, Party leaders are using long-standing socialist principles of 'people's mastery' and 'socialist democracy' that advocate popular supervision of state institutions to justify a more representative democracy. As a recent amendment to the Constitution attests, the state believes that people's mastery is necessary to develop 'a prosperous people, strong country, equitable, democratic and civilised society' (Pham Van Hung 2001:66–9).

It is also interesting to speculate whether differences in the public's respect for the Party in China and Vietnam affect the importance attached to socialist values. There are grounds for arguing that the Communist Party of Vietnam enjoys considerably more public support than its Chinese counterpart (Kerkvliet et al. 1999). There was no cultural revolution in Vietnam to discredit Party decision-makers and only a generation has passed since the Party delivered the country from foreign invaders.

Finally, Dowdle's structural explanations for institutional change envisage possible pragmatic legal reform. Quarantined from underlying political and social discourse that may constrain change, Dowdle argues that Party élites freely accept ideas that provide political advantage. Élites reject ideas that compromise the system that gives them privileged access to power, such as Party leadership, but other reforms, such as constitutionalism, are acceptable because they have the potential to extend power over rivals.

In contrast, Gillespie (Chapter 3) argues, using discourse theory, that while Vietnamese socialist legal thinking has always been fragmented it remains important. At the outset he notes that the Democratic Republic of Vietnam administration borrowed uncritically and extensively from the Soviet Union. While the legal borrowing was comprehensive, its implementation, argues Gillespie, was always mediated by practical policymaking.

Challenges for those commenting on socialist legal systems identified by Gillespie include the need to move any analysis beyond an exclusive focus on socialist legality to include the other equally abstract but significant notions of democratic centralism and collective mastery. It is too easy to miscast the role of law in contemporary socialist states if Western lawyers only concern themselves with narrow debates about changes to socialist legality. Gillespie argues persuasively that, historically, the Vietnamese Party–state variously invoked all three tenets to legitimate its leadership and govern. It is not possible to trace the changes to the role of law and its many implications unless all three precepts are analysed.

Looking to the contemporary period, it is Gillespie's thesis that it is not possible to characterise Vietnamese legal change as consistent across jurisdictions. More particularly, Gillespie contends that an analysis of the way law is legitimated, debated and reformed suggests that the legal discourses within the economic, legal and cultural spheres of Vietnamese society produce very different interpretations, both between the discourses and within them. For example, it is suggested that legal transplantation debates within Vietnam reveal both a continuing instrumentalist conception of law and a local commentary drawing on Western socio-legal insight into the ways laws permute and transform.

While cautious of overcasting his interpretation of the three identified discourse areas within Vietnam, Gillespie ultimately concludes that where law and politics are 'interwoven' politics dominates. For example, he suggests that where the debate concerns the extent to which law will regulate or 'constrain party political power' Western rule of law precepts are not admitted into the debates. In contrast, where the state seeks to regulate emerging market activity Marxist-Leninist conceptions of 'socialist legality' have been adapted to become 'more legalistic and rule-oriented' to enable East Asian developmentalism to flourish. Thus Gillespie concludes that the regulation of the market has shifted from being based upon moral and Party edicts and policies to an increased use of normative laws.

Nghia (Chapter 4) emphasises the role of pre-modern values such as Confucianism in contemporary legal discourse more than Dowdle (Chapter 2) and Gillespie (Chapter 3). Nghia examines the interplay between traditional legal thinking, socialist law and rights-based law in Vietnam. His main contention is that Confucian and socialist precepts continue to provide moral values that bind society and determine the social relevance of law. Like other authors (Gillespie, Chapter 2; and Painter, Chapter 12) Nghia argues that imported ideas have formed hybrids with local precepts and practices.

Although he concedes that Confucian, Buddhist and Daoist values coexisted, Nghia believes that Confucianism created the standard norms for Vietnam's society. He bases this view on work by Vietnamese scholars such as Dao Duy Anh and does not engage with Western scholarship (for example, Giebel 2001) that contests the existence of uniform Confucian values throughout the country. Contrasting with the negligible impact of French colonial legalism, Nghia argues that socialism profoundly changed Confucian thinking. He argues that socialism merged with Confucian values that privileged communitarianism, state management of society and instrumental legalism. These norms continue to play a prominent role in economic regulation. For example, the *xin cho* (application grant) approach to economic regulation is attributable to Confucian-socialist notions of state management.

The introduction of the 'law-based state' doctrine in the 1992 Constitution has not fundamentally changed the underlying Confucian-socialist norms. Even though the Soviet term 'socialist legality' is no longer fashionable, its message that public interests should prevail over private interests, that states should 'manage' (*quan ly*) societies, and that law is an instrument of state power, remains intact. Nghia concludes that hasty legal borrowing has left Vietnam with a 'jungle of law' and that there is much to be learnt from legal borrowing from Japan and Singapore where more care is taken to adjust imported norms to suit local social norms. As an interim measure, he speculates that certain Confucian values could augment and even compete with imported laws to build 'social trust, discipline and order'.

ENDURING SOCIALIST IDEOLOGY AND PRACTICE

Moving from the insight offered by discourse theory, Chao Xi (Chapter 5), St George (Chapter 6), Bui (Chapter 7), Nicholson (Chapter 8) and Nguyen and Steiner (Chapter 9) take up the story of socialist legal transformation in Chinese and Vietnamese institutions. As noted previously, each author invokes the theory–practice gap to investigate how socialism, and more particularly democratic centralism, socialist legality and people's mastery, enable or constrain legal change. In each of these studies the authors explore what is meant by socialism theoretically and then investigate how socialist ideology has been transformed, marginalised or retained.

In examining the development of the enterprise law, Chao Xi contests the view that legal reforms in China have proceeded largely without the benefit of socialist thinking. He shows that the first enterprise law evolved from a series of compromises between socialist ideology and economic efficiency during the 1970s and 1980s. Each compromise eroded the state sector. Enterprise reforms commenced with the creation of joint-stock companies. But these hybrid state–private entities were only permitted to operate in economic sectors neglected by state-owned enterprises. Later, the government sought greater efficiency gains by separating ownership and management over state-owned enterprises. During that period 'the socialist economic road' and Marxist-Leninist theory influenced lawmakers.

More recently, Jiang Zemin informed the National Congress in 2002 that, in order to remain a socialist country, the state must keep public ownership its core economic policy. Lawmakers drafting a revised Corporations Law were instructed to take what was useful from capitalism while retaining socialist principles of state ownership and economic management. The resulting tensions between 'the socialist road' and managerial efficiency produced incremental reforms. For example, although the new Company Law applies to both state and private entities, a complex shareholding system gives the state a controlling interest in an estimated 84 per cent of privately listed companies.[6] In addition, the law permits the Party to establish committees in every private company.

Chao Xi observed that Russian lawmakers were unconstrained by socialist ideology and adopted Western corporate laws with disastrous results (Black, Kraakman and Tarassova 2000). He concludes that 'Chinese enterprise reforms are but a means to bolster socialism and its economic foundations'. Although Marxist-Leninist orthodoxy has conceded ground to economic efficiency, company law remains an instrument used to secure state ownership and Party leadership.

St. George (Chapter 6) identifies a mismatch between Party-stated objectives for the Vietnamese higher education curriculum and the manner in which education is evolving as a partly privatised activity. She analyses the impact of socialist doctrine (defined as Marxism–Leninism with Ho Chi Minh thought) on the development of the Vietnamese 1998 Education Law. Before turning her attention to the Education Law of 1998, she notes the problematic role for law in a socialist state, noting the ways in which the Party has sought to legitimate law as an instrument of 'all' classes rather than as a bourgeois instrument reflective of the capitalist mode of production. St.George's analysis then turns to higher education, and specifically considers the socioeconomic and political role of education.

St George contends that Vietnamese education is cast as 'intrinsically ideological'. She notes that socialism is explicitly invoked as an aim of education in Articles 2, 3 and 23 of the Law and that Article 36 provides that the 'content of higher education' must include the 'scientific subjects of Marxism–Leninism and Ho Chi Minh thought'.

She characterises these inclusions as 'committing the national education system to building socialism in the country, as well as to creating people who are socialist in character'. She also correctly notes that invoking socialism is not a feature of all Vietnamese laws.

Having established the rhetorical commitment of the Party-led drafting committee, St George notes that, in certain vital respects, the law departs from its ostensible commitments to socialist ideology. In particular, she cites the practice of allowing private education facilities and schools to establish their own relations with community (particularly donors) as indicating the dominance of practical politics over consistent socialist policymaking. In relation to fees, she notes that the law is internally inconsistent in allowing no 'commercialisation' of education, but permitting the use of economic activities to generate funds for schools. Looking at the issue of administration of schools generally, St George identifies that the law should be interpreted as much by what is left out as by what was included. She notes that in the final, twenty-third draft the administration of education is dealt with only cursorily. While a leadership role is retained for central government, the law specifically states that educational institutions are to establish their own regulations affecting relations between schools, families and community.

In conclusion, St George contends that Marxism–Leninism and Ho Chi Minh thought feature as the doctrines that should be taught in curriculum and inculcated in students. Yet the practical realities of an educational system starved of funds and straining to accommodate all those who wish to participate has produced a situation where the Party, at least partly, relinquishes control over the delivery of education.

Bui (Chapter 7) argues, unlike St George, that legal teaching remains infused by Marxist-Leninist doctrine. She examines changing notions of socialist law in Vietnam's legal education system. The State Education Development Strategy for 2001–10, she notes, envisages a 'scientific education system with a socialist orientation and nationalist nature. It should be based on the foundation of Marxist-Leninist theories and Ho Chi Minh thought'. The state has the capacity to implement this policy because law courses are well funded and taught by state-managed institutions and staffed by public servants.

She finds that law school curricula reflect Marxist-Leninist theories, but Ho Chi Minh thought is not yet taught. Before studying substantive legal subjects, students are first instructed that law reflects the will of the working class and state economic management (*quan ly nha nuoc ve kinh te*). These doctrines are considered necessary in the mixed-market economy to protect the working class from exploitive capitalism. As Bui observes, even though students are later exposed to subjects about market laws, 'ideologies of state economic management are often well rooted and continue to develop during the four year course'. Since most legal issues are approached from a state management perspective, students soon learn that law's main function is to privilege state interests.

Bui believes that legal education lags behind other social sciences in adapting its curriculum to market conditions. She attributes this discrepancy to the prominence given in legal education to socialist theories that classify 'social relationships' into 'independent law branches'. For example, land law is considered an independent branch because land is a 'special commodity' owned by the state. This classification system constrains teachers from creating new legal taxonomies that reflect the introduction of rights-based laws into the legislative framework.

Bui also shows that structural factors reinforce socialist values. Consensual decision-making used to review curricula discourages teachers from engaging in the controversial debates required to promote reforms. A didactic pedagogy also discourages students from asking questions that may expose gaps between law as taught and actual economic and social conditions. Teaching reforms that encourage problem solving may eventually create more demand for relevant legal instruction. But law teachers have recently been forbidden from working in the legal profession, a decision that distances the most progressive teachers from law-in-action.

She finishes her chapter by considering the impact legal education has on the legal system. University mission statements stress that legal education should improve 'political and moral qualities and the consciousness to serve the people', but neglect to mention the skills required to equip students as members of the legal profession. Only 3–4 per cent of students find work in the legal system, yet legal study is considered prestigious and worthwhile because most students find employment as state officials. Bui gloomily concludes that the purpose of legal education is to train state officials to perpetuate socialist management practices. Her finding that the education system inculcates core socialist values corroborates Nicholson (Chapter 8) and Nguyen and Steiner (Chapter 9), who argue that socialist ideals still profoundly shape decision-making in state institutions.

Nicholson (Chapter 8) examines tensions between long-standing socialist approaches to law and reforms strengthening law-based processes in Vietnamese courts. She finds mixed messages about the trajectory of law reform in the 2002 Politburo Resolution No. 8 on Forthcoming Principal Judicial Tasks. The Resolution reaffirmed decades-old socialist legality doctrine that the Party leads the state. Judges, for example, are enjoined not only to follow laws, but also the Party line. In addition, the Party reserves the right to direct political, organisational and personnel policies within courts.

Counterbalancing socialist legality, Resolution No. 8 also instructs courts to guarantee citizens' equal treatment before the law, real democracy, fair trials based on merit and rights for lawyers to collect evidence and represent clients before and during trials. Broadly reflecting the law-based state doctrine adopted in the 1992 Constitution, these reforms appear to show the Party responding to social demand for more predictable, efficient and transparent courts.

But Nicholson wonders whether lawyers will seize, or be permitted to seize, the opportunity under the new adversarial court procedures to shift judicial decision-making closer to the law; this issue is taken up in the following chapter by Nguyen and Steiner (Chapter 9). Nicholson finds support for both continued Party leadership over courts and a greater emphasis on law-based judicial outcomes in theoretical discourse. She describes orthodox socialist legality as a 'policy–law dichotomy' in which law and Party policy (and state plans) are interchangeable. Applying this doctrine, courts have historically considered law only one means of implementing Party policies. Although Resolution No. 8 reaffirmed the 'policy–law dichotomy', socialist legality is now modified by the law-based state doctrine that promotes self-managed courts, law-based judicial decision-making and an increased role for the private legal profession.

Nicholson reconciles these contradictory positions by suggesting that although in principle courts are expected to follow law, in practice open-ended legislative drafting gives the Party numerous opportunities to direct judicial outcomes by influencing the interpretation of law. She also presents evidence that other socialist doctrines, such as democratic centralism and collective mastery, influence judicial practices. For example, democratic centralism insists on strict top-down judicial decision-making, and vague echoes of collective mastery are discernable in the Party's decision to allow lay people's assessors to judge cases with professionally trained judges.

Nicholson concludes that reforms promoting law-based decision-making in the courts have not displaced long-standing socialist norms such as Party leadership, democratic centralism and collective mastery. But she acknowledges that procedural changes giving courts self-management powers and modest adversarial proceedings may act as catalysts for more far-reaching reforms. A practical confirmation of Nicholson's theorising is found in Chapter 9 by Nguyen and Steiner.

Nguyen and Steiner use the changing role of lawyers in Vietnam to assess the contemporary relevance of socialist legal concepts. They argue that socialist legality and democratic centralist principles imported by revolutionary leaders, extirpated colonial legality from Vietnamese legal institutions. Rather than balancing conflicting rights, courts in the new society followed democratic centralism by vertically implementing Party rules and policies. Independent bar associations established under French rule were closed and most French trained lawyers fled or were purged. The few who proved their loyalty to the new regime became state officials entrusted to implement state policy.

Starting with the 1980 Constitution, which provided for the establishment of organisations for lawyers, the authors argue the state has incrementally given lawyers more autonomy. The Ordinance on Lawyers' Organisations, passed in 1987, paved the way for the reintroduction of bar associations and the possibility of a private (non-state) legal profession. The Ordinance on Lawyers 2001 codified Party policy that acknowledged the role the legal profession play in protecting the democratic and legal rights of citizens.

The authors then assess whether high-level policy has influenced the way state officials administer the interaction between lawyers and clients. They show that lawyers require 'good relationships' and the payment of bribes to secure access to state officials and cooperation to mediate on behalf of their clients.

In the court system, new criminal and civil procedures codes have introduced modest adversarial procedures that now place lawyers on a similar, if not equal, footing with procurators in criminal trials. But the authors note that the judicial practices developed over many decades when judges and procurators dominated trials are unlikely to change without considerable encouragement. For example, they convincingly show that in the notorious Nam Cam criminal trial the state was not prepared to allow lawyers to depart from the prosecution's script and fully represent their clients' interests. The authors assert that lawyers acting for a high-ranking Party member broke the democratic centralism principle of prearranging outcomes in important trials. More particularly, defence counsel contested the accusations rather than delivering a plea in mitigation in this instance. In contrast to the Minh Phung criminal trial conducted five years earlier, in this instance the Chairman of the Bar Association and some media outlets were prepared to support the rights of lawyers to represent their clients fully and vigorously.

Chapter 9 primarily focuses on state-directed reforms, but it also postulates how lawyers will change the legal system. Implicit in the authors' narrative is Weber's assumption that lawyers work towards the formally rational elements of law, because these instruments provide the self-contained doctrinal rules that inform predictable and consistent legal opinions. For example, Nam Cam's lawyer used legal arguments to expose shortcomings in the prosecution's case and commercial lawyers argued with state officials to protect statutory legal rights from bureaucratic interference.

In Vietnam's state-directed legal landscape it is also possible that, rather than promoting private legal rights, lawyers will prefer to mediate and negotiate their clients' interests with state authorities. Evidence presented in Chapter 9 shows lawyers forming 'good relationships' with bureaucrats and judges and altering outcomes with bribes. This behaviour undermines 'formal rationality' and is entirely consistent with the situational and discretionary outcomes promoted by socialist legality. That lawyers pursue both strategies, sometimes simultaneously, implies a transitional and fragmented legal space. Whether lawyers decide that formal legal rationality is the most persuasive strategy depends not only on changes with the state, but also on the kinds of interests clients want protected.

SOCIALIST TRANSITIONS: THE CENTRE AND THE LOCAL

In part three, Biddulph (Chapter 10), Fforde (Chapter 11) and Painter (Chapter 12) each explore the intersections and conflicts between centre-led and locally-instituted change. Both Fforde and Painter explore the extent to which state-owned enterprise and administrative reforms respectively reflect endogenous change, rather than the implementation of Party-led legal reform. Biddulph, on the other hand, uses Bourdieu's (1987) device of the 'legal field' to find evidence of central legal influence in the local administration of detention powers in China. She argues this at once enables the Party–state to reconstitute its powers legally, while not diminishing them.

More particularly, Biddulph explores the changing role of law in China in the context of administrative detention powers. In particular, she asks whether Chinese administrative detention powers are debated and defined in legal or political terms. Through a study of the Chinese police detention power, 'Detention for Investigation' (*shourong shencha*), Biddulph examines how the Chinese state manages legal reform and change to maintain social order.

Biddulph argues that it is possible to discern local contests concerning whether administrative powers should be maintained and how they might be legitimised. Further, she argues that without the use of the 'field' as an analytical tool it is all too easy to cast Chinese law reform as inevitably producing a thin version of the 'rule of law' (Peerenboom 2004). Biddulph's preference is not to see Chinese legal reform reflecting a transitional paradigm, inevitably replicating Western-style legal institutions and processes. Rather, she argues that the emerging contests of the role and place of administrative law bring to the fore the ways in which the state, and particularly the Party, produce and manage legal change. She argues that, while it appears that the Chinese Party–state, and its various agencies, appropriates the rhetoric of the rule of law and reform, it in fact continues to pursue various policies for control and social order.

Biddulph characterises socialism in terms of state power. She does not trace developments in Chinese socialist ideology, preferring instead to cast Party–state instrumentalism as local, pragmatic and increasingly harnessing the language and rhetoric of law to produce new patterns of social order. She demonstrates that the administrative power to detain Chinese has not been lost, but instead has been recast and legitimised by its reintroduction in the Chinese Criminal Procedure Law. This transformation is cast as a largely indigenous exercise played out among the new 'law' professionals, including police, academics and lawyers.

Unlike Biddulph, Fforde (Chapter 11) does not define socialism in ideological terms. Rather he contends that Vietnamese 'socialism' is a local political force: more pragmatic than ideological. He characterises its 'political' objectives as enabling stable transition to an enhanced role for the 'law of value' while concurrently retaining the Party–state as the mediator of public–private interests. This characterisation of the role of the state as more affected by 'rule than by law' leaves socialist doctrine and law *per se* of little relevance in the context of Vietnamese state-owned enterprise reform.

More particularly, Fforde takes up three questions: whether and how socialism shapes law and law-related institutions, whether external or internal factors explain legal change, and, finally, whether socialist doctrine inhibits legal change. To answer these, he undertakes surveys of laws relating to state-owned enterprises and media commentary in two time periods. First, Fforde looks at the interaction between law and state-owned enterprise practice in the early 1990s and then compares this with their interaction between 2000–02. Second, he considers the role played by law in media reporting of state-owned enterprise activities, again over these two time periods.

Fforde demonstrates the Party–state's pragmatic understanding of its socioeconomic reality to explain how it is that the state can officially enable state-owned enterprise reform and concurrently constrain it. This constraint is legitimised because too many shocks could harm the Vietnamese economy and its citizenry. In this sense, a pragmatic political sense produced *ad hoc* Party interventions in the early 1990s rather than systemic policy or law-based reforms.

Moving to the early twenty-first century, Fforde contends that while state-owned enterprises are now ostensibly managed more systematically, they in fact continue unshaped by law. While law generally has become more detailed, Fforde cites the ongoing ambiguities of particular laws and the leadership's continued *ad hoc* style in support of this thesis. This analysis forms a part of Fforde's wider thesis that law and even economic policy ought not be seen as shaping Vietnamese socialist transformation (or indeed perhaps any transition?). Instead, he characterises regulation of state-owned enterprises as a fluid context-driven phenomenon where the state selectively and sporadically invokes policy to give effect to their pragmatic preferences.

Fforde's findings contrast with those of some other commentators. For example, Gainsborough (2003) argues that economic decisions in Vietnam are pragmatic in the sense that they do not consistently follow particular ideals, but in forming decisions, Party leaders draw on predetermined sets of ideas, many of which are socialist. In studying the 'hollowing-out' of the state sector in Ho Chi Minh City during the 1990s, he concluded that neoliberal economic ideas have not penetrated the thinking of senior state officials deeply. Instead, privatisation followed compromises between socialist thinking and personal gain.

Returning to the questions Fforde asks upfront, he concludes that practical politics, and not ideologies, shape law. This view contrasts with Chao Xi's and Gainsborough's summation that law reforms aim to reconcile state ownership ideology with economic efficiency and personal interests. Further, Fforde's argument implicitly suggests that internal factors (a local understanding of what is needed) dominate policy and lawmaking affecting state-owned enterprises. Finally, he argues that it remains hard to answer the question of whether socialism impedes legal change, as the relationship between the two is at best dynamic and fluid. He rejects the notion that law drives transition and remains sceptical about its relevance to transition.

Painter (Chapter 12), writing about transforming socialist ideals in the context of public administrative reform in Vietnam, is also sceptical of the local impact of centrally determined reform policy. He identifies three factors that influence the interaction between local and imported ideas about administrative reform. First, how important is political rhetoric to change? Second, what institutional factors make competing ideas about reform appear attractive to policymakers? Third, are reform ideas assessed according to their compatibility with Party doctrine?

For Painter, Party policies and theories dominate public administrative reform. He notes that public administrative reform stresses linkages joining state reform and Party reform, grassroots democracy and mass-organisation reforms. These objectives reflect long-standing Marxist-Leninist notions of Party leadership over the state, democratic centralism and collective mastery. Less importance is given, he believes, to imported Western reforms that stress administrative efficiency and rational bureaucratic processes.

Drawing from administrative and legal transplantation literature, Painter maintains that imported public administrative reform initiatives rarely follow prescribed patterns. Rather than applying set solutions for identified problems, reforms are fragmented into multiple agendas that 'have a life of their own, solutions look for problems as much as vice versa'. He borrows the metaphor of 'cropping up' to describe the phenomena where global 'talk' or discourse about administrative reforms produce similar solutions to problems in different localities.

The case for 'cropping up' reform is tested in a study concerning Vietnamese salary reform. Painter contends that the state sought to increase public sector salaries by implementing a series of local adaptations that clearly reflected 'themes and models that are very familiar in the global context'. In other words, the ideas used to reform public administration were largely borrowed, but the selection and adaptation of these ideas followed local political imperatives. He concluded that multilateral donors did not impose the public administrative reforms that were eventually adopted by local authorities. Borrowed ideas were merged with local precepts and practices to produce homegrown hybrid solutions. His observations about public administrative reforms are based on salary reform and do not contest the broader view that other initiatives, such as administrative streamlining and judicial accountability reflect a global agenda (Vichit-Vadakan 1996).

Painter leaves his readers with the important insight that borrowed ideas frequently take on new roles in host countries. As Luhmann (1987) puts it, transplants act as 'irritations' or 'perturbations' that give rise to new and unpredictable political and legal meanings. What is left unsaid is how core socialist notions, such as Party leadership, democratic centralism and collective mastery, are reconciled with imported administrative reforms promoting a Weberian meritocracy. Finally, what is the transformative potential for imported ideas to create what Dowdle calls 'runaway legitimation' and generate their own momentum for change?

RECONCILING IDEOLOGIES: INTERNATIONALISM AND CATHOLICISM

The final two chapters take up the issue of reconciling ideologies, each arguing that socialism is reconcilable with other ideologies. In particular, Bryant and Jessup (Chapter 13) (on international law) and Hansen (Chapter 14) (on Catholicism) argue that socialism impacts on Vietnam's capacity to integrate other ideological commitments. Hansen argues forcefully that Vietnamese socialism *per se* has not precluded Catholicism, rather historical antagonisms between church and state have caused tensions. Bryant and Jessup argue that Vietnamese socialism is preventing the systematic incorporation of international law, but international law is introduced in an *ad hoc* manner.

More particularly, Bryant and Jessup argue that the legacy of Vietnamese socialist ideology undermines Vietnam's apparent preparedness to allow those international treaties it has ratified automatically to become a part of Vietnamese domestic law. They note that the incorporation approach to international law (one that provides if you have signed a treaty it automatically becomes a part of a state's law without need for a separate legal instrument) is not explicitly adopted in Vietnam. Rather, the 1998 Ordinance on the Conclusion and Implementation of International Agreements only countenances incorporation in Vietnam where the treaties are either consistent with Vietnamese law or address areas currently not covered by Vietnamese law. But, Bryant and Jessup argue, accepting this qualification, the Vietnamese fail consistently to give legal effect to ratified treaties.

The authors note that Vietnamese scholars and commentators on international law consistently argue that international laws ought not be binding on Vietnam, unless they are specifically transformed. They note that this is consistent with Marxist-Leninist jurisprudence, which conceives of law as reflecting the economic base. Within such a framework it is not possible uncritically to adopt international laws as these laws would, by definition, reflect the capitalist bases of the nations that produce them. Further, they note that a preoccupation with sovereignty, which they ascribe to ideological tenets, has stymied the incorporation of ratified treaties.

The result, as this chapter documents, is a law–practice gap in Vietnam. The provisions enabling the direct incorporation of treaties consistent with Vietnamese law or filling in gaps in domestic law are rarely cited. Rather, treaties are given effect through regulations and policies introduced by the responsible ministry or agency and not through a high-ranking legal instrument, such as an ordinance or law passed by the National Assembly. The result is that international law is implemented through policy or low-ranking laws in an *ad hoc* fashion. In effect, practical politics subverts the ideological argument against the incorporation of treaties, but it does so covertly rather than through National Assembly lawmaking. In conclusion, the authors call upon the Vietnamese state explicitly to adopt an incorporation approach to the international treaties to which it is a signatory.

In contrast, Hansen contends that church–state relations in Vietnam ought not be seen as constrained by Marxist ideology. Rather, he argues, that the mutual distrust between church and state in contemporary Vietnam, where evident, is a function of history. He bases his contention on two arguments. First, through an analysis of the constitutional and criminal law provisions affecting the ability of citizens to maintain their Catholic faith, Hansen argues that the Communist Party of Vietnam never intended to wrest spiritual leadership of Vietnamese Catholics from Rome. In particular he argues that, unlike China, Vietnam never required the ordination of bishops not in communion with Rome. Put another way, while the Vietnamese state has at various times been unsympathetic toward Catholics, Hansen suggests it has never systematically sought to sever structural links between the local church and its leadership in Rome.

Second, Hansen investigates the incarceration of Father Ly in Vietnam and concludes that his agitation went beyond issues of faith to engage directly with political issues of the day. For that reason the Vietnamese state's prosecution of Father Ly can be defended. Hansen contends again that it is not ideology that results in Father Ly's prosecution, rather his overt political actions in a one-party state.

Hansen notes the increasing freedom to practise religion and also describes unenforceable constitutional guarantees of freedom of religion, he does not attribute either manifestation of church–state relations in Vietnam to ideology. He reiterates his characterisation of an antagonism that evolved as a result of the long history of mutual distrust of the political agendas of church and state to explain each phenomenon.

Hansen writes as a cleric and lawyer arguing persuasively that the Vietnamese Party–state has, in recent times, softened its restraint of religious freedom *vis-à-vis* Catholics. Not all will be persuaded by a thesis that does not address why it is that contemporary Catholics are still, in the main, distrusted by the political élite and remain prevented from maintaining their faith and holding political posts. But Hansen argues forcefully that ideology has been overcast as an explanation of church–state relations in Vietnam. This is a bold analysis downplaying the importance of Marxism to state–church relations and casting the contest as about power rather than beliefs.

In summary, several themes emerge from the diverse and insightful accounts of legal and institutional change in China and Vietnam. Most authors agree that, despite the changes instituted by market reforms, certain core socialist ideas continue to order state–society relationships. But the authors also think that understandings of socialism are both ideologically and contextually constructed. These chapters demonstrate how certain socialist ideals change their meaning and significance according to context. Those studying socialist precepts in tightly controlled institutions such as courts and universities found relatively low levels of adaptation and hybridisation in official thinking, whereas those studying the interaction of socialist concepts with market and non-state institutions reported high levels of adaptation. These studies also show that Party and state leaders selectively plunder the socialist canon for situationally appropriate ideas, producing fragmented meanings that retain their authority in some social arenas, but not in others. Finally the chapters point to a set of questions and methodologies to guide further studies in the dynamism of law and legal institutions within socialist Asia.

NOTES

[1]   See, for example, Lubman (1999); Peerenboom (2002); Chen (1999); Potter (2001); Vermeer and d'Hooghe (2002); Chi (2000); Turner et al. (2000); Otto et al. (2002); Otto et al. (2000).

[2]   See, for example, Bergling (1999); Gillespie (2004); Nicholson (2002); Pham Duy Nghia (2002); Quinn (2002); Sidel (2002).

[3]   For an excellent treatment of the comparative transformative experience of Asian socialism, but not confined to a discussion of legal change see *The China Journal*, Special Issue on Transforming Asian Socialism, Vol. 40, July 1998. See also Chan et al. (1999); Abuza (2001).

[4]   See, for example, Barry (1992); Frankowski and Stephan (1995); Varga (1995); Kornai (1990).

[5] Nguyen Chi Dung, Comment at the Law and Governance: Socialist transforming Vietnam and China conference, Asian Law Centre at the University of Melbourne and Law School, Deakin University, Melbourne, Australia 12–13 June 2003.

[6] Vietnamese Ministry of Finance figures show that the state retains a major (51 per cent or more) stake in 47 per cent of privatised state owned enterprises and a controlling stake in many more (*Dua Tu Chung Khoan*, 12 April 2004:16).

REFERENCES

Abuza, Z., 2001. *Renovating Politics in Contemporary Vietnam*, Lynne Rienner, Boulder, Colorado.

Barry, D.D. (ed), 1992. *Toward the 'Rule of Law' in Russia: political and legal reform in the transition period*, M. E. Sharpe, New York.

Bergling, P., 1999. *Legal Reform and Private Enterprise: the Vietnamese experience*, Volume 1, Umea University, Sweden.

Black, K., Kraakman, R. and Tarassova, A., 2000. 'Russian privatisation and corporate governance: what went wrong?', *Stanford Law Review*, 52(6):1731–21.

Bourdieu, P., 1987. 'The force of law: toward a sociology of the juridical field', *Hasting Law Journal*, 38(5):805–53.

Chen, J., 1999. *Chinese Law: towards an understanding of Chinese law, its nature, and development*, Kluwer Law International, Boston.

Chi, F. (ed), 2000. *China's Economic Reform at the Turn of the Century*, Foreign Languages Press, Beijing.

Fforde, A. and de Vylder, S., 1996. *From Plan to Market*, Westview Press, Colorado.

Frankowski, S. and Stephan, P.B. (eds), 1995. *Legal Reform in Post-Communist Europe: the view from within*, M. Nijhoff, Boston.

Gainsborough, M., 2003. *Changing Political Economy of Vietnam: the case of Ho Chi Minh City*, RoutledgeCurzon, London.

Giebel, C., 2001. 'Museum-shrine: revolution and its tutelary spirit in the village of My Hoa Hung', in Hue-Tam Ho Tai (ed.), *The Country of Memory: remaking the past in late socialist Vietnam*, University of California Press, Berkeley:77–105.

Gillespie, J. (ed), 1997. *Commercial Legal Development in Vietnam: Vietnamese and Foreign Commentaries*, Butterworths, Sydney.

——, 2004. 'Concepts of law in Vietnam: transforming statist socialism', in R. Peerenboom (ed.), *Asian Discourses of Rule of Law*, Routledge, London:146–82.

Kerkvliet, B., Chan, A. and Unger, J., 1999. 'Comparing China and Vietnam: an introduction', in A. Chan, B.J.T. Kerkvliet and J. Unger (eds), *Transforming Asian Socialism: China and Vietnam compared*, Allen and Unwin, St Leonards:1–14.

Kornai, J., 1990. *The Road to a Free Economy: shifting from a socialist system the example of Hungary*, W.W. Norton & Company, New York.

Lubman, S., 1999. *Bird in a Cage: legal reform in China after Mao*, Stanford University Press, Stanford.

Luhmann, N., 1987. 'The unity of the legal system', in G. Teubner (ed.), *Autopoietic Law: a new approach to law and society*, W. de Gruyter, New York:335–48.

Nicholson, P., 2002. 'The Vietnamese court and corruption', in T. Lindsey and H. Dick (eds), *Corruption in Asia*, Federation Press, Sydney:201–18.

Otto, J.M., Polak, M.V. and Chen, J. (eds), 2000. *Law-making in the People's Republic of China*, Kluwer Law International, The Hague.

Otto, J.M., Chen, J. and Li, Y. (eds), 2002. *Implementation of Law in the People's Republic of China*, Kluwer Law International, London.

Peerenboom, R., 2002. *China's Long March Toward Rule of Law*, Cambridge University Press, Cambridge.

—— (ed), 2004. *Asian Discourses of Rule of Law*, Routledge, New York.

Pham Duy Nghia, 2002. *Vietnamese Business Law in Transition*, The Gioi Publishers, Hanoi.

Pham Van Hung, 2001. 'Tu Tuong Ho Chi Minh Ve Viec To Chuc va Xay Dung Quoc Hoi Thuc Hien Quyen Luc Cua Nhan Dan' (Ho Chi Minh's thoughts on the National Assembly as an institution to perform people's power), *Nghien Cuu Luat Phap*, 4:65–69.

Potter, P., 2001. *The Chinese Legal System: globalization and local legal culture*, Routledge, London.

Quinn, B.J.M., 2002. 'Legal reform and its context in Vietnam', *Columbia Journal of Asian Law*, 15(2):219–91.

Sidel, M., 2002. 'Analytical models for understanding constitutions and constitutional dialogue in socialist transitional states: re-interpreting constitutional dialogue in Vietnam', *Singapore Journal of International and Comparative Law*, 6(1):42–89.

Turner, K., Feinerman, J. and Guy, R.K. (eds), 2000. *The Limits of the Rule of Law in China*, University of Washington Press, Seattle.

Varga, C., 1995. *Transition to the Rule of Law On the Democratic Transformation in Hungary*, Faculty of Law of Lorand Eotvos University and Hungarian Academy of Sciences, Budapest.

Vermeer, E.B. and d'Hooghe, I. (eds), 2002. *China's Legal Reforms and their Political Limits*, Curzon, Richmond.

Vichit-Vadakan, V., 1996. 'Reforming the policy and institutional framework for a market oriented economy', in UNDP (ed.), *International Colloquium on Public Administrative Reform*, United Nations Development Program, Hanoi:1–22.

2

Of 'socialism' and 'socialist' legal transformations in China and Vietnam

Michael Dowdle

One of the great tragedies of modern constitutionalism is that it has remained largely insulated from the concerns that socialism was developed to address. These concerns are real, and deserve more constitutional attention then they generally receive. The insights gleaned from Vietnam's experience with the process of legal transformation perhaps can go some way toward rectifying this tragedy. We cannot presume, however, that it is enough that Vietnam chooses to call itself, its laws and its constitution 'socialist'. In order for the 'socialist' experiences of Vietnam to contribute to a meaningfully 'socialist' vision of legal transformation, their self-described 'socialism' must be somehow amenable to the experiences of others.

In the search for a possibly socialist legal transformation of Vietnam, one needs to be clear about the parameters of the discussion. On the one hand, since Vietnam is identified as a 'socialist' country, any legal change experienced by that country could credibly be termed a 'socialist legal transformation'. Such tautologies have little analytic utility, however. In order to constitute a meaningful topic of discussion and enquiry, the idea of socialism that informs our search for a socialist legal transformation has to function as an independent, rather than dependent, variable.

Of course, the Vietnamese are free to define 'socialism' and 'socialist law' as they see fit, just as if I decided to define 'cat' as a colour midway between red and fuchsia, I am perfectly within my rights to do so as a fully autonomous member of humanity. I would, however, find it well nigh impossible to participate in any meaningful discussion with others about the nature of cats. Similarly, to the extent that the idea of a 'socialist legal transformation' seeks to refer to something more than Vietnam's *sui generis* experiences, it must reference something beyond Vietnam's own, and possibly self-styled, 'socialist' interpretations of those experiences.

This is not to suggest that Vietnam's 'socialist' interpretation or actual experience of 'law' and 'legal transformation' must conform to outside expectations or even be intelligible to others. Nevertheless, as a cognitive matter, we need a minimal set of common points for reference. A lack of common points will not delegitimate the truths—relative or otherwise—that reside within the Vietnamese experience. It would, however, effectively prevent this experience from contributing to our larger appreciation of the human condition.

Even if we agree that the idea of a socialist legal transformation in Vietnam is something beyond whatever the Vietnamese say it is, we still leave room for divergence about what socialist legal transformation in Vietnam is, or could be. What follows is an exploration of how one particular variant of this phenomenon, what we will call a 'socialist constitutional transformation', could be conceptualised so as to allow the Vietnamese experience to contribute to a more global appreciation for the potential of that idea.

I have selected this 'constitutional' variant of socialist legal transformation because I believe that it offers a better opportunity for meaningful Vietnamese contribution than does the 'rule of law' metric that more commonly informs comparative legal analyses. Underlying the idea of a socialist legal transformation has to be some non-tautological conception of what constitutes a 'legal system'. The traditional rule of law conceptualisation, what Peerenboom (2002) and others have referred to as a 'thin' rule of law conception, sees 'law' simply in terms of certain mechanistic attributes. Examples of these attributes include the presence of a robust set of transparent and predictable rule-based definitions of both private and public competencies and powers, an independent judiciary capable of enforcing these rules free from the pressures of politics or expediency, and so on. Such a definition, however, would reduce the quest for a 'socialist' legal transformation to one of mere bookkeeping—a routine recording of whether or not a particular society does or does not have these requisite 'legal' structures. It would allow us to determine whether or not Vietnam has a legal system, but its ultimately deductive character would prevent Vietnam's particular 'socialist' experiences from contributing anything meaningful to our understanding of the phenomenon of law.[1]

In order to allow Vietnam's 'socialist' experiences to contribute meaningfully to our own ongoing learning about the nature of the rule of law and legal development, we need to adopt a 'thicker'—or what Rawls (following Kant) would have called a more 'comprehensive'—vision of rule of law, one that perceives the possibility of normative linkages between the phenomenon of 'law' and whatever human values might be implicated by Vietnam's particularly 'socialist' transformation (see Pogge 2002). The idea of constitutionalism fills this bill quite nicely. Our common understanding of 'constitutionalism' embodies some reference to the idea of law, and in this way it can inform our understandings of legal transformation. But as we shall see further below, it also refers to something that is more than law, and in this way embeds that reference to 'law' within a larger web of ideas about the nature of human society.

The remainder of this chapter explores what a Vietnamese socialist 'constitutionalism' would look like in a way that could contribute to our knowledge about the nature and function of law within human society. It does not make any claims, however, about whether or not such phenomena as Vietnamese socialist constitutionalism or socialist legal transformation actually exist, or whether they should exist as a moral or practical matter. It could be the case, for example, that the particular aspects of human society that concern, or should concern, Vietnamese socialism are not coterminous with the particular aspects of human society that effect notions of constitutionalism. Such a condition would not delegitimate Vietnamese socialist understandings of society or government, but I am not interested in the legitimacy or lack thereof of Vietnam's 'socialist' experiences. I am simply interested in exploring how we might determine whether these experiences do indeed have something to contribute to our own understanding of the larger human phenomena of 'constitutionalism' and its role in 'legal transformation'.

To do this, I will adopt an unabashedly functionalist approach to understanding and defining constitutionalism. This is because the concept of constitutionalism emerges in response to assumptions and concerns that were originally distinctly 'Western' and distinctly capitalist (or more precisely 'mercantilist'). A rigorous focus on functionalism would tend to objectify these particular assumptions by expressing them in terms of explicit cause–effect relationships. This makes it easier to account for this phenomenon in the translation to different cultures and political–economic systems. Of course, functionalism has also come under attack for its cultural presumptuousness. Functionalist arguments too often presume that the particular functional needs of societies are universal, or that correspondence in structural form evinces correspondence in functional need. I will attempt to avoid such an analytic pratfall by allowing cultures to speak for themselves as to the particular functionality of their self-styled 'constitutional' systems.

The functionality of constitutionalism lies in its political epistemic character. More specifically, it lies in its recognition that valid political understandings are not monopolised by discrete and insular elements of society. To make such a demonstration, I will begin in the second section to explore what a political epistemology is and why it is important. As I will explain, 'political epistemology' refers to the normative criteria that political institutions use to determine whether a particular claim deserves to be taken into account in political decision-making. We shall also see that, despite their ethereal, metaphysical character, political epistemologies can significantly affect the patterns of decision-making made by the polity.

I will then explore why the idea of 'constitutionalism' gained purchase in the United States and Europe. We will see that what constitutionalism did was describe a new opening-up of political epistemology. Previously, European political epistemology had assumed that valid political insight could only come from a particular, insular segment of society. To the extent this assumption was ever valid, it was rendered obsolete with the onset of mercantilism. The appeal of US constitutionalism lay in the fact that it recognised this new political–epistemic situation. I will then engage in a comparative exploration of constitutional functionality in the People's Republic of China to show how despite its socialist and generally non-Western predicates, China's use of constitutionalism evinces this same particular functionality.

Finally, I examine some of the implications of all this for an exploration into a distinctly 'socialist' legal transformation in Vietnam. I begin by taking particular notice of the fact that, despite being a strongly self-identified socialist country, China's idea of constitutionalism operates largely outside of its idea of socialism. As we shall see, this is because the Chinese idea of socialism exists within a largely closed epistemic framework, which effectively renders it irrelevant to the particular, epistemically-opening functionality of constitutionalism. Analogous to this phenomenon is the failure of the early Anglo-American constitutionalism to associate itself with Christianity, despite the defining role that Christianity played in the self-identity of both England and the United States during the time of their respective constitutional formations. In both countries, the early constitutionalists recognised that Christianity's ultimately closed epistemic character rendered it incompatible with constitutionalism as they saw it.

Of course, none of this is to suggest that Vietnam's own idea of socialism is similarly epistemically closed or otherwise similarly constitutionally irrelevant. What it does suggest, however, is that to the extent our interest in Vietnam's 'socialist' legal transformation is motivated by a desire to see how that experience might rectify oversights in Western visions of law and constitutionalism, the epistemology that informs the phenomenon of Vietnamese socialism will have to be, perhaps for that purpose only, epistemically open.

OF INSTITUTIONS AND INSTITUTIONAL EPISTEMOLOGIES

The particular functionality of constitutionalism lies in its ability to encapsulate institutionally a particular kind of political epistemology. In this section I will examine what a political epistemology is and why it is important.

Political society is itself a kind of institution. In order to function effectively, institutions must have agreed-upon criteria for determining which of the myriad of competing factual claims confronting the institution will be taken into account in intra-institutional decision-making. We will call such a collection of criteria an 'institutional epistemology'. In other words, an institutional epistemology refers to the normative collection of rules and methods a particular institution uses to determine whether particular claims are to be afforded institutional respect, that is, whether they are to be treated as 'true'.

Of course, many will often question the degree to which actual institutional decision-making comports with that institution's purported normative epistemology. Kuhn (1962) famously demonstrated, for example, that scientific 'truths' were frequently informed by factors such as reputation, professional opinion and intellectual fad that science itself claimed should be irrelevant to truth determinations. Similarly, both critics of the common law and even some common law judges claim that judicial decision-making in common law courts is frequently informed by factors that are not recognised as valid by the formal epistemology of that institution (see Posner 1990; and Singer 1984).

But institutional epistemologies can have important institutional effects even where they are not perfectly adhered to. For example, they significantly affect the capacity of an idea to propagate through the system. Studies have found that epistemically consistent information propagates more readily through an institution than does epistemically inconsistent information, even where the technologies and ideas operating outside of received normative understandings of the institution prove useful in addressing institutional problems (see Roger 1995; Elster 1995; Barenberg 1994).

In this way, institutional epistemologies significantly shape institutional evolution. This is true even where decision-makers do not personally take the institution's own epistemology particularly seriously. Studies of institutional behaviour and dynamics have also found that institutional leaders and opinion makers who successfully introduce new ideas and norms for strategic, instrumental purposes often lose control of these ideas and norms after they become accepted by the institution (Elster 1995; Barenberg 1994). For example, authoritarian governments in Eastern Europe and Latin America frequently sought to assuage pluralist, interest-based opposition by setting up state-corporatist interest organisations operating ostensibly on behalf of these classes. The strategic design behind this move was, on the one hand, to secure the political support of these interests by symbolically recognising and legitimating their particular concerns, while on the other hand preventing these concerns from interfering with governance by ensuring that these organisations would operate as an agent of the state rather than as an agent of the target interests. In numerous instances, however, the state-corporatist organisation originally set up simply to provide the appearance of interest-based empowerment actually began working on behalf of its constituency in direct contradiction of the original strategic intent of their founders. The simple symbolic act of recognising the legitimacy of these interests, incorporating them into the state's formal political epistemology as it were, ultimately opened the door to these interests' more effective participation in political decision-making (see Baohui Zhang 1994; Elster 1996).

Institutional epistemology can also shape actual institutional decision-making by dictating particular organisational structures to the institution. To see how this is so, let us compare two legal institutions with two different formal institutional epistemologies: juries and forensic laboratories. The institutional epistemology employed by a jury is essentially conventionalist, in the sense that it holds simple consensus as the defining feature of institutional truth (see Reichenbach 1938). Insofar as a jury is concerned, a claim becomes 'true' simply by virtue of the fact that a certain portion of that jury accepts it as true. The reasoning behind the decision is largely irrelevant, as is the possibility that that truth might lie in direct contradiction of other truths found by that same jury (Abraham 2001). The institutional epistemology employed by a forensic laboratory, on the other hand, is primarily positivist. A forensic laboratory will ostensibly recognise the truth of a claim of culpability only when that claim can be rationally, consistently extrapolated from other truths recognised by forensic institutions (see Gadamer 1996). The mere presence of some sort of consensus among a selected group of individuals is epistemically[2] irrelevant.

Of course, Kuhn (1962) has famously demonstrated that, despite their formal objection to conventionalism, scientific communities—like forensic laboratories—are, in fact, governed by conventionalist epistemic forces. Assuming this to be the case, does it mean that the decision-making patterns of juries and laboratories are really indistinguishable?

This is clearly not the case. The different institutional epistemologies of laboratories and of juries have caused each to assume a distinct organisational structure and these structures give very different shapes to their respective decision-making patterns. In order to activate its democratic, conventionalist function, service on a jury is determined largely by lottery (Abramson 1994). At the same time, however, the conventionalist nature of a jury decision renders the process by which that decision is made inherently opaque—a jury does not articulate the reasoning that underlies its determination—which, in turn, gives rise to the possibility that some jury decisions could be founded on unfair or unjust biases (Harvard Law Review 1997). For this reason, the information on which a jury may base its decision is strictly filtered.[3] Service in a forensic laboratory, by contrast, is not democratic, but limited (at least insofar as the forensic decision-makers in that laboratory are concerned) to persons who possess specialised knowledge and training (see Schroeder 1992). Since the validity of a scientific truth–claim derives from the transparency of the relationship between that claim and other established scientific truths (Kahn 2001), there is thought to be no need for institutional filtering of the knowledge that these specialists are allowed to view.[4]

Obviously, the decision-making pattern of a largely random collection of citizens viewing carefully filtered evidence in an opaque decision-making environment will differ significantly from that of a homogeneous selection of trained specialists with unfiltered access to evidence but whose decision-making processes must be transparent in order to be credible. Thus, even accepting Kuhn's claim that scientific determinations are ultimately as conventionalist as jury determinations, the differing normative character of the forensic laboratory's decision-making epistemology, vis-à-vis that of the jury, nevertheless produces very different patterns of decision-making.[5]

HISTORICAL DIMENSIONS: CONSTITUTIONAL DEVELOPMENT IN EARLY MODERN AMERICA AND WESTERN EUROPE

The emergence of constitutionalism in early modern America and later in Western Europe is directly associated with the appearance of a new, institutional epistemology for political decision-making. Under feudalism, statecraft skills were effectively cultivated only within a small, distinct and insular class of the population. As a result, the knowledge, understandings and skills associated with statecraft were effectively limited to members of that particular population, a condition we will refer to as being 'epistemically closed'. With the rise of mercantilism, however, many of these skills became increasingly deployed within and comprehensible to persons outside this aristocratic élite and political knowledge became progressively open.

However, Europe's standard state-level forms of political organisations, which had developed in and reflected the presumption of the feudal era, were slow to adapt to this new epistemic condition. US constitutionalism, by contrast, developed initially and primarily in the context of a mercantile society, and thus both recognised and encapsulated political dynamics associated with this new open political epistemology. As the political capacities and ambitions of epistemically-excluded populations increasingly clashed with the political monopolies of the old European order during the nineteenth century, European polities began turning to US constitutionalism as a means for opening political epistemology in a nevertheless controlled, regulated manner. Herein resides the real functionality of modern constitutionalism—its capacity to conceptualise political systems founded on a largely open political epistemology.

On the reproduction of political knowledge

Institutions are complex phenomena. On the one hand, they frequently endure and are intended to endure for generations, but they are ultimately comprised primarily of individuals that endure for much shorter spans. Moreover, these individuals must possess particular skills and knowledge necessary for the effectiveness of the institution. In order to survive and be effective, institutions must therefore be able to ensure that the individuated knowledge necessary for its survival and effectiveness is continually being 'reproduced' in new individuals who can take over from older individuals when they leave the institution.

Institutions can reproduce institutional knowledge in a number of ways. For example, an institution might seek to instil relevant skills and knowledge itself via internal training processes. An example of this would be the apprenticeship arrangements found in many craft and artisan communities. Where other institutions within the society are producing the relevant skills and knowledge, however, the reproducing institution can save time and money by simply 'raiding' these other institutions for its personnel. When a large US public corporation needs a new CEO, it often simply hires someone with significant prior experience as an executive officer from another US corporation because the particular knowledge demanded of a CEO is now produced in a myriad of institutional sites throughout the corporate world.

Obviously, how a particular institution goes about reproducing itself depends to a large extent on factors within the larger society from which that institution draws its members. Where the relevant skill is highly fungible within the larger society of which that institution is a part (for example, literacy in industrialised economies), the institution will find it cheaper to rely on other institutions for reproduction (for example, public schools). The less fungible the skill (for example, violin-making), the more incentive there is to develop and reproduce that knowledge in-house (for example, apprenticeship systems) (see Becker 1975).

Government is itself an (intergenerational) institution. Its long-term success clearly depends in part on its ability to ensure that the particular skills and understandings that underlie effective governance—what we will refer to somewhat misleadingly as 'political knowledge'—are being continually and effectively reproduced in new generations of personnel. As per our discussion above regarding the different strategies for reproducing institutional knowledge, different governments adopt different approaches to this problem, depending in part on particulars in the larger society of which that government is a part.

The reproduction of political knowledge in feudal Europe: closed versus open epistemic systems

During the early formation of the European state system, the skills and techniques associated with political leadership in Europe were not produced by society at large. They had to be produced by political institutions 'in-house'. This was the ultimate functional basis for feudalism. Feudalism effectively created a specialised sub-community—the nobility—that sought to ensure the (re)production of persons with the skills and understanding necessary for governmental effectiveness. This reproductive aspect of feudalism was most clearly reflected in the original English–Norman system of feudal tenures, a system in which the King (and other higher-level nobility) would grant perpetual land-rights to another in exchange for a pledge to provide particular forms of service. Under this system, the principal source of knights for the King's armies was those families vested with military tenure, who were obligated to provide 'knight's service' in exchange for their dominium over a parcel of the King's land. Similarly, public administrators often came from families vested with civil tenure. Such a system made perfect sense in a society in which both effective military talents (such as wielding a lance while on horseback and wearing heavy armour) and effective literacy required years of specialised training that society at large did not, and could not, provide.[6]

One by-product of creating distinct and insular institutional environments for the reproduction of particular institution-specific skills and understandings is that these environments would generally enjoy a kind of monopoly in the production and reproduction of that kind of knowledge. Where a particular kind of knowledge is monopolised by a particular, discrete and insular community, I will refer to it as 'epistemically closed'. There are at least two kinds of epistemic closure. One is a kind of closure, which I will call 'functional', that occurs when the institution is the only one that is able produce the particular knowledge relevant to that institution. During the tenth and eleventh centuries, the University of Bologna functionally monopolised the reproduction of what would later become known as the Civil Law in Western Europe, because it was the only institution in Western Europe with access to the historical materials from which principles of civil law derived, Justinian's *Corpus Juris Civilis* (of which it had the only copies) (Vinogradoff 1968; Haskins 1957).

Monopolising institutions can also develop what we might call deontological closure. Deontological closure results when the institution's epistemology refuses simply as a formal matter to accept or consider potential knowledge that originates from outside the institution, without regard as to whether or not that knowledge could actually contribute to institutional effectiveness. When the Catholic Church determined in the sixteenth century, via the Council of Trent, that theological truths could henceforth only be issued from properly recognised Catholic theologians (Pelikan 1984), it produced a particular institutional epistemology that would be called 'deontologically' closed.

To be clear, few, if any, actually functioning institutional epistemologies are completely closed or completely open. In general, most, if not all, institutional epistemologies are simply more closed or more open, depending on the degree to which they limit *pro forma* possible sources of knowledge. Similarly, with regards to those institutions that do evince some degree of epistemic closure, that closure is most frequently due to a combination of mutually reinforcing natural and deontological conditions. Nevertheless, as we shall see, these admittedly very unclear and ambiguous distinctions can still be useful in explaining constitutional functionality.

Mercantilism[7] and the 'opening up' of political knowledge

It was noted that under feudalism the reproduction of political knowledge basically was monopolised by a particular sub-community of the feudal system, the nobility. The resulting epistemic closure may well have originally been functional, as would be the case where literacy and chivalry were not being effectively reproduced by society at large (Keen 1990). Over the centuries, however, economic and technological development conspired to destroy whatever functional advantages these epistemic monopolies enjoyed. The military discovery first of the longbow and, later, of the firearm, freed military effectiveness from its previous dependence on years of specialised knights-service training. Effective armies could now be produced from the general populace in a matter of months. Similarly, mercantilisation and the printing press meant that a widening diversity of non-enfeoffed communities were producing literacy and other administrative skills used to administer, or at least understand, government (see Keen 1990; Zaret 2000).[8]

As these other populations gained force in society, the insular and distinct political sub-communities that had descended from those used to reproduce feudal government sought to maintain their epistemic monopolies by buttressing their deteriorating functional monopolisation of political knowledge with a more deontological monopolisation. As noted above, the Catholic Church, for example, justified its continued monopoly over the promulgation of canonical law by claiming that only the Catholic Church could comprehend divine truths. Secular aristocracies adapted a similar tactic, creating an 'artificial aristocracy'—in the words of Thomas Jefferson—in which the mere formality of being born into the feudal nobility supposedly evinced unique access to divinely bestowed political knowledge (Jefferson 1984 [1813]). Both the concept of a 'natural law', which linked traditional political practices to divine inspiration, and the 'divine right of kings', which linked the formality of Kingship with divinely-ordained truths, would be examples of this phenomenon.[9] Another example of this tactic is found in how many political thinkers, such as Edmund Burke, associated the reproduction of effective political knowledge with something akin to animal husbandry (see, for example, O'Neill 2004).

The advent of US constitutionalism

As national political systems increasingly relied on deontological rather than functional means for maintaining control over the generation of political knowledge, their political epistemologies became increasingly ineffective in generating and maintaining social coherence. In England, increased tensions between the state's formal epistemology that 'the King can do no wrong' and the growing belief of a new mercantile class that it could in fact see the King actually doing wrong ultimately produced a series of crises in the seventeenth century: the Long Parliament, a Civil War, Oliver Cromwell's Interregnum and finally, the Restoration (North and Weingast 1989). The overall result of this century-long tension was to kludge the underlying epistemic disagreement via the well-established common law device of the legal fiction (Dicey 1967). On the one hand, the English system maintained the appearance of a closed political epistemology, for example by formally continuing to recognise the classical doctrine that 'the Queen could do no wrong'. On the other hand, it also established that the Queen's omnipotence could be effectively manifested only where the action in question was the responsibility of someone else in government.

Unfortunately, this particular kludge did not work insofar as American (and other English) colonialists were concerned, since they were not represented in the English parliament (Bailyn 1967). Therefore, when the American colonists sought to justify their independence from their English overseers, they did so in part by disputing the closed character of England's official political epistemology.[10]

Of course, the American colonists did not invent the idea that political epistemology was inherently open. Such an idea was a defining product of the Enlightenment, and even before then was very much present in the mercantilist city–state 'republics' of fourteenth-century Italy (Skinner 1989). American revolutionaries expressly drew from both sources in developing their advocacy for a particularly 'open' political epistemology. The real American contribution was not to invent this kind of epistemology, but to embed it within a particular, institutionalised framework of government, what they and I refer to as a 'constitution'.

The marriage between the idea of a constitution and the notion that political knowledge was open was particularly apparent in the Federalist–Anti-Federalist exchange that accompanied the founders' campaign to ratify the constitution. The Federalist–Anti-Federalist exchange was remarkable if for no other reason than for being the first extended deliberation on the future shape and path of government to take place in public newspapers. Moreover, although by-and-large penned by political élites, the newspaper articles that constituted this exchange were frequently written under *noms de plume* that suggested a more common origin (for example, 'Publius', 'The Federal Farmer').

In this exchange, both sides commented with pride on the presumptiveness of the ordinary American citizen's willingness to proffer political insight. In opening this exchange in October of 1787, Publius (Alexander Hamilton) remarked: 'It has been frequently remarked that it seems to have been reserved to the people of this country...to decide the important question, whether societies of men are really capable or not of establishing good government from reflection and choice' (Hamilton 1961 [1787]:89). The Anti-Federalist 'Brutus' began his first essay by noting

> When the public is called to investigate and decide upon a [such a great] question...the benevolent mind cannot help feeling itself peculiarly interested in the result. In this situation, I trust the feeble efforts of an individual, to lead the minds of the people to a wise and prudent determination, cannot fail of being acceptable to the candid and dispassionate part of the community. Encouraged by the consideration, I have been induced to offer my thoughts upon the present important crisis of our public affairs (Brutus 1981 [1787]:363).

Diffusion to England and beyond

To the rest of the world, this new open political epistemology was the defining feature of this American 'constitutionalism.' In an appendix to his 1803 edition of Blackstone's *Commentaries on the Law's of England*, the English legal scholar St. George Tucker noted

> The American Revolution has formed a new epoch in the history of civil institutions, by reducing to practice, what, before, had been supposed to exist only in the visionary speculations of theoretical writers...The powers of the several branches of government are defined, and the excess of them, as well in the legislature, as in the other branches, finds limits, which cannot be transgressed without offending against that greater power from whom all authority, among us, is derived; to wit, the people (St. George Tucker 1999 [1803]:19).

Perhaps nowhere is the defining linkage between 'constitutionalism' and an open political epistemology made more obvious than in the way this concept of 'constitutionalism' began affecting nineteenth-century English politics. Up until the middle nineteenth century, English political thinkers had regarded the structure of English government as—in Dicey's words—a kind of 'sacred mystery of statesmanship' (Dicey 1967:2; see also Harrison 1996), one whose wisdom and logic ultimately lay beyond rational critique by ordinary mortals (see Epstein 1994). The mere existence of a cabinet, for example, was not formally acknowledged in English constitutional scholarship until the early nineteenth century (Harrison 1996).

Beginning in the early nineteenth century, working-class radicals began introducing a new notion of 'constitutionalism' into British political debate, one derived expressly from the American experience that linked political legitimacy with widespread capacity to participate in the development of political knowledge. An example of this development can be seen in the radical publisher T.J. Wooler's use of constitutional argument in his courtroom defence against charges of seditious libel in 1817. Inspired to a considerable extent by Thomas Paine's articulation and defence of American theories of governance, Wooler used the term 'constitutionalism' to refer, not to a closed creed, but to a much more inclusive way of interpreting English political history. Over the objection of both the prosecutor and the presiding judge, he argued that interpretations and understandings of constitutional principle should be open to anyone. Wooler used this idea effectively to undermine efforts by the court and by government prosecutors to constrain courtroom discussion to technical points of law, and dramatically transformed the trial into a debate about the properly public character of England's 'constitutional' rights (Epstein 1994).

Within a generation, the popularisation of Wooler's alternative, the American-derived vision of 'popular constitutionalism', engendered a cultural split within England over the meaning of English 'constitutionalism' (Dicey 1967; Kammen 1986; Epstein 1994). The split had two related dimensions. On the one hand was the epistemic disagreement, outlined above, over the source of constitutional authority. On the other hand, there was a related political justice disagreement over the fairness of the particular distribution of political privilege within English society. England's modern vision of constitutionalism, as famously introduced by Walter Bagehot and Albert Venn Dicey, compromised the two dimensions of this dispute: accepting the radical's constitutionalist epistemic claims while rejecting their political justice arguments (see Schneiderman 1998; Tulloch 1977; Kammen 1986). In Dicey's words, the wisdom of the English political system lay in its ability 'to give to constitutions resting on the will of the people the stability and permanence which has hitherto been found only in monarchical or aristocratic states' (Dicey 1886c).

The epistemic experiences that caused first the Americans and later English reformers to reject England's closed vision of political epistemology were not unique to them. Beginning in the late eighteenth century, the idea of an inherently open political epistemology spread across first to Europe, and then beyond. And with it spread the new, American idea of constitutionalism. The French Revolution, which rejected *in extremis* any aristocratic claim to innate privilege or superiority, also ushered in the enactment of France's first self-described 'constitution' (the Constitution of 1791), an enactment that was expressly inspired by the American interpretation of its own experience (Billias 1990; Bourne 1903). Reformers in the post-Napoleonic German states then used both French and American visions of constitutionalism to begin urging the constitutionalisation of their own governments, a development that culminated in its initial stages in 1849 with the aborted Paulskirche Constitution of 1849 (Nipperdey 1996; Hartmann 2002). Towards the end of the nineteenth century, Japan and China began using the clearly-imported concept to refer to new forms of government that soften their respective monarch's formal monopolisation of political knowledge—both inventing entirely new words (*kenpo* and *xianfa* respectively) to capture this new notion.

COMPARATIVE DIMENSIONS: CONSTITUTIONAL DEVELOPMENT IN SOCIALIST CHINA

The comparative strength of this concept, and its reference to the epistemic opening of political knowledge, is well demonstrated by recent events in the People's Republic of China. China has recently experienced a constitutional emergence. As we shall see below, behind the emergence of this self-styled constitutionalism is an ongoing re-evaluation of the nature of political knowledge in China.

Constitutionalism, socialism and political epistemology in China

We noted above that the notion of 'constitutionalism' (*xianfa*) originally entered Chinese political discourse in the late nineteenth century, imported from Japan by scholars interested in replacing China's absolutist monarchy with a more open political system. The monarchical system was formally dismantled in 1911. By the 1920s, the idea that the political environment was to be governed by a constitution resembling that of Western countries was well-accepted within China. In the 1930s, when civil war broke out between the factions in power, the Republicans and the Communists, both sides adopted self-styled 'constitutions' to govern their respective territorial holdings (Fitzgerald 2002).

During this same timespan, however, an alternative political epistemology— called socialism—was also shaping notions of governance within the communist faction. Socialism began in China as an epistemically open concept, finding its conceptual shape in debates among public intellectuals during the early part of the twentieth century (Li Yu-ning 1971). It was also one of the principal ideological bases for the Communist Party of China (CPC), but the CPC was an inherently closed epistemic community (van de Ven 1995). Modelling itself after the Communist Party of the new Soviet Union, it embraced what James C. Scott termed a 'high modernist' vision of social organisation, that is, one that saw effective social development purely in terms of top-down planning and organisation (led by the Party) (Schwartz 1968; cf. Scott 1998). Inherent in the act of placing yourself and your own designs uniquely at the pinnacle of social development is an assumption that no-one from the outside could possibly possess independent knowledge relevant to that endeavour.

During the civil war period, the epistemic tension between the CPC's closed, Leninist vision of socialism, on the one hand, and its use of a constitutional-style government on the other, was buffered somewhat by an institutional pragmatism brought about by the need to respond creatively to a number of serious threats to the Party's survival (Fitzgerald 2002). Once the CPC succeeded in gaining control of the mainland from the Republicans, however, its internal epistemic contradiction became more manifest. In 1954, the new People's Republic of China enacted its first constitution, one which tried to establish a particular power balance between the constitutional and party systems (Jiang Jinsong 2003). Nevertheless, when the constitutional system—namely the national parliament, the National People's Congress (NPC)—and the Party began to disagree on the Party's role in the new Chinese state (specifically, over the viability of a multiparty political system), the CPC effectively dismantled the constitutional apparatus (Jiang Jinsong 2003). With the onset of the Cultural Revolution in the mid 1960s, a very epistemically-closed vision of socialism became the only institutionally recognised source of political knowledge in China (Schwartz 1968).

The re-advent of Chinese constitutionalism

By the mid 1970s, the Cultural Revolution was widely regarded within China, even among CPC political élite, as a social and political disaster. A new leader, Deng Xiaoping, sought to begin extracting China from the utter chaos caused by the CPC's long string of failed policies. Political authority in China, however, continued to rest overwhelmingly on CPC affiliation. By famously characterising his reforms as 'socialism with Chinese characteristics,' Deng therefore legitimated himself and his ideas by linking them with the CPC's unique competence to understand the truths of socialism (Kluver 1996; Chan 2003).

At the same time, however, Deng also found it useful to resurrect the constitutional system, albeit more out of strategic, rather than epistemic, concerns. On the one hand, a resurrected constitutional system allowed him, symbolically, to distinguish his newer high-modern reformism from the disastrous high-modern reformism of the earlier CPC. Additionally, Deng's support for economic transformation was not without opponents, some of whom enjoyed considerable prestige and respect within élite political circles. In order to promote his reforms, Deng sought ways to marginalise his more prestigious oppositions' capacity to affect political decision-making without denying the CPC's wisdom in affording such people respect. Placing such opponents in the resurrected, but still moribund, constitutional apparatus allowed him to recognise their political prestige while at the same time isolating them from political decision-making.

One such opponent was Peng Zhen. Peng had been part of the CPC's inner circle since at least the 1930s. He had participated in the Long March, a distinct badge of honour in the CPC, and served as mayor of Beijing during the 1950s. He was a protégé of Zhou Enlai, one of China's most respected and admired political figures. However, he opposed significant aspects of Deng's reforms, and Deng therefore had him assigned to the leadership of the newly reconstituted NPC. Technically the supreme constitutional body, the NPC was expected to, and for the most part did, operate largely as a 'rubber stamp' legitimator of important Party directives. The conventional wisdom is that Deng expected that Peng's assignment to the rubber-stamp NPC would effectively remove his voice from high-level political decision-making (Tanner 1999).

This was not to be the case, however. Having been removed from an élite position in the CPC decision-making hierarchy, Peng sought to develop potential alternative sources of political authority, sources that existed outside the CPC's direct bureaucratic control (Tanner 1999). Obviously, Peng could not appeal to truths of socialism in such efforts, since doing so would have required him either to work through decision-making pathways of the very institution from which he was effectively isolated, or alternatively to contest the closed character of socialism from outside of the CPC and thus alienate the very institution he was seeking to influence. Indeed, throughout the 1980s, moves to expand discussions about the nature of Chinese 'socialism' beyond the scope of the CPC were quickly quashed by the CPC (Sun Yan 1995).

In seeking to promote the NPC's role in political decision-making in China, Peng thus had to appeal to legitimate epistemologies that had purchase within the CPC but whose reproduction was not monopolised by the CPC. He solved this problem in part by reviving the CPC's earlier articulated support for constitutionalism (Tanner 1999; Potter 2003). This strategy benefited him in a number of ways. First, the demise of the CPC's interest in constitutionalism corresponded with the onset of the now discredited Cultural Revolution and this gave significant historical weight to his arguments (see, for example, Peng Zhen 1990a, 1990b; Jiang Jinsong 2003). Second, Peng was head of the NPC after 1983, which in turn was formally China's paramount constitutional body. An appeal to constitutionalism thus gave some comparative advantage to the NPC, and through it, to Peng (O'Brien 1999).

The epistemic nature of China's new constitutionalism

Peng's epistemic machinations evinced the same appeal to an epistemically open political knowledge as we earlier saw in the emergence of constitutionalism in England and the United States. As noted above, at the core of Peng's argument for a re-invigorated constitutionalism was a conceptual linkage between the collapse of the constitutional order and the onset of the Cultural Revolution. Of course, Peng was not the only member of the Chinese political élite to criticise the Cultural Revolution. In fact, the CPC had effectively delegitimated the Cultural Revolution when it tried and convicted the 'Gang of Four'.[11] The prosecution and conviction of the Gang of Four both signalled official acknowledgment that the Cultural Revolution had been a mistake and laid responsibility for that mistake wholly at the feet of particular individuals.

By contrast, Peng argued that the Cultural Revolution was due to the CPC's systemic failings, rather than merely to the personal failings of particular individuals. He attributed the Cultural Revolution to a lack of information and understanding within the party-system itself. This lack of information, he argued, had been caused by the dismantling of the constitutional system. He claimed that, because of the uniquely representational nature of the NPC, constitutionalism provided special access to knowledge that was vital to preventing the kinds of Party mistakes the Cultural Revolution represented (Peng Zhen 1990b). In this way, Peng's argument clearly linked the benefits of constitutionalism with what we are calling the opening-up of political epistemology. What he was saying, in effect, was that by itself the CPC hierarchy inherently lacks access to particular sources of knowledge that can be crucial to political decision-making, and that such knowledge can only come from representational institutions—institutions like the NPC that are able to directly perceive and reflect the diversity of experiences found in larger society.

Of course, many have suggested that Peng's appeal to constitutionalism was strategic—that in fact he was not actually interested in establishing 'constitutionalism' as a normative matter. But since we are looking at constitutionalism from a functionalist perspective, what we are really interested in here is institutional effect, not personal intent. And regardless of Peng's actual motivations, his arguments did seem to trigger a growing institutionalisation of constitutionalism in China, and institutionalisation that is indeed characterised by what we are claiming to be constitutionalism's ultimate purpose, namely, to open political epistemology to input from sources outside the CPC or any other discrete and insular segment of society (see Dowdle 2002).

For example, beginning in the late 1980s, the NPC began consulting with an increasingly diverse collection of societal interests when drawing up or reviewing draft laws and regulations. In some cases, it rejected draft legislation because it felt that the drafters had failed to take sufficient account of particular societal perspectives. It encouraged greater autonomy in NPC representatives and promoted the need for private capacity to challenge political decision-making. These 'constitutional innovations' have since diffused to other areas of China's constitutional apparatus. All this can be directly traced to Peng Zhen's initial promotion of constitutionalism and to the need he articulated to free political epistemology in China from monopolisation by a discrete and insular collection of decision-makers (Dowdle 2002, 1997).

WHITHER 'SOCIALIST' CONSTITUTIONAL DEVELOPMENT?

One of the things curiously absent from China's evolving constitutional evolution is any distinctly 'socialist' aspect. Socialism and self-styled 'socialist' political doctrine have been the defining focus of Chinese political thought during the last half of the twentieth century (Schwartz 1968; Sun Yan 1995; Chan 2003). Nevertheless, Chinese constitutional discourse has yet to identify a distinctive correspondence between any of the key socialist doctrines to emerge in China and any of the particular structures, doctrines or procedures that constitute China's constitutional system.[12]

Our discussions above offer an explanation for this curiosity. If constitutionalism involves an opening-up of political epistemology, and if the epistemology of 'socialism' as it has evolved in China is monopolised by the CPC as I suggested, then the two discourses would be epistemically incompatible. The reason why China's socialist discourse remains in the main so irrelevant to China's constitutional development (at least insofar as its comparative relevance is concerned) is because the 'truths' of Chinese socialism would have very little purchase in the epistemic environment that governs Chinese constitutionalism.

A similar phenomenon can be seen in the absence of any association between Anglo-American constitutional structures or practices and Christianity. Arguably, Christianity was as much a defining element of Anglo-American political communities during their respective periods of constitutional formation as socialism has been with regards to that of China. At the time of their respective constitutional formations, American and English constitutionalists readily identified themselves as members of distinctly 'Christian' nations, and were not shy about drawing parallels between Anglo-American political and constitutional acumen and their Christian piety (Bradford 1993)—just as Chinese constitutionalists today readily draw parallels between China's political and constitutional acumen and their socialist piety. Nevertheless, Anglo-Americans, including Anglo-American Christian theologians, have largely rejected the idea that our respective constitutions have anything distinctly 'Christian' about them (Dreisbach 1999).

This phenomenon can not simply be due to some misplaced strain of constitutional imperialism. Our respective constitutionalist founders were well aware that they were engaging in a very particularist venture, one that to them was by-and-large distinctly Anglo-Saxon (Kammen 1986). Today, we continue to acknowledge our constitutional particularism when we uncontroversially see in our constitutionalism distinctly 'capitalist' or distinctly 'liberal' elements. Nor is Anglo-American conceptual blindness in this regard unique to us. Even self-professed non-Christians in self-professed non-Christian countries (such as those in China, or in the Middle East, or in the former Soviet bloc) who have sought to resist universal application of Anglo-American constitutional models by-and-large have not founded their resistance on any distinctly 'Christian' aspect to Anglo-American constitutionalism.

We find a particularly clear demonstration of Anglo-American constitutionalism's intellectual resistance to Christian-theological doctrine in the intellectual history of the privilege against self-incrimination, a privilege that is prominent in both the US and English constitutional systems (1 Blackstone 1783 [1765]:*68). Until recently, contemporary jurisprudence has held that the privilege emerged in the common law in opposition to competing ecclesiastical law doctrine (Levy 1986). In fact, that privilege actually emerged initially in ecclesiastical law itself. Its initial justifications were founded in significant part in Christian theological doctrine. From there, it migrated into English and later into American constitutional law. It was there that it shed its religious underpinnings (Langbein 1994; Helmholtz 1990).

What could have caused the constitutional law of two strongly self-identified Christian polities to repudiate the Christian origins of one of its fundamental maxims? The answer would seem to lie in precisely the kind of epistemic incompatibility that we saw above in the context of the conceptual disconnect that separates constitutionalism from socialism in socialist China. Particularly during the Enlightenment, and perhaps so even today, many saw the fundamental epistemology of Christianity as being incompatible with the demands of the post-feudal European constitutionalism. The foundational epistemic building block of Christianity is faith. As described by John Locke, '[f]aith [in contrast with reason] is the assent to any proposition...upon the credit of the proposer as coming from GOD, in some extraordinary way of communication' (Locke 1979). As per Locke, the very nature of faith prevents persons other than the believer from being competent to assess the truths inherent in the belief. Capacity to contribute to the truths of the belief thus is monopolised by the believer. Thus, under Locke's description, faith comports with what we are calling a closed epistemology.

American constitutionalists were strongly influenced by Locke's views about the conflict between faith-based religion and reason-based constitutionalism (Walzer 1983). This epistemic incompatibility between faith-based Christianity and reason-based constitutionalism also caused many leading religious figures to similarly reject the idea of a Christian constitutionalism (or what they tended to call a 'Christian commonwealth'). John Witherspoon, a leading Presbyterian clergyman and President of the College of New Jersey (later to be known as Princeton), argued that

> Another reason why the servants of God are represented as troublesome is, because they will not, and dare not comply with the sinful commandments of men. In matters merely civil, good men are the most regular citizens and the most obedient subjects. But, as they have a Master in heaven, no earthly power can constrain them to deny his name or desert his cause (1802:415).

Elder John Leland, leader of the Virginia Baptists, expressed the same sentiment more bluntly when he urged that '[t]he notion of a Christian commonwealth, should be exploded forever' (Green 1845:118).[13]

Of course, none of this is to deny that Christianity has often had decisive influence over various aspects of Anglo-American constitutional development. Nor is it to suggest that Christianity—or religion in general—should not have such influence (Greenawalt 1988). But just as Judaism's significant influence on Albert Einstein (Jammer 1999) did not result in a discernibly 'Jewish' theory of relativity, Christianity's epistemic incompatibilities with constitutionalism have caused its influence on Anglo-American constitutional development, like socialism's influence on China's constitutional development, to remain outside the cognition of 'constitutionalism' per se.

All this suggests another important point regarding our efforts to identify a 'socialist' legal-constitutional transformation in Vietnam. Our analysis of the way that Christianity did and did not affect Anglo-American legal-constitutional development 200 years ago argues that, insofar as Vietnam's 'socialist' legal or constitutional transformation is concerned, we need to be careful and not confuse a hypothesis that Vietnam's constitutional or legal transformation has not been particularly 'socialist' with a hypothesis that Vietnam's constitutional or legal transformation has not in fact been strongly and positively influenced by 'socialism'. If it were to be found that Vietnam's legal transformation was not distinctly 'socialist', that would not denigrate at all socialism's contributions or potential contributions to that country. It would not imply that socialism in Vietnam is a meaningless sham. It would not mean that socialism does not contribute anything valuable or important to Vietnam's ongoing legal and constitutional transformation. It would simply mean that socialism's particular contributions to Vietnam's constitutional, political and social development remain, at least for the time being, outside the limits of constitutionalism's particular *Gestalt*.

CONCLUSION

As I noted at the outset, the fact that Western constitutionalism continues largely to ignore the particular economic and societal injustices that socialism seeks to address should be of significant concern to us. To date, our experience has been that the burdens of 'transformation' tend to fall disproportionately—and, many argue, unjustly—on those very populations that socialism seeks to protect. The idea(l) of a socialist legal transformation is thus very enticing (Stiglitz 1994), and one hopes that Vietnam's socialist heritage would allow it to contribute to our understanding of how such an ideal might be reified in humanity at large. But hope *per se* does not alleviate the need for hard and critical analysis. If Vietnam's 'socialist' experiences are to point us in the direction of a distinctly 'socialist' form of human legal transformation, then the 'socialism' that defines those experiences must itself be the product of human reflection—not simply that of some distinct if valuable subset.

NOTES

[1]   For more on the problem of deductive legal models, see Dowdle (forthcoming).
[2]   Such consensus does have important ramifications, insofar as the sociology of forensic truth is concerned.
[3]   See, for example, Daubert v. Merrell Dow Pharm., Inc., 509 U.S. 579, 590 (1993).
[4]   See Hsu (1999), which shows broad constitutional recognition of social need to protect unfiltered scientific access to information.
[5]   One particularly visible example of this might have been the O.J. Simpson Trial. See Arenella (1996) and Thompson (1996).
[6]   See generally Keen (1990). The feudal tenures system is described in Baker (1990).
[7]   My use of the term 'mercantilism' in this context derives from the definition offered by Minchinton (1969:vii):
      'Mercantilism' can therefore be described as the striving after political power through economic means, which, given the circumstances of the time [ca. 1400–1700], meant through encouragement of trade and manufactures rather than the improvement of the land.
[8]   See Keen (1990) and Zaret (2000). See also Dickson (1967) and Clapham (1958), who both describe the merchant class's increasing penetration of governmental decision-making.
[9]   With regards to the epistemic implications of the English doctrine natural law, see Jeremy Bentham (1996). With regards to the epistemic implications of the divine right of kings, see, for example, Jean Bodin (1992).
[10] There is no questioning that this new, open 'American' political epistemology was very much developed in pursuit of very strategic and self-serving ends. See also Howard Zinn (1995). I described above, however, how one important feature of *institutional* epistemologies is that they can reproduce and strengthen themselves simply by affecting institutional structures and other processes of runaway legitimation.

[11] The 'Gang of Four' referred to four élite Party members (including Mao's wife) who allegedly convinced Mao to initiate and perpetuate the Cultural Revolution in order to further their own personal ends.

[12] Constitutional scholars and intellectuals in China readily associate their constitution in general with something called Chinese 'socialism.' But as noted above, simply saying that China's constitutional system is 'socialist', without linking distinctive aspects of its socialism with distinctive aspects of its constitutionalism, is comparatively meaningless (or more precisely, tautological): similar to one saying that Chinese food is 'socialist'. Of course, to reiterate, the fact that the Chinese have not yet drawn particular links between their socialist experiences and their constitutional experiences does not diminish at all the importance or legitimacy of either China's socialist system or its constitutionalist system. Nor does it diminish the legitimacy of their claims that their constitution is in fact a 'socialist' constitution. It simply means whatever 'socialist' aspects there may be to these experiences, they are aspects that—unlike many other aspects of Chinese constitutional experiences (see Dowdle 1997)—as yet remain inherently outside the realm of to meaningful *comparative* understanding.

[13] For a similar argument as made by a more modern Christian theologian, see Powell (1993).

REFERENCES

Abraham, K.S., 2001. 'The trouble with negligence,' *Vanderbilt Law Review*, 54(3):1187–224.

Abramson, J., 1994. *We the Jury: the jury system and the ideal of democracy*, Basic Books, New York.

Arenella, P., 1996. 'People v. Simpson: perspectives on the implications for the criminal justice system—Foreword: O.J. lessons', *Southern California Law Review*, 69(4):1233–66.

Harvard Law Review, 1997. 'Developments in the law: the civil jury,' *Harvard Law Review*, 110(4):1408–537.

Bailyn, B., 1967. *The Ideological Origins of the American Revolution*, Belknap Press of Harvard University Press, Cambridge, Massachusetts.

Baker, J.H., 1990. *An Introduction to English Legal History*, Third edition, Butterworths, London and Boston.

Baohui Zhang, 1994. 'Corporatism, totalitarianism, and transitions to democracy', *Comparative Political Studies*, 27(1):108–36.

Barenberg, M., 1994. 'Democracy and domination in the law of workplace cooperation: from bureaucratic to flexible production', *Columbia Law Review*, 94(3):753–983.

Becker, G.S., 1975. *Human capital: a theoretical and empirical analysis, with special reference to education*, National Bureau of Economic Research and Columbia University Press, New York.

Bentham, J., 1996. *An Introduction to the Principles of Morals and Legislation*, Clarendon Press, Oxford [ed. J.H. Burns and H.L.A. Hart].

Billias, G.A., 1990. 'American constitutionalism and Europe,' in G.A. Billias (ed.), *American Constitutionalism Abroad: selected essays in comparative constitutional history*, Greenwood Press, New York.

Blackstone, W., 1783 [1765]. *Commentaries on the Laws of England*, Ninth edition, W. Strahan, T. Cadell, London.

Bodin, J., 1992 [1576]. *On Sovereignty: four chapters from six books on the commonwealth*, Cambridge University Press, Cambridge and New York [tr. and ed. Julian H. Franklin].

Bourne, H.E., 1903. 'American constitutional precedents in the French National Assembly', *American Historical Review*, 8(3):466–86.

Bradford, M.E., 1993. *Original Intentions: on the making and ratification of the United States constitution*, University of Georgia Press, Athens.

Brutus [R. Yates], 1981 [1787]. 'Essay I, 18 October 1787', in H.J. Storing (ed.), *The Complete Anti-Federalist*, Volume 2, University of Chicago Press, Chicago: 363.

Chan, A., 2003. *Chinese Marxism*, Continuum International Publishing Group, London and New York.

Clapham, J.H., 1958. *The Bank of England: a history*, The University Press, Cambridge.

Dicey, A.V., 1886a. 'Americomania in English politics', *Nation*, 42(1073): 52.

——, 1886b. 'Can the English Constitution be Americanized?', *Nation*, 42 (1074):73.

——, 1886c. 'Democracy in Switzerland – II', *The Nation*, 41:494–96.

——, 1967. *Introduction To The Study Of The Law Of The Constitution*, Tenth edition, Macmillan, London and St Martin's Press, New York.

Dickson, G.P.M., 1967. *The Financial Revolution in England: a study in the development of public credit, 1688–1756*, Macmillan, London.

Dowdle, M.W., 1997. 'The constitutional development and operations of the National People's Congress', *Columbia Journal of Asian Law*, 11(1):1–125.

——, 2002. 'Of parliaments, pragmatism, and the dynamics of constitutional development: the curious case of China', *New York University Journal of International Law and Politics*, 35(1):1–200.

——, forthcoming. 'Visabilizing invisible hands: exploring for new paradigms of public accountability,' in M.W. Dowdle (ed.), *Public Accountability: law, society and beyond*.

Dreisbach, D.L., 1999. 'In search of a Christian Commonwealth: an examination of selected nineteenth-century commentaries on references to God and the Christian religion in the United States Constitution', *Baylor Law Review*, 48(4):927–1000.

Dyzenhaus, D., 1997. *Legality and Legitimacy: Carl Schmitt, Hans Kelson, and Hermann Heller in Weimar Republic*, Clarendon Press, Oxford.

Elster, J., 1995. 'Strategic uses of argument', in K. Arrow, Ross, L., Tvershy, A. and Wilson, R. (eds), *Barriers to Conflict Resolution*, W.W. Norton and Co., New York:236–57.

——, 1996. *The Roundtable Talks And The Breakdown Of Communism*, University of Chicago Press, Chicago.

Epstein, J.A., 1994. *Radical Expression: political language, ritual, and symbol in England, 1790–1850*, Oxford University Press, New York.

Fitzgerald, J., 2002. 'The politics of the civil war: party rule, territorial administration and constitutional government', in W. Draguhn and D.S.G. Goodman (eds), *China's Communist Revolution: fifty years of the People's Republic of China*, RoutledgeCurzon, London:50–81.

Gadamer, H., 1996. *Truth and Method*, Second revised edition, Continuum International Publishing Co., New York [tr. J. Weinsheimer and D.G. Marshall].

Greenawalt, K., 1988. *Religious Convictions and Political Choice*, Oxford University Press, Oxford and New York.

Hamilton, A., 1961. 'The Federalist No.1', in C. Rossiter (ed.), *The Federalist Papers*, New American Library, New York [ed. Clinton Rossiter].

Harrison, B., 1996. *The Transformation of British Politics ,1860–1995*, Oxford University Press, Oxford.

Hartmann, B.J., 2002. 'How American ideas traveled: comparative constitutional law at Germany's National Assembly in 1848–1849', *Tulane European & Civil Law Forum*, 17:23–70.

Haskins, C.H., 1957. *The Renaissance of the Twelfth Century*, Meridian Books, New York.

Helmholtz, R.H., 1990. 'Origins of the privilege against self-incrimination: the role of the European Ius Commune', *New York University Law Review*, 65(4):962–90.

Hsu, M.B., 1999. 'Banning human cloning: an acceptable limit on scientific inquiry or an unconstitutional restriction of symbolic speech?', *Georgetown Law Journal*, 87(7):2399–430.

Jammer, M., 1999. *Einstein and Religion: physics and theology*, Princeton University Press, Princeton, New Jersey.

Jefferson, T., 1984 [1813]. 'Letter from Thomas Jefferson to John Adams (October 28, 1813)', in T. Jefferson, *Writings*, Viking Press: Literary Classics of the US, New York:1304–1305.

Jiang Jinsong, 2003. *The National People's Congress of China*, Foreign Languages Press, Beijing.

Kahn, P.W., 2001. 'Approaches to the cultural study of law: freedom, autonomy, and the cultural study of law', *Yale Journal of Law & Humanities*, 13(1): 141–71.

Kammen, M., 1986. *A Machine That Would Go Of Itself: the constitution in American culture*, Knopf, New York.

Keen, M., 1990. *English Society in the Later Middle Ages, 1348–1500*, Penguin Press, London.

Kluver, A.R., 1996. *Legitimating the Chinese Economic Reforms: a rhetoric of myth and orthodoxy*, State University of New York Press, New York.

Kramer, L.D., 2001. 'The Supreme Court 2000 Term—Foreword: We the Court', *Harvard Law Review*, 115(1):4–169.

Kuhn, T., 1962. *The Structure of Scientific Revolutions*, University of Chicago Press, Chicago.

Langbein, J.H., 1994. 'The historical origins of the privilege against self-incrimination at Common Law', *Michigan Law Review*, 92(5):1047–85.

Greene, L.F., 1845. *The Writings of the Late Elder John Leland Including Some Events in His Life, Written by Himself, With Additional Sketches &c*, G.W. Wood, New York.

Levy, L.W., 1986. *Origins of the Fifth Amendment: the right against self-incrimination*, Second edition, Macmillan, New York.

Li Yu-ning, 1971. *The Introduction of Socialism into China*, Columbia University Press, New York.

Locke, J., 1979 [1690]. *An Essay Concerning Human Understanding*, Clarendon Press, Oxford [ed. P.H. Nidditch].

Minchinton, W.E., 1969. 'Introduction' in W.E. Minchinton (ed.), *Mercantilism: system or expediency?*, D.C. Heath, Lexington, Massachusetts.

Nipperdey, T., 1996. *Germany from Napoleon to Bismarck 1800–1866*, Princeton University Press, Princeton, New Jersey [tr. Daniel Nolan].

North, D.C. and Weingast, B.R., 1989. 'Constitutions and commitment: the evolution of institutions governing public choice in seventeenth-century England', *Journal of Economic History*, 49(4):803–32.

O'Brien, K.J., 1999. 'Hunting for political change', *China Journal*, 41:159–69.

O'Neill, D.I., 2004. 'Burke on democracy as the death of Western civilization', *Polity*, 36(2):201–25.

Peerenboom, R.P., 2002. *China's Long March toward Rule of Law*, Cambridge University Press, New York.

Pelikan, J., 1984. *The Christian Tradition, A History of the Development of Doctrine 4: reformation of church and dogma (1300–1700)*, University of Chicago Press, Chicago.

Peng Zhen, 1990a. 'Zai Zhongyang Zhengfa Weiyuanhui Kuoda Huiyi Shang de Jianghua [Speech before Enlarged Meeting of the Central Political–Legal Committee]', in National People's Congress Standing Committee General Office Research Department (ed.), *Zhong Renmin Gongheguo Chuanguo Renmin Daibiao Dahui Wenxian Ziliao Huanbian 1949–1990* [Collection of Documents and Materials of the National People's Congress 1949–1990], Zhongguo Minzu Fazhi, Beijing:582.

——, 1990b. 'Bujin Yao Kao Dang de Zhengce, Erque Yao Yi Fa Banshi [Not only Follow Party Principles, Also Work According to the Law],' in *Zhong Renmin Gongheguo Chuanguo Renmin Daibiao Dahui Wenxian Ziliao Huanbian 1949–1990*, Zhongguo Minzu Fazhi, Beijing.

Pogge, T.W., 2002. 'Is Kant's *Rechtslehre* a "comprehensive liberalism"?', in M. Timmons (ed.), *Kant's Metaphysics of Morals: interpretive essays*, Oxford University Press, Oxford:133–58.

Posner, R., 1990. *The Problems of Jurisprudence*, Harvard University Press, Cambridge, Massachusetts.

Potter, P.B., 2003. *From Leninist Discipline to Socialist Legalism: Peng Zhen on law and political authority in the PRC*, Stanford University Press, Stanford.

Powell, H.J., 1993. *The Moral Tradition of American Constitutionalism: a theological interpretation*, Duke University Press, Durham.

Reichenbach, H., 1938. *Experience and Prediction: an analysis of the foundations and the structure of knowledge*, University of Chicago Press, Chicago.

Roger, E.M., 1995. *Diffusion of Innovations*, Fourth edition, Free Press, New York.

Schneiderman, D., 1998. 'A.V. Dicey, Lord Watson, and the law of the Canadian Constitution in the late nineteenth century', *Law and History Review*, 16(3):495–526.

Schroeder, J.L., 1992. 'Subject: object', *University of Miami Law Review*, 47:1–119.

Schwartz, B.I., 1968. *Communism and China: ideology in flux*, Harvard University Press, Cambridge, Massachusetts.

Scott, J.C., 1998. *Seeing Like a State: how certain schemes to improve the human condition have failed*, Yale University Press, New Haven.

Singer, J.W., 1984. 'The player and the cards: nihilism and legal theory', *Yale Law Journal*, 94(1):1–70.

Skinner, Q., 1989. 'The state', in T.Ball, J.Farr, R.L. Hanson (eds), *Political Innovation and Conceptual Change*, Cambridge University Press, Cambridge and New York:90–131.

St. George Tucker, 1999 [1803]. 'On sovereignty and legislature', in *Blackstone's Commentaries*, Appendix A, reprinted in St. George Tucker, *View of the Constitution of the United States with Selected Writings*, Liberty Fund, Indianapolis, Indiana:18–20.

Stiglitz, J.E., 1994. *Whither Socialism?*, MIT Press, Cambridge, Massachusetts.

Sun Yan, 1995. *The Chinese Reassessment of Socialism 1976–1992*, Princeton University Press, Princeton, New Jersey.

Tanner, M.S., 1999. *The Politics of Lawmaking In Post-Mao China: institutions, processes and democratic prospects*, Clarendon Press, Oxford and Oxford University Press, Oxford:97–98.

Thompson, E.P., 1968. *The Makings of the English Working Class*, Penguin, Harmondsworth.

Thompson, W.C., 1996. 'Proving the case: the science of DNA—DNA evidence in the O.J. Simpson trial', *University of Colorado Law Review*, 67(4):827–58.

Tulloch, H.A., 1977. 'Changing British attitudes towards the United States in the 1880s', *The Historical Journal*, 20(4):825–40.

van de Ven, H.J., 1995. 'The emergence of the text-centered party', in T. Saich and H. van de Ven (eds), *New Perspectives on the Chinese Communist Revolution*, M.E. Sharpe, Armonk, New York:5–32.

Vinogradoff, P., 1968. *Roman Law in Medieval Europe*, Speculum Historiale, Cambridge.

Walzer, M., 1983. *Spheres of Justice: a defence of pluralism and democracy*, Basic Books, New York.

Witherspoon, J., 1802. 'The charge of sedition and faction against good men, especially faithful ministers, considered and accounted for', in *The Works Of The Rev. John Witherspoon*, Volume 2, William W. Woodward, Philadelphia:415–17.

Zaret, D., 2000. *Origins of Democratic Culture: printing, petitions, and the public sphere in early-modern England*, Princeton University Press, Princeton, New Jersey.

Zinn, H., 1995. *A People's History of the United States: 1492–present*, HarperPerennial, New York.

3

Changing concepts of socialist law in Vietnam

John Gillespie

Few aspects of the Vietnamese legal system are more uncertain and controversial than the meaning of socialist law. It influences the way the Communist Party of Vietnam 'leads' the state, the way the state 'manages' society and the way officials and the public implement and obey laws. Socialist law resists definition.

'Socialist law' generates confusion because it was introduced more than forty years ago to regulate the command economy, but the term is still in use to describe contemporary mixed-market regulation. This flexible usage raises the question what is socialist about socialist law? Does the term have immutable and intrinsic meanings or has it become a convenient label for state law?

There are two main problems in assessing continuity and change in the meanings attached to 'socialist law'. First, core Marxist-Leninist notions underpinning socialist law—socialist legality, democratic centralism and collective mastery—operate at too high a level of abstraction to convey concrete meanings. Marxist-Leninist ideology informs us that law has a class element that reflects state ownership over the means of production, but says little about other social relationships such as housing, family or traffic regulations. Western 'rule of law' ideas smuggled into the recently adopted law-based state (*nha nuoc phap quyen*) doctrine are equally uninformative. They maintain that socialist law should be equal, transparent and consistent, but rarely discuss broader normative issues. Socialist law needs middle-level propositions (an epistemological context) to acquire specific and systematic meanings.

The second analytical problem is caused by the rapidly changing and fragmenting conceptual environment shaping 'socialist law'. Socialist notions that the state owns the 'means of production' to safeguard workers' interests have dissolved into Party policies that encourage foreign investment, international economic integration and equitisation (*co phan hoa*) of state-owned companies. Ho Chi Minh's declaration that '[i]f the people are hungry, it is the fault of the Party and the government, if the people are cold, it is the fault of the Party and government; if the people are sick, it is the fault of the Party and the government' seems utopian compared with contemporary 'user pays' 'socialisation' policies (Thanh Duy 1997:27–8).

Our analysis needs to distinguish social change from social motion. Societies everywhere are in constant motion. Economies strengthen and weaken, social institutions rise and fall, and technology and global interaction move everyone. Yet, social motion rarely alters underlying legal meaning (Grossman 1971). We need to search for new legal meanings in the successive waves of social and legal changes that have transformed Vietnamese institutions and law.

This chapter searches for change by comparing the narratives shaping the importation of Soviet political-legal ideas forty years ago with contemporary thinking about law. Rather than attempting an authoritative definition—a project doomed by fragmented social meanings—the discussion looks for representative meanings in written records and interviews with officials within the Party and state orbit. By determining which historical contexts convey the most representative meanings, the analysis gains insight into continuity and change in 'socialist law'.

This discussion needs a framework in which to place and compare different contextual understandings about socialist law. Discourse analysis is a useful tool, since political–legal ideas are largely generated through communicative processes (Luhmann 1987; Teubner 1993; Beck 1994). Discourse is taken to mean 'all forms of spoken interaction, formal and informal, and written texts of all kinds', especially political, economic, moral, cultural and legal modes of communication (Potter and Wetherell 1987:7).

Discourse analysis does not capture every meaning of 'socialist law'. Party and state writings deterministically portray Vietnamese culture as forged in the crucible of Red River Delta culture, based on moral rule, 'led' by a morally perfected Party and possessing a low level of legal consciousness. These storylines serve to remind us that, in focusing on Party and state discourse, this investigation is limited to one (admittedly highly influential) contextual understanding of socialist law. It is important to remember that there are many legal understandings fragmented throughout the numerous discursive communities in Vietnam. The views of those from outside the Party and state orbit are discussed in another setting.

This discussion starts by mapping the main political-legal principles imported into the Democratic Republic of Vietnam from the Soviet Union. It then reflects on approaches to legal borrowing, asking why Soviet law was imported with few concessions to local practices and whether contemporary attitudes to imported laws have changed. The discussion argues that differences in the way Vietnamese policymakers borrowed ideas profoundly changed the meanings given to the 'core' Marxist-Leninist canon. It then examines contemporary narratives about law to ascertain whether core legal meanings are more responsive to change in some discourse modes than in others. The chapter concludes that meanings invested in socialist law are fragmenting as core socialist political-legal principles are exposed to new thinking.

BUILDING A SOCIALIST LEGAL STATE

It was not until the First Congress of the Vietnam Workers Party (*Dang Lao Dong Viet Nam*) in September 1951 that legal cadres were instructed to 'build up socialist law' (Hoang Quoc Viet 1962:14–15). Officials in the incipient Democratic Republic of Vietnam previously characterised legality according to the French civil law concept of 'democratic legality' (*phap che dan chu*). The Third Party Congress in 1960 adopted the Soviet 'socialist legality' (*sotsialisticheskaia zakonnost'*) doctrine, which translated into Vietnamese as *phap che xa hoi chu nghia* [a state legal ideology] (Tran Hieu 1971:108).

At first, prominent legal writers such as Dinh Gia Trinh argued that economic conditions in people's democracies like the Democratic Republic of Vietnam were insufficiently evolved to sustain Soviet-style socialist legality.[1] Eventually the Soviet view, that legality in people's democracies and in socialist republics was equivalent, prevailed. By the 1970s, Vietnamese writers uniformly accepted imported socialist legal thinking as their own and unreflectively equated Soviet law with socialist law (Pham Van Bach 1970; Ngo Van Thau 1982). Assertions that Soviet law was really a public law analogue of European civil law never entered Vietnamese legal discourse.

Three doctrines constituted the 'core' socialist political-legal canon—socialist legality, democratic centralism and collective mastery.

Socialist legality

Socialist legality (*phap che xa hoi chu nghia*) is the main socialist legal doctrine. It was defined in Vietnamese writings during the 1960s as a tool of proletarian dictatorship (*chuyen chinh vo san*) to defeat enemies and to protect the revolution and collective democratic rights to organise, manage and develop a command economy (Dinh Gia Trinh 1961).

Vietnamese writers reasoned from Marxist theory that worker-controlled societies required legal systems that reflect proletarian aspirations.[2] The connection between law and class was explained by the familiar assertion that law is part of the 'superstructure', which reflects the 'will of the ruling class' (*y chi cua giai cap thong tri*) and its control over the means of production. As the executive committee of the ruling class, the Party determined the content of law. The conflation of Party policy and law enabled the Party and state to use law as a 'management tool' (*cong cu quan ly*) to adjust or balance (*dieu chinh*) social relationships—a practice permitting the substitution of policy for law.

That law was primarily seen as a political tool is further implied by the low priority accorded to defining legal terminology. Words such as *hieu luc* (validity) and *tinh hop phap* (legitimacy) were used interchangeably with *phap che* (legality). Rather than legal certainty, writers were preoccupied with generating social compliance. In an effort to make legal terms appear more familiar to villagers, scholars replaced many Sino-Vietnamese legal terms with neologisms created from everyday, but imprecise, Vietnamese terms (Dinh Gia Trinh 1965).

Democratic centralism

Democratic centralism (*tap trung dan chu*), as conceptualised by Lenin, was an organisational principle binding Party and state (Lavigne 1985). A facsimile of the doctrine appeared in the political report delivered by President Ho Chi Minh to the Second National Congress of the Vietnamese Workers Party (VWP) in 1951 (Ho Chi Minh 1994:127). By the time it was formally adopted in the 1959 Constitution, it had matured into a two-pronged doctrine linking popular participation in state activities with centralised Party and state power.

Party documents indicate that democratic centralism was introduced to consolidate central Party control over regional Party cadres, state officials and the general public (Le Van Luong 1960; Nguyen The Phung 1960). According to socialist strategic thinking, Party power constituted the most potent remedy to 'regionalism' (*dia phuong chu nghia*) and 'departmentalism'. Only a hierarchically organised, disciplined Party could deliver the social and bureaucratic unity required for command economic planning. Article 10(f) of the VWP Statute 1960 explains the meaning of 'centralism'

> Individual Party members must obey the Party organisations. The minority must obey the majority. Lower organisations must obey higher organisations. Party organisations throughout the country must obey the National Delegates' Congress and Central Executive Committee (Le Van Luong 1960:33).

The second arm of democratic centralism was based on Lenin's assertion that democracy is only possible where the working class 'centralise[s] power in their hands'.[3] Socialist democracy (*dan chu xa chu nghia*) was understood in two ways. Theorists argued that popularly elected legislatures (National Assembly and provincial legislative councils) should supervise state power on behalf of the people. Socialist democracy also encompassed Lenin's revolutionary view that bourgeois democracy transferred the people's democratic rights to elected representatives. He believed the working class had comparatively few opportunities to participate in government by influencing political decision-makers through 'lobbying' (*chay lo thu tuc*) and popular demonstrations. Democratic rights were better safeguarded by 'proletarian dictatorship' (*chuyen chinh vo san*) that empowered the 'ruling class' to supervise state organs directly through their proxies: the Communist Party and mass organisations. Democratic centralism validated Party leadership (*su lanh dao cua dang*) within state and society.

Collective mastery

The ideas that eventually coalesced into the 'collective mastery' (*lam chu tap the*) doctrine appeared in Party publications from the 1950s onwards (Pham Van Dong 1952). Unlike socialist legality and democratic centralism, collective mastery was officially imagined through revolutionary Chinese thinking, though it drew inspiration from Lenin's assertion that true democracy is only possible where workers exercise mastery over society.

Vietnamese leaders were captivated by radical Maoist mass mobilisation theories, long after Stalinist jurists in the 1930s rejected public participation in state administration as 'the old twaddle about the mobilisation of socially active workers' (Vyshinski 1982 [1936]:81). This utopian vision enlisted law to 'fundamentally remake the conscience of the people'.

Party General Secretary Le Duan discussed collective mastery during the 1960s and 1970s, but the doctrine did not take hold until the euphoria surrounding reunification in 1975 made radical social transformation seem possible (Le Duan 1994:242–3). At the Fourth Vietnam Workers Party Congress in 1976, collective mastery was described as a system where 'the true and supreme masters are the social community, the organised collective of working people, with the worker–peasant alliance as the core' (Pham Van Dong 1977:K11–K12). The slogan 'the Party is the leader, the state is the manager and people are the masters' (*dang lanh dao, nha nuoc quan ly, nhan dan lam chu*) unified Party, state and public relationships under collective mastery (Le Duan 1979:4).

Theorists claimed that the path to collective mastery lay in eliminating conflict between the state and individuals (Le Thi 1977). This goal is evident in the Party slogan: 'The important target of the revolution is to strengthen the unification between politics and the spirit of the people [*tang cuong su nhat tri ve chinh tri va tinh than cua toan dan*]'. In classless societies, collectivism replaced individualism, enabling people to live harmoniously without the laziness, individualism, selfishness and corruption associated with the 'old society' (*xa hoi cu*). Collective mastery rejected civil society or individual space outside state and collective orbits as bourgeois individualism. As a corollary, the doctrine was hostile to private legal rights.

Collective values were encouraged in mass mobilisation campaigns led by the Party leadership. Early moral campaigns purged residual French cultural influences (1946–52), reformed land ownership (1953–56) and attacked 'feudalistic property ethics and Confucian morals' (Weggel 1986:415). During the 1970s and 1980s, the Party used mass organisations to mobilise popular support to 'revolutionise the whole of life' by remodelling society along state-lines (Le Phuong 1994).

Taken together, socialist legality, democratic centralism and collective mastery generated four core socialist legal principles that closely resembled the imported Soviet ideas. First, law is not above the state, but rather emanates from the state. As an extreme manifestation of legal positivism, there is no space in socialist law for customary rules or natural rights. Second, the Party and state possess prerogative powers to substitute policy for law. Law facilitates and orders, but never constrains state power. Third, the central 'Party leads' (*su lanh dao cua dang*) the state and society. Fourth, individual legal rights give way to the collective public good.

IMPORTING SOCIALIST POLITICAL–LEGAL THOUGHT

Explanations for the similarities between Soviet and Vietnamese legal thinking are found in Vietnamese approaches to legal borrowing during the 1960s and 1970s. Ignoring their own warnings against unreflective borrowing, Party leaders imported socialist law with few concessions to local conditions. Truong Chinh denounced 'gulping down raw other people's culture, parrot-fashion learning, or the mechanical introduction of a foreign culture into our own without taking into account the particularities and concrete conditions of the country and its people' (Truong Chinh 1948:251). Ho Chi Minh wrote in 1924 that 'Marxism is to be revised with respect to its historical basis, and to be consolidated by the ethnology of the East'. Later he was more direct: '[W]e are not like the Soviet Union; they have different habits and customs, history and geological conditions. We can take another road to socialism' (Ho Chi Minh 1995:338).

Their concerns rarely surfaced in the extensive Vietnamese literature concerning legal borrowing from the Soviet Union. This reluctance to localise Soviet legal reasoning is partially attributable to Marxist–Leninist hostility to the notion that culture plays a role in determining the characteristics of legal systems. Since both law and culture are located in the superstructure, their interaction is considered unimportant. The elaborate historical materialist explanations for legal development focused on linkages between European economic production and law, and said little about 'Asiatic' production (East Asian rice-growing economies) (Avineri 1969). Vietnamese theorists faced a choice between uncritically applying Marx's Eurocentric legal theory to Vietnam or comprehensively rethinking Marxist theory in the context of 'Asiatic' production. Like the Chinese, they adopted a Maoist land-reform program, but applied the Soviet legal template to other social spheres.

Marx also followed a well-established European intellectual tradition that depicted Asian societies in undifferentiated ways as 'barbarians' or 'semi-barbarians', portrayals that generated socialist antipathy to neo-Confucian and 'feudal' culture (Marx 1969 [1877]:6). Truong Chinh evinced this orientalist thinking when he blamed the 'Asian mode of production' for backward economic and social conditions in Vietnam. He vilified traditional cultural precepts as 'unscientific', promoting 'superstition, idealism, mysticism, bungling, carelessness, all those habits that are irrational or retrograde' (Truong Chinh 1948:25–52). Vietnamese leaders sought a 'new democracy culture' based on 'rational, progressive socialist legislation'. They considered the Soviet Union the most advanced socialist state and thought Soviet 'proletarian culture' should link the working classes in different countries. National cultural barriers based on 'Asiatic' and 'feudal' modes of production were supposed to dissolve in the face of this unifying force.

The adaptation of imported ideology to local conditions was further constrained by ethnocentric Soviet jurists, who encouraged 'satellite' nations to 'build socialism' through imitation, rather than experimentation. In exhaustively reviewing Soviet commentaries on Vietnamese legal development, Ginsburgs (1973) blamed political policy for the reluctance to localise legal borrowings. He wrote that the

> academic exploration of the distinctive attributes of socialist experimentation in the countries of the Soviet bloc became both safe and fashionable—as long, of course, as the main accent remained on the common heritage and the disparities were treated either as necessary tactical adoptions to 'objective conditions' or components in a pragmatic region-wide search for better solutions to existing socialist problems (1973:661).

Vietnamese officials working in the legal sector during the 1960s recalled that law reform sought to transplant 'proletarian culture', and Soviet advisers discouraged local adaptation as 'dangerous nationalism' (*chu nghia dan toc cuc doan*).[4] A general reluctance to address local conditions and diverge from the Soviet legal template is revealed in a series of articles written by Soviet jurists about Vietnamese legal development (Letsoni 1963). They seldom acknowledged, much less analysed, incongruities between imported Soviet ideals and local institutional and cultural conditions. Instead, they steadfastly focused on abstract political-legal principles such as socialist legality or procedural issues affecting civil and criminal codes (Sarogoratisk 1961). On the even rarer occasions when Vietnamese writers examined legal transplantation, discussion concentrated on narrow procedural differences between court practices (Ta Thu Khue 1963). An extensive review of the Vietnamese legal literature over this period has failed to find a single article analysing local political, economic and cultural barriers to Soviet law and organisational practices.

Finally, Marxist-Leninism promised a socialist utopia built on an infallible scientific methodology. Party leaders promoted the belief that 'Marxist doctrine is omnipotent because it is true. It is complete and harmonious' (Truong Chinh 1968:547). As an all-embracing philosophy the doctrine could only accommodate other viewpoints from a Marxist perspective. By adopting Marxist 'scientism'—a comprehensive search for the fundamental guides to life—Vietnamese leaders created a doctrinaire intellectual environment. Because the Party and state determined the class relationships that generated legal consequences, legal concepts were by definition limited to subjects approved by the state. Critical analysis of legal ideology challenged Marxist-Leninist infallibility and was politically unacceptable.

The preceding discussion suggests various factors combined to constrain local Vietnamese discourses from reshaping Soviet legal ideology

- the deterministic link between the economic base and superstructure discouraged investigation into links between law and cultural factors
- Marxism discredited East Asian economic and cultural practices
- socialism promoted a global workers' culture that de-emphasised regional differences

- as a holistic ideology Marxist-Leninism created a closed epistemological structure that only permitted analysis from its own self-referential perspectives
- Vietnamese were reluctant to offend Soviet aid providers
- Vietnamese lawmakers reconciled law and society through pragmatic experimentation (learning by doing) rather than theorising.

ADAPTING SOCIALIST LAW: SEARCHING FOR VIETNAMESE LEGAL DISCOURSE

Unlike socialist legality, Soviet organisational principles (democratic centralism and collective mastery) were consciously applied to and mixed with local political and moral ideas. Following independence, Party leaders soon discovered that imported egalitarian Soviet ideals could not easily displace neo-Confucian values and hierarchical practices (Hoang Quoc Viet 1964). While authorities struggled to apply socialist legality in everyday life, they pragmatically mixed Soviet organisational principles with pre-modern moral principles to get 'in touch with the people' (*duong loi quan chung*) (Thanh Duy 1997:27–8). Since people responded to *tinh cam* (sentiment) more readily than to abstract socialist legality, revolutionary morality was used to mobilise public support (collective mastery).

Party theorists developed revolutionary morality by mythologising continuities between pre-modern morals and Marxist-Leninism (Nguyen Khac Vien 1974). Revolutionary morality promoted shared communitarian values—the idea that people are 'a totality of their social relationships', 'collective discipline' and the 'fulfilment of social obligations'. Confucianism and Marxist-Leninism were not entirely compatible because Marxist materialism discredited Confucian spirituality social hierarchies.

More generally, revolutionary morality not only shared a similar moral outlook, but also a comparable administrative style with pre-modern governance. Ho Chi Minh frequently stressed the importance of moral leadership by the Party (Nguyen Khac Vien 1974; Quang Can 2001). He opined that '[i]f one does not have morality, one can hardly lead the people, however talented one can be' (Ho Chi Minh 1995:338). Party leaders were expected to 'display higher knowledge than ordinary people…act with lucidity and clear-sightedness and…look farther and wider than others' (Song Thanh 1995:6). Once Party leaders had attained a higher revolutionary morality—like mandarin 'first knowers'—they were obliged to instruct and guide those with less 'class sentiment or awareness' (*tinh cam giai cap*).

Like Confucian rule, revolutionary morality personalised state–society relationships. Theorists aimed to 'strengthen the unification between politics and the spirit of the whole people' (*tang cuong su nhat tri ve chinh tri va tinh than cua toan va phap*) by infusing personal relationships between cadres and the people with class sentiment or awareness.[5] If the masses were awakened (*giac ngo*) to class sentiment or awareness, they would respect the Party as the highest 'revolutionary moral' (*dao duc cah many*) authority. Party cadres in practice complained that the people followed orders from those they liked and ignored those from whom they disliked. Many officials were not originally from the working class and required constant reminding to remain close to the people.

Pre-modern and socialist organisational principles converged in three areas: raising public interests over individual interests, promoting the state to lead society and treating law as a tool to maintain social order.

The preceding discussion implies that socialist legality and socialist organisational principles (for example, democratic centralism and collective mastery) engaged different Vietnamese narratives. Soviet-trained Vietnamese lawyers imported socialist legality into a reified Soviet-influenced legal environment that rarely engaged the world outside élite legal institutions. Despite potent political and epistemological constraints, Soviet legal reasoning was not entirely isolated from local discourse. Through cultural osmosis it slowly acquired meanings from residual imperial Vietnamese and French legal epistemologies. Take, for example, the Sino-Vietnamese term *phap che*, which was used to translate the Soviet word for 'legality' (Dinh Gia Trinh 1964a). While *phap che* retained its Soviet meaning in scholarly discourse, in political discourse it reverted to its pre-modern legal meaning—to 'ensure legal compliance' through mass legal or moral education campaigns.

Vietnamese legal personnel extended the process of acculturation by pragmatically adapting Soviet laws to suit Vietnamese legal institutions (Nicholson 2001). But they were content with highly contextualised, technical adjustments and did not meditatively theorise a distinctly Vietnamese socialist law.

Various factors discouraged lawmakers from conceptually reconfiguring Soviet legal theory to suit local ideas and practices. Marxist-Leninist theory disassociated law from cultural relationships. It also assumed that a global workers' culture would flatten out regional differences separating socialist countries. Most policymakers presupposed the infallibility of Soviet thinking and sought ways to make society resemble law, rather than making laws resemble society. They placed socialist law in a closed epistemological system with few points of communication with local moral and cultural thinking.

In contrast with socialist legality, democratic centralism and collective mastery concepts were interwoven with local political and moral arguments promoting Party 'leadership' (Nguyen Khanh Toan 1964). They stressed hierarchies and communitarian sentiments that were analogous to, and easily blended with, Ho Chi Minh's revolutionary virtue-rule. Moreover, they primarily addressed Party and state cadres—the group most influenced by the imported socialist 'workers' culture'. In the end, Soviet organisational principles established the Party and state architecture and the revolutionary virtue-rule regulated governance practices.

Incompatibilities between imported legality and political and moral virtue-rule did not especially matter in the command economy, where the state primarily used discretionary powers to order society. Legality began to assume more importance when the Sixth Party Congress in 1986 formally agreed that 'management of the country should be performed through laws rather than moral concepts'. By this time, market forces were already undermining the administrative apparatus used to dispense virtue-rule. After decades without significant change, external conditions forced a discourse between socialist legality and local deliberations.

CONTEMPORARY LEGAL BORROWING

This section examines contemporary political, economic, moral, cultural and legal discourses for new meanings about socialist law. Following the *doi moi* reforms in 1986, lawmakers began searching beyond the socialist world for legal inspiration. It is argued that the conceptual debates used to justify importing capitalist legal norms into commercial laws have significantly reconfigured some core beliefs underpinning socialist law.[6]

Political discourse

The Seventh Party Congress in 1991 changed the socialist political–legal canon by adding law-based state (*nha nuoc phap quyen*) concepts to socialist legality, democratic centralism and collective mastery (Do Muoi 1992). The law-based state promoted a procedural 'rule of law' based on stable, authoritative and compulsory law; equality before the law; and the use of law to constrain and supervise enforcement and administration. It also proposed a separation of Party and state functions where the Party was supposed to formulate socioeconomic objectives, leaving the state apparatus to enact and implement the Party line.

Far from producing legal certainty, the law-based state failed to clarify whether the Party retained prerogative powers to substitute policy for law. The Constitution in 1992 appeared to place the Party under the rule of law, but it also reaffirmed the constitutionality of socialist legality, democratic centralism and collective mastery, doctrines that promoted Party paramountcy over law.

Dao Tri Uc (1999:18), a prominent legal scholar, recently confirmed the Marxist-Leninist basis of law, stating that

> [l]egality (*phap che*) in general is the way to organise society, to put social life into the order that fits with the will of the ruling class. If laws are the legalised will of the ruling class, arising from the contemporary needs and social conditions of the ruling class, legality must be understood as the process to put that will into real life, making it reality. Thus, for us, legality has the same meaning as the need to institutionalise the requirement that state administration and social administration benefit the working people.

Recalling Marxist 'scientism', this narrative first asserts that Marxist-Leninism and the thoughts of Ho Chi Minh are infallible and eternal truths. It then applies this *a priori* 'truth' to show that law reflects the 'will of the ruling class' (*y chi cua giai cap thong tri*). As the executive committee of the 'ruling class', the Party decides which laws 'benefit the working people' (Nguyen Van Thai 1996:3, 7).

This political image of socialist law has been so successfully inculcated through Party policy, university and professional training courses and workplace practices that many Vietnamese legal officials treat socialist law as indigenous thinking (Le Honh Hanh 1998; Le Minh Tam 1998). Recycling decades-old notions that Vietnam belongs to an international socialist family (*gia dinh xa hoi chu nghia*), many officials believe that socialist law is compatible with Vietnamese precepts because it originated from a similar 'political system' (*he thong chinh tri*). In the socialist family, the Soviet Union was considered the 'elder brother' and 'family members' followed what they were told.

Some theorists have reconfigured class theory to make it more relevant to lawmakers, who are now required to borrow laws from non-socialist sources. Using class-based law as his theoretical compass, Dao Tri Uc (1995) developed a methodology to guide lawmakers borrowing norms from the Lê and Nguyen dynasty codes. He reasoned that Imperial Laws were composed of two basic elements— social norms that regulate common interests and rules designed to advance imperial families. 'One should not jump to the conclusion', he wrote, 'that the first aspect [norms regulating common interests] is progressive and should be inherited, while the second aspect [laws promoting imperial families] is counter-progressive and therefore should not be inherited' (Dao Tri Uc 1995:39). On the contrary, in his estimation, feudal laws were 'progressive' and worth borrowing, provided they did not conflict with common interests or the national interests. Departing from orthodox class-based thinking, he urged contemporary lawmakers to select laws from pre-modern sources that reflected the interests of the working class or that promoted national goals.

For Dao Tri Uc, law in the superstructure should reflect both national and worker interests. His reformulation of the link between the will of the working class and law gave lawmakers a theoretical licence to borrow laws from capitalist countries. He ultimately concluded that the purpose of law was to implement the Party line— a formulation that is consistent with the principles of orthodox democratic centralism and collective mastery (now renamed people's mastery or *lam chu nhan dan*). It remains to be seen whether theorists working in other disciplines are prepared to change core Marxist-Leninist principles fundamentally and constrain Party political power with law.

Economic discourse

Market reforms have influenced legal discourse more than any other single factor. Economic arguments have challenged legal thinking about Marx's causal link between the 'economic base and superstructure', 'state economic management' (*quan ly nha nuoc kinh te*) and international legal harmonisation.

Party resolutions recognising private ownership have emboldened some economic writers to adapt the Marxist canon imaginatively to market conditions (Vu Anh Tuan 1998; Vo Khanh Vinh 1997). Some writers reaffirmed old orthodoxies that the 'economic system of a society determines the nature and form of its legal system', but used this argument to assert that changes in the 'base' or 'mode of production' induced by private ownership should be reflected by corresponding legal changes in the 'superstructure'. By this, they mean market laws in the superstructure should reflect mixed-market economic relationships. This new application of conventional Marxist thinking removes conceptual obstacles to importing rights-based market laws into the superstructure.

Strongly influenced by Chinese Marxist theorists (Shih 1996), other Vietnamese writers insist that 'laws have their relative independence and influence on the economic system' (Vu Anh Tuan 1998:26–7; Le Minh Quan 1997:28–31). In other words, the economic base and superstructure co-exist with 'relative autonomy'. This radical revision of Marxist orthodoxy not only removes conceptual obstacles to borrowing laws from non-socialist economies, it also abandons the core socialist idea that law reflects class interests.

State economic management. Especially after the Fourth Vietnam Workers Party Congress in 1976, Soviet state economic planning became the primary regulatory instrument (Cong Tac Ke Hoach 1976). State planners needed administrative mechanisms to implement plans. Devised in the Soviet Union to link planning and economic production, 'state economic management' (*quan ly nha nuoc kinh te*) unified political and economic leadership in the state (Nguyen Nien 1976:34–6). 'State economic management' possessed a 'party nature' (*tinh dang cong san*), which gave Party and state authorities broad 'prerogative' powers to fine-tune economic production (Hoang Quoc Viet 1973:8–12; Le Thanh Nghi 1975).

Calls by legal writers in the 1970s to legalise and systematise command planning with an economic code were rejected. Party leaders argued that prerogative powers were needed to 'organically link' the Party's economic line with economic regulation. 'State economic management' gave the Party and state extra-legal prerogative powers to micromanage the economy.

Following *doi moi* reforms, regulatory tensions between imported market liberalism and 'state economic management' have increasingly surfaced in legal discourse (Doan Trong Truyen 1997). Views range from the neoliberal claim that states should only intervene to prevent market failures to orthodox state managerial models.[7] Neoliberal theorists argue for a facilitative legislative framework administered by reactive state institutions such as courts. This regulatory formula limits state intervention to correcting market pathologies and deregulating 'asking giving' (*co che xin cho*) discretionary business licences. Neoliberal economic ideas are clearly evident in foreign donor-funded legal reforms, such as in the Comprehensive Legal Needs Assessment (LNA) Report,[8] which provides that

- citizens may do everything not expressly prohibited by law
- the 'state must not do anything, except that which is expressly permitted by law'
- citizens should have increased powers to 'know, discuss and check' state power.

There is little discernable support for neoliberal economic ideas in the legal literature. A small number of Vietnamese legal academics are convinced 'state economic management' compromises liberal market rights, such as freedom to conduct authorised business activities (Pham Duy Nghia 2002; Pham Duy Nghia 2000). However, they remain sceptical about whether sweeping economic deregulation designed to remove bureaucratic discretion is an appropriate economic policy for a poor country experiencing uneven wealth creation. Instead, they support the Keynesian view that states should proactively redistribute wealth according to need.

Other commentators favour a Japanese-style proactive regulatory model.[9] They agree with neoliberal theorists that transparent legal systems encourage market stability and predictability, but believe that economic growth requires 'Rhine capitalism', where proactive states regulate economic producers (Vu Tuan Anh 1994:253–4). They believe there is an ongoing role for 'state economic management' in controlling large state-owned enterprises and micro-managing the private sector. In their estimation, legal rules should constrain the exercise of prerogative 'state management' powers.

At the other end of the regulatory spectrum, most commentators still support orthodox 'state economic management' that gives regulators extra-legal prerogative powers to manage the economy (Vu Ngoc Nhung 1999). They stress the compatibility between socialism and mixed-market economies—'commodity production is not the opposite of socialism'. They also consider 'the marriage of the private sector with a "socialist orientation" is one of convenience, not true love' and the 'market economy following a socialist orientation' (*kinh te thi truong theo dinh huong xa hoi chu nghia*) is a necessary transitional stage on the road to socialism (Luu Ha Vi 1997:1–4). 'State economic management' is thought necessary to ensure the economy follows the 'socialist' way.

Party enthusiasm for 'state economic management' likewise seems undiminished by market reforms. Although the Resolution of the Fifth Plenum of the Party Central Committee in 2002 endorsed private sector development, it also reaffirmed that the 'socialist-oriented market economy is placed under state management'.

Perhaps because it directly concerns politically sensitive prerogative powers, published writings rarely critically evaluate the relevance of 'state economic management' in a mixed-market economy. This reticence is also found in unpublished postgraduate dissertations that discuss the application of 'state economic management' to new commercial sectors such as the stock market or foreign banking. Rather than questioning the relevance of a command economy regulatory system, researchers have searched for ways to strengthen state control. Support for 'state economic management' is also found in some academic writings. Mai Huu Thuc (2001:23–4) obliquely argues that 'state economic management' is required to realise Party-mandated socioeconomic objectives. Hoang The Lien, the author of the 'Legal Needs Assessment Legal Institutions Report', was more explicit in recommending legal institutions reform to 'improve leadership by party organisations over economic and financial management' (Ministry of Justice 2002:40).

International economic integration. Arguments supporting international economic integration have profoundly influenced legal thinking. Contrasting with the cryptic and coded references to 'state economic management', international economic integration is vigorously debated. By the mid 1980s, Party leaders concluded that central planning, trade with Eastern bloc countries and import-replacement strategies could not replicate the economic growth experienced by Vietnam's neighbours (Fforde 1999:44–63). In 1986, the Party adopted an 'open door' (mo cua), adopting policies of cautiously opening the economy to foreign trade and investment from capitalist countries. Most Vietnamese commentators attribute this reorientation more to economic necessity than to an ideological shift towards free trade. Nevertheless, officials realised

> the biggest factor that may influence the direction of Vietnam's future trade policy is the integration of this country into regional and international economic organisations. The process of joining the WTO compels Vietnam to adjust its whole trade system in accordance with the rules and disciplines of this organisation (Tran Thu Hang 1999:121).

Entry into a bilateral trade agreement (BTA) with the United States in 2001 in some ways overshadowed WTO accession, which is currently scheduled for 2006. The BTA contained most WTO entry conditions and some additional provisions requiring Vietnam to change institutional structures to improve administrative review over 'state economic management' and widen market access for foreign legal practitioners.[10]

Opinions concerning international economic integration are polarised. Most government sources uncritically promote integration (Nguyen Minh Tu 1999). Numerous studies have attempted to demonstrate that integration has improved domestic economic growth and reduced poverty (Giang Chau 2003; Minh Khuong 1999). The 2001–10 Socio-Economic Development Strategy, issued by the Ninth Party Congress in 2001, endorsed this position.

Not everyone in the Party supports economic integration. Nguyen Tan Dung, a Politburo member, cautions that integration and globalisation will erode national sovereignty

> Economic independence and sovereignty means first of all not being governed by or dependent on the outside for economic development lines and policies, on the economic and/or political conditions they wish to impose on us for assistance, bilateral or multilateral cooperation, the conditions which will cause harm to our national sovereignty and national basic interests (Nguyen Tan Dung 2002:3).

Underlying his concern is the fear that international integration may compromise the capacity for state-owned enterprises to 'constitute an important material force and macro instrument for the state to orient and regulate the economy'. Put more generally, the national interest (that is, food, energy, environment and socioeconomic infrastructure) and economic growth supported by local capital and technology should be protected from foreign economic influence. Such views are heavily coloured by nationalism and deeply ingrained notions of 'self-sufficiency' (phat huy noi luc; literally, to promote internal strengths). Those advocating self-reliance believe the erosion of national sovereignty outweighs the putative benefits of international trade and investment (Pham Van Chuc 2002).

For different reasons, other economists have questioned the government's assertion that international economic integration is an unqualified good (Tran Viet Phuong 1999). Their research shows that international trade and investment can increase social inequality, a topic that is conspicuously absent from most government literature. Rather than passively accepting economic globalisation, they argue that careful state intervention can anticipate and reduce many harmful side-effects. Their writings are free of the visceral fears about foreign dependency animating political critiques.

Unsurprisingly, government legal writings unreservedly embrace international economic integration. The Final Report of the Legal Needs Assessment is unequivocal in its support

> The concept of proactive international economic integration must be instilled in the development and completion of the legal system of Vietnam in all fields, from lawmaking and implementation, to legal education and dissemination. Vietnam's legal system should not only reflect the specific features of this country, but also must meet international standards in order to be able to help Vietnam perform her international commitments based on the principles of national independence, self-determination and socialist orientation (Ministry of Justice 2002:25).

International integration was put beyond doubt by the LNA action plan, which gave priority to legislative reforms required for BTA and WTO membership.

Critiques by commentators following the government's integrationist line generally considered narrow technical issues. Some have reviewed domestic statutory changes required to satisfy Most Favoured Nation, National Treatment and international intellectual property conditions imposed by the WTO (Tran Van Nam 2002; Nguyen Thanh Tam 2001). Others have described the reforms to administrative review required to meet treaty obligations (Hoang Phuoc Hiep 2001). Their work is distinguished by a reluctance to link legal harmonisation with broad economic arguments that legal harmonisation will create economic winners and losers. Only a few academic legal writers have queried government policy by suggesting that legal harmonisation should aim to minimise domestic economic dislocation (Pham Duy Nghia 2001).

To summarise, shifts in Marxist economic thinking have made legal borrowing from capitalist countries theoretically respectable, but at the same time the role of 'state economic management' in the mixed-market economy is unresolved. Legal discourse reflects this uncertainty. It oscillates between the neoliberal legal language that permeates foreign donor discourse and the ambiguous messages in Party and government writings about 'Party leadership' over the economy.

With some notable exceptions (discussed below), legal discourse rarely considers the institutional and epistemological incompatibilities generated by superimposing a rights-based legislative framework over a Soviet-inspired legal system. Most contemporary writers focus on narrow legal technicalities without engaging in broader discursive narratives. In dismissing indigenous business culture as sub-optimal or non-existent, writers assume that international legal harmonisation is simply a technical adjustment between legal systems. Further, unreflective borrowing is politically prudent, because critical research may implicitly fault Party policy by questioning economic integration.

Uncritical law reform did not especially matter in the command economy, because officials could reconcile gaps between law and reality with 'state economic management' discretionary powers. This strategy is becoming less tenable in contemporary Vietnam, because foreign investors are prepared to test legal rights introduced in borrowed capitalist laws. Legal contests will bring into focus competition between extra-legal prerogative powers and legal rights, and the political, moral and legal rationales underpinning these regulatory approaches.

Morality

There is a long-standing tension between moral and legal discourse in Vietnam. Moral discourse was historically privileged over legal arguments (Ta Van Tai 1982). As we have seen, virtue-rule more than legality regulated pre-*doi moi* Vietnam. Legality was officially encouraged by the Sixth Party Congress in 1986, but rule through law was not formally accepted until the Seventh Party Congress endorsed the 'state-based law' (*nha nuoc phap quyen*) doctrine in 1991 (Do Moi 1992:30–8). By this time, most legal writers recognised that the separation of law and morality is a prerequisite of rights-based legal systems (Nguyen Nhu Phat 1997).

Although it has significantly reconfigured socialist legality, law-based state discourse has had little impact on the Soviet organisational principles (democratic centralism and collective mastery) that legitimise Party moral 'leadership' (*su lanh dao cua dang*). For every official pronouncement that law governs state–society relations, other narratives strongly imply that moral rule is still a vital source of legitimacy and normative standards for Party leadership. The Party and state insist that 'the CPV is the political force leading the whole system…and reforms of the political system should absolutely not touch the decisive point that the CPV has the sole leading role' (Hoc Vien Hanh Chinh Quoc Gia 1991:11–9).

The contemporary importance of moral rule is inferred from the unrelenting efforts to portray the Party as infallible—a moral exemplar. Reprising Ho Chi Minh's assertion that the 'Party is morality', Tran Xuan Truong (2002) recently declared 'our Party is civilisation'. Nguyen Phu Trong (1999:7), a member of the Politburo, grandiloquently described the Party as 'the intellect, the honour, the conscience of our time; the Party is the embodiment of the wisdom, quality, the quintessence of the nation'.

Moral rule is further implied by the Party's preoccupation with moral perfection. The Central Committee's Political Report to the Ninth Party Congress in 2001 proposed the following measures to strengthen Party leadership: forge revolutionary ethics, combat individualism, promote exemplary behaviour, and concentrate on self-improvement (Communist Party of Vietnam 2001). Public administration reforms aiming for meritorious recruitment and promotion were also recommended, but as an adjunct to the moral perfection underpinning 'Party leadership'. Government reports are also full of accounts attributing the gap between legislative objectives and social behaviour to poor implementation by officials who lack ideological knowledge and deviate from Party morality (Ngo Cuong 1997). They resemble in substance and tone the moral justifications for legal violations in legal writings during the 1960s.

It is important to recognise the potential for transformative change. Evidence suggests that market forces and international treaty obligations are compelling the Party to replace moral regulation with due process and legal transparency. As foreign and domestic investors increasingly challenge the discretionary outcomes produced by moral rule, it is plausible that the Party and state will search for alternative sources of institutional order—legal sources of order. Moral solutions are difficult to sustain in a socially pluralistic mixed-market economy.

Preliminary research suggests the shift from moral to legal regulation is already well advanced in the economic arena (Nguyen Thi Oanh 1998:3). Once moral rule declines in importance as a regulatory instrument, it is possible that the Party will open moral discourse to public debate. In the meantime, legal writers rarely mention moral rule, much less the appropriateness of political morality. Their silence contrasts with the vigorous exchanges concerning cultural borrowing.

Culture

Vietnamese writers are fascinated with the role culture plays in social and economic development.[11] Many themes run through this discourse, but two concepts support the proposition that attitudes to cultural identity shape the way people approach legal borrowing. The first account infers from traditional village practices an authentic national culture (*van hoa dan toc*) surrounded by layers of received external influences (Dao Minh Quang 1993). Some writers in this tradition deride mandarin literati for 'worshipping' Chinese culture and consigning indigenous Vietnamese state and legal apparatus to a quagmire of neo-Confucian dogmatism and conservatism (Vu Khieu 1999; Dao Tri Uc and Le Minh Thong 1999). Like articles of faith, certain Vietnamese institutions like Red River Delta villages are placed within the traditional core, while other practices, particularly those derived from colonial and foreign sources, are relegated to the social margins. Such views are especially evident in political tracts designed by Party leaders to highlight a culture in opposition to foreign influences (Le Kha Phieu 1998).

Contesting this nationalistic portrayal of the Vietnamese as heroic resisters against foreign domination, a second counter-narrative portrays Vietnamese culture in dialogue with foreign influences. Some commentators maintain that during the initial stages of anti-colonial resistance most Vietnamese intellectuals treated French culture with disdain (Dao Tri Uc and Le Minh Thong 1999). Later, when traditional values proved unable to combat colonial domination, prominent Vietnamese began to selectively borrow imported precepts and practices. Nationalist leaders such as

Phan Boi Chua and Phan Chau Trinh were influenced by French legal ideas such as civil rights and constitutionalism. Later still, lessons learnt by Ho Chi Minh in Europe, the Soviet Union and East Asia during the 1930s are described as having revitalised opposition to colonial rule (Quang Can 2001). The message for contemporary leaders is that cultural exchange invigorates and renews domestic values.

Commentaries regarding foreign cultural borrowings are strongly influenced by perceptions about Vietnamese cultural identity. Those promoting cultural exchanges warn against an exaggerated national identity that inhibits learning from others (Nguyen Tran Bat 2002). They believe that foreign cultural values should be evaluated according to their capacity to increase social and economic competitiveness.

Counter-narratives stressing Party-led resistance to foreign domination focus instead on how 'global' culture spread by foreign trade, media, Internet communications, cinema and tourism has the potential to subvert confidence in local traditions (Tran Van Giau 1995). This discourse theme reinforces xenophobia by characterising foreign influence as 'peaceful evolution' (*dien bien hoa binh*)—foreigners undermining Party and state authority. Its potency is demonstrated by the demotion of Le Dang Doanh, a prominent market reformer, for allegedly associating too closely with foreigners, especially Americans.[12]

Borrowed cultural elements are portrayed as tainting or disrupting 'core' Vietnamese values. For example, foreign ideas are blamed for alienating the young from Vietnamese culture, causing them to lose their roots (*mat goc*), and breeding individualism and consumerism. Party resolutions echo these concerns: 'the market economy, with its tremendous spontaneous power, has encouraged individualism and made the people attach importance to individual interests while forgetting the interests of the community'.[13]

Rather than evaluating cultural imports according to their capacity to benefit society, this nationalistic narrative uses politically determined criteria to guide cultural borrowing. As the nation's moral guardians, Party theorists select and promote core political and moral ideas that 'protect the "beautiful traditions" (*truyen thong tot dep*) and values of the country' (Le Kha Phieu 1998:42). The central concern is that 'internal factors must have the leading role in directing the relations with and deciding the choice of external factors.'

Cultural debates rarely appear in legal writings, but their influence is evident in approaches to law reform. Differences between Western laws and core Vietnamese cultural values were explored in research conducted by the Legal Research Institute (*Vien Nghien Cuu Khoa Hoc Phap Ly*), a body attached to the Ministry of Justice.[14] Their search for legal norms in Vietnam's Imperial Codes was strongly influenced by the 'Asian values' thesis. Promoted by Asian leaders such as Singapore's Lee Kuan Yew and Malaysia's Mohamad Mahathir, this nationalisitic rhetoric maintains that Asian states can withstand 'negative' global pressures and preserve social stability and élite power by asserting core 'traditional', mainly Confucian, moral values. This approach was partially discredited when the East Asian economic crisis exposed deep structural flaws in the East Asian development model. Research, nevertheless, proceeded on the untested assumption that 'East Asian' cultural values will produce beneficial economic outcomes in Vietnam.

Researchers plundered Vietnam's pre-modern Imperial Codes, searching for quintessential Vietnamese-Confucian laws. In treating pre-modern legal norms as autonomous regulatory instruments, however, they detached these rules from the social, economic and cultural context that gave them meaning. Traditional preference for non-adversarial dispute resolution, for example, was attributed to a traditional Vietnamese communalism that discouraged 'individuality' and the 'self' (Dao Bao Ngoc 1999:32–5). Pre-modern political and economic constraints on court-based adjudication were ignored.

Researchers also employed a dubious methodology that read history backwards. They used prevailing cultural values to assess the contemporary utility of pre-modern legal norms. For example, commentators imagined the early Lê Dynasty (fifteenth century) as a golden age of political-legal innovation when indigenous commercial practices crystallised into legally enforceable rights. This construction misconstrued the stated purpose of the Lê Code, which was to reproduce an imported Chinese social order (*tam cuong*). To the Confucian mind, close textual readings made limited sense, since legal meaning resided primarily in the moral teachings of mandarin literati (Whitmore 1995). Appeals to the letter of the law implied a disregard for morality, or worse, moral weakness. Commercial provisions in the Lê Code served a public law function to preserve village harmony and were never intended to confer private rights (Vu Van Mau 1963).

Despite voluminous writings, researchers failed to find meaningful ways to incorporate traditional norms (*duc tri*) based on pre-industrial village life into a legal system regulating an educated and internationally integrated mixed-market society (Dao Tri Uc 1995). Researchers did not give legislative drafters the contextual information needed to ascertain whether pre-modern legal norms could regulate contemporary life.

Without cultural frames of reference, legal drafters must rely on vague cultural stereotypes and the perceived prestige of particular legal systems to decide whether Chinese law, for example, is intrinsically more compatible with Vietnamese culture than US or Japanese law. Cultural compatibility seemed relatively unimportant to legal borrowing during the 1960–70s, when the Party was convinced that society was evolving into a transcultural Soviet-socialist utopia. But unreflective legal borrowing is untenable in contemporary Vietnam, where the state is borrowing laws from an eclectic range of legal sources. It is also difficult to explain by reference to either inward or outward-looking cultural discourses, as both caution against wholesale legal borrowing from foreign cultures. What remains unclear is why contemporary legal borrowers have been reluctant to bring lawmaking into conversation with economic, moral and cultural discourses.

LEGAL BORROWING DISCOURSE

Like Soviet borrowing in the 1960s, post-*doi moi* legal borrowing has again superimposed foreign legal concepts over indigenous institutional and epistemological legal structures. This section examines whether contemporary lawmakers are more prepared than their predecessors to adjust borrowed law to local political, economic, moral and cultural concerns.

Three analytical threads run through the literature. First, most writers use technical legal language to analyse foreign laws. Second, some writers have reconfigured Marxist-Leninism to make legal borrowing from capitalist countries a theoretical possibility. Third, a few commentators have quietly replaced Marxist-Leninism with borrowed Western sociological theory that embeds borrowed law in a broad discursive context.

Returning to the first analytical thread, most legal writers avoid sensitive political, economic and moral comparisons between imported law and domestic conditions by narrowly focusing on technical legal rules (Dao Bao Ngoc 1999; Pham Duy Nghia 2000). Consider Hoang The Lien's (1996) comparative consideration of legal capacity in the European and Vietnamese Civil Codes. His analysis examined the surface text without engaging underlying legal doctrines, much less the political, economic and moral discourses shaping legal preferences. For example, the legal capacity of companies was analysed by comparing the textual meaning of different statutory provisions, without explaining that these provisions operated in profoundly different legal systems and political economies.

There are undoubtedly many explanations for this 'black letter' law approach to legal borrowing, such as a lack of comparative law and research skills. Never far below the surface is the political concern that law should reflect the 'will of the ruling class', as interpreted by the Party. The LNA project, coordinated by the Ministry of Justice, illustrates this problem. It assessed the suitability of Vietnamese laws and legal institutions according to their capacity to realise the four socioeconomic development strategies approved by the Ninth Party Congress in 2001. Ministry officials ignored economic reports showing that the Party's economic integration policy produces inequitable outcomes and committed the government to legal reforms required to 'meet international standards in order to help Vietnam perform her international commitments' (Ministry of Justice 2002:25). Political and cultural arguments that legal imports may erode 'core' Vietnamese cultural values were also disregarded.

If legal needs are primarily assessed from Party and state political perspectives, it is comparatively unimportant whether legal imports are compatible with local conditions. Although lawmakers are generally well aware that incongruent laws are unlikely to produce desired outcomes, they feel constrained from localising law in a closed epistemological environment where legal discourse is subordinate to political imperatives. Borrowed laws are consequently treated like technical fragments detached from a political, economic, moral and cultural context.

The second analytical thread reveals the tension between political constraints over legal thinking, and government policies that now encourage lawmakers to consider the social impact of new law.[15] This policy has emboldened some theorists to find new ways to localise borrowed law. While retaining the belief that Marxist-Leninism 'is still the most scientific and creative ideology in the world', they stress the need to apply socialist theory flexibly to new conditions (Le Honh Hanh 1998:319).

Dialogue with Soviet lawyers slowed after the Russian Federation was formed, and Vietnamese theorists began looking for new sources of legal thinking. Most theorists lacked the linguistic skills to engage deeply with Chinese theory and, in any event, considered Chinese legal thinking comparatively underdeveloped. Some theorists turned to internal sources for new ideas, while others looked outside Vietnam for inspiration.

Dao Tri Uc was among those many theorists who sought new ideas from local discourse. As previously mentioned, he attempted to make borrowed Soviet theory more relevant by reconfiguring Marx's base–superstructure metaphor to justify legal borrowing from capitalist regimes. Others creatively used Ho Chi Minh's eclectic blend of Western, Marxist-Leninist and pre-modern Vietnamese thinking as a 'political umbrella' to smuggle new concepts into the legal discourse. They selectively plundered Ho Chi Minh's thoughts for 'rule of law' or Confucian aphorisms to open the epistemological environment to ideas beyond the narrow parameters permitted by class-analysis (Tran Dinh Huynh 1999; Le Minh Tong 2000).

Borrowing from external discourses, some theorists have attempted to expand the epistemological repertoire by increasing the narrow range of legal relationships recognised by orthodox Soviet legal taxonomies (Nha Nuoc va Phap Luat 1996). Soviet jurisprudence received into Vietnam during the 1960s used law instrumentally to 'adjust social relationships' (*dien chinh*). The state first classified 'social relationships' (*quan he xa loi*) according to shared class characteristics and then enacted laws to regulate social relationships within predetermined 'independent law branches' (*nganh luat doc lap*). Soviet legal taxonomies functioned well enough in a command economy, but now constrain Vietnamese lawmakers from thinking about market laws in conceptually coherent ways.

Soviet finance law taxonomies illustrate the problem. They were developed to classify financial transactions in a centrally planned economy and influence the way legal actors conceived law. For example, Soviet taxonomies classify tendering rules as public finance law, because money is paid from the state budget. Consequently, it is difficult for lawyers to see the private law underlying tendering rules.

The imported notion that 'fair and equitable' laws (*cong bang cua phap luat*) must balance social interests directly challenges the instrumental Soviet notion that law adjusts social relationships. As one writer put it, 'law should be attached to politics but is not a servant of the state' (Nha Nuoc va Phap Luat 1996:116-7). In other words, laws implement political policy, but are not 'management tools' (*cong cu quan ly)*. This new thinking allows lawyers to move beyond top-down Soviet taxonomies and conceptualise horizontal legal relationships.

Other theories have attempted to blend Marxist thinking with Western thoeries that stress linkages between law and culture, especially legal culture (*van hoa phap ly*). Their writings unconsciously borrow from Durkheim's 'collective consciousness'—the notion that if society is an invisible moral environment surrounding individuals, then law is the visible manifestation of 'community sentiment' (Durkheim 1960). Though arguing that law reflects social mores and 'community sentiment' (*tinh lang nhia xom*), they are unwilling to repudiate the Marxist base–superstructure metaphor and embrace a fully realised alternative social theory that explains the interdependence between law and society (Le Minh Tam 1998). Without taking this final step, their theorising lacks the methodological tools lawmakers need to codify ideas from local discursive narratives.

The third analytical thread contrasts with the previous theoretical approaches, because it uses Western sociological theory to bypass Marxist-Leninism. This subtle shift in thinking is revealed as much by what is not said as by explicit arguments. These writers rarely mention Marxist-Leninist formulas and clearly separate political, economic, moral and legal arguments. Unfettered by the base–superstructure metaphor, they are free to conceptualise complex interactions between borrowed law and society.

Some German-trained academic lawyers argue from Weberian theory that imported foreign commercial laws (*du nhap luat kinh te nuoc ngoai*) will only induce desired behaviour where they are popular with the people (*tinh pho thong*), well-defined (*xac dinh on dinh*), predictable (*co the du doan truoc*) and transparent (*tinh ro rang*) (Pham Duy Nghia 2000, 2001). They maintain that hastily borrowed Western legal rules laws are incompatible with domestic 'legal ideology' (*tu duy phap ly*) and will not transplant successfully.

Pham Duy Nghia (2000) argued that many Western commercial legal norms introduced capitalist political and economic ideals that were incompatible with the small-scale family structures and sentimental bonds that characterise Vietnam's 'peasant legal culture' (*nen phap ly nong dan*). He illustrated this point with Articles 8 and 9 of the Commercial Law 1997, which imported Western unfair competition and consumer protection principles that functioned like idealistic political slogans (*khau hieu*) in Vietnam's highly state-directed economy. He concluded that borrowed Western law is generally incompatible with domestic economic and cultural conditions, but legal importation is the only practical means of quickly enacting the commercial legal framework required for international economic integration. 'Legal harmonisation' (*hai hoa phap luat*) is a long-term project requiring the state to devote more resources to researching and reconciling imported precepts with local social conditions.

CONCLUSION

The introduction of the law-based state doctrine in 1991 opened up legal debate by allowing Vietnamese commentators to re-evaluate long-standing socialist legal concepts. Their richly variegated legal discourses, considered in this chapter, convey multiple understandings of socialist law. In some areas socialist law has assimilated capitalist legal rights; in other areas it resembles decades-old Soviet discourse.

It is also possible to infer from the legal discourse three interrelated propositions that suggest the potential for legal change. First, law is a process used by competing social agents to order state power. Second, power struggles determine whether epistemological settings governing legal discourse are closed and self-referential, or open and willing to engage new ideas. Third, rules that control the levers of power are more strongly contested than legal ideas on the periphery of power relations (Dezalay and Garth 2002).

Democratic centralism and collective mastery rapidly became the central organisational principles governing power relationships among Vietnamese Party and government structures. These principles remain deeply embedded in political and moral narratives and resist conceptual changes that may disrupt longstanding power sharing arrangements.

In contrast, socialist legality was for decades enmeshed in a quasi-Soviet legal language understood by only a few élite Soviet-trained lawyers. As a peripheral discourse with little direct bearing on political power, socialist legality was less constrained by political discourse than democratic centralism and collective mastery. Especially in the commercial arena, where the Party actively encouraged legal change, socialist legality has rapidly evolved in response to new economic ideas. Imported commercial laws are now beginning to supply the normative rules that were once almost exclusively the prerogative of Party edicts and moral campaigns. Change is much slower where legal thinking impinges on Party and state power. For example, commentators discussing the capacity for socialist law to constrain Party political power are not permitted to consider Western 'rule of law'.

Power-sharing arrangements have also influenced the epistemological conventions that allow socialist ideas to change. Responding to market forces, rigid base–superstructure determinism has partially given way to a Durkheimian and Weberian conceptual framework that places law in a broad social, political and economic matrix. Legal discourse is learning from new economic ideas, especially concepts sponsored by international trade agreements. Other epistemological barriers are also dissolving. Marxist antipathy towards East Asian culture has been replaced by a 'reality' manufactured to support contemporary development objectives. Utopian yearnings for a model socialist society have been discarded in favour of East Asian developmentalism with 'socialist' characteristics. In the arenas where legal discourse has emerged from the shadow of political discourse, socialist law has become noticeably more legalistic and rule-oriented.

The Party and state have not been able to quarantine sacrosanct socialist principles entirely from change. Those advocating market regulation and a facilitative legal system openly challenge 'state economic management', which is a central component of Party 'leadership'. Marxist-Leninist 'scientific' infallibility, another concept closely allied to Party 'leadership', is also being eroded by sociological arguments that law belongs in a social context and is not merely an instrument of Party power. For the present, however, Party 'leadership' over politically sensitive national security issues remains beyond the reach of legal accountability.

This analysis locates the meaning of socialist law in 'officially' sanctioned discursive narratives. As legal thinking increasingly interacts with local 'unofficial' discourses, core Marxist-Leninist principles are giving way to new regulatory approaches. This trend is especially evident in the commercial arena, where imported laws interact and form hybrids with local norms and practices. In other social arenas, where political and moral discourses remain more powerful than legal discourse and without compelling reasons to legalise or constitutionalise political processes, 'socialist law' is likely to remain faithful to longstanding Marxist-Leninist concepts.

NOTES

[1] As editor of the Supreme Court journal *Tap San Tu Phap*, Dinh Gia Trinh was a prolific and influential writer (Dinh Gia Trinh 1961).

[2] Writing in the Vietnamese Court Review (*Tap San Tu Phap*), several Soviet law professors set out the basic principles of Soviet law (Lets Noi 1961).

[3] Vietnamese writers cited V. I. Lenin in *Nha nuoc va Cach Mang* [State and Revolution], Chapters Two and Three. Lenin proposed that the working class should centralise power in their hands and power should be distributed on the basis of democracy. This ideology gave political and social meaning to democratic centralism (Dinh Gia Trinh 1964a).

[4] Interviews with Le Kim Que, President, Bar Association of Hanoi, Hanoi, 1 October 1999, and Nguyen Thuc Bao, Former Legal Adviser to the Ministry of Agriculture, Hanoi, 11 September 2000.

[5] Interviews with Pham Huu Chi, former adviser to the Minister of Justice, Vice Rector of the Hanoi Law College and member of the Company Law Drafting Committee, 1992–94.

[6] Current legal thinking has been gleaned from political, economic, moral, cultural and legal discourse in Party and state publications, and also from interviews with state officials and academics.

[7] Interviews with Nguyen Dinh Cuong, Director of the Enterprise Department, CIEM, July 2002; March 2003.

[8] Most of the report was written in 2002 by John Bentley and Theodore Parnell, UNDP legal advisers to the Ministry of Justice.

[9] Interviews with JICA long-term legal representatives Legal Coordinator Kawazu Shinsuke and Judicial Expert Takeuchi Tsutomu, Hanoi, January 2002. See generally Lawrence Tshuma (1999:75–96).

[10] Resolution No. 48/2001/QH10 on the Ratification of the Agreement between the Socialist Republic of Vietnam and the United States of America on Trade Relations, Annex F.

[11] Cultural discourse, understood as arguments concerning the framework that gives meaning and sense to people's lives, comprises many interwoven discourse modes, such as moral, political and legal communication. It is treated as a separate discursive category, partly because it is difficult to unravel the discrete discursive modes and partly because for centuries the Vietnamese have evaluated their interaction with foreigners through a cultural framework.

[12] Interview with Le Dang Doanh, Hanoi, January 2001.

[13] Resolution of the Fifth Plenum of the Central Party Committee, 2001.

[14] The project was initiated by the Minister of Justice, Nguyen Dinh Loc, to overcome some of the problems experienced by drafting committees in reconciling borrowed law with Vietnamese conditions. Interview with Duong Thi Thanh Mai, Deputy Director of the Institute of Law

Research, Ministry of Justice, Hanoi, March 1999.

15   Law on the Promulgation of Law Instruments (amended 2003).

REFERENCES

Avineri, S., 1969. 'Introduction', in S. Avineri (ed), *Karl Marx on Colonialism and Modernization,* Doubleday, New York:6–16.

Beck, A., 1994. 'Is law an autopoietic system', *Oxford Journal of Legal Studies,* 14(3):401–18.

Communist Party of Vietnam, 2001. 'Political report of the Party Central Committee, 8th tenure, to the 9th National Congress', reproduced in Communist Party of Vietnam, *9th National Conference Documents,* The Gioi Publishers, Hanoi:75–82.

Cong Tac Ke Hoach, 1976. 'Carrying out good national economic planning and summarizing national economic planning well', April, 9, 9-11; JPRS 67923. 16-22.

Dao Bao Ngoc, 1999. 'Regional integration in Asia: from the perspective of the interaction between legal culture and legal regimes', *Nha Nuoc va Phap Luat* [State and Law], 7:30.

Dao Minh Quang, 1993. 'History of land tenure in pre-1954 Vietnam', *Journal of Contempary Asia,* 23(1):84–92.

Dao Tri Uc, 1995. 'Introduction to the study of Vietnam's state history and law', *Vietnam Law and Legal Forum,* 1(8):38–40.

——, 1999. 'The principle of legality ('Phap che') and its presentation in the criminal code of Vietnam', *Tap Chi Cong San* [Communist Review], January:18–22.

—— and Le Minh Thong, 1999. 'Su Tiep Nhan Cac Gia Tri Phap Ly Phuong Dong va Phuong Tay Doi Voi Su Phat Trien Cac Tu Tuong Phap Ly Viet Nam' [Reception of oriental and occidental legal values in the development of Vietnamese legal ideology]', *Nha Nuoc va Phap Luat* [State and Law], 5:3–16.

Dezalay, Y. and Garth, B.G., 2002. *The Internationalization of Palace Wars,* University of Chicago Press, Chicago.

Dinh Gia Trinh, 1961. 'May Y Kien Dong Gop Ve Van De Bao Ve Phap Che [Some opinion on the protection of legality]', *Tap San Tu Phap,* 3:20–32.

——, 1964a. *Nghien Cuu Nha Nuoc va Phap Quyen* [Studies about State and Legality], Nha Xuat Ban Su Hoc, Hanoi.

——, 1964b. 'Phap Che [Legality]', *Tap San Tu Phap,* 4:28–29.

——, 1965. 'May y kien ve tinh dan toc va tinh khoa hoc cua thuat ngu luat hoc— Nhan xet phe phan ve mot so thuat ngu thong dung [Nationalistic and scientific use of legal terminology: criticisms of common legal terms]', *Tap San Tu Phap,* 3:24–26.

Do Moi, 1992. *Sua Doi Hien Phap Xay Dung Nah Nuoc Phap Quyen Viet Nam, Day Minh Su Nghiep Doi Moi* [Amending the Constitution, Establishing a Law-based State and Promoting *Doi Moi* Achievements]', Nha Xuat Ban Su That (Truth Publishing House), Hanoi.

Do Muoi, 1992. 'Sua Doi Hien Phap, Xay Dung Nha Nuoc Phap Quyen Viet Nam, Day Manh Su Nghiep Doi Moi [Revising the constitution, building a law-governed state and promoting renovation]', *Tap Chi Cong San*, 5:6.

Doan Trong Truyen, 1997. 'Market economy and state management', *Vietnam Social Sciences*, 4:10–16.

Durkheim, E., 1960. *Sociology and its Scientific Field*, Free Press, New York [tr. G. Simpson].

Fforde, A., 1999. 'From plan to market', in A. Chan, Kerkvliet, B. and Unger, J. (eds), *Transforming Asian Socialism: China and Vietnam compared*, Allen and Unwin, Sydney:44–63.

Giang Chau, 2003. 'Trade to firm up after solid promotion during first year', *Vietnam Investment Review*, 10 February:1.

Ginsburgs, G., 1973. 'Soviet sources on the law of North Vietnam', *Asian Survey*, 13(7):659–76.

Grossman, J.B., 1971. 'Introduction', in J.B. Grossman and M.H. Grossman (eds), *Law and Change in Modern America*, Goodyear Publishing Co, Pacific Palisades, California:1–10.

Ho Chi Minh, 1994. 'Political report at the second national congress of the Vietnam Workers Party', in *Selected Writings of Ho Chi Minh*, Gioi Publishers, Hanoi:101–29.

——, 1995a. *Complete Works*, Volume 5, The National Political Publishing House, Hanoi.

——, 1995b. *Complete Works*, Volume 8, The National Political Publishing House, Hanoi.

Hoang Phuoc Hiep, 2001. 'Hiep Dinh Thuong Mai Viet Nam—Hoa Ky va Van De Nghien cuu Lap Phap o Viet Nam [The Vietnam-US bilateral trade agreement and legislative issues in Vietnam]', *Tap Chi Nghien Cuu Lap Phap* [Legislative Studies Review], 2:60–78.

Hoang Quoc Viet, 1962. 'Viec Xay Dung Phap Che Xa Hoi Chu Nghia va Giao Duc Moi Nguoi Ton Trong Phap Luat [Building up socialist legality and educating people to respect laws]', *Hoc Tap* [Study Review], 6:14–18.

——, 1964. 'Can Dam Bao Cho Phap Luat Duoc Ton Trong Trong Cong Tac Quan Ly Linh Te Cua Nha Nuoc [We must ensure the enforcement of law in state economic management]' in *Nghien cuu Nha Nuoc va phap quyen* [Studies about State and Law], Truth Publishing, Hanoi:31–41.

——, 1973. *Tang Cuong Che Xa Hoi Chu Nghia Trong Cong Tac Quan Ly Xi Nghiep* [Strengthening Socialist Legality in Management Enterprises], Nhan Xuat Ban Su That, Hanoi.

Hoang The Lien, 1996. 'Subject system in Vietnam's civil code', *Vietnam Law and Legal Forum*, 2(18):22–25.

Hoc Vien Hanh Chinh Quoc Gia (The National Administrative School), 1991. *Ve Cai Cach Bo May Nha Nuoc* [On the Reform of the State Apparatus], Truth Publishing House, Hanoi.

Lavigne, P., 1985. 'Democratic centralism', in F.J.M. Feldbrugge, G.P. Vanden Berg and W.B. Simons (eds), *Encyclopedia of Soviet Law*, Second edition, Martinus Nijhoff Publishers, Dordrecht:31–53.

Le Duan, 1979. Nhan Dan Lao Dong Lam Chu Tap The la Sui Manh, la Luu Duy Cua Chung Chanh Vo Sau [The Labouring People Hold Collective Mastery which is the Force Driving Proletarian Dictatorship], Unpublished speech given by Le Duan, Hanoi, 2 April.

——, 1994. *Le Duan: selected writings*, The Gioi Publishers, Hanoi.

Le Honh Hanh, 1998. *Giao Trinh Ly Luan Nha Nuoc va Phap Luat* [Themes of State and Law], Nha Xuat Ban Cong An Nhan Dan, Hanoi.

Le Kha Phieu, 1998. 'Party leader addresses cultural officials', *Nhan Dan*, 9 October:1, 5 [tr. FIBIS East Asia Daily Reports 98–289].

Le Minh Quan, 1997. 'On the necessity to build a social law-governed state in Vietnam', *Vietnam Social Sciences*, 5:27–33.

Le Minh Tam, 1998. *Giao Trinh Ly Luan Nha Nuoc va Phap Luat* [Themes of State and Law], Nha Xuat Ban Cong An Nhan Dan, Hanoi.

Le Minh Tong, 2000. Mot So De Ve Nha Nuoc Pha Quyen Trong Boi Canh Viet Nam [Some Issues about the Law Based State in the Context of Vietnam], Unpublished paper presented to conference on Rule of Law and its Acceptance in Vietnam, Institute of State and Law, 11 September, Hanoi:1–2.

Le Phuong, 1994. Civil Society: From Annulment to Restoration, Unpublished paper presented at the Vietnam Update Conference *Doi Moi,The State and Civil Society*, Canberra, 5 November.

Le Thanh Nghi, 1975. *Mot So Van De Co Ban Trong Quan Ly Kinh Te Xa Hoi Chu Nhgia* [Several Basic Matters of Socialist Economic Management], Nhan Xuat Su That, Hanoi.

Le Thi, 1977. 'Create a correct relationship between the collective and the individual in the socialist system', *Tap Chi Cong San*, 8:54–58.

Le Van Luong, 1960. 'Tang Cuong Che Do Tap Trung Dan Chu Trong Dang Ta' [Strengthening the democratic centralism in our party], *Hoc Tap*, 6:27–31.

Lets Noi, B.M., 1961. 'Phap Che Xa Hoi Chu Nghia Xo Viet: Tinh Lich Su va Tinh Giai Cap Cua Phap Che [Socialist legality historical and class features], *Tap San Tu Phap*, 6:36–41.

Letsoni, V., 1963. 'Nen Tu Phap Cua Nuoc Viet Nam Dan Chu Cong Hoa [The judiciary of the Democratic Republic of Vietnam]', *Tap San Tu Phap*, 11:26–28.

Luhmann, N., 1987. *A Sociological Theory of Law*, Routledge, London [tr. by E. King and M. Albrow].

Luu Ha Vi, 1997. 'Vietnam: industrialization viewed from the interplay between productive forces and relations of production', *Economic Development Review*, 1 January:20.

Mai Huu Thuc, 2001. 'Characteristics of market economy with socialist orientation in Viet Nam', *Vietnam Social Sciences*, 1:20–25.

Marx, K., 1969 [1877]. 'Otechestvenniye Zapiski', reproduced in S. Avineri (ed.), *Karl Marx on Colonialism and Modernization*, Doubleday, New York:6.

Minh Khuong, 1999. 'Efficiency and competitiveness of the Vietnamese economy', *Vietnam's Socio-Economic Development*, 19:3-13.

Ministry of Justice, 2002. *Report on the Comprehensive Needs of Developing Law Making Bodies, Law Implementation and Enforcement, International Treaty Reception and Dispute Resolution*, Ministry of Justice, Hanoi.

Ngo Cuong, 1997. 'Vietnam fatherland front presidium conference contributes ideas to third plenum draft', *Dai Doan Ket*, 29 May:1, 2 [tr. FBIS East Asia Reports 97–119].

Ngo Van Thau, 1982. *Tim Hieu ve Nha Nuoc* [Studies about State and Law], Nha Xuat Ban Phap Ly, Hanoi.

Nguyen Khac Vien, 1974. *Tradition and Revolution in Vietnam*, Indochina Resource Center, Berkeley.

Nguyen Khanh Toan, 1964. 'Nha nuoc va phap quyen xa hoi chu nghia va cong tac nghien cuu luat hoc [State and Law: socialist state and legal research]', in *Nghien cuu Nha Nuoc va phap quyen* [Studies about State and Law], Truth Publishing, Hanoi:7–19.

Nguyen Minh Tu, 1999. 'Integration of Vietnam's economy into the regional and world economy at present', *Vietnam Social Sciences*, 6:91–96.

Nguyen Nhu Phat, 1997. 'The role of law in Vietnam during the formation of the market-driven mechanism in Vietnam', in J. Gillespie (ed.), *Commercial Legal Development in Vietnam: Vietnamese and foreign commentaries*, Butterworths Asia, Singapore:398–413.

Nguyen Nien, 1976. 'Several legal problems in the leadership and management of industry under the conditions of the present improvement of economic management in our country', *Luat Hoc* [Juridical Science], 14:33 [tr. J.P.R.S., 30 September 1976:34–36].

Nguyen Phu Trong, 1999. 'Effect a new change in the study of political theory of cadres and Party members', *Tap Chi Cong San* (*Communist Party Review*), 7 November:6–9.

Nguyen Tan Dung, 2002. 'Building a socialist-oriented independent and sovereign economy', *Quan Doi Nhan Dan* [People's Army], 13 September:3.

Nguyen Thanh Tam, 2001. 'Phap Luat So Huu Tri Tue Cua Viet Nam Trong Hoi Nhap Quoc Te [Vietnamese intellectual property laws in international integration era]', *Tap Chi Nghien Cuu Lap Phap* [Legislative Studies Review], 2:46–54.

Nguyen The Phung, 1960. *Nguyen Tac Tap Trung Dan Chu: Dam Bao Thuc Hien Tot Nhiem Vu Cach Mang Truoc Mat* [The Principle of Democratic Centralism: a justification for implementing the revolutionary task before us], Nha Xuat Ban Su That, Hanoi.

Nguyen Thi Oanh, 1998. 'Tu Phim Nghiep Chuong Thu Ban Ve Van Hoa' [Let's discuss culture from the film 'Causes and Consequences'], *Tuoi Tre* [Youth], 18 October:3–8.

Nguyen Tran Bat, 2002. 'Culture in recognition of its value', *Essays*, collection of unpublished papers, Hanoi, 1.

Nguyen Van Tai, 1996. 'On the state ruled by law and a multipartisan regime', *Vietnam Social Sciences*, 1:3–8.

Nha Nuoc va Phap Luat [Institution of State and Law], 1996. *Nhung Van De Ly Luan Co Ban Ve Nha Nuoc va Phap Luat* [Basic Theoretical Issues about State and Law], Nha Xuat Ban Chinh Tri Quoc Gia, Hanoi.

Nicholson, P., 2001. Borrowing Court Systems: the experience of the Democratic Republic of Vietnam, 1945-1976, PhD Thesis, University of Melbourne, Melbourne.

Pham Duy Nghia, 2000. 'Phap Luat Thuong Mai Viet Nam Truoc Thach Thuc Cua Qua Trinh Hoi Nhap Linh Te Quac Te [Commercial law faces the challenges of international economic integration]', *Nha nuoc va phap luat*, 6:9–18.

——, 2001. 'Mot So Anh Huong Truc Tiep Cua Qua Trinh Hoi Nhap Kinh Te Khu Vuc va The Gioi Doi Voi Phap Luat Viet Nam [Some direct influences of the world's and regional economic integration into Vietnamese law]', *Tap Chi Nghien cuu Lap Phap* [Legislative Studies], 2:3–8.

——, 2002. 'Tiep Nhan Phap Luat Nuoc Ngoai—Thoi Co va Thach Thuc Moi Cho Nghien Cu Lap Phap [Transplantation of foreign law: chances and challenges for legislative studies in Vietnam]', *Tap Chi Nghien cuu Lap Phap* [Legislative Studies], 5:50–57.

Pham Van Bach, 1970. 'Le Nin Voi Van De Phap Che Xa Hoi Chu Nghia [Lenin and socialist legality]', *Tap San Tu Phap*, 3:9–16.

Pham Van Chuc, 2002. 'Dang Co Chang Mot Toan Cau Hoa Cho Moi Nguoi [Is there now a globalisation for all people?]', *Tap Chi Cong San*, 12:33–37.

Pham Van Dong, 1952. *May Van De Cot Yeu cua Chinh Quyen Dan Chu Nhan Dan Viet Nam* [Some Crucial Aspects of the People's Democratic Regime in Viet Nam], Ban Chap Hanh Trung Uong, Hanoi.

——, 1977. 'Strengthen the Party leadership, carry out the state's managerial functions and develop the people's right to ownership in order to successfully fulfil the 1977 state plan', *Ho Chi Minh City Domestic Service*, 22 January:4. Reproduced in FIBIS East Asia Daily Service 16, 25 January:K9, K11-K13.

Potter, J. and Wetherell, M., 1987. *Discourse and Social Psychology*, Blackwell, London.

Quang Can, 2001. 'Some reflections on Marxist philosophy in the perspective of Eastern culture', *Vietnam Social Sciences*, 1:8–11.

Sarogoratisk, 1961. 'Vai Tro va Quan He Giua Cuong Che va Thuyet Phuc Cua Phap Luat Trong Thoi Ly Xay Dung Chu Nghia Cong San Tren Quy Mo Rong Lon [Roles and relations between enforcement and legal education in the communist period]', *Tap San Tu Phap*, 11:41–57.

See Huu Tho, 1998. 'Some problems concerning ideological work in the new situation', *Tap Chi Quoc Phong Toan Dan* [People's Army Review], 9(September):10–15.

Shih, C-Y., 1996. 'China's socialist law under reform: the class nature reconsidered', *The American Journal of Comparative Law*, 44(4):627–646.

Song Thanh, 1995. 'President Ho Chi Minh laid the foundation for a law-governed state in Vietnam', *Vietnam Law and Legal Forum*, 1(9):3–6.

Ta Thu Khue, 1963. 'Can Than Trong Trong Viec AP Dung Kinh Nghiem Lien-xo Voa Trinh Tu Phuc Tham [We need to be cautious in applying soviet experience in appellate procures], *Tap San Tu Phap*, 2:12–14.

Ta Van Tai, 1982. 'Vietnam's code of the Lê dynasty (1428-1788)', *American Journal of Comparative Law*, 30(3):523–53.

Teubner, G., 1993. *Law as an Autopoietic System*, Blackwell, Oxford.

Thanh Duy, 1997. 'Co So Khoa Hoc va Van Hoa Trong Tu Tuong Ho Chi Minh Ve Nha Nuoc va Phap Luat [Scientific and cultural basis of Ho Chi Minh's ideas of state and law], *Tap Chi Cong San*, January:26–28.

Tran Dinh Huynh, 1999. 'Moi Quan He Giua Tri Luc—Dao Duc—Phap Luat Trong Quan Ly Dat Nuoc Cua Chu Tich Ho Chi Minh [Relationship between intelligence—morality-law in Ho Chi Minh's thought on administration], *To Chuc Nha Nuoc*, 5:3–5.

Tran Hieu, 1971. *25 Nam Xay Dung Nen Phap Che Viet Nam* [25 Years of Building Vietnamese Legality], Nha Xuat Ban Lao Dong, Hanoi.

Tran Thu Hang, 1999. 'Vietnam's trade in the course of international integration', *Vietnamese Studies*, 2:113–23.

Tran Van Giau, 1995. 'Methodologies for incorporating cultural factors into development projects and planning', in Pham Xuan Nam (ed.), *Methodologies for Incorporating Cultural Factors into Development Projects and Planning*, Social Sciences Publishing House, Hanoi:169–75.

Tran Van Nam, 2002. 'On the ordinance on the most favoured nation and the national treatment in international trade', *Vietnam Law and Legal Forum*, 8(96):25–26.

Tran Viet Phuong, 1999. 'Globalisation and integration into the world economy', *Vietnam Social Sciences*, 6:79–84.

Tran Xuan Truong, 2002. 'Our Party is morality, civilisation', *Tap Chi Cong San* [Party Review], 3 February. Available online at www.tapchicongsan.org.vn.

Truong Chinh, 1948. Marxism and Vietnamese culture, Report delivered to the Second National Cultural Conference, July 1948, reproduced in *Truong Chinh Selected Writings*.

——, 1968. 'Forward along the path charted by Ho Chi Minh', reproduced in Truong Chinh, 1994. *Selected Works*, The Gioi Publishers, Hanoi, 547.

Tshuma, L., 1999. 'The political economy of the World Bank's legal framework for economic development', *Social and Legal Studies*, 8(2):75–96.

Vo Khanh Vinh, 1997. 'Mot So Van De Ve Xa Hoi Hoc Xay Dung Phap Luat [A number of issues in sociological lawmaking]', *Nha Nuoc va Phap Luat* [State and Law], 8:14–20.

Vu Anh Tuan, 1998. 'Voi Mat Trai Cua Kinh Te Thi Truong [Laws and negative aspects of the market economy]', *Nghien Cuu Ly Luan* [Journal of Theoretical Studies], 3:26–31.

Vu Khieu, 1999. 'President Ho Chi Minh and culture', *Nhan Dan on-line*, www.nhandan.org.vn/english/people/19990517.html.

Vu Ngoc Nhung, 1999. 'Role of state in market economy with socialist orientation', *Vietnam Social Sciences*, 6(74):19–24.

Vu Tuan Anh (ed.), 1994. *The Role of the State in Economic Development: experiences of the Asian countries*, Social Sciences Publishing House, Hanoi.

Vu Van Mau, 1963. 'Le Driot Prive Vietnamien Moderne Compare Avec Les Droits Occidentaux', in *Quelques Aspects Technique de la Reception des Driots Occidentuax*, Association Nationale de Droit Compara, Saigon:3–22.

Vyshinski, A., 1982 [1936]. 'Raise the red banner of socialist legality', *Sots. Zak.*, November, cited in G.B. Smith, 'Development of "socialist legality" in the Soviet Union', in F.J.M. Feldbrugge and W.B. Smith (eds), *Perspectives on Soviet Law for the 1980s*, Martinus Nijhoff Publishers, The Hague, 81–82.

Whitmore, J., 1995. 'Chung-hsing and Cheng-t'-ung in texts of and on sixteenth-century Viet Nam', in K.W. Taylor and J.K. Whitmore (eds), *Essays Into Vietnamese Pasts*, Studies on Southeast Asia 19, Cornell University Press, Ithaca:116–32.

4

Confucianism and the conception of the law in Vietnam

Pham Duy Nghia

Confucianism in Vietnam originated from the Vietnamese people's agricultural lifestyle and continues to influence society today. As a set of social norms, Confucianism not only substitutes for the law in many aspects of life, but also contributes heavily to the conception of the law in Vietnam. Analysing Confucianism's impact will help us to understand better the role and limitations of the Vietnamese legal system today.

With the growth of the market-oriented economy, legal reform in Vietnam has entered a new stage where emerging paradigms are challenging the outdated doctrine of 'socialist legality'. Western legal models are increasingly providing the basic framework for new legislation, as can be seen in recently enacted legislation on business organisations (The Law on Enterprises 1999), contracts (The Commercial Law 1997, Civil Code 1995), dispute resolution, and bankruptcy (Ordinance on Commercial Arbitration 2003, Bankruptcy Law 1993). The increased levels of discussion on the Constitution, the protection of individual rights, and the need for a 'socialist state ruled by law has been coupled with increasing levels of awareness amongst civil society' (Amendment of the Constitution in 2001). As citizens become increasingly wealthy, however, they tend to become increasingly reflective of their historic and cultural roots. As a consequence, Confucian classic literature is enjoying a period of revival in Vietnam.

Following a long period of isolation, food shortages and emigration, Vietnamese society is undergoing rapid change, a crucial element of which is evolution of the law. In this transitional stage, enforcement of the law is imperative. Legal ideas adopted from the West face difficulties when implemented into a society where traditional forces resist change. In economic, political and cultural fields, the divergence between the written law and its application is widely evident. While the Constitution protects citizens' rights, the authorities' wide scope for misinterpretation is not effectively constrained by public claims and denunciation alone. For instance, the freedom of citizens to conduct business and compete fairly in the market faces ostensible restrictions imposed by the administrative authorities. Public faith in the judicial system is still limited, and the number of cases being heard before Vietnam's economic courts is, in fact, decreasing every year, despite the steady economic growth.[1]

To appreciate the current situation in Vietnam, one needs to look back to the past to understand the way in which the Vietnamese govern their society based on their beliefs and culture. Although laws to facilitate business activities are badly needed, they cannot substitute for the social norms that have dominated the Vietnamese agricultural society for centuries. Thus, when concepts such as limited liability in corporate law, for example, are introduced into the Vietnamese legal system, their application will take different forms from that in Germany or the United States. Thus, despite the various ways of harmonising the law and legal practice in the age of globalisation, one cannot ignore the impacts of tradition and cultures in forming the conception of the law in a given society (Örücü 1999).

The process of legal harmonisation in Vietnam has not been smooth. One contributing factor is that Vietnamese legal scholars, trained in former Soviet Union and East Germany, are surprisingly unfamiliar with their own legal traditions. Textbooks used in courses at major law schools, such as *General Theory on State and Law*, define the law according to *Klassenkampf*—the law is considered substantially as a tool used by the ruling class to exploit the working class. In legal history courses, legal development is described to fit the Marxist vision of a society progressing from slavery to feudalism, capitalism and finally towards a socialist communist state. Students learn by rote the five different types of state and laws, and try to place all statutes and laws within this prescribed format. Although courses in the 'History of Political Doctrines' are taught, their aim is to introduce the evolution of political philosophy according to the Marxist view.

The role of traditional law and its interaction with ethics and other social norms is not well researched within Vietnam. The discrepancy between the recent development in Vietnam and the backward style of research and teaching is a negative reflection, not only of the development of legal jurisprudence, but also most other social sciences in Vietnam (Phan Dien 2003).

In other countries, such as Japan, Korea, Taiwan, Singapore, and more recently China, ideas such as 'Asian values' and 'Confucian society' indicate the impact of traditional culture on contemporary legal and economic development. What lessons, if any, can Vietnam learn from the experiences of these countries? How can the traditional conception of the law continue to be protected and promoted as Vietnam moves to adopt laws based on Western models?

This chapter seeks to discuss the role of social norms in Vietnamese society, and in particular the contribution of agricultural social norms to the formation of Confucianism. It also uses the concept of 'Vietnam's Confucianism', initially presented by the scholar Kim Dinh (1969, 1970) to evaluate the past and present role of the law and its limitations in Vietnamese society. To this end, I will try to indicate the extent to which traditional agricultural social norms have influenced legal practice in Vietnam today.

ORIGIN AND MAIN FEATURES OF VIETNAMESE CONFUCIANISM

Vietnam was, and still is, a country that depends on its agricultural industry, with approximately 80 per cent of the workforce employed in that sector. At the same time, most of the urban population still lives in, or feels a connection to, the village of their ancestors.[2] The success and failure of any contemporary reform in Vietnam cannot be explained without taking into account the problems facing Vietnamese farmers.

As a set of enforceable rules imposed or recognised by the state power, the law has never had supremacy in Vietnamese society. The social norms that govern Vietnamese society have been drawn largely from Vietnamese agricultural life, and continue to live in the beliefs of the people. The way people think influences the way they act; learning from their beliefs helps to explain their actual behaviour. It is therefore appropriate to search for the sources of Vietnamese indigenous norms in order to understand the present legal practice.

From a Western perspective, with the exception of the penal rules in the traditional codes (Le Code 1460 and Nguyen Code 1813), the indigenous norms in Vietnam remain somewhat unclear, originating as they did from the interchange between three leading religions in East Asia—Daoism, Buddhism and Confucianism. Historians often view Vietnam's culture as a mixture incorporating Chinese and Indian influences into the indigenous culture. Marxist materialists have little interest in researching and promoting such religious thinking. It is well known that Marx saw religion as the 'opium of the people' and an expression of the hope of the suppressed mass for a brighter future. Given that generations of Vietnamese, including the Communists and their followers, continue to maintain the cult for their ancestors, and given the increasing public interest in Daoism, Buddhism and other natural beliefs, it is surprising that Vietnamese religious thinking is rarely researched in contemporary Vietnamese Marxist literature.

It is thus an appropriate time to rediscover the role of Confucianism in contemporary Vietnamese society. Following discussion about Nguyen Truong To's work in the second half of the nineteenth century and the reprint of Tran Trong Kim's standard work on Confucianism, a number of scholars have raised questions relating to the role of Confucianism in contemporary society (Tran Van Giau 1988). The work of Vu Khieu (1997) and Phan Dai Doan (1998) reverberated in academic circles as a signal for a possible change in public opinion towards the once-leading ideology of Vietnam: Vietnamese Confucianism.

Confucianism is the only term known in the West for 'Nho giao'. During the chaotic Spring–Autumn and Warring States period, Confucianism emerged as one of many schools of thought that sought to provide order to society. Although Confucius was its the most famous teacher, he was not the creator of a new religion; the five classical works incorporated the wisdom of many generations (Tran Trong Kim 1971; Nguyen Hien Le 1958; Tran Le Sang 2002). During the ten centuries of Chinese domination in Vietnam, Confucianism was introduced into the modern-day areas of North and Middle Vietnam (Nguyen Dang Thuc 1967), and continued to exist in harmony with other religions, such as Dinh, Ly and Tran, under Vietnam's first independent dynasties. During this time, the three religions used different 'ways' to reach the same goals (*tam giao dong nguyen*). In the transition from the Tran to the Ho dynasty, the influence of Confucianism intensified and extended from the capital down to the district levels. Confucianism became the leading ideology of the Vietnamese monarchy from the Le dynasty, particularly under the reign of Le Thanh Ton (1460–97). From that time until the early twentieth century, the traditional state of Vietnam, the recruitment of mandarins, and the organisation of society as a whole, were based on Confucian values and examinations (Phan Dai Doan 1998, Nguyen Dang Thuc 1967). The last Confucian examinations were conducted between 1915–18 in Northern and Middle Vietnam respectively (Tran Truong Kim 1971).

It is noteworthy that, as a system of rules governing people's behaviour, the face of Confucianism was dynamic and constantly changing, and incorporated both indigenous beliefs and norms. As a result, Confucianism took different forms in China, Japan, Korea and Vietnam. For example, loyalty in Japan was interpreted to mean loyalty to only one imperial family; loyalty in Vietnam, by contrast, focused on loyalty to the country as a whole and on defence of the nation.[3]

Vietnam's Confucianism cannot be viewed simply as being the ideology of the Chinese occupiers. Long after the occupiers had gone, the ideology remained and expanded to generate the standard norms that would govern the society for centuries. In this regard, the following explanations appear most plausible

- convergence between Vietnamese indigenous agricultural norms and Confucian values may have enhanced the broadening of Confucian values in Vietnam centuries after independence from China in 939 AD
- in comparison to Buddhism and Daoism, Confucianism offered a doctrine more appropriate for the ruler's class to govern Vietnamese society
- based on archaeological, historical and anthropological evidence, relevant sources indicate that the ancestors of the Vietnamese people must have occupied the areas south of the Yangtze River in China. Under pressure from the Hoa people, they moved southwards, and the resulting meeting and mutual integration of Vietnamese agriculture and the nomadic Hoa culture possibly formed the wisdom that Confucius referred to as the wisdom of ancestors (Dao Duy Anh 1937, 1950; Nguyen Dang Thuc 1967; Kim Dinh 1970).

The scholarly works of Kim Dinh sought to trace the contribution of the Vietnamese people in establishing Confucian values, but what are the specific characteristics of Vietnamese agricultural life that contributed to this? Which features dominant in Vietnamese culture helped promote the convergence of Confucianism with the indigenous beliefs and traditions? A number of features of agricultural life appear relevant

- **Collectivism.** Vietnamese collectivism is distinct from communitarian attitudes in the West. A human being is born to be a member not only of a family, but a village and, in a broader sense, a member of a country. He or she lives in natural connection with other members of the society, as an integrated part of one organic body. Under such a system, the collective interest of society is supreme over individual interests; people who fight for their own interests are often viewed as selfish and egotistical (Marr 2000). This natural mindset of collectivism is born from the common efforts to cultivate crops. It is a major characteristic of the Vietnamese mentality and, at the same time, an essential factor hindering the emergence of individualism in Vietnam.

- **Rule of causality.** As a nation of farmers, the Vietnamese learnt the rule of causality (*nhan-qua*) very early. This rule suggests that whatever happens today has been caused by past events. In the views of the people, justice practised by the heavens is absolute and the actions of parents affect the destiny of their children. Accordingly, success or failure, wealth or poverty, peace or war are not random events; their reasons lie deep in human behaviour (Nguyen Tai Thu 1993).

- **Life is to endure.** Living in the highly populated river deltas, struggling to survive under the steady pressure of the dominant neighbours in the North and coping with endless obstacles, the Vietnamese have learnt to endure life. As a result, the Vietnamese life motto is to endure all challenges. As the Vietnamese say, 'if you are too clever, you will perish; if you are too stupid, you will also perish; but if you know how to live, you will survive [*Khon chet, dai chet, biet thi song*]'. This mentality may explain the elasticity and flexibility of Vietnamese people's behaviour.

- **Harmony and consensus, not conflict.** The need to maintain balance and harmony is stressed in all aspects of life, from family, to lineage, to village and state issues, and acknowledged by most Vietnamese. Although the man is traditionally considered head of the family, Vietnamese women have also enjoyed considerable equality and rights. In issues relating to the lineage of people with the same ancestors, decisions were usually made by consensus. The same principle may be seen in the structure of the villages, where consensus building is the major force keeping the village in order. Even though there were some indications of power struggles, instances of personal politics or cult-infused leadership were quite mild in communist Vietnam compared to China or North Korea.

- **Face saving and relationship keeping.** As a consequence of collectivism, the respect and opinion of the community is crucial to the life of each individual in Vietnam. The success of a person is dependent their trustworthiness and their ability to build and maintain relationships with other people. Fear of bad public opinion still motivates the Vietnamese.

- **Respect for elders.** Cultures based on agriculture have great respect for the elderly. This respect is reflected in decision-making in the villages, and frequently also in traditional law. As the demographic structure and socioeconomic conditions in Vietnam change, the traditional respect accorded to the elderly may face serious challenges.
- *Nhan-Nghia.* The Vietnamese term *nhan* corresponds to the Chinese counterpart *ren*, and remains one of the most difficult concepts of Confucianism. This term can only roughly be translated into the English 'benevolence'. According to Tran Trong Kim (1971), the purpose of lifelong self-cultivation is to learn benevolence, mercy, charity and humanity. As a result of this lifelong learning a man will receive the ability to love and hate, virtues that form the kernel of his behaviour. The extent of knowledge of the *nhan* will essentially distinguish the gentleman from the uneducated. The Vietnamese *nghia* corresponds to a notion of 'righteousness' and noble obligation towards family and the community. If *nhan* refers to a man's virtues, *nghia* refers to his responsibility towards other people and the society where he lives. This unwritten, undefined ethical rule creates the framework and boundaries to distinguish the Confucian gentleman (*quan-tu*) from the uneducated (*tieu-nhan*). Naturally, the particular ethical values of this rule governing human beings may change occasionally, but over time this rule encourages people to behave well towards others and society generally.

When one considers the social norms governing the agricultural life of the Vietnamese people, similarities with Confucian values become apparent. Historians often discuss the question, first presented by Kim Dinh (1969, 1970), whether the Vietnamese culture contributed to Confucian values, or whether Confucianism, once introduced, became deeply rooted in, and a guide to, the behaviour of the Vietnamese. Regardless, social norms continue to govern Vietnamese society from one generation to another, alongside the written law.

THE DECLINE OF CONFUCIANISM IN VIETNAM AND THE EMERGENCE OF SOCIALIST LEGALITY

A class of Vietnamese Confucian scholars emerged during the first Chinese domination from 111 BC to 937 AD, but their presence went unnoted in historical reports. Their role in the first independent dynasties did not seem significant, since the sword had more power than philosophy. The most literally educated élite class in Vietnam at that time was the Buddhist monks, who served as advisers to the courts, helped receive Chinese ambassadors, and whose temples served as educational centres (Nguyen Dang Thuc 1967). As the influence of Confucianism grew in the thirteenth century, however, the monks' role in politics decreased.

Vietnamese scholars used Confucianism to fight against the Chinese occupiers during the wars against the Chinese Minh dynasty. Thereafter, the social prestige of Confucian scholars improved—mandarins were recruited based on Confucian examinations, and a state bureaucracy began to form based on Confucianism (Phan Dai Doan 1998).

Confucianism became a political doctrine in the hands of the ruling class. Le Thanh Ton codified the Confucian values in books that were widely distributed to the villages, and private Confucian schools helped to broaden the Confucian values from the élite class down to all levels of the population. In addition, during its expansion, Confucianism also incorporated the values of other religions, such as Buddhism, Daoism and other natural beliefs. For this reason, even though it was not created as a religion, the population had already been practising Confucianism, albeit in an indirect manner.

As Confucianism is a political doctrine, the following features may help to understand the role of the law in Confucian society.

- Confucianism recognises the divisions within society between different classes—each man shall learn to act appropriately for his status in society. Gentlemen shall know the way to live, shall know the 'li' as rituals and rules governing relationships among people. By doing so, the man educates himself to become a gentleman, thus keeping his family, country and the state in order. The law seeks to enforce good behaviour amongst individuals by punishing those people who don't know the 'li'. Individuals therefore have an incentive to learn and practise the 'li' in a way that enhances social order, and the law is consequently subordinated under the moral rules of 'li'. Despite some provisions in regard to property and contracts in the traditional codes, one can assume that the private law tradition in Vietnam is rather weak, suggesting that there was no need for such a set of legal regulations.

- The hostility inherent in legalism was criticised as being contrary to Confucian principles. Confucian values, however, may be interpreted as arbitrary because of the lack of clear, systematic and transparent rules. The people were once considered to be the roots of the country and the ruler's mission was to serve the people. Later, the feudal mandarins shifted this to focus more on the obedience of the subjects to the rulers, thus making the ruler like a god—the son of heaven. Moral values have their limitations, especially in times of economic strain. The backward-thinking style of Confucianism sometimes produced reactionary forces that opposed reform. In Vietnam, for example, reformers like Ho Quy Ly, Nguyen Hue and later, Nguyen Truong To, faced resistance, particularly from Confucian scholars and mandarins.

- The question is not to make a choice between legalism and Confucianism, but rather to 'Confucianise' the law, as was done during the Chinese Han dynasty. Law reform was enhanced under the Le and Nguyen dynasties, and particularly under Minh Mang. Legislation, including the formal requirements for lawmaking and the scope of regulation, was codified and standardised. Confucian values were newly underpinned by penal sanctions—thus Confucian values were transformed into enforceable norms.

Numerous peasant uprisings at the end of the seventeenth century signalled a reaction to the backward thinking of Confucianism and its weaknesses in managing the country.

1 The intellectual class had confined itself to the classics of Confucius and Mencius. The social and natural sciences were not taught. The teaching style, moreover, focused on rote learning, thus blocking new ideas and learning from Western civilisations.

2 The ruling class—from the king to the mandarins—relied on the bureaucratic style of government and required absolute obedience from the subjects.

3 The peasants were mentally and physically closed from the world behind village walls. Vietnamese society, from its rulers to the peasants, remained a relatively closed society until the late eighteenth and early nineteenth centuries. Foreign merchants settled in Pho Hien (North Vietnam) and Hoi An (South Vietnam) but left the country (partly because of the hostile policies of the Trinh and Nguyen lords toward Christianity) without being able to make any notable changes to the Vietnamese attitude towards the outside world.

The enemy keeping Vietnam impoverished lies deep in the Vietnamese soul. Reformers in the nineteenth century attempted to redefine traditional values in order to open up the country by promoting trade, consumption and by enabling foreigners to invest and conduct business within the country. These benefits were lost, however, in the silence of the closed and traditional society. Confucianism heavily exploited the popular belief in the necessity of obedience to the rulers, even in the face of their backward thinking. Not surprisingly, when faced by Western civilisations, this did not succeed.

Vietnamese intellectuals looked to foreign ideas for ways to rescue the independence of their country. This had already failed under French domination, when Vietnam was heavily exploited and suppressed by the colonialists. Having no chance to explore liberalism, the Vietnamese people bitterly learned of the dark side of capitalism. They therefore began to embrace socialism and socialist ideals under the influence of French colonialists. Nationalism, combined with Communism's general principle of equality, essentially helped the Communists to succeed. Confucian values and ethical standards were frequently borrowed in the effort to mobilise the masses, and new interpretations were made to fit the needs of long-lasting liberation and a war against the foreign occupiers.

Once in power, the Vietnamese Communists did not fight Confucianism as bitterly as did their Chinese counterparts, but the social prestige of Confucianism was essentially destroyed. In the political sphere, Marxism–Leninism replaced the Confucian worldview—the puppet son of heaven abdicated its power and was replaced by the people's republic, which again was replaced by the 'dictatorship of the proletariat'. Heaven, gods and other supernatural forces and beliefs had no place in the orthodox materialism. Only recently have the people's traditional beliefs enjoyed a certain amount of freedom and protection from the state authorities. In the cultural sphere, the ideals of a 'new kind of socialist man' replaced the outdated Confucian gentleman. Socialist collectivism replaced the Confucian three yokes and five relationships (*tam-cuong, ngu-thuong*). A political campaign against individualism dismantled the tradition of strong leadership in the family and society—the Confucian family leader (*gia truong*) being considered a remnant of the feudalism that socialist society sought to erase.

The socialist conception of social equality destroyed the Confucian views of class. For example, new rich families recruiting household servants now often allege that their servants lack obedience, and when Vietnamese women are sent to work as household servants in Taiwanese families, similar complaints often emerge. This is not surprising given that the 'socialist collective leadership' did not know the terms 'employer and employees'. Instead, people were divided into units (*don-vi*), where everyone had the right to know, discuss and decide on issues relating to this unit. This characteristic may make the training of the Vietnamese workforce somewhat difficult.

Yet tradition persists. The new ideology has embedded itself in the major aspects of society, from the rules in family matters, to business networks, through to the relationships with public authorities. Indications suggest, however, that the Confucian tradition may have changed in appearance but that the substance is still important in modern Vietnamese life. In the political sphere, the Vietnamese press and political documents sometimes use the term 'Communist' mandarins to refer to this phenomenon. In the economic sphere, the increased autonomy of state-owned enterprises and other institutions, and decreased control of business by bureaucrats and managers, have opened up the possibility of traditional, family-style governance.

From another perspective, Marxism and Confucianism have converged in a number of respects; for example, the primacy of public or common interests over individual interests, the broad and active role of the ruler or state to serve the common interests of the people, and the conception that law is just one of the tools used by the state to maintain social order. This also explains why the Confucian authoritarian style of government may also have contributed its characteristics to Asian Communism (Peerenboom 2002).

Socialist legality, borrowed from the former Soviet Union, broadened its influence and was far more extensive than the French civil law heritage in Vietnam. In essence, the Soviet doctrine saw the law as a tool that the state could use to ensure socialist revolution. More generally, under this doctrine, the legal system existed to serve the interests of the working class. Such a system had to be enforced, even through dictatorship of the proletariat if necessary. Under this system, the written legal documents defined the limits of individuals' behaviour, the courts and justice system were reorganised to provide greater justice to the population, and the privileges available to lawyers and judges were curtailed.

In the economic sphere, the socialist production mode was premised on the dominance of state-owned enterprises operating in the framework of a centrally planned economy. Peasants were organised into Soviet-style cooperatives, and private enterprise was extremely limited. In this regard, the Vietnamese state came close to achieving its goal—that people would only be allowed to do what was prescribed by the law. The economic reform occurring today in both agriculture and industry would have been characterised as law-breaking or 'breaking the wall' (*vuot-rao*) at the time of the centrally planned economy.

During the 1990s, people wishing to open businesses had to apply for numerous licences in order to prove the legality of their actions, and this complex system remained in place until it was simplified in the 1999 Law on Enterprises. This liberalisation, however, was not backed by equivalent changes to contract law and the laws concerning dispute resolution. The power and discretion of the state authorities to intervene in the activities of contracting parties remained unconstrained. Business contracts, for example, may be declared void, often arbitrarily, based on outdated and conflicting regulations.

In the political sphere, the doctrine of 'socialist legality' led to the liquidation of the Ministry of Justice, leaving only one department—'Legality' (*Vu Phap Che*)–within the Office of the Government. Even today, the names of some legal departments in certain ministries (Department of Legality, *vu phap che*) still refer back to the doctrine of that time. Under 'socialist legality', communal autonomy was extremely limited; traditional village structures were abolished and replaced by the People's Committee and People's Council, similar to the Soviet model. Distribution of funding and other resources was governed by a system of top-down distribution known as 'applications and grants' (*xin cho*),[4] in which the resources controlled by the local governments were limited. Only in recent years have local governments enjoyed increased autonomy.

With the new slogan 'socialist state ruled by law', Soviet-style 'socialist legality' disappeared from Vietnamese legal jargon, but its effects on society are far from disappearing. In the justice system, judges still wait for instructions from the Supreme Court and are unable to develop law (make law) in cases where the written legal documents are silent on a particular issue. Likewise, local authorities still wait for circulars and official letters distributed by the ministries to implement a given law, thus making a law merely a set of general principles and leaving the administrative authorities wide discretion in interpreting it. Engaging in business is neither expressly allowed nor prohibited by the law, but may still be interpreted as illegal, as has happened in recent cases where businesspeople were essentially defined as tax frauds or evidencing an intention to break the law.[5]

LEARNING FROM ASIAN NEIGHBOURS: WHAT CAN CONFUCIANISM CONTRIBUTE TO CONTEMPORARY LEGAL DEVELOPMENT IN VIETNAM?

After a century of struggle, the Vietnamese have recognised that learning from their Asian neighbours, Japan, China, Korea and other ASEAN countries, may bring more order and prosperity to their homeland than drawing from the experiences of the former Soviet Union or the Middle East and East Europe. Given their phenomenal growth in the second half of the twentieth century, the East Asian economies' experiences of borrowing Western commercial laws, while also consolidating traditional institutions, appear to carry the most valuable lessons for Vietnam.

The new advances in comparative economics and law show that different circumstances require different institutions to balance the fundamental trade-off between disorder and dictatorship (Djankov et al. 2003). The obstacles that prevent the emergence of rule of law in the former Soviet Union are distinctive from those in China (Stiglitz and Hoff 2002). While the 'big bang policy' may have led to stagnation and disorder in the former Soviet Union, the gradual dual-track economic reform in China has promised to be more successful (Sachs and Woo 1997). By consolidating traditional institutions to promote a market-oriented economy, Confucianism offers a rich source of norms and institutions that could underpin economic and social development in Asia in general, and Vietnam in particular.

Traditional Confucian society is well-known as a 'no law society', where law and legal litigation do not have the same importance as in the West. The ratio of residents to lawyers in the United States is 400:1; 7,000:1 in Japan; and 20,000:1 in Vietnam (Keleman and Sibbitt 2002). Confucian ethics can substitute for some functions of law; hence family capitalism is preponderant in Asia, and Confucian-based government and collectivism substitute and supplement the law to maintain social order and discipline (Kheng-Boon Tan 2000; Branson 2001).

Experiences in other Asian countries where Confucian values have been integrated into legal development may be of interest to Vietnam.

- **Confucian heritage.** Vietnam shares the common heritage of Confucianism with other East Asian countries. Although Confucianism is based on the received wisdom of generations, it is flexible and can be redefined to meet the modern needs of ensuring harmony and social order. Confucian values and faith can help form new patterns of behaviour and thus contribute informally to achieving the aims of law.
- **Confucian state.** The process of change from an agricultural nation to an industrialised nation is not possible without strong and careful state intervention. The Confucian state is more responsible than most Western states for serving the interests of the people, and is thus more focused on promoting export-oriented policies and certain other sectoral policies. This intervention encompasses a wide range of activities, from holding

large shares of public ownership in enterprises to controlling financial resources, facilitating networks and building consensus amongst business and government.

- **Confucian view of the primacy of public over individual interests.** In times of economic difficulty, collective interests trump individual and civil rights. This approach does not deny outright that stability and economic growth are to some extent concerned with individual liberty, but, when translated into political or economic law, the Confucian views seem to clash with the Western concept of liberal democracy and the rule of law. This trade-off, however, may be of essential importance in Asia's economic growth.

- **Culturally specific institutions.** Law and social norms need appropriate institutions to transmit behavioural forms to the mass population. The Confucian society reproduced its own institutions to enforce the norms. Despite widespread adaptation of corporate forms, family-based management styles are still prominent, evident in the way that business operators in these countries frequently rely on traditional networks as a way of managing risk. The role of contract, dispute resolution, and bankruptcy laws can only be understood in this context.

- **Seeking convergence.** The intense integration of Confucian values into the world economy as a result of globalisation emphasises the need to redefine these values to allow them to converge to, and exist alongside, other harmonised legal standards. The economic benefits that would follow lie in the possibilities that Western-based commercial laws offer for more advanced modes of organising and governing business, raising capital, managing risks, and enhancing transactions. The examples of Japan, Korea, Taiwan, Singapore and China show that these capitalist institutions are crucial in facilitating a market-oriented economy. The Japanese and Singaporean governments in particular have taken the initiative in adopting Western commercial law, without being coerced by foreigners. From fine literal translations to borrowing sophisticated theories, the Japanese carefully combined traditional values with Western liberalism, thus promoting the convergence of their cultural roots with foreign ideas. The translation of the Greek word for 'economy' into 'serving the country, helping the world', indicates a mastery in the art of borrowing traditional values for the new needs of modern times. It links the realisation of the Western ego with the Eastern sacrifice for the country, thus making conducting business ethically a highly honoured work. In the same way, Asian business schools, drawing on the long Chinese tradition of the 'art of war', describe business as being similar to military combat. It comes as no surprise then that, in Western eyes, the Japanese and Chinese engage in economic competition as though they are engaged in war.

CONCLUSION

After decades of reform, the Vietnamese legal system today resembles a jungle of laws. It is evident that much has to be done if the mess is to be resolved. The scandal of the Nam Cam case and the emergence of criminal networks illustrates not only the weakness of the legal and juridical system, but also the unique response of the market economy to the lack of efficient institutions in this country. Where the long arm of the law cannot reach, traditional norms and structures informed by Confucian values continue to dominate. Confucian values, thus, may positively supplement and strengthen the law but may also challenge and compete with it. In the long run, newly redefined Confucian values may continue to establish social trust, discipline and order in Vietnam.

NOTES

[1]   See the Annual Report of the People's Supreme Court, also Duong Dang Hue (2003).
[2]   For updated economic data of Vietnam, see CIEM (2002).
[3]   See Tran Van Giau (1998:136), and for a comparative perspective Chongko Choi (1997).
[4]   'Xin cho' literally means 'ask and give'.
[5]   See Report of the Working Team of the Government to Implement the Law on Enterprise, available at www.vnexpress.net of May 16, 2003; also the Governmental Decree No 61/1998/ND-CP dated 15 August 1998 on Inspection of Enterprises.

REFERENCES

Branson, D.M., 2001. 'The very uncertain prospect of global convergence in corporate law', *Cornell International Law Journal*, 34(2):321–61.

Central Institute for Economic Management, 2002. *Vietnam's Economy 2001*, National Politics Publishing House, Hanoi. Available online at www.ciem.org.vn, www.worldbank.org.vn.

Chongko Choi, 1997. *Asian Jurisprudence in the World*, Seoul National University Press, Seoul.

Dao Duy Anh, 1930. *Vietnam's Culture History*, Quan Hai Tung Thu Publishers, Hue.

——, 1950. *The Origin of the Vietnamese People*, The Gioi Publishers, Hanoi.

Dao Tri Uc and Le Minh Thong, 1999. 'Reception of East and West legal values into Vietnam's legal ideology', *State and Law*, 5: 3–17.

Djankov, S., Glaeser, E.L., La Porta, R., Lopez-de-Silane, F. and Schleifer, A., 2003. *The New Comparative Economics*, Working Paper 9608, National Bureau of Economic Research, Cambridge, Massachusetts. Available online at www.nber.org/papers/w9068.

Duong Dang Hue, 2003. 'The role of the Bankruptcy Law in present Vietnam', *State and Law*, 1:30–40.

Dvor, B.A., 1999. 'What is the connection? Vietnam, the rule of law, human rights and antitrust', *Houston Journal of International Law*, 21:427–49.

Head, J.W., 2003. 'Codes, cultures, chaos and champions: common features of codification experiences in China, Europe and North America', *Duke Journal of Comparative and International Law*, 13(1):1–94.

Hizon, E.M., 1999. 'Virtual reality and reality: the East Asian NICs and the global trading system', *Annual Survey of International and Comparative Law*, 5:81–162.

Keleman, D., and Sibbitt, E., 2002. 'The Americanization of Japanese law', *University of Pennsylvania Journal of International Economic Law*, 23:269–323.

Kim Dinh, 1969. *Differences between East and Western Philosophy*, Khai Tri Publishers, Saigon.

——, 1970. *Origin of Vietnam's Philosophy*, An Tiem Publishers, Hanoi.

Le Van Quan, 1997. *Introduction to History of Chinese Ideology*, Giao Duc Publishers, Hanoi.

Le Van Sieu, 1968. *National Tradition*, Hoang Dong Phuong Publishers, Saigon

Ly Te Xuyen, 1961. *Viet Dien U Linh Tap*, Khai Tri Publishers, Saigon [tr. Le Huu Muc].

Marr, D.G., 2000. 'Concepts of "individual" and "self" in twentieth-century Vietnam', *Modern Asian Studies*, 34(4):769–96.

Ngo Tat To, 1940. *Critic of Confucianism*, Mai Linh Publishers, Hanoi.

Nguyen Dang Dung, 2001. *Some Issues of Constitution Law and State Apparatus*, Giao Thong Van Tai Publishers, Hanoi.

Nguyen Dang Thuc, 1967. *History of Vietnam's Ideology*, Ministry of Education, Saigon.

——, 1992. *Lich su tu tuong Vietnam* [History of Vietnam's Ideology], Volume VI, Ho Chi Minh City Publishers, Ho Chi Minh City.

Nguyen Hien Le, 1958. *Confucianism: a political philosophy*, Ministry of Education, Saigon.

——, 1992. *Iking: the way of gentlemen*, Van Nghe Publishers, Westminster

Nguyen Ngoc Huy and Ta Van Tai, 1987. *The Le Code: law in traditional Vietnam*, Ohio University Press, Athens.

Nguyen Tai Thu, 1993. *History of Vietnam's Ideology*, Social Sciences Publishers, Hanoi.

——, 1997. *Influences of Ideologies on Vietnam's Culture*, National Politics Publishers, Hanoi

Nguyen The Anh, 1968. *Economy and Society under the Nguyen Dynasty*, Trinh Bay Publishers, Saigon

Örücü, E., 1999. *Critical Comparative Law: considering paradoxes for legal systems in transition*, Geschriften van de Nederlandse Vereniging voor Rechtsvergelijking 59, Nederlandse Vereniging voor Rechtsvergelijking, Kluwer International Law, Deventer.

Peerenboom, R., 2001.'Globalization, path dependency and the limits of the law: administrative law reform and the rule of law in the PRC', *Berkeley Journal of International Law*, 19(2):161–264.

Peerenboom, R., 2002. 'Let one hundred flowers bloom, one hundred schools contend: Debate rule of law in China', *Michigan Journal of International Law*, 23(2):471–544.

Phan Dai Doan, 1998. *Some Issues of Vietnam's Confucianism*, National Politics Publishers, Hanoi.

Phan Dien, 2003. 'Improvement of the ideological work of the Party [Nang cao hon nua cong tac tu tuong, van hoa cua Dang]', *Tap chi Cong san*, 9 (3/2003).

Phan Ke Binh, 1983. *Vietnam's Customs*, Song Moi Publishers, Hanoi.

Ruskola T., 2002. 'Legal Orientalism', *Michigan Law Review*, 101(1):179–235.

Sachs, J.D. and Woo W.T., 1997. *Understanding China's Economic Performance*, Working Paper 5935, National Bureau of Economic Research, Cambridge, Massachusetts. Available at www.nber.org/papers/w5935/.

Shin Yi Peng, 2000. 'The WTO legalistic approach and East Asia: from the legal culture perspective', *Asia-Pacific Law and Policy Journal*, 1(2):1–69.

Stiglitz, J., and Hoff, K., 2002. *After the Big Bang? Obstacles to the emergence of the rule of law in post communist countries*, Working Paper 9282, National Bureau of Economic Research, Cambridge, Massachusetts. Available at www.nber.org/papers/9282/.

Stoltenberg, C.D., 2000. 'Globalization, Asian values and economic reform: the impact of tradition and change on ethical values in Chinese business', *Cornell International Law Journal*, 33:711–29.

Tan, E. Kheng-Boon, 2000. 'Law and values in governance: the Singapore way', *Hong Kong Law Journal*, 30(1):91–119.

Tran Le Sang (ed.), 2002. *Five Classical Works*, Social Sciences Publishers, Institute of Chinese Studies, Hanoi

Tran The Phap, 1960. *Linh Nam Chich Quai*, Khai Tri Publishers, Saigon [tr. Le Huu Muc].

Tran Trong Kim, 1971. *Confucianism: introduction into Chinese philosophy*, Tan Viet Publishers, Saigon (reprinted by Ho Chi Minh City Publishers frequently from 1992–2002).

Tran Van Giau, 1988. *Philosophy and Ideology*, Ho Chi Minh City Publishers, Ho Chi Minh City.

Truong Ba Can, 1988. *Nguyen Truong To: person and literature*, Ho Chi Minh City Publishers, Ho Chi Minh City.

Vu Khieu, 1997. *Confucianism and Development*, Social Sciences Publishers, Hanoi.

Vu Van Khien, 1968. *Vietnam's Customs*, Duong Sang Publishers, Saigon.

Vu Van Mau, 1958. *Introduction into Civil Law*, Ministry of Education, Saigon.

——, 1963. *Quelques Aspects Techniques de la Réception des droits Occidienteux*, Association Nationale de Droit Compare, Saigon.

5

Transforming Chinese enterprises: ideology, efficiency and instrumentalism in the process of reform

Chao Xi

Historically, the roots of the contemporary Chinese legal system are deeply embedded in the Soviet Union model of the socialist legal system (see Butler 1983). Even today, the Soviet influence can easily be identified, largely reflected in China's constitutional organisation, which replicates to a significant extent that of the former USSR (especially in its 1936 Constitution) (A.H.Y. Chen 2000). This significance, however, has been fading. The economic reforms carried out in the 1980s in China were apparently much more dramatic and liberal than those occurring in the Soviet Union at that time—particularly in terms of development of the non-public sector in the economy and the rapid expansion of foreign investment in, and foreign trade with, China. Soviet legal models were not adequate for China's attempt to create 'socialism with Chinese characteristics'. An increasing number of civil and common law legal doctrines and institutions have found their way into recent Chinese legislation and exert ever-increasing external influences on Chinese legal development.

It may be wrong, however, to conclude that the diminishing influence of the Soviet legal system indicates that socialist ideology will play no part in shaping the future of the Chinese legal system. Indeed, in an attempt to construct a new theory of law, upon which Chinese legal development is based, Chinese jurists have successfully discarded the rigid Vyshinsky-type socialist theory of law (Lo 1997). They have not, however, ventured further to challenge the official socialist ideology of Deng Xiaoping's 'four cardinal principles', which sets the boundaries of legal development in China. In the final analysis, China is one of the few countries in the world that still upholds socialism as an ideological pursuit. So long as China remains a socialist country, socialism will continue to play a substantial role in shaping law and law-related institutions in China. The question to be answered is what role does socialism play?

This chapter attempts to present an answer to this question by examining the development of Chinese enterprise law, particulary in terms of enterprise/corporate governance. Having officially abandoned the centrally-planned economy, China is now embracing a 'socialist market economy'. As part of the economic reform, state-owned enterprises (SOEs)—the basic unit implementing production plans and providing social welfare in the centrally-planned economy—are gradually being transformed into modern companies, the dominant vehicle for conducting business in the market economy. The prevalent legal instrumentalism has resulted in the development of Chinese enterprise law, in particular its governance aspects, embodying the intricate interactions between socialist ideology and economic efficiency in the process of reform. It is therefore of particular relevance to the central question of this chapter. The second part of this chapter places this analysis in context by briefly outlining enterprise reforms since 1978 and their economic and policy impetus. The third part identifies the two fundamental ideological doctrines of socialism in the context of enterprise reforms, namely, predominance of public ownership of the means of production[1] and leadership of the ruling Communist Party. The chapter then examines how the two socialist doctrines have shaped law and law-related institutions in China and concludes by presenting some thoughts about socialism and the future of Chinese enterprise law.

CHINESE ENTERPRISE REFORMS: A LONG MARCH TOWARD EFFICIENCY

The subservience of law to policy and the instrumental use of law in China[2] make an understanding of the Party's policies on enterprise reforms indispensable if one is to comprehend the development of Chinese enterprise law. As the issue of Chinese enterprise reforms is one that has been explored by numerous works in various disciplines, I will present a brief and necessarily simplified account of the evolution of Chinese enterprise reform policies.

Initial conditions of enterprise reforms

The Communist Party of China (CPC) gained control over Mainland China and established the PRC in 1949. At the outset of socialist rule, private ownership amounted to 90 per cent of the state economy and public ownership was only of nominal significance. When the CPC was attempting to gain control of the country, the foremost task was to expand the magnitude of public ownership in the economy. Rigorous measures were taken to confiscate state-run enterprises owned by the defeated Kuomintang government, the so-called 'bureaucratic-capital', and enterprises and capital owned by 'hostile' entrepreneurs and governments.[3] The national bourgeois and the private sector were, however, largely left untouched. As a result, a multi-ownership economy, with public ownership controlling economic 'lifelines', took shape.

The next stage of development (1953–57) followed a debate within China's leadership over economic development strategies. One side of the debate advocated maintaining the existing mixed ownership economy, whereas the other side called for transformation to a socialist economy (Gao Shangquan and Yang Qixian 1999b). Those favouring transformation won the day, and the first 'Five-Year Plan' was launched in 1953 to carry out 'socialist transformation' with Soviet assistance. The process of socialist transformation resulted in the state assuming control over virtually all industrial organisations by 1956 and restructuring them into SOEs governed and operated in a manner similar to those operating within the Soviet model of command planning.[4]

From 1957 to 1965, China's SOEs underwent huge upheavals, propelled by various forms of political movements and readjustments.[5] The development of SOE policies was terminated abruptly by the onset of the Cultural Revolution in 1966, though restored ten years later.

Enterprise reforms in the transitional period (1978–92)

A historical shift in CPC policy took place in 1978. In December 1978, the Third Plenary Session of the CPC Central Committee was held. Among many decisions was that of enterprise reform. The policy orientation of initial enterprise reforms (*The People's Daily*, 24 December 1978) separated state administration from SOE management, which entailed a delegation of managerial autonomy to the SOEs and their management (*The People's Daily*, 24 December 1978). A variety of measures, including the retention of a proportion of profits and economic accountability, were implemented.

These efforts barely made any improvements, largely because policy priority was given to reforms in the rural sector prior to 1984. Chai's observation that post-Mao China adopted an incremental approach to economic reform helps to explain why rural reforms took place first. Reforms were first carried out in the sector where resistance was weakest, and then spread to those sectors where the reform measures were more complex and less popular (Chai 1997). Obviously, less political risk was involved in reforming the rural collective economy than reforming the urban command economy and SOEs, as the latter were associated with much more intractable, deep-rooted and politically explosive problems.

Nevertheless, the task of reforming SOEs was undeniably crucial. Despite their overwhelming dominance in China's economy, SOEs suffered chronically from inefficiency and low productivity. A majority were in debt, incurring an ever-increasing and staggering amount of losses, and the subsidies to keep them afloat were an intolerable burden on the central government (Wang 1992). On the other hand, the taxation system was poor, and SOE profits formed the primary source of fiscal revenue for the central government (Lin Zhijun 2001). Given the government's dependence on SOEs for revenue, the ever-deteriorating performance of the state sector threatened to drag down the nation's economy. The need for reforms in the SOE sector could no longer be ignored.

Inspired by the triumph of the reforms in the rural sector,[6] the Chinese leadership was determined to place SOE reforms at the top of the economic reform agenda, focusing in particular on fostering SOE efficiency. An efficient state sector was set as the ultimate goal of the SOE reforms, reflecting persistence of the ideological notion that socialism (and hence state-led economic activity) is superior to capitalism (Deng Xiaoping 1994:221–3).

The ground-breaking SOE reforms were initiated in 1984. Blaming SOE inefficiency on the state's direct management of SOEs, the CPC's 'Decision on Economic Structure Reform' (CPC Central Committee 1984) proclaimed that ownership and management of SOEs 'should be appropriately separated'. State-owned enterprises should become independent legal entities, responsible for their own profits and losses (CPC Central Committee 1984). It is worth noting, however, that, while daily managerial autonomy was largely delegated to the SOEs, ownership of SOE property remained with the state and was never intended to be transferred to the enterprises.

In 1988, the CPC adopted a bolder mechanism, the 'contract responsibility system', to divide state administration from SOE management. Enterprise directors signed contracts with their supervisory authorities, setting targets for enterprise performance. Tackling the enterprise inefficiency problems, once thought to be the panacea, resulted, however, in little improvement (Qi Duojun 2003). It seemed all reforms that avoided removing enterprise property from the regime of the monopolised state ownership ran into barriers and failed to provide meaningful autonomy or incentives for enterprise efficiency.

The Chinese leadership's concerns about SOE efficiency led them to search for an alternative approach to enterprise reform. The fact that stock companies serve as a robust engine for the prosperous capitalist economies meant that establishing a similar shareholding system in China was a tantalising option, but ideological obstacles existed. The concept of establishing a shareholding system and issuing stocks to the public was thought to be inconsistent with, even heretical to, socialist public ownership (Qian 1993).

Starting from the mid 1980s, however, Chinese economists, building on a reference by Karl Marx, claimed that this corporate form developed in capitalist countries could also benefit the socialist economy (Wang 1992). The concept received endorsement from Deng, who was in favour of employing some 'capitalist methods' to build socialism (Deng Xiaoping 1994:151–3), and the policy reversal prompted the Chinese government to open a new path to enterprise reform. Vigorous steps were taken towards establishing a shareholding system, including pilot schemes to transform SOEs into so-called shareholding companies and the opening of stock exchanges in Shanghai and Shenzhen.

Related to the shareholding system reform, a far-reaching ideological breakthrough came from the CPC Thirteenth National Congress in 1987, which proclaimed that China was a socialist country still in the first stages of socialism (Zhao Ziyang 1987). At this point, it was thought that public ownership had to predominate, but a private sector could contribute production and employment that the state could not. This shift in policy reflected an intention to permit the existence of private ownership as a supplement to state ownership, which continues to play the leading role in the Chinese economy. Released from the stringent ideological restraints imposed on it, a flourishing private sector soon emerged and provided the resources necessary to support the shareholding system.

Corporatisation: enterprise reforms in the socialist market economy

Following Deng Xiaoping's triumphant tour of south China in late 1992, the CPC's Decisions on Socialist Market Economy System[7] of 1993 finally cast aside the concept of a planned economy and marked the eventual adoption by the Chinese leadership of a more liberal and market-oriented reform strategy. The orientation of enterprise reform was declared to be establishing a 'modern enterprise system' with public ownership as its mainstay. Instead of accurately defining the vague term 'modern enterprise system',[8] the 1993 Decisions delineated it as a system that has 'clarified property rights, designated authorities and responsibilities, separated government and enterprise functions, and established scientific management' (section 2).

Two approaches were identified to modernise the inefficient SOE regime. The first approach was 'converting SOE's operational management mechanisms' while leaving their fundamental ownership and organisational structure unaltered. It is indeed a continuation of the conventional line of enterprise reform. The second approach was corporatising SOEs, particularly large and middle-sized SOEs, in a gradual and realistic way (1993 Decisions, section 6). It signalled that the CPC officially endorsed the shareholding system as a useful instrument to reform SOEs, after many years of experiments, as noted above. Indeed, it was this formal endorsement of the shareholding system that accelerated the enactment and promulgation of the first national company law in 1993.[9] Given that the first approach was simply an improved version of the already failed 'contract responsibility system' (Qi Duojun 2003:28), it is not surprising that policy priority was attached to the second approach—corporatising SOEs. By corporatising SOEs, the Chinese leadership intended to separate government administration from enterprise management, release the state from its unlimited responsibility for SOEs, raise funds to diversify SOE risks, and, consequently, improve enterprise efficiency (1993 Decisions, section 6).

Notwithstanding the backing of the 1993 Decisions, fears about the capitalist attributes of the shareholding system remained and, from time to time, frustrated the CPC's endeavours to corporatise SOEs. More radical ideological breakthroughs took place in 1997. In his report to the CPC National Congress, Jiang Zemin (1997) redefined the public sector of the economy, which included not only state and collectively-owned sectors, but also the state and collectively-owned elements in the sector of mixed ownership. The dominant position of public ownership could be maintained by the state sector controlling (rather than monopolising) major industries and key areas of the national economy. Along this line, Jiang continued boldly to assert that the shareholding system is one of the forms of materialising public ownership, as long as the state or a collective holds the controlling share. This controlling position, Jiang maintained, may indeed expand control capacity and eventually bolster the dominant role of public ownership.

This policy determinacy eventually paved the way for the market-oriented corporatisation and ownership diversification, and prompted the enactment of the long-awaited national securities law in 1998.[10] To date, most large and medium SOEs have corporatised themselves, although the process has not yet been completed. Ownership diversification is taking place in two main forms: listing on domestic and international stock exchanges in the case of larger SOEs, and sales to domestic and foreign investors in the case of small and medium SOEs.[11]

Ideology

It has been demonstrated above that the main theme of China's enterprise reform policies has been improving enterprise efficiency. This does not, however, end this observation; rather, it poses another question, namely, what has distinguished China's enterprise reforms from those carried out in the former Soviet bloc, which has also been in search of increasing enterprise efficiency? It is submitted that China's adherence to socialism (with Chinese characteristics) when undertaking enterprise reforms may help to explain the divergence of paths to enterprise reforms.

Through various forms of mass privatisation, most Eastern European and former Soviet Union countries attempted to cut their ties with socialism by radically transforming their communist economies into market economies with 'big bang' strategies (see Coffee 1998; Stiglitz 1999). Conversely, while reforming its SOE regime, China has officially proclaimed its constant adherence to socialism. China has never radically departed from the socialist practicalities of the past. Indeed, the top leaders of the Party have used an efficient SOE regime and the market economy merely as a means to bolster public ownership and socialism. For instance, Deng once bluntly stated

> ...taking advantage of the useful aspects of capitalist countries, including their methods of operation and management, does not mean that we will adopt capitalism. Instead, we use those methods in order to develop the productive forces under socialism. As long as learning from capitalism is regarded as no more than a means to an end, it will not change the structure of socialism or bring China back to capitalism (1995:239).

Nonetheless, it would be wrong to assume that China's top leaders would stringently and rigidly adhere to socialist ideology. On the contrary, as this chapter has illustrated, the Chinese leaders have taken a pragmatic and flexible stance in interpreting the socialist ideology in a bid to accommodate reforms aimed at increasing enterprise efficiency, which they believe will in turn enhance socialism. The interaction and tension between the concerns to increase efficiency and adherence to socialist ideology also help to explain the conventional observation that China's enterprise reforms are a progressive and incremental process, rather than a significant leap forward.

This *ad hoc* interaction has a momentous bearing on legal development in China. Western observers have observed that law in China is still conceived as, and still operates as, an instrument to carry out and consolidate institutional (primarily economic) changes according to predetermined policies (see, for example, Epstein 1994). This legal instrumentalism reflects the assertions of Party leaders that the Chinese legal system is but a means to serve and safeguard economic constructions (Xin Chunyun 1999) and that its development must be conducive to economic development (Chen Jianfu 1999). Law, as an instrument, reflects and substantiates Party policies shaping economic development and enterprise reforms, and the latter guides lawmaking and legal enforcement (Zhang Youyu and Wang Shuwen 1989). Given that enterprise reform policies have been the result of interactions between the concerns about efficiency and the pursuit of socialism, the operation of legal instrumentalism renders it perfectly logical for Chinese enterprise law to be shaped by socialism, although enterprise law also serves to foster enterprise efficiency.

Before turning to examine how socialism has shaped the development of enterprise law in China, it is important to identify the socialist doctrines of direct relevance to enterprise law; it may not be as constructive to discuss socialism in the abstract sense.

In his renowned talk in 1979, Deng enunciated that the ideological prerequisite of China's economic reform was the so-called 'four cardinal principles', namely: upholding the leadership of the Communist Party, upholding the socialist road, upholding the dictatorship of the proletariat; and upholding the Marxist-Leninism and Mao Zedong Thought. In 1987, he maintained that, of the four cardinal principles, upholding the leadership of the Party and upholding the socialist road were of the utmost importance. While the principle of upholding the leadership of the Party is self-explanatory, the principle of upholding the socialist road seems vague. In Deng's view, predominance of public ownership is one of the two fundamental features of the socialist road.[12] When elaborating on his strategy of economic reform and development, Jiang Zemin (1997) also stated that 'being a socialist country, China must keep public ownership as the foundation of its socialist economic system'. To conclude, in the context of enterprise reforms, predominance of public ownership and leadership of the Party are the two fundamental socialist doctrines that have prevailed in China since Deng assumed power in 1978.[13]

These two fundamental socialist doctrines were constitutionalised in the 1982 PRC Constitution. Article 6 of the Constitution provides that 'the basis of the economic system is socialist public ownership of the means of production' and thus endorses the predominant position of public ownership of the means of production as a constitutional principle. The Party's leadership, together with Deng's three other cardinal principles, is enshrined in the Preamble.[14] It can also be inferred from Article 1 of the Constitution, which reads, 'the PRC is a socialist country under the people's democratic dictatorship led by the working class and based on the alliance of workers and peasants', where the Party is supposedly representative of the working class (von Senger 2000).

Few have doubted China's adherence to the fundamental socialist doctrines while reforming its SOE regime during the 1980s and early 1990s. However, the move to incorporation and ownership diversification since the mid 1990s (always by listing larger SOEs at stock exchanges and selling small or medium SOEs to private investors) has prompted some Western commentators to argue that China is heading toward mass privatisation (for example, Tam 1999) and an eventual abandonment of socialism.

This scenario is clearly not the intention of Chinese leaders and it seems unlikely to occur in the foreseeable future. In a pivotal policy document setting forth the orientation of enterprise reforms to 2010, the Decision on Major Issues Concerning the Reform and Development of State-Owned Enterprises,[15] the CPC reaffirms its guiding principles for future SOE reforms as upholding public ownership as the mainstay of the socialist market economy, and giving full play to the core role of Party organisations within enterprises. This position was recently reiterated by Jiang Zemin in his 2002 report to the Sixteenth CPC National Congress.

Having identified the fundamental socialist doctrines in the context of enterprise reforms, that is, predominance of public ownership of the means of production and the leadership of the Communist Party, I will now examine the extent to which, and the way in which, the CPC has shaped and influenced the development of the Chinese enterprise law.

PREDOMINANCE OF PUBLIC OWNERSHIP OF THE MEANS OF PRODUCTION

1949–78: SOEs subordinated to the state

Largely due to Mao's philosophy of class struggle and, consequently, his hostility towards formal law, Chinese society under his rule was one in which legal nihilism prevailed. Apart from some basic laws enacted while heavily under the influence of the Soviet model of 'socialist legality' in the early 1950s, essentially no formal law existed. Having said that, however, the Measures of State-Run Industrial Enterprises Work (Draft)[16] is, by its nature, a legal document regulating matters in relation to the governance of SOEs. The moderately comprehensive 1961 Measures, as will be illustrated below, exemplify that socialism could determine the contents of law and that the function of law was simply to render the highly abstract and conceptual ideology more concrete, substantial and operable.

Bluntly stipulating that 'the whole people ownership of state-run industrial enterprises must be firmly preserved and must not be violated' (Para. 1, Article 1), the foremost undertaking of the 1961 Measures was to safeguard public ownership of the means of production of SOEs. To this end, the state, pursuant to the then prevailing socialist ideology, not only owned the means of production on behalf of the people, but was also directly involved in the day-to-day management of SOEs.

Indeed, direct management of SOEs by the state was instituted as the guiding principle, equal in importance to the principle of public ownership of the means of production. On behalf of the state, different levels of state agencies exercised excessive and rigid control over the daily management of SOEs, directing their production, controlling their pricing, and allocating their output. State-owned enterprises remitted any profits to the state, which, in turn, subsidised others' losses.

State-owned enterprises were subordinates or, in Chinese terms, 'appendages' to the state's administrative system and were subject to direct control by the state, as well as its mandatory plans.[17] A SOE was supervised and directed chiefly by a 'higher authority' (1961 Measures, Para. 5, Article 4), which might be a ministry, provincial government or local government.[18] The higher authority assigned the production plans to the SOEs in its control. These plans were given to the higher authority by an even higher level of authority. As one Western commentator vividly delineated, the state was one giant vertically-integrated productive firm. Ministries were divisions within the firm and enterprises were factories (Clarke 1992; Jiang Yiwei 1985). State-owned enterprises typically had minimal decision-making powers over their production and business management—even their monthly production plans needed to be verified by their higher authorities (1961 Measures, Para. 1, Article 10).

Another manifestation of the subordinate position of SOEs was that Party Committee members and the management personnel of SOEs were appointed—and could be dismissed—by the higher authority. Indeed, SOE leadership was an integral part of the general governmental framework. Party Committee members and the management personnel of SOEs were entitled to political and economic treatment equivalent to cadres serving the Party and governmental agencies (Schipani and Junhai Liu 2002). They were held accountable to the higher authority, which took account of the fulfilment of the assigned production plans rather than the profitability of the SOE.

1978–82: excessive state control over SOEs remained

State ownership of the means of production was reaffirmed and direct management by the state of SOEs remained the norm between 1978 and 1982. The Interim Regulations on State-Owned Industrial Enterprises[19] made it clear that SOEs should conduct their production and business operations under the leadership of their higher authority (Article 5). The latter decided on all important issues ranging from production quota and plans to the direction of product development (Articles 23, 28, 62, 64). Moreover, the SOE director and other senior executives were appointed, dismissed and assessed by the higher authority. State-owned enterprises were not allowed to make decisions that contradicted those of the higher authority (Articles 63, 66).

1984–92: separating government from enterprises

While state ownership of the means of production remained an unshakeable socialist doctrine, the Stalinist ideology of direct state management of SOEs was largely abandoned. An 'appropriate' separation of state administration from enterprise management was seen as necessary to improve efficiency.

Law was reformed to accommodate this ideological breakthrough. These reforms meant that SOEs were explicitly vested with significant managerial powers that they were not entitled to before 1984. More significantly, law attempted to provide legal guarantees to safeguard these managerial powers. The Law on Industrial Enterprises Owned by the Whole People[20] prohibited any state organ or unit from encroaching upon the managerial powers of SOEs (Article 58). The Regulations on Transforming Operational Management Mechanisms of Industrial Enterprises Owned by the Whole People[21] further equipped SOEs with legal remedies in case any organ or individual was to interfere with their 'operational rights'.[22]

In spite of these notable legal developments, the law still left a few crucial powers in the hands of the state and its agencies, that is, the higher authorities of SOEs. This was largely because the Chinese leaders aimed for an 'appropriate' rather than a complete separation between the government and enterprises. These crucial powers included issuing unified mandatory plans to SOEs; examining and approving important plans; and appointing or approving the nomination of the director and other senior executives.[23] It was these powers that various governmental agencies took advantage of to justify their excessive interference with enterprise affairs. In practice, these powers severely undermined the effectiveness of the provisions that had granted SOEs remarkable managerial autonomy and attempted to safeguard their autonomy. It is therefore not surprising that a senior Chinese policy advisor maintained as late as 1997, that the utmost imperative mission of Chinese enterprise reforms was the separation of the government from enterprises (Liu Ji 1997).

From 1993: the state as the company property owner and the majority shareholder

Compared to pre-1993 national enterprise laws, the 1993 Company Law presents a key progression as it categorised an enterprise in accordance with its liabilities rather than the attributes of its owner (see Jiang Ping 1994). Moreover, the 1993 Company Law has universal application to all companies incorporated under it,[24] and may have disallowed mandatory requirements in companies for state ownership of the means of production. These remarkable legal developments do not imply, however, that socialist ideology was abandoned in the 1993 Company Law. After all, the legislative backdrop of the 1993 Company Law was the corporatisation of SOEs (see also Art and Minkang Gu 1995), as evidenced by one of its legislative purposes, 'to promote the development of the socialist market economy' (Para. 5, Article 1). It is interesting to examine how the socialist ideology of predominance of state ownership of the means of production penetrates the 1993 Company Law and other related regulations.

To begin, the foremost (and conventional) issue to be addressed by company law is the ownership of the property and assets of a company. Given that pre-1993 enterprise laws invariably mandated state ownership of SOEs' means of production, the 1993 Company Law represents an important step forward by incorporating the doctrine of corporate personality. Generally, a Chinese company has full entitlement to the so-called 'property right of legal person' created by the collective investment of its members. Despite the vagueness of the 'property right of legal person',[25] this provision seems to conform to the essence of corporate personality in both common law[26] and civil law.[27]

However, Article 4(3) of the 1993 Company Law, which reads 'the ownership of state-owned assets in a company shall vest in the state', apparently contradicts the provision in Article 4(2) and casts doubt on whether the property of Chinese companies is genuinely distinct and separate from its members.[28] Jurists have made efforts to interpret Article 4(3) to bring it in accordance with the doctrine of corporate personality (see, for example, Schipani and Junhai Liu 2002). These efforts, however, seem to be frustrated by the Provisional Regulations Concerning Supervision and Administration on State Assets in Enterprises,[29] in which 'state assets' are defined as 'the various forms of investments in enterprises by the state and rights and interests derived from such investments' (Article 3). This definition may well mean that the property of the company (in which the state has investments) is not separate from its member—the state—and that the state still retains ownership of the assets that it has invested in companies. Obviously, the extraordinary provision of Article 4(3) only has the effect of safeguarding the state's ownership of the company but may not necessarily lead to the dominant position of state ownership.

To secure the dominant position of state ownership in larger companies transformed from SOEs[30] (which always take the joint-stock company corporate form), the state employed a legal strategy dividing shares of companies into three classes, namely, state-owned shares, legal person shares and social shares. State-owned shares are typically held by the central and local governments (represented by local financial bureaus, state asset management companies or investment companies) and by the parent of the joint-stock company (typically an SOE or a wholly state-owned company). Legal person shares are shares held by such domestic institutions as industrial enterprises, non-bank financial institutions and technology and research institutes. State-owned shares and legal person shares are not tradable on the stock exchange. Social shares are shares held mostly by individuals (including enterprise employees) and by private institutions in some cases. Social shares of listed companies are generally tradable on stock exchanges. It is apparent by definition that such categorisation is based on the attributes of the shareholders, a practice already abandoned by the 1993 Company Law.

Official statistics show that each of the three classes account for about one-third of all outstanding shares of Chinese listed companies.[31] It is worth noting, however, that these statistics merely reflect the state's direct shareholding in listed companies, because they do not take the 'state-owned legal person shares' into account. This sub-category of legal person shares was introduced by the Tentative Measures

Concerning Administration of State-Owned Equities of Joint Stock Companies.[32] Legal person shares held by SOEs, state-owned institutions and other work units fall under this sub-category (1994 Tentative Measures, Article 2). State-owned shares and state-owned legal person shares, which are collectively referred to as state-owned equity in the 1994 Tentative Measures mandate (Article 2), must be in the position of control in joint stock companies (Article 3). This controlling position can be achieved by means of either an absolute control (over 50 per cent) over most of the listed company, or a relative control (30–50 per cent)[33] over the listed companies with a dispersed ownership structure (1994 Tentative Measures, Article 11).

In terms of the state-owned legal person shares, the direct and indirect shareholding of the state may account for a significantly higher proportion than one third of all outstanding shares in listed companies. A recent study has shown that the state is the majority shareholder in 53.6 per cent of Chinese listed companies and the state is in absolute control (control over 50 per cent of votes) of 24.3 per cent of Chinese listed companies (He Jun 1998). Another empirical observation is that the ultimate control of 84 per cent of Chinese listed companies is in fact in the hands of the state (Liu Shaojia et al. 2003).

The state's position as the majority shareholder, as has been observed above, calls for sufficient legal safeguards to protect the state's interests in the companies. One of the legal strategies utilised by the Chinese legislature is vesting an extraordinarily wide range of decision-making powers in the shareholder's general meeting under the 1993 Company Law (Article 38(103)), including managerial powers normally exerted by the board of directors in other jurisdictions.[34] The roots of this corporate governance arrangement may be in the political governance philosophy expressed by the PRC Constitution (Schipani and Junhai Liu 2002). More practically, reserving vital decision-making powers exclusively to the shareholders' general meeting limits the managerial power of the board of directors, thus potentially helping to reduce the adverse effects of any abuse of powers or wrongdoing by directors. This legal strategy seemed desirable in light of the 'insider control' problems and the associated problem of managerial asset stripping. It may, however, cause inefficiency in decision-making, as one shareholders' general meeting per year would not be able to respond to the constantly changing market.

The government's overwhelming concerns about its own interests as the majority shareholder may also help to explain the 1993 Company Law's ignorance of minority protection and the failure to provide practicable legal mechanisms to protect the minority shareholders. This lack of minority protection has resulted in widespread malpractice in the Chinese stockmarket, whereby the majority shareholders abuse their position and exploit the public minority shareholders (see, for example, Anderson 2000; Wei Xinjiang 2002).

THE LEADERSHIP OF THE COMMUNIST PARTY

1949–78: the Party taking the paramount leadership in SOEs

To bring the ideology of the Party's leadership into practice, leadership of the unified Party at the factory level was the norm. The prevailing model was the 'director responsibility system under the leadership of the Party Committee',[35] adopted at the Eighth National Congress of the CPC in 1956. The essence of the system was that the Party Committee played a monistic and all-encompassing role in SOE internal governance. All major enterprise decisions were to be made collectively by the Party Committee pursuant to the majority rule.[36] The director was under the leadership of the Party Committee, acting as its executive.[37] In practice, the Party Committee even deprived the directors of limited autonomy relating to enterprise production (Jiang 1985).

This unified Party leadership provided an institutional setting by which it penetrated into every corner of enterprise internal governance. Given that the Party Committee assumed all major decision-making powers, SOEs were in effect appendages not only of the state, but also of the ruling Party. Together with the higher authority, the Party Committee functioned to unify decision-making vertically, execution and control into one all-encompassing and centrally administered hierarchy (You 1998).

The collective leadership represented by the Party Committee induced inefficiency in decision-making. The director did not have the authority to make business policies, while the Party Committee, which had this authority, had little interest in issues of daily management and in any case did not possess relevant expertise. Moreover, unified leadership posed a problem of accountability, that is, of failing to identify who should take responsibility for any losses caused by a wrong decision. Indeed, Deng himself was aware of the accountability problem, saying that, 'nominal responsibility of the committee for decision-making means no responsibility, or nobody to be really responsible for decisions' (cited in Zhang Zanlun 1987:9).

1978–84: first attempt to apportion decision-making

The director responsibility system under the leadership of the Party Committee was upheld in 1981 and 1983 (Article 1, 1981 Interim Regulations; Article 4, 1983 Interim Regulations). The director remained liable for decisions implemented by the Party Committee on enterprise production and administration. Nevertheless, attempts were made to reduce the influence of the Party Committee and to limit its direct involvement in daily management. The director was allowed to play a more vigorous role in two ways. First, the director was able to propose important matters to the

Party Committee and the higher authority for their approval. These issues included business policies, long-term and annual plans and appointment of senior executives. Second, the director was granted full powers to decide on matters other than those mentioned above. In addition, a so-called 'factory-level meeting', comprising the deputy director and other senior executives, was accountable to the director rather than to the Party Committee. This bolstered the director's position. Theoretically, at least, when the director was given more decision-making power, a new decision-making hub slowly emerged. The state and the Party no longer monopolised the decision-making of SOEs (Zheng 1988).

These legal changes marked one of the first attempts[38] to establish a sound and clear apportionment of decision-making between governance organs in the Chinese legal system, a classical question addressed by all modern company laws. They echoed the moderate pre-1984 ideological shifts, which attempted to equip SOEs with more managerial autonomy. However, these legal changes were destined to yield only marginal results due to policy indeterminacy (Tang Guodong 1987). The boundaries of decision-making of the state, the Party Committee and the director remained blurred and, as a result, past practicalities barely changed (Wang Baoshu and Cui Qingzhi 1984), although the general trend pointed to weakened state and Party roles in SOEs.

1984–92: power sharing between the Party Committee and the management

The director responsibility system (not subject to the Party Committee's leadership) was first endorsed in the 1984 Decisions. A circular jointly issued by the CPC Central Committee and the State Council in 1986 overtly claimed that

> [t]he director of an industrial enterprise owned by the whole people is the head of the enterprise and the representative of the 'enterprise legal person', assuming the overall responsibility for the enterprise, occupying the central position and playing the central role.[39]

This delineation of the director's role was partly reproduced in the 1988 Enterprise Law (Article 45). Indeed, the three Regulations issued in 1986 and the 1988 Enterprise Law all unambiguously provided for the director responsibility system.[40] The director was empowered to decide on important matters for the SOE,[41] with the assistance of a management committee acting in an advisory manner.

These provisions marked the end of the three decades of the Party Committee command system practicalities. The dominant role of the Party Committee in everyday factory life was greatly curtailed. The Party Committee was intentionally kept out of the enterprise management[42] and its role was confined to conducting 'ideological education' and 'guaranteeing and supervising the implementation of guidelines and policies of the Party and the state'.[43] It is a striking feature of the pre-1993 enterprise law that the Party organs were increasingly marginalised in enterprise production and administration.

This legal move, which had the *prima facie* effect of undermining the Party's leading role in SOEs, seems to be inconsistent with the ideological doctrine of the

Party's leadership. Indeed, it again manifests the Chinese leadership's pragmatic stance towards the interactions of enterprise efficiency and socialist ideology. It was indisputable that most Party cadres (including the Party secretary, the *de facto* controller of the Party Committee in SOEs) were laymen to enterprise management. Stringently adhering to the Party Committee unified leadership system at the factory level inevitably led to inefficiency. It was thus a more efficient allocation of decision-making to have the Party Committee focus on the areas in which it had expertise,[44] leaving the business operations to the director. A new legal regime was thus created at the micro factory level in which the Party Committee was accorded a core role in leading the factories' political life, paralleling the management's central position in leading the factories' economic life (You Ji 1998). In the meantime, the Party's leadership still manifested at a more macro level by formulating economic and enterprise reform policies and guidelines and by appointing and, where necessary, removing the director through the higher authority.

From 1993: the Party Committee returns?

The 1993 Company Law appears to have gone further to make sure that the Party Committee was not involved in enterprise management. Article 17 provides that the activities of grassroots organisations of the Party within companies (which always take the form of Party Committee) must abide by the Party's Constitution. On the face of it, this provision is one that applies merely to internal affairs of the Party Committee. Apart from this provision, the 1993 Company Law says nothing more about the Party Committee's role in the company.[45] Considering the connection with the legislative trend of phasing out the Party Committee's involvement in enterprise management, it appears that the Party Committee will play an increasingly insubstantial role, if any, in companies.

However, an alternative interpretation of Article 17 also appears. First, Article 17 may provide a solid justification for the Party Committee to exist and operate in the company. More significantly, by providing for the exclusive application of the Party's Constitution to the Party Committee in the company, it may in effect preclude the application of the 1993 Company Law to the Party Committee and give the Party's Constitution implicit statutory authority to supplement the 1993 Company Law. This interpretation of Article 17 seems more constructive if one examines the Party's Constitution.

The Party's Constitution confers on the Party Committee in the company not only the power of 'guaranteeing and supervision', which it was entitled to under the previous enterprise laws, but also the power to participate in company decision-making, which previous legislation attempted to phase out. Article 32 of the Party's Constitution[46] reads

> The Party's grassroots organisation acts as the political nucleus and works for the operation of the enterprise. [It] guarantees and supervises the implementation of the principles and policies of the Party and the state in its own enterprise and backs the shareholders' general meeting, the board of directors, the supervisory board and the manager (factory director)

in the exercise of their functions and powers according to law. [It] relies wholeheartedly on the workers, supports the work of the workers' congress and *participates in the decision-making of major matters in the enterprise...*[emphasis added]

If the Party's Constitution is but a set of rules applicable to the Party Committee and has no binding legal effect on the company, it makes one wonder what Article 32 was supposed to achieve. Therefore, it is more sensible to understand Article 17 as one that has the legal effect of allowing the Party's Constitution to supplement the 1993 Company Law in many aspects. In this sense, the 1993 Company Law allows the possibility of the Party Committee in the company becoming a governance organ, if the Party's Constitution so provides.

The way in which the Party Committee may act as a governance organ, as noted, is determined by the Party's Constitution. Being a set of general norms, the Party's Constitution itself is silent in this regard. It is the fundamental principle of the Party's Constitution, however, that the lower Party organ is subordinate to its superiors and must comply unconditionally with decisions, resolutions, instructions and directives from superiors.[47] To be sure, these decisions, resolutions, instructions and directives are not normally deemed legally binding. Article 17 does not give them legal authority, but the aforementioned principle of the Party's Constitution lends them authority and elevates them to become legally binding on the Party Committee in the company and on the company itself. It follows that the Party Committee may lawfully participate in corporate governance in the way that decisions, resolutions, instructions and directives from its superiors (in particular, the CPC Central Committee) prescribe.

A momentous CPC Central Committee Circular issued in 1997[48], dealing with companies transformed from SOEs, covers the major issues relating to the extent and ways that the Party Committee may act as a governance organ in these companies. It clarifies that the 'major matters in the enterprise' described by Article 32 of the Party's Constitution refer to all matters discussed and decided by the shareholders' general meeting and the board of directors. Decision-making by the board of directors on these matters is closely scrutinised and supervised by the Party Committee. To elaborate, the board of directors must solicit and show respect to the Party Committee's opinions on these matters before making its own decisions. They then notify the Party Committee of the implementation of the decisions. The Party Committee may require the board of directors to rectify the decisions if it finds they contradict Party policies, guidelines and laws. Second, the Party Committee plays an active and vital part in nominating and appointing medium-level managers, a power that the 1993 Company Law has reserved exclusively to the general manager.[49] More significantly, Party cadres are encouraged to be directly involved in the day-to-day management of the company, and the Party secretary may serve concurrently as the chairman of the board of directors. Other members of the Party Committee may become members of the board of directors, the supervisory board and the senior management, in accordance with law, and vice versa.

These measures exemplify the Party's intention to take the leading role in, and steer the orientation of, the process of corporatising SOEs (1997 Party Central Committee Circular), by maintaining the Party's leadership at the company level and directly or indirectly participating in corporate governance. Realistically, these measures are useful in confining the imprecise—but in practice extensive—decision-making power of the Party Committee and, consequently, in aiding the full functioning of new governance organs.[50] Nevertheless, there are inconsistencies with the 1993 Company Law. For example, the decision-making power of the Party Committee overlaps those of the other governance organs, blurring the boundaries of decision-making of various governance organs prescribed by the 1993 Company Law. Moreover, it is problematic that the directors' legal duties and liabilities are inapplicable to the Party Committee and its members, which virtually means the Party Committee is in effect a governance organ with remarkable powers but little accountability. These drawbacks add difficulties to the attempts of reforming the already defective Chinese corporate governance law regime. Building up a sound system of corporate governance in line with internationally recognised standards in China is also made very difficult.

WHITHER REFORM? SOCIALISM AND THE FUTURE OF CHINESE ENTERPRISE LAW

The efficiency-oriented Chinese enterprise reforms have been the key component of China's transition from a traditional planned economy to a socialist market-oriented economy. In this process, an impressive body of enterprise law has emerged, with the recent legislation increasingly embracing corporate forms and business practices in the Western market economies in a bid to improve efficiency.[51] However, the development of the Chinese enterprise law regime has involved socialist ideology so extensively that one Western commentator once disappointedly concluded that 'the state is merely changing the form, but not the substance of economic relationships' (Howson 1997:172–3). This disappointment is inevitable, given that Chinese enterprise reforms are simply a means to bolster socialism and its economic foundation and that law has long been used as an instrument to implement the Party's enterprise reform policies. The orthodox ideology is, no matter how far enterprise and legal reforms progress, the bottom line will always be there—socialism with Chinese characteristics must be adhered to.

In spite of socialist orthodoxy, the fate of Chinese enterprise law may change owing to a number of far-reaching recent developments. First and foremost, the interpretation of the nature of 'socialism with Chinese characteristics' may shift. As noted, the Chinese leaders have been pragmatic in adjusting the interpretations of socialist ideology to accommodate economic development. The incorporation of the 'three represents' thought[52] into the Party's Constitution in 2002 and the promulgation of the CPC Central Committee's Decisions on Perfecting the Socialist

Market Economy in 2003 may well signal such a shift. Second, China amended its Constitution in 1999 to endorse the principle of 'ruling the country in accordance with law'. Although it is unlikely that the Chinese leadership would favour the liberal democratic version of rule of law (see Peerenboom 1999, 2002), the constitutionalisation of the rule-of-law principle may help to curtail the instrumental use of law in China. Finally, China's commitments under the World Trade Organisation (WTO) expose Chinese enterprises to increasingly fierce international competition, adding to the urgent need for reforms of the defective Chinese enterprise law regime to build a sound corporate governance system and provide sufficient protection to investors.[53]

An amendment of the 1993 Company Law is reportedly part of the NPC legislative blueprint in the future. This scheduled amendment will present us with a new opportunity to observe the intractable interactions of socialist ideology, economic efficiency and legal instrumentalism in socialist China.

ACKNOWLEDGMENT

The author would like to thank Michael Palmer for helpful comments. The usual disclaimer applies.

NOTES

[1]   Or *sheng chan zi liao*, which refers to the facilities and resources for producing goods.
[2]   See Lubman (1999). Legal instrumentalism and the relationship between policy and law in China will be dealt with in more detail later.
[3]   Those who took a hostile attitude towards the newly established communist People's Republic of China, in particular, the United States and its then allies.
[4]   Although the Stalinist line of economic development strategy was abandoned, the Soviet pattern of command economy and enterprise management remained and had dominated China for several decades (see Howe et al. 2003).
[5]   They were the 1957–61 decentralisation and Great Leap Forward, and in 1962–65 the period of readjustment. For a detailed account, see Riskin (1987) and Gao and Yang (1999).
[6]   Deng Xiaoping, the late paramount Chinese leader, acknowledged, 'we started the reform first in the rural areas. It was only after it had produced results there that we had the courage to launch it in the cities. In fact, the urban reform is a reform of the economic structure as a whole and is very risky' (Deng Xiaoping 1994:134).
[7]   Decisions of the CPC Central Committee on Some Issues Concerning the Establishment of a Socialist Market Economy System, adopted by the Third Plenary Session of the CPC Fourteenth National Congress on 14 November 1993 (hereinafter, '1993 Decisions').
[8]   For an illustration of the debate concerning the meaning of the 'modern enterprise system', see Wang Baoshu (2002).
[9]   The Company Law of the People's Republic of China (promulgated on 25 December 1993, and in effect on 1 July 1994. Hereinafter the '1993 Company Law'). See Yongqing Zhao (1996); Jiang Ping (1994).
[10]   The Securities Law of the People's Republic of China (promulgated on 29 December 1998, and in effect on 1 July 1999. Hereinafter the '1998 Securities Law').
[11]   See Tenev and Chunlin Zhang (2002:1). Official statistics show that by 2002, 442 companies transformed from larger SOEs have become listed companies and that more than 80 per cent of small-sized county-level SOEs and 60 per cent small-sized city-level SOEs have been sold to private investors. See also http://www.sasac.gov.cn/ldjh/ldjh_0068.htm.

12 The other feature is common prosperity, which is related to the wealth distribution system and not the direct concern of this chapter. See Deng Xiaoping (1994d).

13 Glendon, Gordon and Osakwe's (1985) comparative work on the socialist legal tradition reached a similar conclusion. Of a number of elements, an uncompromising recognition of the supreme leadership of the Communist Party and state ownership of the dominant means of production and distribution were identified as two of the elements of the ideology of the socialist legal system.

14 Legal scholars have, however, expressed different views on the exact force of the Preamble (Chen 1998).

15 Adopted at the Fourth Plenum of the Fifteenth CPC Central Committee on 22 September 1999.

16 Issued by the CPC Central Committee in 1961 and implemented on a trial basis nationally (hereinafter '1961 Measures').

17 Para. 1, Article 4 of the 1961 Measures reads, 'unified leadership, hierarchical governance, is the principle of the state's administration on state-run industrial enterprises ...'.

18 The assignation of the higher authority depends largely on the scale of the SOE in question and may change over time. The larger firms are likely to be held accountable to an appropriate ministry. Medium and small-sized firms are supervised at a level appropriate to the market they serve. See Hay et al. (1994).

19 Issued by the State Council on 1 April 1983. Hereinafter the '1983 Interim Regulations'.

20 Adopted by the Seventh NPC on 13 April 1988 and came into force on 1 August 1988. Hereinafter, the '1988 Enterprise Law'.

21 Issued by the State Council and came into force on 23 July 1992. Hereinafter, the '1992 Regulations'.

22 The 1992 Regulations, Article 22. The SOEs may choose to appeal or inform the government or its competent department, or go straight to the court to litigate against the organ or individual.

23 The 1988 Enterprise Law, Article 55; *Regulations on the Work of Director of Industrial Enterprises Owned by the Whole People* (issued by the CPC Central Committee and the State Council on 15 September 1986 and became effective on 1 October 1988. Hereinafter the 1986 Director Regulations), Article 9.

24 Indeed, the State Council's 1992 draft of company law, which proposed to apply merely to state-owned companies, failed to pass through in the NPC. See Bian Yaowu and Li Fei (1994).

25 Keith and Zhiqiu Lin (2001) present an excellent elaboration of jurisprudential discourse of the 'property right of legal person' in China.

26 In English law, the fundamental attribute of corporate personality is that a company is an entity separate and distinct from its members, and the property of the company is clearly distinguished from that of its members (Davies 2003; Sealy 2001).

27 The core element of legal personality in civil law is that the firm owns its own assets, which are distinct from the property of other persons (Kraakman et al. 2004).

28 Kong Xiangjun (1994), when reviewing Article 4 of the 1993 Company Law, sharply argued the state has ownership over the state-owned assets.

29 Issued by the State Council on 13 May 2003. Hereinafter, 2003 Provisional Regulations on State Assets.

30 Normally, large or medium-sized SOEs were corporatised.

31 By the end of 1998, state-owned shares totalled 86.6 billion shares, 34.25 per cent of the total equity of Chinese listed companies; legal person shares totalled 71.6 billion shares, 28.35 per cent of the total equity; tradable shares totalled 86.2 billion shares, 34.11 per cent of the total equity (among which A shares 24.06 per cent, B shares 5.30 per cent, H shares 4.75 per cent). Statistics available on the China Securities Regulatory Commission (CSRC) website: http://www.csrc.gov.cn/CSRCSite/eng/esmintr.htm.

32 Co-issued by State Administration of State-Owned Assets and State Commission for Economic Restructuring on 3 November 1994. Hereinafter, the '1994 Tentative Measures'.

33 Notably, La Porta et al. (1999) define that a corporation has a controlling shareholder if this shareholder's direct and indirect voting rights in the firm exceed 20 per cent.

34 For example, Article 70 of Table A, 1985 UK Companies Act, provides that '... the business of the company shall be managed by the directors who may exercise all the powers of the company'. In practice, the shareholders of larger companies in the United Kingdom, United States and Germany generally delegate decision-making extensively to the board (Davies 2003).

[35]   Para 2, Article 6 of the 1961 Measures stipulates that the director responsibility system under the leadership of Party Committee is the fundamental enterprise governance system.

[36]   The 1961 Measures, Para 3, Article 6; Paras 1 and 3, Article 62.

[37]   The 1961 Measures, Para 3, Article 55; Paras 2 and 3, Article 54.

[38]   The 1979 Equity Joint Venture Law also dealt with the question.

[39]   Article 1, The Supplementary Circular of the CPC Central Committee and the State Council Concerning Carefully Carrying Out and Implementing the Three Regulations on Industrial Enterprises Owned by the Whole People (issued 11 November 1986).

[40]   Article 1, 1986 Director Regulations; Article 2, The Regulations on the Work of Grass-Root Organizations of the CPC of Industrial Enterprises Owned by the Whole People (jointly issued by the CPC Central Committee and the State Council on 15 September 1986 and became effective on 1 October 1988. Hereinafter the '1986 CPC Grass-Root Regulations'); Article 2, The Regulations on the Work of Workers' Congress of Industrial Enterprises Owned by the Whole People (jointly issued by the CPC Central Committee and the State Council on 15 September 1986, effective 1 October 1988. Hereinafter '1986 Workers' Congress Regulations'); Article 7, The 1988 Enterprise Law.

[41]   Article 47, 1988 Enterprise Law; Article 10 and 11, 1986 Director Regulations.

[42]   Indeed, to ensure the independence and integrity of managerial autonomy of the director, the Party Committee secretary was generally not allowed concurrently to assume the position of director under 1986 CPC Grass-Root Regulations.

[43]   Article 8, The 1988 Enterprise Law.

[44]   Namely, 'ideological education' and 'guaranteeing and supervising the implementation of guidelines and policies of the Party and the state'.

[45]   In fact, this provision did not even appear in the final draft of the 1993 Company Law. It was the NPC Law Committee that added the provision during their deliberation of the final draft. Some of its members felt it necessary to make some provisions in respect of the activities of the Party in companies. See Xiang Chunyi's *Report of Amendment Opinions Concerning the Company Law (Revised Draft) and the Decision to Amend the Accounting Law* to the NPC on 29 December 1993.

[46]   Amended and adopted at the CPC Sixteenth National Congress on 14 November 2002.

[47]   The 2002 Party Constitution, Article 10(1).

[48]   The Circular Concerning Further Strengthening and Improving the Party's Construction Work in State-Owned Enterprises, issued by the CPC Central Committee on 24 January 1997. Hereinafter the '1997 Party Central Committee Circular'.

[49]   The 1993 Company Law, Articles 50(7) and 119(7).

[50]   Tenev and Chunlin Zhang (2002) observed that the incremental approach to enterprise reforms resulted in new governance organs emerging alongside the old ones, which are groping their way to becoming functional.

[51]   One example is the introduction of the role of independent directors into Chinese listed companies in 2002, whereas the Chinese board structure is a two-tier one with a supervisory board.

[52]   This calls for the CPC to represent the development trend of China's advanced social productive forces, the orientation of China's advanced culture, and the fundamental interests of the overwhelming majority of the people of China.

[53]   Empirical studies have shown that capital tends to flow to the financial markets with strong investor protection and effective corporate governance. See, for example, La Porta et al. (2000).

REFERENCES

Anderson, D.M., 2000. 'Taking stock in China: company disclosure and information in China's stock markets', *Georgetown Law Journal*, 88(6):1919–53.

Art, R.C. and Minkang Gu, 1995. 'China incorporated: the first Corporation Law of the People's Republic of China', *Yale Journal of International Law*, 20(2):273–308.

Bian Yaowu and Li Fei (eds), 1994. *Theory and Practice of Company Law* [Gongsifa de Lilun yu Shiwu], China Commerce Press, Beijing.

Butler, W.E., 1983. *The Legal System of the Chinese Soviet Republic 1931–34*, Transnational Publishers Inc, Dobbs Ferry, New York.

Chai, J., 1997. *China: transition to a market economy*, Oxford University Press, New York.

Chen, A.H., 1998. *An Introduction to the Legal System of the People's Republic of China*, Butterworths (Asia), Singapore, Malaysia and Hong Kong.

Chen, A.H.Y., 2000. 'Socialist law, civil law, common law, and the classification of contemporary Chinese law', in J.M. Otto, M.V. Polak, Jianfu Chen and Juwen Li (eds), *Law-Making in the People's Republic of China*, Kluwer Law International, The Hague:55–64.

Chen Jianfu, 1999. *Chinese Law: towards an understanding of Chinese law, its nature, and development*, Kluwer Law International, The Hague and Boston.

——, 2000. 'Coming full circle: law-making in the PRC from a historical perspective', in J.M. Otto, M.V. Polak, Jianfu Chen and Juwen Li (eds), *Law-Making in the People's Republic of China*, Kluwer Law International, The Hague:19–40.

Clarke, D.C., 1992. 'Regulation and its discontents: understanding economic law in China', *Stanford Journal of International Law*, 28:282–322.

Coffee, J.C., 1998. 'Inventing a corporate monitor for transitional economies: the uncertain lessons from the Czech and Polish experiences', in K. Hopt, H. Kanda, M.J. Roe, E. Wymeersch and S. Prigge (eds), *Comparative Corporate Governance: the state of the art and emerging research*, Oxford University Press, New York:67–138.

CPC Central Committee, 1984. Decisions of the CPC Central Committee on the Economic Structure Reform, adopted by the Third Plenary Session of the CPC Twelfth National Congress, Beijing, 20 October 1984.

Deng Xiaoping, 1994. *Selected Works of Deng Xiaoping*, Volume 3, Foreign Language Press, Beijing.

——, 1995. *Selected Works of Deng Xiaoping*, Volume 2, Second edition, Foreign Language Press, Beijing.

Davies, P.L., 2003. *Gower and Davies' Principles of Modern Company Law*, Sweet and Maxwell, London.

Epstein, E.J., 1994. 'Law and legitimation in Post-Mao China', in P. Potter (ed.), *Domestic Law Reforms in Post-Mao China*, M. E. Sharpe, New York and London:19–55.

Gao Shangquan and Yang Qixian (eds), 1999. *China's State-Owned Enterprise Reform* [Zhongguo Guoyou Qiye Gaige], Jinan Press, Jinan.

Glendon, M.A., Gordon, M.W., and Osakwe, C., 1985. *Comparative Legal Traditions: text, materials and cases*, West Publishing Co, St. Paul, Minnesota.

Hay, D., Morris, D., Liu, G. and Shujie Yao, 1994. *Economic Reform and State-Owned Enterprises in China, 1979-1987*, Oxford University Press, New York.

He Jun, 1998. 'An empirical analysis of corporate governance of the listed companies [Shangshi Gongsi Zhili Jiegou de Shizheng Fenxi]', *Economic Research Journal* [Jingji Yanjiu], 5:50–57.

Howe, C., Kueh, Y.Y. and Ash, R., (eds), 2003. *China's Economic Reform: a study with documents*, RoutledgeCurzon, London.

Howson, N.C., 1997. 'China's company law: one step forward, two steps back? A modest complaint', *Columbia Journal of Asian Law*, 11(1):127–73.

Jiang Ping, 1994. 'The modern enterprise system established under the Company Law [Gongsi Fa suo Jianli de Xiandai Qiye Falu Zhidu]', *Study and Exploration of Theories* [Lilun Xuexi yu Tansuo], 3:2

Jiang Yiwei, 1985. 'On the leadership mechanism of Socialist enterprises [Lun Shehui Zhuyi Qiye de Lingdao Tizhi]', in Jiang Yiwei (eds), *Discussions on Certain Issues of Economic System Reform and Enterprise Management* [Jingji Tizhi Gaige he Qiye Guanli Ruogan Wenti de Taolun], Shanghai People's Press, Shanghai:16–40.

Jiang Zemin, 1997. Hold High the Great Banner of Deng Xiaoping Theory for an All-round Advancement of the Cause of Building Socialism with Chinese Characteristics to the 21st Century, Report to the CPC Fifteenth National Congress, Beijing.

——, 2002. Build a Well-off Society in an All-Round Way and Create a New Situation in Building Socialism with Chinese Characteristics, Report to the CPC Sixteenth National Congress, Beijing.

Keith, R.C. and Zhiqiu Lin, 2001. *Law and Justice in China's New Marketplace*, Palgrave, Basingstoke.

Kong Xiangjun, 1994. 'On Ownership Structure of Modern Companies: also reviewing provisions on company ownership in the Company Law of our country [Lun Gongsi Chanquan de Jiegou: Jianping Woguo Gongsifa dui Gongsi Chanquan de Guiding]', *Tribune of Political Science and Law* [Zhengfa Luntan], 4:31–35.

Kraakman, R., Davies, P., Hausmann, H., Hertig, G., Hopt, K.J., Kanda, H. and Rock, E.B., 2004. *The Anatomy of Corporate Law: a comparative and functional approach*, Oxford University Press, New York.

Lin Zhijun, 2001. 'Recent development of tax system reforms in China: challenges and responses', *The International Tax Journal*, 27(1):90–103.

Liu Ji, 1997. 'Separating government and enterprises', in Guanzhong Wen and Dianqing Xu (eds), *The Reformability of China's State Sector*, World Scientific Publishing Co., Singapore:16–36.

Liu Shaojia et al., 2003. 'The theory of ultimate ownership, ownership structure and firm's performance [Zhongji Chanquan Lun, Guquan Jiegou yu Gongsi Jixiao]', *Economic Research Journal* [Jingji Yanjiu], 4:51–62.

Lo, Carlos Wing-Hung, 1997. 'Socialist legal theory in Deng Xiaoping's China', *Columbia Journal of Asian Law*, 11(2):469–86.

Lubman, S., 1999. *Bird in a Cage: legal reform in China after Mao*, Stanford University Press, Stanford.

Peerenboom, R., 1999. 'Ruling the country in accordance with law: reflections on the rule and role of law in contemporary China', *Cultural Dynamics*, 11(3):315–52.

——, 2002. *China's Long March Toward Rule of Law*, Cambridge University Press, Cambridge.

La Porta, R., Lopez-de-Silanes, F. and Shleifer, A., 1999. 'Corporate ownership around the world', *Journal of Finance*, 54(2):471–517.

—— and Vishny, R., 2000. 'Investor protection and corporate governance', *Journal of Financial Economics*, 58(1):3–27.

Qi Duojun, 2003. *Studies on Legal Problems Concerning Reorganising State-Owned Enterprises by Incorporatisation* [Guoyou Qiye Gufen Gongsi Gaizu Falu Wenti Yanjiu], China Fangzheng Press, Beijing.

Qian, Andrew Xuefeng, 1993. 'Riding two horses: corporatizing enterprises and the emerging securities regulatory regime in China', *UCLA Pacific Basin Law Journal*, 12:62–97.

Riskin, C., 1987. *China's Political Economy: the quest for development since 1949*, Oxford University Press, Oxford.

Schipani, C.A. and Junhai Liu, 2002. 'Corporate governance in China: then and now', *Columbia Business Law Review*, 1:1–69.

Sealy, L.S., 2001. *Cases and Materials in Company Law*, Seventh edition, Butterworths, London.

von Senger, H., 2000. 'Ideology and law making', in J.M. Otto, M.V. Polak, Jianfu Chen and Juwen Li (eds), *Law Making in the People's Republic of China*, Kluwer Law International, The Hague:41–54.

Stiglitz, J.E., 1999. Whither Reform? Ten years of the transition, Keynote Address to the World Bank Annual Bank Conference on Development Economics, Washington, DC, 28–30 April. Available online at http://www.worldbank.org/research/abcde/pdfs/stiglitz.pdf.

Tam, On Kit, 1999. The Development of Corporate Governance in China, Edward Elgar, Cheltenham.

Tang Guodong, 1987. *An Introduction to Industrial Enterprise Law*, China's People's University Press, Beijing.

Tenev, S. and Chunlin Zhang, 2002. *Corporate Governance and Enterprise Reform in China: building the institutions of modern markets*, World Bank and International Finance Corporation, Washington, DC.

Wang Baoshu, 2002. Legal System of Enterprise Systems [Xiandai Qiye Falu Zhidu], Standing Committee Legal Lecture to the Twentieth National Party Congress, Beijing, 31 May. Available online at http://www.npcnews.com.cn/gb/special/class000000033/1/hwz210144.htm.

Wang Baoshu and Cui Qingzhi, 1984. 'On the legal status of directors of state-run enterprises [Lun Guoying Qiye Changzhang de Falu Diwei]', *Legal Research* [Faxue Yanjiu], 1:28–35.

Wang, Wallace Wen-Yeu, 1992. 'Reforming state enterprises in China: the case for redefining enterprise operating rights', *Journal of Chinese Law*, 6(2):89–136.

Wei, Xinjiang, 2002. 'People's Republic of China: the legal features of Chinese capital markets in the light of the Zhengzhou Baiwen case', *Company Lawyer*, 23(3):100–4.

Xiang Chunyi, 1993. Report of Amendment Opinions Concerning the Company Law (Revised Draft) and the Decision to Amend the Accounting Law (Legislative Report to the NPC)

Xin Chunyun, 1999. *Chinese Legal System and Current Legal Reform*, The Law Press, Beijing.

You Ji, 1998. *China's Enterprise Reform: changing state/society relations after Mao*, Routledge, London and New York.

Zhang Zanlun, 1987. *The Director Responsibility System* [Changzhang Fuzezhi], Economic Press, Beijing.

Zhang Youyu and Wang Shuwen (eds), 1989. *Forty Years of the PRC's Legal Science* [Zhongguo Faxue Sishi Nian], Shanghai People's Press, Shanghai.

Zhao Yongqing, 1996. 'The Company Law of China', *Indiana International & Comparative Law Review*, 6:461–92.

Zhao Ziyang, 1987. 'Advance along the road of Socialism with Chinese Characteristics—Report delivered at the Thirteenth National Congress of the CPC', in *Documents of the Thirteen National Congress of the Communist Party of China*, Foreign Language Press, Beijing.

Zheng, H.R., 1988. *China's Civil and Commercial Law*, Butterworth & Co (Asia), Singapore.

6

Socialist ideology and practical realism: the process of compromise in Vietnam's law on education

Elizabeth St George

As part of the overall theme of this book, this chapter seeks to analyse how socialism has been influential in shaping law by examining the specific example of the Education Law of Vietnam, passed in 1998. Socialism, in its many incarnations, played a particularly important role in the development and elaboration of the Vietnamese Education Law, linked in part to the significance of the education sector as the principal vehicle for the transmission of socialist theory and ideology—even as its importance is being downplayed in other sectors. Socialism, in its various different forms, has had a variety of impacts on the structure and content of the Education Law. At times these have been in contradiction with the practical realities facing the Vietnamese education sector, leading to certain contradictions within the law itself.

While the Education Law covers all education levels, this chapter draws its practical examples principally from developments in higher education. This sector saw the most far-reaching changes while the law was being drafted, and was one where developments had a strong influence on shaping the way in which many important issues were addressed. The first section looks at the theoretical role of law in Vietnamese socialism, and shows that this role is far from resolved. Against this background, the chapter then goes on to look at the Education Law itself and the references to socialism and socialist theory (particularly Marxism–Leninism) it contains. Finally, it focuses on the issues surrounding three specific areas in the law—those of administration, financing and the role of education itself—and argues that, while socialist central planning and socialist theory have had a strong influence on the shape of the law, many areas show a break from these paradigms where they did not fit with wider social values or were contradictory to the perceived development path of the country. In short, this chapter argues that, while the Education Law purports to be supporting a socialist direction, that direction is focused very much on solving the practical realities facing Vietnamese society and theoretical paradigms are readily altered in the face of necessity.

The question of what is socialism is a particularly complex one, beginning as it does in political economic theory that has then been applied in practice to a number of different societies around the world. Consequently, the term has acquired many layers of meaning both from vigorous intellectual debate and from its concrete application in different countries for more than a century. Vietnam is avowedly a socialist republic, and the debate over the nature of socialism has become even more vigorous since the official acceptance of a market economic direction at the Sixth Party Congress in 1986. While the country has maintained the name adopted since the reunification of the country—the Socialist Republic of Vietnam—the particular socialist path the country should take has not always been clear and the role of law within the country remains problematic.

This section seeks to understand the Education Law from the internal theoretical paradigm from within which it was written. This is a double challenge, first because a large number of people were involved in the formulation of the law, each with their different backgrounds and perspectives on the role of the law, and second because, while an outsider can bring important insights to a process that may not be evident to those involved, this perspective is necessarily based on second-hand accounts that may not fully reflect the complex considerations involved at the time. Despite these concerns, it is difficult to explain the socialist aspects of the Education Law fully, without reference to wider contemporary debates about the role and nature of socialist law in Vietnam.

The dominant paradigms from which those formulating the Education Law were operating were those of Marxist-Leninist theory, and the practical experience of Vietnamese education leaders over the past fifty years or so of Vietnam's history (also based in part on a long-standing Confucian heritage, emphasising respect for education).

In principle, all state and political activities in Vietnam must accord with the country's path to socialism, as decided by the Communist Party of Vietnam (CPV), on the basis of Marxism–Leninism and Ho Chi Minh thought. In other countries, 'Marxism' may refer not only to the writings of Marx and Engels, but also to a plethora of subsequent literature concerning the state, labour or a multitude of other topics, as well as the platforms of Marxist-inspired parties. In Vietnam, however, Marxism–Leninism and Ho Chi Minh thought refer specifically to the original writings of Karl Marx, Frederick Engels, V.I. Lenin and Ho Chi Minh, which are then reinterpreted in light of current circumstances and the 'objective realities' prevailing in the country at the time. Marxist-Leninist theory and Ho Chi Minh thought are the affirmed foundations on which the CPV bases its platform and leads the country. As stated at the opening to the Ninth Party Congress in 2001, the nation has a 'precious heritage—Ho Chi Minh thought which, combined with Marxism–

Leninism, constitutes the ideological foundation and the lodestar for all actions of the Party and Vietnamese Revolution' (Communist Party of Vietnam 2001:4).

The place of both education and the law within this theoretical framework is an ambiguous one. In a theoretical system in which the driving forces of history are the relations of production between different classes, both the law and education are part of the superstructure, instruments that the ruling class is able to manipulate by virtue of its position of superiority. Under capitalism, therefore, where the ruling class is the bourgeoisie, law is an instrument that the bourgeoisie manipulates in its own favour. 'Law, morality, religion, are to [the proletarian] so many bourgeois prejudices, behind which lurk in ambush just as many bourgeois interests' (Marx and Engels 2000 [1887]:9). Marx was also suspicious of formal education. In his one specific reference to the subject in *The Critique of the Gotha Program*, he argues that the state and the church have had a very negative impact on the education of the people, and instead '...the state has need, on the contrary, of a very stern education by the people' (Marx 1947:42). Lenin was only slightly more positive about the role of education. While he recognised the importance of education campaigns to educate the masses about the nature of socialism, communism and revolution, '[l]ike the state, schools were held to be compulsory institutions that obstructed a truly socialist construction, and they should be allowed to wither away' (Lilge 1968:560).[1]

Marx and Engels distinguished five principal phases of historical progression that nations must pass through, based on their particular relations of production: slavery, feudalism, capitalism, socialism and finally communism. According to the CPV, Vietnam is a country 'developing along the path to socialism'[2] or, in more detail, the Ninth Congress in 2001 asserted that '[t]he path forward of our country is transitional development to socialism, bypassing capitalism, in other words bypassing the establishment of the dominance of the production relations and the superstructure of capitalism'.[3] In practice this should mean that capitalist characteristics—both governing through a system of laws, and developing a formal education system—are elements that should be bypassed. In the case of Vietnam, however, both are being strengthened.

In attempting to come to terms with this complicated and potentially contradictory situation, Dinh Van Mau and Pham Hong Thai (2002) in their foundational text for law school students, support the introduction of law in Vietnam by arguing that instead of automatically asserting that law is an instrument of the bourgeoisie, it is necessary to ask certain questions to understand the foundations on which the law is based: 'What is the economic basis of the law?' and 'Whose class interests are best served by the law?' (Dinh Van Mau and Pham Hong Thai 2002:210). They then go on to argue that laws in feudal societies supported the rule of kings and religion (Dinh Van Mau and Pham Hong Thai 2002), while the essence of capitalist law is to reinforce the interests of the capitalist class, among other things by protecting private property (Dinh Van Mau and Pham Hong Thai 2002) and excluding communist parties, which represent the interests of workers, from politics (Dinh Van Mau and Pham Hong Thai 2002). Under socialism the working class becomes the ruling class. Consequently, socialist law, by contrast with other forms of law, must necessarily reflect the will of the working class. The situation presented by the authors for Vietnam, however, does not fit this clear periodisation.

> [S]ocialist law is the synthetisation of the rules of behaviour that give expression to the will of the working class and workers under the leadership of the Communist Party, and is decided by state offices and those with jurisdiction according to the order and the procedures laid down by the law, in order to readjust social relations in accordance with a market economy during the transition to socialism (Dinh Van Mau and Pham Hong Thai 2002:233).[4]

Although they do not mention Vietnam specifically, it is clear that the aim of the authors is to justify the use of law in Vietnam. They are left in a quandary, however, because they recognise that Vietnam has not yet reached the socialist stage of development and Vietnam is supporting a market economy. From a classical Marxist-Leninist point of view their argument is highly suspect, if not contradictory in paradigm. In order to assert that laws in Vietnam are socialist, the authors argue that they reflect the will of the working class, and yet at the same time they recognise that the country has a market economy and is in transition to socialism—it has not yet reached socialism. According to the 'objective laws' of Marxism–Leninism, where the nature of the superstructure (law) depends on the relations of production and the nature of the economy, a market economy and pre-socialism (that is, effectively where capitalist relations are still present) are objectively highly unlikely to give rise to socialist laws that represent the interests of the working class.

While implicitly recognising this contradiction, the authors attempt to bypass it in order to justify the current Vietnamese situation. Although they recognise that the law is an instrument of the state, they argue that the state is guided by the Communist Party, which itself represents the interests of 'labourers, peasants and other types of labourers' (Dinh Van Mau and Pham Hong Thai 2002:238). Consequently they argue that the law is unlike that of capitalist countries which serves only those few who have taken over leadership of the state; rather, the 'socialist' law of Vietnam serves the will of all classes (Dinh Van Mau and Pham Hong Thai 2002:238).[5]

The authors not only justify the socialist nature of Vietnamese law, but also describe its particular content. They argue that socialist law is an instrument of the state that defines the operations and administration of the state, ensures the participation of all people in the state, and defines the limits of power between the different parts of the state. It also protects the different internationally recognised human rights and, importantly, it is a means to concretise the policies of the CPV and ensure their unified implementation (Dinh Van Mau and Pham Hong Thai 2002). Many of these concerns are present in Vietnam's Education Law.

The authors conclude that in the transitional phase to socialism there is a need for a system of laws so that the market economy can operate efficiently and guide the country to a higher stage of development (Dinh Van Mau and Pham Hong Thai 2002), when implicitly laws will no longer be needed. In theoretical terms, the leading role of the Communist Party in Vietnam is central to justifying the introduction of 'bourgeois' laws. In short, socialist law in Vietnam is principally a set of instruments by which the state manages the country in accordance with the guidance of the CPV.

While this argument represents the view of only two authors, their work, as a basic university textbook, necessarily received high-level scrutiny and approval before it was introduced. That their conclusions are widespread is supported by a number of primary texts. The Ninth Party Congress documents, for instance, refer to the law instrumentally as a means to fight corruption and bring order to the civil service (Communist Party of Vietnam 2001), and the need to build socialist state law under the leadership of the Party (Communist Party of Vietnam 2001).[6] The *Textbook on Socialist Science*, prepared by the Central Steering Committee for the Editing of National Textbooks for the Study of Marxism–Leninism and Ho Chi Minh thought, also emphasises the instrumental nature of laws. The fundamental aim of strengthening the legal system it argues—including the role of the National Assembly and the division of responsibilities in formulating laws—is to improve the administrative results of the state and the democracy of the people.[7] It also emphasises that the democracy of the people is guaranteed by the leadership of the CPV guiding the state (Communist Party of Vietnam 2001:272).

Taken together, the arguments presented above lead to the conclusion that socialist law is a set of guiding rules and regulations that are formulated and implemented by the state (consisting principally of the different ministries and their local offices) under the guidance of the CPV in accordance with the process of political compromise that necessarily goes into documents based on wide consensus (such as the Documents of the Ninth Congress, national textbooks, and the Education Law). It is also an administrative tool that serves to ensure that the policies of the CPV are better applied than in the previous system of diffuse ordinances and regulations, combined with an appeal to people's morality (Dinh Van Mau and Pham Hong Thai 2002). In no instance is there any suggestion that the law exists as a means to ensure checks and balances within the system of governance or as an equal partner in the sense of executive, legislative and judicial branches of state. In practice, this situation creates a certain amount of ambiguity and tension because the law is simultaneously intended as a centralised administrative instrument of the Party–state, and, in the context of a burgeoning market economy, it regulates the areas in which the market economy—in this case the schooling system—is able to develop its own separate regulations and funding arrangements. It must walk the line between a background of socialist central planning and the practical realities where socialist central planning has already failed as a viable system of state management. These contradictions were carried through into the drafting process of the Education Law, and were evident in the final compromises that were reached.

Prior to the Education Law in 1998, education was managed by an *ad hoc* system of decrees and decisions produced by different authorities concerning their (overlapping) jurisdictions, and also by unwritten practices that were developed over time.[8] The responsibilities of higher education institutions , for example, and their relationship to the state were decided by the individual regulations established on a case-by-case basis, in accordance with the general regulations governing the founding of HEIs in Vietnam established in 1963 (171/CP, 20/11/1963). These individual regulations were decided on application to the government by the MOET (or other ministry or provincial government office) and the State Planning Committee, with the submission of documents stipulating the institution's 'mission statement, planned teaching program, curriculum, method of teaching, enrolment and structure' (Minh Vu 1994:11).

Regulations concerning other issues—everything from the level of financing to the responsibilities of teachers—were dealt with by the particular department (*vu*) responsible for that area. The department would examine a problem and issue a decision, frequently with little consultation with any other department that might be concerned with the issue. The situation was further complicated at the provincial and district levels with extra levels of vertical and horizontal administrative hierarchies that administer secondary level schools and below. The decrees were signed by the minister or vice-minister, who was supposed to act as a filter to ensure that the decrees did not overlap or contradict each other. In fact, however, a number of contradictory decrees continued to be promulgated, allowing the institutions often to do much as they pleased.[9] In 1995 Tran Chi Dao complained that

> [t]here is a deficiency of current legal statutes that are relevant and appropriate to management of the changing situation in Vietnam's higher education institutions. This lack tends to make some institutions excessively dependent on the MOET while others exercise newly found initiative. Both patterns can affect the quality of education (Tran Chi Dao et al. 1995:89).

Case-by-case decision-making simultaneously gave institutions the leeway to interpret the decisions according to their interests, and created a climate of uncertainty in which institutions were unwilling to act. As there was no formal delineation of decision-making responsibilities between institutions and the central government, the latter could theoretically intervene in any area it deemed important. In the mid 1990s, for example, two national universities in Hanoi and Ho Chi Minh City were created on the basis of existing institutions. These universities were given special powers to develop and establish their own courses and open experimental classes in new subject areas. In practice, however, the MOET still required that all new courses be submitted for approval before beginning operation (St. George 2003). Effectively, the founding regulations governing the two new universities overlapped with the general regulations governing universities as a whole, leading to confusion and contradiction in their implementation, as well as delays in the introduction of new courses.

The first limited attempt to bring order to the very diffuse system of regulations in higher education appears to have taken place in 1985 with the introduction of the Provisional Regulation on the Responsibilities, Organisation Structure and Operation of Higher Education Institutions (17 July 1985). This regulation defined the general duties and responsibilities of institutions, including regular reports to the Ministry of Education and Training (MOET) and the overseeing ministry, the organisation structure and duties of different bodies within the institutions, and the rights and responsibilities of students, teachers and the rector (Minh Vu 1994:11).

Following further efforts to bring some order to the regulatory framework in education, the government continued to recognise the need for a comprehensive system of legislation, in which the roles and responsibilities of the different decision-makers in the education sector were clearly spelt out. The situation was finally addressed in a comprehensive manner through the introduction of the Law on Education. This law underwent 23 drafts before the twenty-fourth was finally passed into law by the National Assembly, after extensive discussion, on 1 December 1998 (Tran Thi Tam Dan 1999).

The process of drafting the Education Law began in October 1995 when the government passed a resolution for work to begin, within the broad framework of building a nationwide system of law (Tran Thi Tam Dan 1999). The law was drafted under the auspices of a special Party cell within the National Assembly, which formally began operation in January 1996 (*Nhân Dân*, 17 May 1997:1, 3).[10] It was given responsibility for guiding the law through a process of consultation with a wide range of groups such as the MOET, government and Communist Party agencies concerned with education within the country, and other education specialists. The twenty-third draft, for example, was presented to 60 of 90 members of the National Assembly, those holding postgraduate degrees, in order for them to examine specifically the legal aspects of the draft (*Nhân Dân Internet Edition*, 21 September 1998). During the process of drafting and re-drafting, regular reports on the law were also presented to the National Assembly (Pham Min Hac 1998).

The extended process of drafting the law was undertaken to ensure a very wide input and opinion from among those with an interest in education. The process brought to the fore particular areas of contention among the interested parties, such as the level of detail the law should contain, administrative procedures, and sources of finance. The final law reflected a complex process of negotiation and compromise between the interested parties, in which the commitment to a socialist order remained an important concern.

In the final event, the Education Law of Vietnam passed by the National Assembly comprises 110 articles that cover in general the aims, levels and types of education, as well as the roles and responsibilities of teachers, students and the state with regards to formal education from crèche through to PhD level.

Within the Education Law, four principal articles contain direct references to socialism, Marxism–Leninism or Ho Chi Minh thought, highlighted above as the foundational texts and guiding lights of Vietnamese socialism.[11] These references to socialism cover two principal areas: the aims of education in Vietnam and the content of the educational curriculum at higher levels of education. The aims and principles of education in Vietnam are contained in Articles 2 and 3. According to Article 2,

[t]he aim of education is to comprehensively develop Vietnamese people through training so that they have ethics, intellectual ability, health, an aesthetic sense and a profession, faithful to an independent nation and socialism.[12]

Article 3 further reinforces the socialist nature of Vietnamese education

Vietnamese education is socialist education that is popular, national, scientific,[13] modern, and laid on a foundation of Marxism–Leninism and Ho Chi Minh thought.[14]

In order to support these general aims, a further specific aim of primary and secondary education is to develop the socialist character of the Vietnamese people (Article 23), so that they can undertake further study.[15]

Article 35 concerning the aims of higher education does not directly mention socialism or socialist thought, instead this is taken up in the following article concerning the content of higher education (including postgraduate education) programs.

The content of higher education must be modern and developed, ensuring an appropriate structure divided between basic scientific knowledge and specialist knowledge, as well as containing the scientific subjects of Marxism–Leninism, and Ho Chi Minh thought (Article 36, Section 1a).[16]

A similar statement is repeated for the content of postgraduate education, although with greater emphasis on developing research capability (Article 36, Section 2a).

The Education Law asserts its socialist character by committing the national education system to building socialism in the country, as well as to creating people who are socialist in character. It confirms that Vietnamese education is socialist in nature, or more specifically that it is based on the teachings of Marxism–Leninism and Ho Chi Minh thought, particularly for university and postgraduate education.

Not only is socialist theory an important basis for the national education system, higher levels of study are also expected to contribute actively to the perpetuation and actualisation of socialism. This is particularly evident in the Law on Science and Technology (*Luat Khoa hoc va Cong nghe*). It is worth pointing out here that the English term 'science' as generally used does not do justice to the multiplicity of meanings of the Vietnamese term *khoa hoc*. Not only does *khoa hoc* refer to the study of physical sciences, but also to higher levels of theoretical study across all fields of enquiry. By extension it also refers to logical methods of enquiry and, further, to research and the application of theory in any discipline. The Law on Science and Technology, then, refers to the duty of science and technology activities as being (among other things) to

creatively develop and apply the reasoning of Marxism–Leninism and Ho Chi Minh thought; to build socialist reasoning and the path to socialism in Vietnam (Article 4, Section 1).[17]

In other words, while educational activities are required to transmit the tenets of socialism, people conducting scientific study (or research) are not only expected to apply them in their own research, but they are also expected to support and build the theoretical foundations underpinning socialism itself. The important political role of research is even more clearly inferred further on, where science and technology activities are strictly forbidden from being used for any activities that 'misrepresent or go against the line or the policy of the Communist Party of Vietnam, the laws of the Socialist Republic of Vietnam or undermine national unity' (Article 8, Section 2),[18] where the 'line or the policy' of the CPV is fundamentally to bring Vietnam along the path to socialism.[19] Clearly, those involved in elaborating both the Education Law and the Law on Science and Technology felt that there were important links that needed to be maintained between education, research and the socialist system in Vietnam.

Explicit references to socialism are not necessarily the norm in Vietnamese laws. The Law on Commerce, for example, only makes explicit reference to socialism in the name of the country, the Socialist Republic of Vietnam. The aims of the law given in the introduction refer to the role of commerce as ensuring the growth of production, improving the lives of the people, and strengthening the nation (among others), rather than to supporting the foundations of socialism.[20] The introduction to the Labour Code (*Bo Luat Lao Dong*) likewise refers to one of the aims of the law as being to implement the CPV's policies, but makes no reference to supporting Marxism–Leninism or upholding socialism.[21]

The significance of references to socialism is not only that they serve to underpin the socialist character of the law, but that they make explicit its political orientation, a characteristic also evident in the largest remaining socialist country, the People's Republic of China. The Law on Compulsory Education of the People's Republic of China, for example, also specifies that the law is 'for the purpose of promoting elementary education and the building of a socialist society that is advanced culturally and ideologically as well as materially' (Article 1), while further on it expresses support for the state policy on education, which, among other things, aims to cultivate 'well-educated and self-disciplined builders of socialism with high ideals and moral integrity' (Article 3) (People's Republic of China 1986). Even the 2002 Law on 'People-founded' Schools specifies that these schools (which are based on non-state funding) are part of the socialist education system (Article 3) and that they serve to construct socialism in the country (Article 4) (People's Republic of China 2002).

By comparison, in Australian legislation on education, for example, references to a particular political orientation are noticeably absent,[22] although many of the other educational aims put forward are virtually the same as those found in the Chinese and Vietnamese laws, including national development,[23] and the intellectual, physical and moral development of students in general education.[24]

David Paris' (1995) analysis of educational reform in the United States argues that the liberal democratic theory on which the US school system is based in fact creates significant difficulties for educational reform because it permits a plurality of perspectives in the approach to, and implementation of, education policies, and this results in a plurality of conflicting ideals guiding policy. Concretely, this means that guiding documents on education tend to avoid presenting higher guiding directions, in favour of setting practical milestones. Consequently, when George

Bush (Snr) put forward the country's new educational strategy in 1989, it was couched in the very practical terms of particular goals to be achieved. Paris argues that, while these goals represented consensus, they avoided the ideological importance of education and became the foundations of conflict in subsequent efforts to achieve these goals (Paris 1995). While Paris is referring to educational strategy rather than education law, it is worth noting that even the 2001–10 Vietnamese education strategy, which contains very detailed education goals (in terms of enrolment, funding, teaching methods and so forth), nonetheless insists on the role of education in following the country's ideological direction by modernising the country and building socialism (Cong Hoa Xa hoi Chu nghia Viet Nam 2001:18). Vietnam's law takes the opposite extreme to that highlighted by Paris for the United States. In Vietnam, the ideological direction is clearly stated, both in the law and in the translation of that law into policy documents, such as the Education Strategy, which concentrates on setting particular targets to achieve educational goals, under the guiding framework provided by the law.

In short, the Vietnamese Law on Education clearly identifies its own socialist nature, which, by its content and concerns, also places it in line with similarly self-avowedly socialist education laws, such as those of China. From this socialist perspective, education is an intrinsically ideological and political activity, and should be asserted clearly at the highest levels of legislation. During the process of drafting the Education Law, therefore, the more contentious issues debated revolved less around whether to include references to ideology, but rather the relative importance that should be given to ideology and to the role of the law in defining levels of authority and responsibility—that is, administrative and organisational issues. They also revolved around the appropriate place of non-state funding, but despite the suspicion with which Marx and Lenin regarded education, there was little debate about the high level of importance that should be attached to this sector.

Administrative issues are best highlighted in a comparison of the sixteenth draft of the law, from December 1996, and the law that was finally passed in December 1998. The introductions to the 1996 draft and the 1998 law set the contrast between the two. In the 1996 draft, the stated purpose of the law is to define the relationship between different organisations responsible for education in Vietnam, and their role in achieving a modern education system. It also serves to 'legitimate viewpoints and directions of education renovation adopted by the Party and State'. It concentrates on the organisation of education, against the background of current policies, although it allows for the possibility that these 'viewpoints and directions' may change. By mid 1997, however, the draft law had begun to emphasise the role of the law as being to structure the policies and work of the Communist Party and the state in education (*Giao duc va Thoi dai* [Education and the Age], 1 May 1997:1, 3), and this was carried through into the law that was finally passed.

The introduction to the 1998 law is principally a Communist Party of Vietnam policy statement, in which the importance of organisation and administration receive only a passing mention. It stresses that the law is aimed at improving education in the country so that it benefits development, and it is virtually a direct copy of statements regarding education made at the Eighth Communist Party National Congress, held in 1996. The education law aims to

> develop education, raise the effectiveness of the state in administering education, raise the people's intellectual standard, train human resources and groom talent to achieve the industrialisation and modernisation of the country, to meet the needs of building and protecting the nation, with the aim of creating a rich, strong, equitable and civilised society.

'Industrialisation and modernisation' in particular are the hallmark slogans of the Eighth Party Congress.

Interestingly, an article that appeared in the Communist Party daily *Nhân Dân* when the National Assembly was considering the twenty-third draft of the law complained that the law had been given to sectoral specialists (that is, educators from the MOET) rather than legal experts and therefore lacked legal standards and was not in line with standardisation across the country (*Nhân Dân Internet Edition*, 10 November 1998). This suggests that the standardisation should comply with broad national policies rather than sectoral objectives, which were the focus of previous drafts.

Compared to the 1996 draft, the 1998 law envisaged a reduced role for the state, and increased responsibilities for educational institutions. Article 105 (1996) specifies that the state organises special schools for disabled students from crèche through to the final year of compulsory education, while Article 58 of the 1998 law states that '[t]he state founds, and *encourages other organisations and individuals* to found schools and classes for disabled people [emphasis added]'. Organisations other than the state are given an opening to take a more active role in educational activities.

In another example, the 1996 draft specifies that the state encourages links between educational institutions, social organisations, businesses and the society at large (Article 95), although schools play the leading role in links between society and education (Article 108). By contrast the final 1998 law specifies that individual educational institutions are to establish their *own* regulations of operation, covering, among other things, the relationship between the school, families and society (Article 48, para 2). In other words, the final law is far more encouraging of educational institutions being pro-active in seeking their own relationships with the wider community, something that would have been unthinkable under socialist central planning.

Another area that shows a reduced role for the highest levels of the state is postgraduate education. In 1976 the Party Central Committee established postgraduate education in the country for the first time (QĐ 224/TTg, 24/5/1976). At that time, matters concerning postgraduate education were to be looked after by a specialist government committee, with the assistance of the Ministry of Higher Education (as it was at the time). Any institutions providing postgraduate training, which were largely research institutes rather than teaching universities, had to report their activities to this committee, and doctoral candidates had to defend their thesis in front of an examination committee appointed by the Prime Minister. Topics of research were also closely coordinated with the relevant ministry responsible for that area of research and the government committee on education. Candidates were expected to be strong supporters of the Communist Party and its policies, and to 'put into practice the path and policies of the Party and government, maintain a truthful attitude and help socialism' (QĐ 224/TTg, 24/5/1976).

Since the early 1990s, universities have been taking a far more active role in postgraduate education, especially at the Master level, but this has continued to receive a very high level of interest from the central government. For doctoral-level study, no committee is guaranteed formal oversight of their provision any longer (although in practice it continues to exist), nor are candidates given preferential treatment based on their involvement with the Party (although many doctoral candidates continue to be members of the Communist Party). One of the areas of hottest contention during the final National Assembly debates on the law was what level of authority (minister or higher education institution rector) should be responsible for awarding postgraduate degrees (*Nhân Dân Internet Edition*, 10 November 1998). The solution adopted was to maintain the *status quo* with regards to PhD degrees—the minister continues to award them (Article 39), but to delegate responsibility for Masters degrees to the rector of the university. In the 1996 draft, the rector first had to seek approval from the Minister of Education (Article 157), but this stipulation was dropped from the final law (see Article 39, para 3), very likely because of the increasingly large number of students who are graduating with Master degrees in Vietnam, which would have heavily increased the workload of the minister or their deputy. Despite the introduction of the law, other regulations govern the requirements and procedures for the award of postgraduate degrees in more detail (QĐ 647/GD-ĐT, 14/12/1996; Minh Vu 1994).

That socialist nature is also in line with the dominant understanding of the role of socialist law as an instrument by which to implement the guiding policies of the CPV. In a close echo of the Eighth Party Congress documents and the introduction to the law, according to the magazine *Education and the Age* [Giao duc va thoi dai], the reason for establishing the law was to structure the policies and work of the Communist Party and the state in education, and to reassert the leadership of the Party, the administration of the state, and the participation of the people. It also seeks to assert the responsibilities of state organisations at each level within education, under the unified management of the state (*Giao du va Thoi dai* [Education and the Age] 1997:1, 3). While the issue of division of responsibility is certainly addressed in the law, and responsibilities of the Ministry of Education and Training at the central level are mentioned, this division remains largely at the level of principles, rather than specifying the concrete measures to ensure that clarification of division of responsibility becomes a reality. For example, the individual school authorities are under the administration 'of all education administration offices'[25] in accordance with the powers delegated by the central government (Article 44).

The scope of authority of different levels of government (provincial, district, and so forth) are only specified in very specific areas, such as the award of graduation certificates and degrees (Articles 27, 33, 39). Other areas are left under the general supervision and administration of the central government, reflecting the strong influence of a recent tradition of socialist central planning.

In the area of curriculum, the division of responsibility remains highly centralised. The central government, through the MOET, maintains the primary responsibility for courses at primary and secondary levels of education, and also has significant responsibility for higher levels. At general education levels, this responsibility is exercised in particular through the compilation and publication of textbooks, which are approved by a national council before being introduced (Article 25). Universities and colleges are able to compile and produce their own textbooks in specialist areas of teaching, after approval by a curriculum committee established by the rector of the institution (Article 37), but only in branches of study (*nganh*) for which the institution has already received permission to teach (Article 55). Given that any new subject may be considered a new branch of learning, the distinction between the two is not always clear, and can be manipulated by the government as well as higher education insitutions to suit their own interests. In subject areas that are prescribed by the MOET for all college and university degrees (such as Marxist-Leninist theory, Marxist-Leninist political economy, national defence, sport), the MOET is also responsible for producing the relevant textbooks and courses of study (Article 37), and their use is further reinforced through subordinate legislation that specifies, for example, how many hours and which chapters of the textbooks should be studied by different groups of students.[26] In fact, the only areas of education for which the state does not produce compulsory textbooks are postgraduate education (where supervision is exercised through the oversight of graduation theses), vocational education, and 'non-regular' (*khong chinh quy*) forms of education, such as literary courses, professional skills upgrading courses and courses specially designed to meet student demands. Part-time courses, distance education, guided study or any course leading to an award within the national education framework must also be approved by the MOET (Article 41).

Despite many areas of the law in which the division of responsibility remain unclear, it is clear that at an official level the development of curriculum remains a highly sensitive and highly centralised undertaking. In other areas there is a clear trend towards greater decentralisation of educational responsibility, in favour of institutions, but the biggest area of contention, and the area that remains most vague in the law is that of the decentralisation of education funding.

If the opening-up of the country and the introduction of *doi moi* were in part a response to the deepening financial crisis of the late 1970s and 1980s, then nowhere was this more evident than in the education sector, where inflation drastically eroded teachers' salaries, and vocational colleges and secondary specialist colleges (*truong chuyên nghiep*) were forced to close (Le Viet Khuyen c1998). Practical experiments with fee-paying students began as early as 1986 in Ho Chi Minh City, and the first fully non-government funded classes in higher education opened in Hanoi in 1988, as a direct response to the crisis situation in the country (St George 2003). From a legal perspective, these activities were in direct contravention of the 1980 constitution, which specified that the provision of education is the prerogative of the state (Article 41), and that education must be provided free of charge (Article 60). In 1992, these provisions were replaced in the revised constitution to allow for a system of 'fees and scholarships' at higher levels of education (Article 59). In other words the constitution was amended to reflect directly the changed practical realities of the Vietnamese education system, at the expense of strict ideological orthodoxy.

The Education Law also acknowledges the need for outside funding of higher educational institutions, by recognising the existence of school authorities in higher education institutions that are public, semi-public, people-founded and private (Article 44),[27] although such institutions are not mentioned for other levels of study. The law also encourages organisations and individuals to contribute financially to education, for which they will receive tax exemptions (Article 91). Despite this acknowledgement of the importance of private contributions to education, there are no further details about the role of such funding in a state dominated education sector, nor any references to clarify the differences between these institutions and their relationship to the state. The final law leaves the founding of all educational institutions up to individual government decisions, such as those that have been used to govern the country in the past (Articles 46 and 47). This is in direct contrast to the 1996 draft (Article 90), which clearly specifies the means for the establishment of private institutions and outlines the responsibilities of such schools.

There are several explanations for the omission in the final law. At the time the law was being finalised there was significant criticism of the quality of private institutions, which were enrolling students at a tremendous rate without always paying attention to the number of teachers, classrooms, or the need for sufficient equipment to ensure the standard of their graduates (St George 2003). Questions were also raised about whether non-government schools and non-regular modes of study should really be considered part of the national unified system of education (Cao Cuong 1998). Finally, those drafting the law discussed, to an extent, the role of the law itself and how specific it should be.[28] The result is that private education's role and rules of operation within the national education system remain vague and subject to subordinate decrees and regulations. On the one hand this shows the reluctance of central government figures to consider privately funded education as a permanent part of the Vietnamese education system (as opposed to a temporary measure to resolve current financial difficulties), on the other hand it reflects the serious concern about the quality of graduates from such institutions.

In general, the issue of income generation for schools apparently remains difficult to reconcile ideologically. Article 17 'forbids all actions commercialising educational activities',[29] but at the same time Article 54 gives permission to higher education institutions to use economic activities (*hoat dong kinh te*) in order to earn money for educational activities. The prohibition against the commercialisation of educational activities implies both that education is in itself a non-productive activity (hence it can be 'non-commercial') and at the same time that education will somehow be contaminated if it is put on a commercial footing. Article 54, by contrast, appears to accept the reality that the state is unable to supply the financial needs of higher education institutions and to recognise the benefits that outside funding can bring. Dang Ba Lam, Director-General of the National Institute for Education Development, who was involved in the drafting of the law, agreed that the law was contradictory to some extent on this point, but argued that the main aim of the injunction against the commercialisation of education was a moral one.[30] This, he suggested, was an appeal to people's moral sense not to misuse the highly respected tool of education for personal gain. The Education Law, therefore, while attempting to bring order to the diffuse system of rules and regulations, and better define the relationship between the state and educational institutions, has nonetheless not abandoned the system of regulating society by 'appealing to people's morals', underscoring the background on which the current law was built. In effect it shows a process of political compromise, in which ideological orientations have been bent, but not entirely forgotten, in the face of real economic necessity.

The issue of funding in education remains ideologically sensitive, as highlighted by the contradictions in the law itself mentioned above, and emphasised even more forcibly by the many funding issues that are left out of the law. At the same time, if state organisation in education and education financing are two areas that show the strong influences of 'socialism', then the issue of education itself is one that has broken radically from its ambiguous status in Marxist-Leninist writing.

As outlined earlier, according to classical Marxist-Leninist theory, education is a part of the superstructure, and its nature depends on the underlying relations of production in the economy. Consequently, both Marx and Lenin only supported education insofar as it raised the socialist conscience of workers. Ho Chi Minh (1972:68–73, 89) emphasised that education needed to have a practical orientation, to support the building of socialism in the country.

Vietnamese leaders in the 1990s have thoroughly laid to rest this hesitant attitude. The constitution adopted in 1992 specifies that '[e]ducation and training is the priority national policy' (Article 35),[31] and this assertion is repeated in the introduction to the Education Law, and again in the Ninth Party Congress documents (Communist Party of Vietnam 2001). In more detail, education is the means to 'bring into play human resources—the basic factor to develop the society, and create rapid and stable economic growth'.[32] According to the consensus represented by the National Party Congress, education is a direct input for economic growth. In other words, it no longer sits in a dependent relationship outside the economy, as part of the superstructure. The Ninth Party Congress further stressed the importance of education as the basis for ensuring that the country achieves the necessary preconditions for advanced technology and science, which are, again, necessary for the development of the country (Communist Party of Vietnam 2001).

The greater importance placed on education is also evident in the practical measures taken by the government to bolster education. Teachers now receive priority salary payments compared to other public servants, and education is the only sector to have its budget proportion fixed and approved by the National Assembly at the high levels of 15 per cent for 2000, 18 per cent for 2005 and 20 per cent for 2010,[33] planned levels that are apparently being achieved (Dang Ba Lam 2003). Student enrolment in higher education institutions, some of the less practically oriented areas of education, has also risen very rapidly, from 593,884 students in 1996/7, to 974,119 students in 2001/2. While the majority of students continue to study in public institutions, the number in non-state institutions has increased significantly as a proportion of the total, from 25,012 in 1996/7 to 100,900 in 2001/2 (from 4.2 per cent to 10.4 per cent of total students), although this proportion has been slowly falling since 1999/2000 (Dang Ba Lam 2003:518).

Prior to 1986, and even in 1991, National Party Congress documents tended to emphasise the role of education in teaching socialist principles and vocational skills, as in classical socialist writings, but during the 1990s, and particularly by the time the Education Law was finalised, the leadership of the country had firmly internalised international thinking about the importance of education as an input for the development of a country (St George 2003), and concretised support for education in practical policies and measures to support its now vital role in the development of the country. This shows a willingness of the part of the leadership not only to be swayed by practical realities, such as allowing private funding for education in the wake of the country's financial crisis, but also to be swayed by alternative theoretical paradigms that had shown their practical importance in other countries, in this case those of human resource development and of the knowledge-based economies (St George 2003). In the case of the latter, this support inadvertently tapped the traditionally high regard accorded to education in a Confucian society, where national examinations for advancement have been held for almost a thousand years. Within this framework, the determination to ensure that socialism and Marxist-Leninist studies are still included in education programs, particular at higher levels of study, can be seen as a compromise—an attempt to maintain the trappings of a socialist education system and guard against accusations that the Vietnamese education system might be becoming bourgeois, or capitalist.

Vietnam's education law purports to be socialist and yet the nature of that socialism is ambiguous. On the one hand it claims to rest on a foundation of Marxism–Leninism and Ho Chi Minh thought, and this background is still evident in the references to Marxism-Leninism and in the highly centralised administrative system provided for in the law. On the other hand, the makers of the law were confronted by a very real set of problems facing education in the 1990s, in terms of administration, finance and the role of education itself. In administration, institutions were hampered in their ability to adapt to a changing world because of a highly centralised decision-making structure. In terms of finance, there was great reluctance to accept non-state funding as a permanent feature of the education system, not only because of ideological and moral concerns, but also because of very real practical concerns about educational quality, and this is evident in the great vagueness of the law on matters of education funding. Finally, in terms of education itself, while Marxism–Leninism treats education with great scepticism, Vietnamese educators have also been keen to take on board international theories of education radically different from those of the nineteenth and early twentieth centuries. They have strongly welcomed international thinking supporting a strengthened role for education in socioeconomic development, to the point where it has been enshrined in the constitution as the 'priority national policy' of the country (Article 35).

In the final analysis, the socialist background of those drafting the Vietnamese Education Law clearly shaped the issues that were (and were not) addressed in the law, as well as the context in which the debates to finalise the law took place. Marxist-Leninist theory and socialist central planning shaped the theoretical perspective from which the Education Law was written, but this theoretical background was tempered by the practicalities of Vietnamese education. While this chapter has focused on the role of socialism in the Education Law, it is worth remembering that the realities of Vietnamese education, as for any other sector, are usually determined less with reference to the law, but rather on a basis that is established through daily social interaction, personal relationships and changing perceptions of the current problematic. Over time, these changing perceptions will no doubt occasion further adjustments to the Education Law in accordance with the changes to the 'objective realities' of socialism in Vietnam.

NOTES

1   Further information on the role of education in Marxism–Leninism and in other socialist writings can be found in St George (2003).
2   'Phat trien theo con duong xa hoi chu nghia' (Communist Party of Vietnam 2001:12).
3   The original text in Vietnamese was 'Con duong di len cua nuoc ta la su phat trien qua do len chu nghia xa hoi bo qua che do tu ban chu nghia, tuc la bo qua viec xac lap vi tri thong tri cua quan he san xuat ve kien truc thuong tang tu ban chua nghia...' (Communist Party of Vietnam 2001:21).
4   The original text in Vietnamese: 'phap luat xa hoi chu nghia la tong hop nhung quy tac xu su the hien y chi cua giai cap cong nhan va nhan dan lao dong duoi su lanh dao cua Dang cong san, do cac co quan nha nuoc, nguoi tham quyen ban hanh theo trinh tu, thu tuc luat dinh, nham dieu chinh cac quan he xa hoi, phu hop voi nen kinh te thi truong trong thoi ky qua do len chu nghia xa hoi chu nghia' (Dinh Van Mau and Pham Hong Thai 2002:233).
5   Clearly this raises another contradiction as to how the Communist Party can represent at the same time the interests of the working class and all other classes equally, and still remain a Communist Party.
6   'Xay dung Nha nuoc phap quyen xa hoi chu nghia duoi su lanh dao cua Dang [Building a state based on socialist law under the leadership of the Party]'.
7   The Central Steering Committee supervises the editing of national textbooks for the study of Marxism–Leninism (The Vietnamese text is 'Hoi dong trung uong chi dao bien soan giao trinh quoc gia cac bo mon khoa hoc Mac-Lenin' (Communist Party of Vietnam 2001:273)).
8   Sections concerning the drafting of the law, including comparisons with the 1996 draft of the law are adapted from chapter 5 of St.George (2003).
9   Personal communication with MOET official, Hanoi, July 1998.
10   Other sources say that drafting of the law began well before these dates, in 1994, but this seems unlikely ('Vietnam Passes First Education Law', AFP News Bulletin, 5 December 1998).

[11]   A quick survey of theoretical articles in journals such as *Tap chi Cong san* [the Communist Party Journal] or *Phap ly va Nha nuoc* [Law and the State] quickly reveal that the majority of references to theoretical works are directly to the original works of Marx and Engels, to the writings of Ho Chi Minh, or less often to the writings of Lenin, rather than the later body of extensive works that now comprise 'socialist theory'.

[12]   The original text in Vietnamese is '*Muc tieu giao duc la dao tao con nguoi Viet Nam phat trien toan dien, co dao duc, tri thuc, suc khoe, tham my va nghe nghiep, trung thanh voi ly tuong doc lap dan toc va chu nghia xa hoi…*'.

[13]   'Scientific' (*khoa hoc*) refers less to the applied sciences as usually meant in English, but rather to all higher level research. See below.

[14]   The original text in Vietnamese is '*Nen giao duc Viet Nam la nen giao duc xa hoi chu nghia co tinh nhan dan, dan toc, khoa hoc, hien dai, lay chu Mac-Lenin va tu tuong Ho Chi Minh lam nen tang*'.

[15]   The original text in Vietnamese is '*Muc tieu cua giao duc pho thong la…nham hinh thanh nhan cach con nguoi Viet Nam xa hoi chu nghia, xay dung tu cach va trach nhiem cong dan…*'.

[16]   The original text in Vietnamese is '*Noi dung giao duc dai hoc phai co tinh hien dai va phat trien, bao dam co cau hop ly giua kien thuc khoa hoc co ban voi kien thuc chuyen nganh va cac bo mon khoa hoc Mac-Lenin, tu tuong Ho Chi Minh…*'.

[17]   The original text in Vietnamese is '*Van dung sang tao va phat trien ly luan cua chu nghia Mac-Lenin va tu tuong Ho Chi Minh; xay dung ly luan ve vhu nghia xa hoi va con duong di len chu nghia xa hoi cua Viet Nam…*'.

[18]   The original text in Vietnamese is '*Loi dung hoat dong khoa hoc va cong nghe de xuyen tac, chong lai duong loi, chinh sach cua Dang Cong san Viet Nam, phap luat cua Nha nuoc Cong hoa xa hoi chu nghia Viet Nam; pha hoai khoi dai doan ket dan toc.*'

[19]   The original text in Vietnamese is '*Dang khang dinh chu nghia Mac-Lenin va tu tuong Ho Chi Minh la nen tang tu tuong va kim chi cho hoat dong cua minh*' in Central Steering Committee for the Editing of National Textbooks for the Study of Maxism–Leninism (2002).

[20]   Luat Thuong mai 1997 [Law on Commerce 1997]

[21]   Luat 35/2002/QH10 cua Quoc Hoi sua doi bo sung mot so dieu cua Bo Luat Lao dong [Labour Code of the Socialist Republic of Vietnam—Amended and Supplemented in 2002].

[22]   See, for example, Commonwealth of Australia, Higher Education Funding Act 1988, Article 2a.

[23]   See the Compulsory Education Law of the People's Republic of China 1986, Article 3; and the Law on Education (1998) of the Socialist Republic of Vietnam, Article 2.

[24]   See the New South Wales Education Act (1990), Article 6.1A; and Socialist Republic of Vietnam (1998), Law on Education (1998) of the Socialist Republic of Vietnam, Article 23.

[25]   The original in Vietnamese is '*cac co quan quan ly giao duc*'.

[26]   See, for example, Quyet dinh so 19/2003/QD-BGDDT ngay 8/5/2003 cua Bo truong Bo Giao duc va Dao tao ve viec ban hanh De cuong mon hoc: Triet hoc Mac-Lenin; Kinh te chinh tri Mac-Lenin (khoi nganh kinh te – quan tri kinh doanh) va Kinh te chinh tri Mac – Lenin (khoi nganh khong chuyen kinh te – quan tri kinh doanh) trinh do cao dang [Decision No.19/2003/ QD-BGDDT, dated 8/5/2003, of the Ministry of Education and Training on the promulgation of the subject: Marxist-Leninist theory, Marxist-Leninist political economy (for economics and business management branches), and Marxist-Leninist political economy (for non-economics and business management specialisation branches) at the college level]. Similar decisions for other branches and subjects appear in the same edition of the national gazette, Cong Bao No. 45, 1 June 2003.

[27]   The difference between these four types of institutions has become increasingly unclear over time. One of the proposed amendments to the Education Law to be put to the National Assembly in 2004 includes reducing the number of types of institutions to two—public (to include semi-public) and private (including 'people-founded'). Personal communication with Dang Ba Lam, Director-General, National Institute for Education Development, Hanoi, 22 May 2003.

[28]   Personal communication with Dang Ba Lam, Director-General, National Institute for Education Development, Hanoi, 22 May 2003.

[29]   The original text in Vietnamese is '*Cam moi hanh vi thoung mai hoa hoat dong giao duc*'.

[30]   Personal communication with Dang Ba Lam, Director-General, National Institute for Education Development, Hanoi, 22 May 2003.

31   The original text in Vietnamese is *'Giao duc va dao tao la quoc sach hang dau'*.
32   The original text in Vietnamese is *'phat huy nguon luc con nguoi - yeu to co ban de phat trien xa hoi, tang truong kinh te nhanh va ben vung'* (Communist Party of Viet Nam 2001:108–9).
33   Communist Party of Viet Nam (2001), and Personal communication with Perran Penrose, UNDP consultant, Hanoi, 3 June 2003.

REFERENCES

Commonwealth of Australia, 1988. *Higher Education Funding Act 1988*, Commonwealth of Australian, Canberra.

Cao Cuong, 1998. 'National Assembly discusses Draft Education Law', *Saigon Times Daily News Brief*, 17 November.

Communist Party of Vietnam, 2001. *Van kien dai hoi dai bieu toan quoc lan thu IX* [Documents from the Ninth National Representative Congress], The Gioi Publishers, Hanoi.

Cong Hoa Xa hoi Chu nghia Viet Nam [Socialist Republic of Vietnam], 2001. *Chien luoc phat trien giao duc 2001–2010* [Education Development Strategy 2001–10], Nha Xuat ban Giao duc, Ha Noi.

Quoc hoi Cong hoa Xa hoi Chu Nghia Viet Nam [National Assembly of the Socialist Republic of Vietnam], 1997. *Luat Thuong mai* [Law on Commerce], Luat so: 5/1997/QH9, Communist Party of Vietnam, Hanoi.

Central Steering Committee for the Editing of National Textbooks for the Study of Maxism–Leninism, 2002. *Giao trinh chu nghia xa hoi khoa hoc* [Textbook on Socialist Science], Nha Xuat ban Chinh tri Quoc gia, Ha Noi.

Dang Ba Lam, 2003. *Giao duc Viet Nam nhung thap nien day the ki XXI - Chien luoc phat trien* [Vietnamese Education in the First Decades of the Twentieth Century], Nha Xuat ban Giao duc, Hanoi.

Dinh Van Mau and Pham Hong Thai, 2002. *Ly luan chung ve nha nuoc va phap luat* [General Theory on the State and Law], Nha Xuat ban Tong hop Dong Nai, Dong Nai.

Giao duc va Thoi dai, 1997. 'Ve du an luat giao duc [Concerning the Education Law project]', *Giao duc va Thoi dai*, 1 May: 1, 3

Ho Chi Minh, 1972. *Ban ve cong tac giao duc* [Discussion on Educational Work], Nha Xuat ban Su that, Ha Noi.

Le Viet Khuyen, c1998. *Dai hoc Viet Nam say 10 nam doi moi* [Vietnamese Universities after Ten Years of Renovation], Mimeo, Hanoi.

Lilge, F., 1968, 1977. 'Lenin and the politics of education', in J. Karabel and A.H. Halsey (eds), *Power and Ideology in Education*, Oxford University Press, New York:556–72.

Marx, K., 1947. *Critique of the Gotha Program*, Foreign Languages Publishing House, Moscow.

Marx, K. and Engels, F., 1848 [2000]. *Manifesto of the Communist Party*. Marx/Engels Internet Archive, http://marxists.org.

Minh Vu, 1994. Legislative Framework for Higher Education in Vietnam, Princeton University, Princeton, New Jersey (unpublished).

New South Wales Government, 1990. *New South Wales Education Act 1990*, New South Wales Government, Sydney.

Paris, D.C., 1995. *Ideology and Educational Reform: themes and theories in public education*, Westview Press, Boulder.

People's Republic of China, 1986. *Compulsory Education Law of the People's Republic of China*, People's Republic of China, Beijing.

——, 2002. *Law to Step up People Founded Schools in the Socialist Republic of China*, People's Republic of China, Beijing.

Pham Minh Hac, 1998. *Vietnam's Education: the current position and future prospects*, The Gioi Publishers, Hanoi.

Socialist Republic of Vietnam, 1998. *Law on Education*, Socialist Republic of Vietnam, Hanoi.

St George, E., 2003. Higher Education in Vietnam 1986-1998: education in transition for development?, PhD dissertation, Department of Political and Social Change, Research School of Pacific and Asian Studies, The Australian National University, Canberra.

Tran Thi Tâm Đan, 1999. 'Luat giao duc—co so phap ly de phat trien giao duc va dao tao [The education law—legal foundation to develop education and training]', *Nhân Dân*, 27 January. Available online at www.nhandan.org.vn.

Tran Chi Dao, Lam Quang Thiep, et al., 1995. 'Organization and Management of Higher Education in Vietnam: an overview', in D. Sloper (ed.), *Higher Education in Vietnam*, Institute of Southeast Asian Studies, Singapore:74–91.

7

Legal education in transitional Vietnam

Bui Thi Bich Lien

The launch of *doi moi* (literally meaning 'Renovation') has resulted in numerous unprecedented changes in Vietnam during the last decade and a half. Moving from a centrally planned society to a market-oriented society, the state has defined law as an important tool to govern society and promote economic development. This transformation process poses great challenges for Vietnam's legal system, as the ambitious targets set by *doi moi* need to be facilitated by qualified legal professionals.

In this context, legal education plays a critically important role. Although it is undeniable that law schools have made significant improvement in terms of teaching and establishing their prestige in society, the pace does not seem fast enough to accommodate legal reform (Legal Needs Assessment Report, 2002). Many practitioners think that the ever-increasing numbers of graduating law students lack the improved professional skills required to serve a transitional society. Despite a number of reform programs, the quality of legal training in Vietnam remains moderate.

This chapter analyses the status of Vietnam's contemporary legal education system, examining the influence of socialist legal doctrines on legal training, and attempts to evaluate the factors that induce resistance to reform.

The chapter starts with a brief description of the law school system and the law curriculum of Vietnam, with special attention on the legal theory subject and its significance to the entire course of study. The teaching and evaluation methods and their consequences are then examined. The efforts to reform legal education are explored, including formal programs launched by the national government and international donors and informal initiatives of law teachers. I will only discuss legal education at the tertiary level, focusing on Hanoi Law University and its training program as this is the largest training institution which plays a prominent role in legal education in Vietnam. Apart from written sources, my analysis is based on various informal interviews with law professors, law students, state officials and legal practitioners.

LAW SCHOOL SYSTEM IN VIETNAM

A brief history

Unlike other socialist countries with a relatively long tradition of law teaching (Macdonald 1980; Tay and Kamenka 1986; Gostynski and Garfield 1993),[1] legal education in Vietnam has a brief, discontinuous history. During the French colonial period, public education was only accessible to a small élite group in large urban areas (Kelly 2000). A law school was established in 1941 with very limited enrolment of Vietnamese students, but there is no evidence that these early law graduates served in the legal education system after their graduation.[2] The harsh period of war did not allow the government in the North to place emphasis on its legal process and training. There was a judicial training school that belonged to the People's Supreme Court, but it only focused on training judges on a small scale. The Ministry of Justice even had to close.

It was not until a few years after reunification that the Ministry of Justice was re-opened and the Hanoi Law University (*Dai Hoc Phap Ly Ha Noi*, later renamed *Dai Hoc Luat Ha Noi*) was established as the first formal tertiary law school (see Sidel 1993). There was a law university in the South before 1975 (*Dai Hoc Luat Khoa Sai Gon*), but in 1976 it was merged with other schools of the old Saigon regime to form the Economic University of Ho Chi Minh City. This new university did not provide formal law training again until 2001. In 1989, Hanoi Law University opened its campus in Ho Chi Minh City. The founding teachers of this branch were sent from the North and were previously trained in the Eastern bloc. This campus was then separated from Hanoi Law University and became an independent law school of the South, the Ho Chi Minh City Law University (HCMCLU).[3] As part of the changes brought by *doi moi*, law has become fashionable and many other institutions offering legal training have flourished.

In summary, legal education in Vietnam is a relatively new area and is largely disconnected from the previous non-socialist legal training. As a part of the national education system, it follows the mainstream track set by the Party and government for education and is consequently targeted at serving the socioeconomic development of the country. According to the Education Development Strategy for 2001–10,[4] Vietnam aims to build a modern, scientific education system that is nationalistic in nature with a socialist orientation, based on the foundation of Marxist-Leninist theories and Ho Chi Minh's thought.[5] Education's objective is to provide qualified human resources for the country's industrialisation and modernisation process.

The law schools and law teaching

The current system of law schools and law teaching in Vietnam is complicated and operates under a number of different forms of administration.

Until the end of the 1980s, Vietnam copied the Soviet education model (Financial Times Information 2002), including two main types of universities (Kelly 2002). The first type, 'specialised universities', such as Hanoi Law University and HCMCLU, focus on a single area of study. These universities are established specifically to train law graduates. Hanoi Law University is the largest law training institution in Vietnam and a subordinate body of the Ministry of Justice. Meanwhile, HCMCLU is under the administration of the Ministry of Education and Training (MOET) (Hanoi Law University 2002), and has quickly established its reputation in the South since becoming independent from Hanoi Law University.

Apart from Hanoi Law University and HCMCLU, universities exist that specialise in other disciplines but which also include a law subject in the curriculum for their non-law students (Hanoi Law University 2002).[6] These universities have a team (*To*) of law lecturers (often a small team) and the courses they teach only provide basic introductions to law.[7]

The second type of universities are 'multi-disciplinary' and offer degrees in different areas, including law. These universities have a Faculty of Law (*Khoa Luat*), most of which were established very recently.[8]

In addition, there are other legal training institutions administered by a research institute or judicial body. These institutions may offer postgraduate law education or focus on legal professional skills training. For example, the Institute of State and Law (under the National Centre for Social and Human Sciences) and the Faculty of State and Law (under the Ho Chi Minh National Political Academy) are authorised to conduct postgraduate law education. Meanwhile, the Higher School of Procuracy (under the People's Supreme Procuracy) and the Legal Professional Training School (under the Ministry of Justice), later renamed the Judicial Academy, train judges, private lawyers and procuracy cadres.

In the early 1990s, Vietnam adopted new forms of tertiary education. 'People-founded universities' (*dai hoc dan lap*) and 'open universities' (*dai hoc mo*) were established as a part of the education reform program. Some of these universities also took part in legal education, but most of their resources, such as lecturers and materials, were drawn from other state law universities on a contractual basis. This type of law training, however, soon ceased because of government concerns over quality.

Law programs

Law training institutions in Vietnam offer a variety of programs, which can be categorised into three main groups.

The first category is applicable to regular full-time students (*sinh vien chinh quy dai han*) who engage in undergraduate education. After completing a four or five year course, students receive a formal Bachelor of Laws degree (*bang dai hoc chinh quy*). Despite tough competition for admission, the number of students enrolled in these courses has increased markedly.[9] In response to the recent popularity of offering several university degrees, some law training institutions have initiated 'second degree courses' (often known as '*lop bang hai*') that provide formal Bachelor of Laws degrees for students who have a degree in another field.[10] These courses are often shorter than the regular program and students are not required to attend classes on a daily basis.

The second category is 'in-service' (*tai chuc*) education.[11] Similar to the Chinese model (Depei and Kanter 1984), in-service training was initially designed for state officials who had not previously undertaken formal education. Students continue to work and attend classes on a part-time basis. They also receive a Bachelor of Laws degree that is specifically issued for in-service courses (*bang dai hoc tai chuc*); such a degree is essential to ensure promotion and job stability. These courses have been expanded to non-state participants due to the decreased demand in the state sector recently. In-service training has been acknowledged as a helpful way to upgrade state officials' knowledge of basic laws and make legal education more accessible to the population. The popularity of this law degree,[12] however, has induced some doubts about its quality. The number of courses is excessive for law teachers, leaving them no time to prepare and update their materials. In addition, a less-valued degree (Certificate of Higher Education in Law or '*bang trung cap luat*') is available for students who only have a basic educational background.

The third type of law program is postgraduate education, which was initiated in 1986 by the Institute of State and Law. Since then, some other institutions, such as the Hanoi Law University, have also begun providing Master and Doctoral degrees in law, and the number of postgraduate students has promptly increased.[13] Many, however, hold the view that this upgrading program does not mean that legal academia in Vietnam is developing. Postgraduate students are concerned that curricula are very similar to those used in the undergraduate programs, and that the courses do not provide them with improved research skills and methodology.

Law curricula

The fact that there are different training institutions providing different law courses does not mean that the law curricula vary. The tension between the increasing demand for a law degree and the lack of resources makes legal teaching heavily dependent on a relatively small number of law teachers and the materials prepared by them. By the end of the 1980s, and during the 1990s, lecturers from Hanoi Law University were intensively mobilised to teach law courses throughout the country. Law textbooks published by Hanoi Law University have also been used widely in other institutions. Although there have been moves to diversify, most of the law schools still share the same syllabus. As such, I will limit my discussion to the undergraduate curriculum studied by full-time students at Hanoi Law University, due to its popularity.[14] I will not refer to the curricula for in-service training,[15] postgraduate and other legal training courses. In addition, my analysis will focus on particular subjects in the curriculum that reflect how socialist legal theories affect the style of law teaching.

Although the length of the course has been changed from time to time,[16] the substantive teaching has not materially changed during the last decade. It looks similar to the curricula followed in other socialist law schools.[17] Marxist-Leninist studies remain compulsory and Soviet legal doctrine decides the design of the entire curriculum. It should be noted, however, that many new subjects have been added to the training program in an effort to bring law education closer to the market place.

The program consists of two phases: fundamental training (*dao tao co ban*) and specialised training (*dao tao chuyen nganh*).

The fundamental training period is mandatory for all law students. For social and humanities studies, it adopts the MOET standards, which obviously have a socialist orientation. Following the introduction of the Education Development Strategy, the prime minister issued a decision in 2002 requiring all universities to invest more human and financial resources in the teaching of Marxist-Leninist theories and Ho Chi Minh's thought. It reconfirms that study of Marxist-Leninist philosophy, political economy, socialist science and history of the Communist Party of Vietnam are compulsory for all university students. From 2004, law students learn the new subject of Ho Chi Minh's thought.[18] Fundamental training in the law schools includes all these topics.

Apart from Marxist-Leninist studies, some other subjects, including physical education (*the duc*), national defence education (*quan su*) and foreign languages, are also taught in this first phase. The time allocated for fundamental training is approximately 30 per cent of specialised legal training (Hanoi Law University 2002).[19]

The specialised legal training focuses on teaching law and other law-related topics. Students learn Marxist-Leninist theories on state and law (*ly luan nha nuoc va phap luat*) and all law branches (*nganh luat*). Each law branch constitutes a mandatory subject. Examples include constitutional, administrative, criminal, civil, economic and labour law.[20] In addition, supplementary and optional subjects are offered separately to students of different departments[21] depending on their 'specialisation' (*chuyen nganh*). Most of these subjects are closely related to the development of a market economy. For example, students in the economic law department take business administration, auditing or securities laws, while students in the international law department study international trade law and international settlement. Although these additional subjects themselves are still influenced by socialist ideologies, the fact that they are included in the curriculum shows a compromise between socialist orientation and a reaction to market needs.

At the end of specialised training, students are sent to different institutions and organisations for an internship to gain some practical experience.[22]

The fundamental training phase is generally controlled by the MOET, while Hanoi Law University has more power in specialised training. Following the timeframe set by the MOET, Hanoi Law University decides on the number of law topics that can be taught and the time allocated to each topic. Changes to the law curriculum, such as the introduction of new subjects or expansion of teaching time, must be approved by the Science Committee (*Hoi Dong Khoa Hoc*) of Hanoi Law University and the Ministry of Justice.

THEMES OF STATE AND LAW

Themes of State and Law [Ly Luan Nha Nuoc va Phap Luat] provides background knowledge on state and law for all law students and is regarded as the conceptual framework in which law is analysed (Le Minh Tam 1998a). As such, it is intended to establish a foundation for law students to deal with legal issues.

The main source of materials used for teaching and studying is a textbook of *Themes of State and Law*. Although it has been updated and revised many times and is now much more comprehensive than it was ten years ago, some basic concepts remain unchanged. Notably, the class nature of state and law, and the approach that law is an instrument of the state to govern society, have been reaffirmed.[23] In addition, Party leadership is among the guiding principles that controls state governance and lawmaking activities (Le Minh Tam 1998c).

Students are taught that the most important function of the state is to manage the economy (*'quan ly nha nuoc ve kinh te'*).[24] State economic management is regarded as a part of the class revolution during the transitional period (*'dau tranh giai cap trong thoi ky qua do'*) to protect the working class from exploitative capitalism. To fulfil this task, the state employs plans (*'ke hoach'*), builds up a 'mechanism of economic management' (*'co che quan ly kinh te'*) and owns essential production tools (*'tu lieu san xuat chu yeu'*), including land (Le Minh Tam 1998d).[25] Since the subject is taught to law students soon after they enter law school, when their legal knowledge is still limited,[26] these ideologies of state economic management are often well rooted and continue to develop during the four-year course.

As mentioned earlier, *Themes of State and Law* divides the legal system into independent law branches (*nganh luat doc lap*). This theory has been the core element that forms the law curriculum. It is based on Marxist arguments of the relationship between the superstructure and infrastructure. Social relations (*quan he xa hoi*) that are subject to law adjustment (known by legal scholars and law students as 'objects of adjustment' or *'doi tuong dieu chinh'*) are part of the infrastructure, while the law belongs to the superstructure.

Once social relations are governed by laws, they become 'legal relations' (*quan he phap luat*). Social relations occurring in a particular field, such as labour or finance, share certain common features. Therefore, they can be categorised into the same group. As a consequence, the laws governing such groups are similarly categorised.

Two standards are used to define the independence of a law branch, namely 'objects of adjustment' and 'methods of adjustment' (*phuong phap dieu chinh*) (Le Minh Tam 1998f:393–94).

The most noticeable disadvantage of this classification theory is that it understates the complexity of the legal system. The 'independent law branch' approach has, to some extent, isolated the 'branches' of law from each other.[27] As learners, law students tend to be attached to simple formulas and channel all legal issues into one (or a few) of the laws that they know. This, in turn, affects their ability to identify a matrix of legal matters that are often associated with social relations. For example, students learn about companies and administrative procedures to set up such entities under economic law. They then learn about land law, tax law and labour law as separate subjects. This way of teaching fails to make students aware that the existence of a company not only involves its establishment formalities, but also involves a series of other complicated legal issues such as land, tax and employment. The compartmentalisation does not prepare students to offer clients practical advice.

Students also face great difficulties dealing with other aspects of the legal system that do not fall into any of the standard law branches, such as import and export regulations and customs laws. Even law teachers tend to limit their knowledge to their 'specialised' topics and the series of issues that are set for teaching within those topics. For example, land law teachers would generally not be interested in researching how land is taxed, as that issue is dealt with by finance law teachers.

Classification theory is also a source of confusion and ambiguity. Legal scholars informally admit that there are numerous social relations that cannot be categorised into any of the current law branches. Even some traditional legal relations, such as contracts, have new forms.[28] As such, law teachers struggle to invent some common features that can represent 'objects of adjustment' of a law branch and maintain their 'independence' from each other.

It is even harder to justify the 'methods of adjustment' proposition. There are only two 'methods of adjustment' that apply to the entire legal system, namely the 'compulsory method' (*phuong phap menh lenh*) and the 'equal method' (*phuong phap binh dang*). It is believed that the 'compulsory method' is suitable for governing vertical legal relations in which the state is one party, such as administrative or criminal laws. On the other hand, the 'equal method' is applied to horizontal relations in which the parties enjoy equal status, such as civil law. Since *doi moi*, all law branches that govern economic activities employ both methods. Therefore, the second element that determines the 'independence' of these branches arguably no longer exists. Although legal writing and teaching has focused less on the reasoning behind the categorisation of the legal system,[29] classification theory is still a part of the formal teaching program, so it continues to generate confusion among teachers and learners.

Themes of State and Law seems to mitigate the interweaving of law and other social spheres. The relationship between law and politics, economics and morality is only briefly addressed (Le Minh Tam 1998d)[30] and is not mentioned again in other law subjects. Thus, students encounter ideologies of instrumentalist law and state management most frequently since these issues are repeated throughout the course. This is another weakness of legal education, since students do not learn about the sophistication of the legal and political system and how law interacts with economic and political development.

Themes of State and Law does not yet reflect the 'nationalism' feature. There has been a series of scholarly discussions about Ho Chi Minh's thought on state and law, but none of this discussion has been introduced to law schools since law teachers are not yet ready. It is expected that this issue will be covered by the new subject of Ho Chi Minh's thought and will be taught by teachers of political science.[31] As such, socialism remains a dominant feature of state and law doctrines.

The following sections will use some law 'branches' as examples to examine further how themes of state and law are incorporated into other law subjects. Although there are currently more than a dozen law branches, a standard model applies to all of them. The first one or two lessons are devoted to providing a theoretical basis to students. This introductory session presents an overview (*khai niem*) of the subject and sets out its scope. Largely based on classification theory, it shows how branches are independent from others.

Land law

Land law is claimed to be different from other laws (in particular civil and economic law) because it has its own 'objects of adjustment' and 'methods of adjustment'.

The 'objects of adjustment' have two salient features. First, land is a 'special commodity' (*hang hoa dac biet*) and therefore social relations concerning land (*quan he dat dai*) are not subject to civil law that governs regular property. This original concept of 'land as a special commodity' is intended to preserve state ownership of land. It remains ambiguous and unclear, as there is insufficient explanation of what makes land a 'special commodity'. Second, land relations are not a type of economic activity since the management and use of land is for community interests rather than for making a profit. Thus, they are not ruled by economic law either. 'Methods of adjustment' is a combination of the 'compulsory method' and the 'equal method' (Tran Quang Huy 2001a:12–16).

The application of the classification theory to land law is confusing because there are certain 'land relations' that do not fit into the ideological framework of 'objects of adjustment'. For example, it is hard to explain why land transactions are not economic activities when they are subject to capital gains tax. In addition, its 'methods of adjustment', as noted earlier, are not different from those of other law branches and therefore cannot be referred to as a distinguishing feature of land law.

Land law also embodies the fundamental principle of Marxist theory that land belongs to 'the people'. Two entire chapters are devoted to state ownership and management of land (*quan ly nha nuoc ve dat dai*) (Tran Quang Huy 2001b:47–76, 2001c:77–110). These chapters reaffirm the themes of state and law and build up the important ideology of state management in relation to land. On the other hand, land law is extended to include a number of lessons on land transactions in recognition of the realities of the market. However, land law teachers rarely question the contradiction between 'state management' and the largely uncontrolled land market in their teaching.

Finance law and banking law

These two subjects are an interesting example of how legal theories and the law curriculum have been adjusted to address economic reform. In the past, they were a single law branch under the name of finance law. Under the central planning regime, finance law governed vertical relations, including budget and tax laws. There were also some insurance and banking regulations but all the insurance companies and banks were state-owned.

The *doi moi* policy and changes in the financial services sector meant that the classification theory was no longer relevant to this law branch. New horizontal relations such as commercial insurance and commercial loans have emerged, prompting law teachers to create a new subject of banking law. The reasoning for this split, however, was still based in the traditional themes of state and law. It was seen that banking law needed to be 'independent' because it has its own 'objects of adjustment' that differ significantly from those of finance law.

Finance law was designed to govern a mixture of vertical and horizontal relations including budget and tax, corporate finance and insurance.[32] Since it is difficult to find common features that represent these groups, scholars changed the approach to list them all as 'objects of adjustment' of finance law. A similar path was adopted for banking law. Although banking law has been made a new subject, law teachers informally and reluctantly acknowledged the unconvincing theoretical basis for its independence. Finance law later was further split into four separate topics; namely, tax law, budget law, commercial insurance law and securities law. All these subjects are still handled by the same team of finance and banking law teachers. However, the concept of 'methods of adjustment' is deliberately silent in the teaching.

As with land law, students learn about state management in the finance and banking sectors (*quan ly nha nuoc trong linh vuc tai chinh va ngan hang*).[33] Although it is not entirely clear, state management is usually referred to as the theoretical basis of almost any exercise of state power. For example, the state management function of the State Bank of Vietnam was invoked to explain why the bank should issue regulations setting a ceiling rate for offshore loans. Later, when the ceiling rate was removed, justification was attributed to the bank's discretion to create a more liberal lending policy for the purpose of state management at that time.

If *Themes of State and Law* introduces the first basis for state management, other law subjects work to consolidate it. When law students reach their final years, the concept has become firmly established. They tend to utilise it to justify virtually all legal issues that arise from state intervention into social relations and, significantly, tend to develop a mentality that assigns priority to state rights and devotes insufficient attention to other parties' interests. In a moot tax case, for example, a student representing—and supposedly defending—a taxpayer, apologised to the tax authority because he felt the principle of state management was being violated.

Design of curricula and course materials

Law curricula for the specialised training phase are prepared by law schools. The first generation of law teachers—now quite senior—was trained in Eastern Europe and is currently the primary force in designing the curricula and writing the textbooks. Due to the lack of resources during the 1980s and early 1990s, course materials, especially the socialist legal doctrines and concepts, were prepared according to law teachers' overseas experiences.

Following *doi moi*, Themes of State and Law and other economic law subjects have been updated to address economic reform. However, changes in law curricula and course content have been relatively slow compared to other disciplines such as economics or other social sciences. Arguably, this can be attributed to the fact that the conceptualised understanding of law—according to which the law is supposed to demonstrate and cement the Party's policies—remains unchanged. As such, the Themes of State and Law have mainly been developed on the basis of Party policy documents. Since the Party's policies promote a socialist legal system (*he thong phap luat xa hoi chu nghia*) in Vietnam, Soviet legal orthodoxies are employed to serve this purpose. For both law teachers and law students, law is an integral part of politics, and the study of state and law is incomplete without referring to the Party's resolutions.[34]

Despite awareness of the need objectively to re-examine the relevance of Soviet legal doctrines in a market economy, law teachers refrain from challenging these entrenched theories. They tend to 'reform' the technical rather than the theoretical aspects of law teaching. This tendency is partly due to the lack of proper research skills and methodologies. However, in many cases teachers are reluctant to touch upon theories because of concerns over political sensitivity. In certain situations where Soviet doctrines appear to be particularly irrelevant, they avoid them by focusing on the practical issues.

While law teachers and scholars were free to adopt Socialist legal writing to prepare their teaching materials, they used legal materials from Western market economies for different purposes. In the latest version of the *Themes of State and Law* textbook, some brief references to US constitutional writing were inserted as examples to illustrate Soviet concepts of state and law. Experience of other Western legal systems has also been sought, but the focus has been on neither doctrines nor concepts.

For example, when banking law was split from finance law, teachers with Australian and British educational experience were consulted on the question of how banking law is treated in these countries. Banking law eventually became an independent subject for teaching partly because of the adoption of a model learned from other developed legal systems (Vo Dinh Toan 2002). However, the classification theory was still used to justify this movement, and references for banking law still include Soviet legal writing from the 1950s and the 1970s (Vo Dinh Toan 2002). Law teachers are urged to introduce the Western experience in certain areas of banking law, such as bank guarantees or syndicated loans, but they are also required to teach the principle of state management of the banking system. It is therefore clear that reformists are reluctant to move away from the politically dominant theme.

Collective decision-making is another factor that may have contributed to resistance to reform of curricula and course materials. Each law subject is often taught by a group of law teachers who work independently to prepare their lecture notes and reference materials. Such materials, however, are required to conform to a standard textbook. New ideas or approaches need to be discussed and approved by the whole team in order to ensure consistency and consensus. While this system aims at compromise and harmonisation, it discourages the introduction of radical views, because their introduction is usually a source of conflict. Teachers tend to avoid presenting individual opinions or controversial views to students because it may cause colleagues to lose face, or expose the team's internal inconsistencies publicly.

Teaching and evaluation

Teaching methodology. Most universities in Vietnam, including law teaching institutions, apply the traditional lecturing style. This method is characterised by one-way communication in which the teachers deliver their lectures while students take notes. There is virtually no interruption for questions or comments from students. Lectures are usually long and classes are large.[35] Junior lecturers are required to attend a course on teaching methodology and skills when starting their careers, and the instructors for this course are from a pedagogy school that emphasises one-way communication and discourages student participation.

Teachers prepare their own lecturing materials, but such materials need to follow standard textbooks to ensure consistency in terms of structure and content. Radical and active teachers may search for external sources such as Western law or even materials used by the Saigon Law School before 1975, but access to these sources is often limited and depends on individual initiative. Most of the law lessons are based on legislation and, as such, can easily become outdated once the legislation changes. Although considerable investment has been put into upgrading teaching and learning facilities, legal updates are often received late by law school libraries. Teachers tend to use their own personal relationships with state officials to obtain new legal documents.

Seminars are also arranged in parallel with lectures. As part of wider reform efforts, the time allocated for seminars has been increased and classes made smaller[36] to give students more opportunities to take part in discussion (Hanoi Law University 2002). This form of teaching is also not very effective, however, as student participation in discussion is often limited. In a typical seminar, teachers have to try hard to get students to speak. This may reflect Vietnamese cultural norms—in

Confucian societies, where education is highly appreciated, students are taught to respect teachers and their opinions. After many years spent in school, they fall into the habit of obeying teachers and following their instructions, and, as a consequence, tend to be shy of presenting their own opinions in public. For those who are confident and outspoken, there is a concern that their perspectives may not be the 'right' ones.

Generally, a seminar is not a forum where students learn how to debate and argue. Rather, it is a modified form of lecturing in which students wait for the right answers and resolutions from teachers. In other words, students rarely work towards a solution for legal problems and their contribution to the outcome of a seminar is minimal. Hypothetical cases are included for discussion, but tend to be relatively simple. Court cases are not yet available from public records, therefore teachers have to be inventive with their own cases.

The biggest disadvantage of this teaching style is that it produces passive learning. Neither the lectures nor the seminars train law students in the problem-solving and analytical skills that are essential for the legal profession. Although reformists have called for the launch of new teaching methods that focus more on skills training, law teachers are confused and torn between traditional lecturing and case studies.[37] Like students elsewhere, students in Vietnam are most concerned about how to pass exams. As the exam scheme (discussed below) focuses on rote learning, students are forced to develop memorising skills. Creative and independent thinking is not promoted and most law graduates are still needlessly immature in this respect after graduation.

Another noticeable shortcoming is the big gap between what is taught at law schools and what is required in legal practice.[38] Although many law teachers are admitted to the bar, only a small number have actually represented clients before the courts or engaged in providing legal consultancy services.[39] The new regulations affecting lawyers have worsened the situation because the legal profession and law teachers are separated indefinitely. According to these regulations, government officials cannot become members of the bar, apparently to avoid conflicts of interest, and those who represent state power cannot simultaneously serve private clients. Since law teachers also have the status of civil servants, they are not allowed to join the bar. From 2004, all law teachers who had previously been admitted to the bar were to quit the bar if they wished to stay with universities.[40]

There have been some arguments that the current methodology applied to law teaching in Vietnam has been influenced by the French style inherited from the French civil law system. However, law teachers who graduated in the Eastern bloc reported that the current teaching style in Vietnam is exactly what they experienced in other socialist law schools.

Although law teachers and students have informally admitted the ineffectiveness of the current teaching methodology, there has been no focus on developing legal trainers' skills. Analysis in the next section will show that legal reform programs at both national and institutional levels assign only an insignificant position to legal education. Meanwhile, government policy on tertiary education demonstrates a contradictory approach to the issue of teaching methodology. Unprecedented by-laws for universities have been issued to promote decentralisation, but at the same time a certain degree of control has been retained.[41] On the one hand, the recent Decision No. 153 entitles lecturers to choose teaching materials and teaching methodology freely in order to promote their individual ability and quality of teaching. On the other hand, teachers are obliged to teach in accordance with curricula and course content designed by MOET and universities.[42]

Since law belongs to the superstructure and is regarded as a state instrument to govern society, the exercise of law is not seen as part of the economic base. Rather, it is a demonstration of state power. Therefore, the concepts of 'legal profession' (*nghe luat su*) and 'legal services' (*dich vu phap ly*) are barely mentioned in legal teaching. This ideology fits with the current institutional structure, where lawyer skills are only taught in a special course which is designed for legal professional training.[43] In addition, professional qualities are often matched with political qualities as law and politics overlap.

The 'general objective' (*muc tieu chung*) of legal training at Hanoi Law University is defined as follows.

> The law program aims at training law graduates with *political and moral qualities and consciousness to serve the people*. Law graduates should have knowledge and capacity to perform their jobs. In addition, they should have good health to meet the demands of the country's modernisation and industrialisation process. They should also contribute to the building of a law-based state, aiming at prosperous people, wealthy nation and civilised society [emphasis added].[44]

The 'political and moral qualities' are positioned as primary targets for legal education. In addition, the requirement that law graduates should have consciousness to serve the people implicitly refers to a socialist state which is 'of the people, for the people and by the people', as defined in the constitution.[45] Other references to modernisation and industrialisation only operate at a high level and thus do not present any particular policy instructions to law teaching.

To achieve this general objective, the policy draws certain specific objectives (*muc tieu cu the*) for legal education

- to provide students with fundamental, comprehensive knowledge about law and the legal system
- to provide students with other law-related social knowledge
- to equip students with scientific mentality and approaches to resolve theoretical and practical legal problems
- to form preliminary concepts about legal expertise in different areas
- to acquaint students with the operation and activities of different institutions so that when they graduate they will be equipped with fundamental legal and practical knowledge, and be able to find and resolve common problems that arise in specialised areas in which they are trained. In addition, they will have a foundation to pursue a higher degree in law.

It is a common understanding among law teachers that 'fundamental knowledge' (*kien thuc co ban*) is limited to the theoretical (*ly thuyet*), rather than the practical side of law and, as such, does not relate to the development of professional skills. They argue that law graduates will develop their own problem-solving skills once they start their careers and deal with law in practice. Although the policy requires training in 'practical skills' (*ky nang thuc hanh*) for students, it simply refers to a preliminary understanding of how institutions (*co quan, to chuc*) operate in practice. In the Vietnamese context, these institutions often mean state organisations such as the court, the inspector office or state-owned institutions. Practical skills are in fact gained when students perform a brief internship in such institutions, rather than in the law school. In addition, the skills acquired frequently concern the exercise of state power using law.

The comprehensive report about legal education in Vietnam completed by Hanoi Law University in 2002 also mentions the need to target professional skills training for law students. Its main focus, however, is the curriculum and no reference is made to teaching methodology.

Exams and assessment

The assessment methods applied in legal education share some common problems apparent in the entire education system of Vietnam. The borrowed Soviet model, spoilt by the local achievement-craving mentality, often leads to dishonest evaluation (Financial Times Information 2002). Different kinds of exams have been trialled, but none seem to be effective in ensuring quality and fairness. In traditional closed-book exams, copying and plagiarism are rampant as students are challenged to memorise large volumes of materials in a few days and seek ways of avoiding this. Open-book exams were trialled, but most papers were returned with the same answers. Oral exams have recently been promoted in a reform effort (Hanoi Law University 2002), but the result has not been overly different and the experiment discomforted both students and teachers. As with closed-book exams, students memorise huge amounts of material, including textbooks, lecture notes and legislation for the oral exams, where they are given a brief time to answer a few questions that constitute a very small part of what they have worked hard to memorise. The teachers, on the other hand, are required to follow a series of assessment instructions which are difficult to apply in practice. Despite strict rules, informal lobbying for good grades is common in both written and oral exams.

LEGAL EDUCATION REFORM

National reform

At the national level, attention to law training reform appears to be modest. In addition, the Party's policy for reform focuses more on management and control than on accommodating legal education to legal and economic development.

Resolution No.08/NQ-TW introduced by the Politburo in January 2002 is an important policy document that sets out a series of institutional reforms for the legal sector. However, it only briefly mentions legal education as a part of the capacity-building program. In particular, the resolution requires tertiary law training to be concentrated in Hanoi Law University and HCMCLU, and calls for unification of curricula and law textbooks. The objective of this reform is to ensure that law graduates will have a firm political view (*quan diem chinh tri vung vang*), high values of morality (*pham chat dao duc tot*) and be professionally qualified. It is unclear how the institutional and curricula restructuring will help reach this objective.

Following the resolution, the prime minister issued Directive No.10/2002/CT-TTg in March 2002 with instructions for implementation, prodding the MOET and the Ministry of Justice to restructure legal training institutions, with a focus on Hanoi Law University and HCMCLU. In addition, it instructs the two ministries to work on a proposal to unify law curricula and textbooks nationwide. The directive does not provide further guidance, and it is up to the discretion of the two ministries to fulfil the instructions.

Restructuring the curricula is one of the first steps that the Ministry of Justice and Ministry of Education have taken to implement the program, with a committee of experts having been formed to work on the issue. Reformists within the group have suggested a modernised curriculum with a Western influence. This approach faces certain tensions and concerns as the majority of the committee were either trained in Eastern Europe or were locally educated. In addition, it exposes some groups of teachers to unfamiliar topics while others have to reduce their lecturing time.[46] For example, there was a proposal that the commercial law subject should also cover insurance regulations. Meanwhile, commercial law teachers have never taught insurance law, as it is regarded as a part of finance law.

In addition to the judicial reform program, the government of Vietnam, following recommendations made by the International Consultative Group in December 2000, established a national inter-agency team to conduct a comprehensive Legal Needs Assessment of the country's legal system. It was intended that the Legal Needs Assessment would serve as a basis for developing a strategy for the development of Vietnam's legal system through until 2010. The inter-agency team, led by the Ministry of Justice, was divided into small groups researching different areas of the legal system, including law training.

The Legal Needs Assessment Report acknowledged the importance of legal education by positioning it as a crucial component of the legal system. Based on the examination of the current status, achievements and shortcomings of legal education, the report provided a set of goals to develop the national law-training regime in the next ten years, as well as an action plan to reach such goals. It was the first time that the country's legal education system and its role in legal reform had been evaluated nationally.[47] The Legal Needs Assessment was rejected after several rounds of reviews and revisions, however, and a new policy document, the Legal System Development

Strategy, was introduced in early 2003. Unlike the Legal Needs Assessment, the Legal System Development Strategy takes the same approach as Resolution No. 8 and places negligible importance on legal education reform. There has been no formal explanation for this shift of focus.[48]

Development projects supporting legal education

Since the early 1990s, reform of Vietnam's legal sector has become attractive to international donors. Many projects have been specifically designed to support legal education.

Together with projects in the area of administrative reform,[49] projects promoting law reform are subject to special governmental control. Regulations on management of international cooperation in the legal sector[50] set out a number of principles for such cooperation. Among other things, law projects must be implemented on the basis of ensuring national sovereignty and respecting local culture. In addition, they should fit within the socioeconomic development policies of the Party and the state. The regulations also establish appraisal and approval procedures for all law projects, including those on legal education. Training institutions like Hanoi Law University are not allowed to have direct relationships with international partners without going through the Ministry of Justice. This filtering regime has resulted in a limited number of projects supporting legal training during the past decade, in comparison to other disciplines. The new by-laws for universities[51] have liberalised this aspect by authorising local universities to set up cooperation programs directly with foreign partners. It is, however, unclear how the conflict between this new by-law and the old regulations will be resolved.[52]

When foreign assistance actually occurs, its impact on local legal education seems to be insignificant. For example, Hanoi Law University, as the largest law training institution in Vietnam, hosts a 'Vietnam–France Law House' (*Nha Phap Luat Viet-Phap*) on campus, which provides library facilities for French language readers and organises seminars on various legal topics. However, the influence of the House seems to be modest given the small French-speaking population in the school. The use of materials and ideas that arise from the seminars is also limited as teachers are still bound in their teaching by the Soviet legal theories and standard textbooks.

Perhaps the most noticeable foreign project is that provided by the generous Swedish International Development Agency. A formal cooperation program has been established between Hanoi Law University, HCMCLU and a Swedish university to improve curricula, teaching capacities and facilities. Seminars have been held and a number of Vietnamese law teachers have gone to Sweden for short and long-term training.[53] Nonetheless, the project remains remote to the educational life at Hanoi Law University. Workshops on teaching methodologies were held but only attended by a small audience of lecturers. After several years in operation, the project's contribution to the improvement of curricula and teaching quality at Hanoi Law University seems to be modest given its relatively large size. These facts have yielded some concerns about the effectiveness of foreign assistance in Vietnam. As Zamboni (2001) noted, this kind of project needs to invest more resources to investigate and scrutinise the actual conditions of the local counterparts.

In addition to formal projects at Hanoi Law University, a number of teachers have benefited from other scholarship programs and have been trained at Western universities. Despite their experience, they remain inactive not influential on their return due to a number of concerns.

Other reform efforts

Apart from the above top-down programs, some bottom-up changes have also emerged, better reflecting local conditions. Examples below of reforms to the curricula and teaching methods are taken from Hanoi Law University.

At Hanoi Law University, more activities have recently been added to the formal teaching program to engage students in public discussion and debate. Moot courts (*phien toa tap su*) and quiz competitions (*cuoc thi*)[54] are organised occasionally. Some new research centres have been established to promote research activities, such as the Centre for Commercial and Investment Law (*Trung Tam Phap Luat Thuong Mai va Dau Tu*) within the Department of Economic Legislation. However, the activities of these centres remain limited as they are not set up as independent units and are therefore not free from control of the department. A new Centre of Comparative Law was also established at university level, but it has experienced difficulties due to a lack of staff and other resources.

A minor project initiated by the Department of Economic Legislation studied the needs of reforming economic law (*luat kinh te*). The question posed by the organiser was whether 'economic law' should retain its current name or whether it should have a new name that better reflected its substance. The two alternative names chosen were 'business law' (*luat kinh doanh*) and 'commercial law' (*luat thuong mai*). In addition, researchers were asked to consider the content of economic law. Diverse opinions expressed in a workshop that reported the results of the project showed how, within the context of legal academia, the traditional Soviet idea of economic law was being challenged by market influence. Though consensus was reached on the importance of reforming the subject, scholars presented different views and perceptions on the issues. Some supported the removal of the name 'economic law' by looking at the experience of the neighbouring Chinese. Senior scholars who were trained in the former Soviet Union described how the idea was imported into Vietnam. They believed that 'economic law' was a mistranslation of Soviet terminology during that transplantation process. A Western approach to commercial law was also introduced as a suggestion for reform. A more pragmatic view cautiously warned that attention should be paid to substance rather than terminology, to avoid the common problem of 'new jar, old wine' (*'binh moi, ruou cu'*). According to these scholars, it was more important to apply new teaching methodologies and make the subject more practically applicable rather than simply change its name.[55]

The frequently mentioned reform idea of 'modern teaching methodology' (*phuong phap giang day hien dai*) also engages a number of radical law teachers in the search for such a method. Collectively or individually, they have tried to experiment with case studies in their teaching. A survey on teaching methodologies was conducted by the Department of Economic Legislation of Hanoi Law University to gather teachers' (mostly junior lecturers) opinions on the issue. Following the survey, a workshop was held to report on the results. Since this event was not formally initiated by the Department or Hanoi Law University, the organisers looked to the Youth Union as a sponsor.

The workshop stirred hot debate about the definition of a 'case study' (*phuong phap tinh huong*) and the 'regular' or traditional way of teaching (*phuong phap thong thuong*). Since most junior teachers are locally trained and have never been exposed to Western training, they were confused about case studies. There was a question whether illustrating examples used in a lecture is a form of case study. Others asked whether a single case should cover most of the legal issues addressed by a law subject. For example, should a single labour case include employment, compensation, strike and dispute settlement issues. Obsessed by the power of modern technology, many believed that the use of slides and projectors is also a new method for teaching (so-called 'projector method' or '*phuong phap den chieu*'). Although the workshop was only an informal reform effort that did not attract much attention from the University authority, it represented the real needs of those who participate in legal education on a daily basis.

CONCLUSION

Observers have been concerned about the failure of legal education in Vietnam during the last one and a half decades. Only three to four per cent of law graduates are finding work in the legal system (Quinn 2002), ringing alarm bells about the law training reform process.

The above analysis has indicated how traditional Soviet legal doctrines and teaching methods affect the quality of training. While state authorities and legal practitioners deal with market participants on a daily basis, law schools are still largely isolated from the process of economic and legal development. Legal academia remains an 'island' where socialist legal ideologies largely dominate. These ideologies, associated with a traditional lecturing style, have equipped law students with rigid ideas about instrumentalist laws and the skill of rote learning. Current curricula still lead law students to simplify the legal system according to the Soviet model and elevate the importance of state control, no longer appropriate in a diverse, market-oriented economy.

The analysis has also shown a conflict between the mandatory teaching of socialist legal doctrines and the need to bring legal training closer to the market place. Reform has been made difficult by a variety of factors, including insufficient policy support, a Soviet institutional structure that promotes collective decision-making, and factors arising from the local culture.

Law students are not trained to practice in the legal profession. Established ideas about the various uses of law equip students with extensive knowledge of how the state can employ law to manage society, but impedes students' capacity to learn about non-state interests and perspectives. Young graduates nowadays are more attracted to the private sector (Nguyen 2002), but often face confusion and great difficulties when starting their careers owing to the nature of their training.

The state sector, with its entrenched psychology of 'state economic management', provides the ideal environment for such law graduates (AusAID 2000). Gillespie has noted that the collision of 'state economic management' ideas with forces for market liberalisation is creating tensions (Gillespie 2002). While the private sector demands greater market access, ministries and local authorites have sought to subvert government reforms and retain power by inventing new forms of control and intervention.[56] The new generation of law graduates will be integral to this process in the future, holding the potential to slow or advance the reforms as they see fit.

It has been widely agreed that better legal education could ease the tensions. Improving teaching methodologies and skills for law teachers is a crucial issue that deserves more serious attention from policymakers. Detailed research of teachers' needs, and formal courses to address them, is likely to yield the best solutions. Such courses should aim at building up the analytical and problem-solving skills of law teachers because creative thinking amongst students will certainly not be promoted if the teachers themselves are not creative thinkers. Once the teachers' skills are upgraded, law students will immediately benefit from the improvements.

Established legal ideologies are not easily changed, but a training program (including curricula and course materials) with an orientation toward practice could make such ideologies less dogmatic. This approach also fits with the trend of the contemporary legal system towards a more pragmatic and rational approach, which would gradually help to improve the quality of legal education and thus reach the ambitious goals of reformers.

NOTES

[1]   Some law schools were established in China in the nineteenth century, and legal education in Poland dates back to the fourteenth century.
[2]   Mr Ngo Van Thau was one of a few professors at the Judicial Training School during the 1960s who speaks fluent French and often refers to French legal materials in his research work. However, his knowledge of the French legal system was obtained through self-learning rather than formal education. Interviewed in Hanoi, 2001. See also Sidel (1993).
[3]   In 1990, a small Faculty of Law was formed at the Ho Chi Minh City University by a group of Saigon attorneys who practised in Saigon before 1975. However, the curricula of this Faculty did not appear very different from other law schools. In addition, the Faculty itself is a controversial institution and not an influential participant in the local legal education market (Sidel 1993).
[4]   Decision No. 201/2001/QD-TTg dated 28 December 2001 of the Prime Minister Approving Education Development Strategy 2001–2010.

5   In Vietnamese: *'Xay dung nen giao duc co tinh nhan dan, dan toc, khoa hoc, hien dai, theo dinh huong xa hoi chu nghia, lay chu nghia Mac-Lenin va tu tuong Ho Chi Minh lam nen tang'.*

6   These include the National Economic University, Ho Chi Minh City University of Economy, University of Civil Construction, University of Commerce, University of Foreign Trade, University of Finance, University of Maritime and Vinh University (see Hanoi Law University 2002).

7   For example, the law team of Vinh University only has 3 lecturers. The Ho Chi Minh City University of Economy, in its ambitious expansion, is an exception in upgrading its law team (*To*) to faculty level (*Khoa*).

8   These include the Law Faculty of the Hanoi National University, Law Faculty of Can Tho University, Law Faculty of Da lat University and Law Faculty of the University of Science of Hue (see Hanoi Law University 2002).

9   There has been no formal survey that shows how fast the number of law graduates has increased during the last 15 years. Legal education has indeed become a 'phenomenon' and as a consequence, law training institutions have mushroomed. For example, in 1988, the Hanoi Law University had approximately 130 students enrolled in the undergraduate program. By December 2001, the University alone had issued Bachelor of Laws degree to 10,000 full-time students and 4,000 others were awaiting completion of their degrees (Hanoi Law University 2002). This is an impressive figure in light of the University's 22 years of education (Legal Need Assessment Report 2002).

10   For example, by the end of 2001, Hanoi Law University had 168 students enrolled in this type of course (Hanoi Law University 2002). The number has increased recently.

11   Hanoi Law University issued 18,000 *'tai chuc'* degrees by the end of 2001 and 7,000 others were in the process of completing the same degree (Hanoi Law University 2002).

12   Twenty-two years after the first formal law training institute was established, the country had 62,236 Bachelors of Laws nationwide (Legal Needs Assessment Report 2002).

13   By the end of 2001, Hanoi Law University alone had trained 314 LLM students (329 others were master candidates), 19 PhD students (55 others were PhD candidates). It set an ambitious target that, by 2005, 70 per cent of the lecturers (232) would have an LLM, and 80 per cent would have that qualification by 2010 (with 50 per cent having a PhD) (Hanoi Law University 2002).

14   Newly opened schools, such as the Law Faculty of Can Tho University, seem to have more flexible curricula. However, the scale of these institutions is relatively small and the materials are still largely based on those prepared by Hanoi Law University and HCMCLU. See further Hanoi Law University (2002). Description of curricula applied in various law teaching institutions is also available in Sidel (1993).

15   The curriculum for in-service training is in fact an abbreviated form of the one used for full-time students.

16   The length for an undergraduate course is four to five years.

17   For an example of curricula used in China, see Tay and Kamenka (1986). For Polish curricula, see Gostynski and Garfield (1993).

18   Decision No. 494/QD-TTg, dated 24 June 2002, of the Prime Minister. The MOET later issued an official letter that provides guidance to implement this Decision (Official Letter No. 7821/CTCT, dated 5 September 2002). In addition, a series of MOET decisions set outlines for the subjects of Marxist-Leninist studies and Ho Chi Minh's thought.

19   Lecturing time is approximately 1,265 hours for general training and 3,265 hours for law training (Hanoi Law University 2002).

20   There are 13 law branches under the current system, among which banking law and environment law have been newly created. International law (including public and private law) is not regarded as a branch of domestic law, but rather as an independent law subject. See details in Le Minh Tam (1998e:399–403) and further discussion on the classification theory below.

21   There are four departments (*Khoa*) at the Hanoi Law University: Administrative Law (*Phap Luat Hanh Chinh*), Economic Law (*Phap Luat Kinh Te*), Judicial Studies (*Tu Phap*), and International Law (*Phap Luat Quoc Te*).

22   After completing the internship, the students are required to submit a brief report and then take a final exam. Internship is waived for those with good grades, who instead submit a graduate thesis.

23   The definition of law is as follows: 'Law is a system of norms that are codified and enforced by the state. It represents the will of the ruling class and is an instrument to adjust social relations

(phap luat la he thong cac quy tac xu su do nha nuoc ban hanh va bao dam thuc hien, the hien y chi cua giai cap thong tri trong xa hoi, la nhan to dieu chinh cac quan he xa hoi)' (Le Minh Tam 1998b:64). This definition has been used for the last one and a half decades.

24   It is said that before reunification, the most important function of the state was national defence. This change in priorities shows that the state is now more concerned with economic development than national defence.

25   This concept of 'state economic management' has been renewed from time to time following Party policy reform. Most of the theory is drawn from Party resolutions.

26   The subject is often scheduled for first year students.

27   Legal scholars have tried to note the 'relative nature' *(tinh chat tuong doi)* of this classification and the interconnection between social relations.

28   For example, a joint-venture contract between a foreign investor and a Vietnamese entity.

29   *Themes of State and Law* contains only a few sentences naming the grounds to categorise law branches, without further analysis (Le Minh Tam 1998f).

30   The textbook is 559 pages long. Only four pages are dedicated to analysis of the relationship between law and other social spheres.

31   The MOET's design for the subject of Ho Chi Minh's thought includes one lesson on Ho Chi Minh's thought about state and law.

32   As part of ongoing reform, finance law was split into three smaller subjects at the end of 2004, namely budget law, tax law and insurance law.

33   State management of land, finance and banking are all subsets of 'state economic management'.

34   The Party's resolutions are the main source of references for *Themes of State and Law*. In fact, students learn about the development of state and law concepts through changes in Party policies.

35   One lecture often lasts for the whole morning or afternoon (four and a half hours), with a ten-minute break every hour. Starting in Autumn 2001, one morning or afternoon session was divided into two subjects at Hanoi Law University. Lectures are often conducted in big halls, containing 100–200 students or more. Depending on the subject, one teacher may have to teach up to 20 hours per week.

36   They are, however, still large, with 70–80 students each.

37   This issue will be discussed at greater length below.

38   It should be noted that this is not only a legal education problem, but rather, a shortcoming of the entire Vietnamese education system. As an article in the Financial Times Information commented: 'teachers often paid too much attention to theoretical knowledge while neglecting practical application. Research institutes within universities and colleges were viewed as ivory towers that were isolated from both training activities and the real demand of the country's social and economic development' (Financial Times Information 2002). A senior official has also remarked on the situation that: 'science is up in the air, while life is down to earth' *(khoa hoc tren troi, cuoc doi duoi dat)*, Available online at Vietnam Net, http://www.vnn.vn/442/2003/3/5081/.

39   Before the new regulations on lawyers were issued, a good network of personal relationships could make it relatively easy for law teachers to join the bar.

40   Articles 8 and 42, Ordinance on Lawyers, dated 25 July 2001.

41   Decision No. 153/2003/QD-TTg, dated 30 July 2003, of the Prime Minister Issuing By-Laws for Universities.

42   Article 46(2), Decision No. 153/2003/QD-TTg, dated 30 July 2003, of the Prime Minister Issuing By-Laws for Universities.

43   Decision No. 34/1998/QD-TTg, dated 11 February 1998, of the Prime Minister Setting up Legal Professional Training School. This school was established to provide on-the-job training for certain court positions, including judges. It was also extended to include courses on lawyer skills for those wishing to join the bar as private lawyers.

44   Decision No. 762/DT, dated 29 July 1999, of the Hanoi Law University Promulgating Curriculum for the Official Training Program at the Hanoi Law University.

45   Article 2, 1992 Constitution.

46   This proposed curricula readjustment would have certain economic consequences because teachers' income will decrease if they are given less lecturing time.

47   It has been acknowledged that the Legal Needs Assessment was an unprecedented government effort to assess the needs of the legal system in general, and legal education in particular. It

showed the serious commitment of leaders to improve the country's legal system in order to facilitate economic and social development (McKinley 2002).

48   Informal interview with Ministry of Justice official and UNDP consultant.

49   Regulations on Control of International Co-operation in the Field of Administrative Reform were issued in conjunction with Decree No. 03/1999/ND-CP of the Government on 28 January 1999.

50   Decree No. 103/1998/ND-CP dated 26 December 1998 of the Government on Management of International Cooperation in the Legal Sector.

51   Decision No. 153/2003/QD-TTg dated 30 July 2003 of the Prime Minister Issuing By-Laws for Universities.

52   The Law on Promulgation of Legal Documents (Article 80) provides a number of principles to interpret legal documents with conflicting provisions. It is unclear how such principles are not applicable in this case.

53   See http://www.undp.org.vn/projects/legal/nofive/ and http://vnexpress.net/Vietnam/Xa-hoi/Giao-duc/2001/.

54   Quiz competitions have become a popular social activity in contemporary Vietnam. At Hanoi Law University, a law-teaching unit (*to*) may have a quiz competition for law students focusing on the subject taught by that unit. Such events are often jointly organised with the Youth Union (*Doan Thanh Nien*) or Students Union (*Hoi Sinh Vien*), as these organisations are in charge of social activities for students.

55   Seminar on Reforming Economic Law, Hanoi Law University: Summer 2002.

56   For further discussion on the implications of 'state economic management' and bureaucratic culture, see AusAID (2000).

REFERENCES

AusAID, 2000. *Vietnam: legal and judicial development*, AusAID, Canberra. Available online at www.ausaid.gov.au/publications/.

Communist Party of Vietnam, 2001. Education System in Vietnam, Communist Party of Vietnam, Hanoi. Available online at http://www.cpv.org.vn/nghiencuu/daihoi9/theky21/docs/3.htm.

Depei, H. and Kanter, S., 1984. 'Legal education in China', *American Journal of Comparative Law*, 32(3):543–82.

Financial Times Information 2002. 'Labour and Education: Vietnam Education Fails Because of Half-Copied Models', *Global News Wire—Asia Africa Intelligence Wire*, Financial Times Information, 11 October. Reproduced at http://www.undp.org.vn/mlist/cngd/102002/post4.htm.

Gillespie, J., 2002. 'Transplanted company law: an ideology and cultural analysis of market-entry in Vietnam', *International and Comparative Law Quarterly*, 51(3):641–72.

Gostynski, Z. and Garfield, A., 1993. 'Taking the other road: Polish legal education during the past thirty years', *Temple International and Comparative Law Journal*, 7(2):243–86.

Hanoi Law University, 2002. Report on Survey of Legal Training in Vietnam, Seminar on Legal Education, Hanoi Law University, Hanoi, 26–27 September.

Ho Chi Minh City University of Economics, 2001. Celebrating Twenty-Five Years of Education of Economic University of Ho Chi Minh City, Ho Chi Minh City University of Economics , Ho Chi Minh City. Available online at http://www.hcmueco.edu.vn/bantin/bantin73/w8.htm.

Kelly, K., 2000. 'The higher education system in Vietnam', E-World Education News and Reviews, 13(3):n.p. Available online http://www.wes.org/ewenr/00may/feature.htm.

Le Minh Tam, 1998a. 'Doi Tuong va Phuong Phap Nghien Cuu Cua Ly Luan Ve Nha Nuoc va Phap Luat [Scope and methodology for studying the themes of state and law]' in Hanoi Law University (ed.), *Giao Trinh Ly Luan Nha Nuoc Va Phap Luat* [Textbook on Themes of State and Law], Nha Xuat Ban Cong An Nhan Dan, Hanoi:5–24.

——, 1998b. 'Ban Chat, Dac Trung, Vai Tro, Cac Kieu va Hinh Thuc Phap Luat [Nature, Features, Roles, Types and Forms of Laws]' in Hanoi Law University (ed.) *Giao Trinh Ly Luan Nha Nuoc Va Phap Luat* [Textbook on Themes of State and Law], Nha Xuat Ban Cong An Nhan Dan, Hanoi:61–82.

——, 1998c. 'Cac Chuc Nang Co Ban Cua Nha Nuoc Xa Hoi Chu Nghia [Main Functions of Socialist States]' in Hanoi Law University (ed.), *Giao Trinh Ly Luan Nha Nuoc Va Phap Luat* [Textbook on Themes of State and Law], Nha Xuat Ban Cong An Nhan Dan, Hanoi:221–42.

——, 1998d. 'Cac Hinh Thuc Nha Nuoc Xa Hoi Chu Nghia [Forms of Socialist States], in Hanoi Law University (ed.), *Giao Trinh Ly Luan Nha Nuoc Va Phap Luat* [Textbook on Themes of State and Law], Nha Xuat Ban Cong An Nhan Dan, Hanoi:243–56.

——, 1998e. 'Ban Chat, Vai Tro, va He Cac Nguyen Tac Co Ban Cua Phap Luat Xa Hoi Chu Nghia [Nature, Role and Fundamental Principles of Socialist Law]', in Hanoi Law University (ed.), *Giao Trinh Ly Luan Nha Nuoc Va Phap Luat* [Textbook on Themes of State and Law], Nha Xuat Ban Cong An Nhan Dan, Hanoi:329–52.

——, 1998f. 'He Thong Phap Luat Xa Hoi Chu Nghia [The Socialist Legal System], in Hanoi Law University (ed.), *Giao Trinh Ly Luan Nha Nuoc Va Phap Luat* [Textbook on Themes of State and Law], Nha Xuat Ban Cong An Nhan Dan, Hanoi:393–414.

Macdonald, R.St.J., 1980. 'Legal education in China today', *Dalhousie Law Journal*, 6(2):313–17.

McKinley, C., 2002. 'In Vietnam, laws are made to be broken', *Dow Jones Newswire*, 29 October. Available online at http://www.usvtc.org/News/2002/.

Nguyen, P.A., 2002. 'Looking beyond Bien Che: the consideration of young Vietnamese graduates when seeking employment in the Doi Moi era', *Sojoun: journal of social issues in Southeast Asia*, 17(October):221–48.

Quinn, B., 2002. 'Legal Reform and Its Context in Vietnam', *Journal of Asian Law*, 15(2):219–93. Available online at http://www.columbia.edu/cu/asiaweb/JAL001.htm.

Sidel, M., 1993. 'Law reform in Vietnam: the complex transition from Socialism and Soviet models in legal scholarship and training', *Pacific Basin Law Journal*, 11(2):221–59.

Tay, A.E and Kamenka, E., 1986. 'Law, legal theory and legal education in the People's Republic of China', *New York Law School Journal of International and Comparative Law*, 7(1):1–38.

Tran Quang Huy, 2001a. 'Khai Niem Chung Ve Nganh Luat Dat Dai [Overview of the Land Law Branch]' in Hanoi Law University (ed.), *Giao Trinh Luat Dat Dai* [Textbook on Land Law], Nha Xuat Ban Cong An Nhan Dan, Hanoi:5–24.

——, 2001b. 'Che Do So Huu Toan Dan Doi Voi Dat Dai [The Regime of People's Ownership with Respect to Land], in Hanoi Law University (ed.), *Giao Trinh Luat Dat Dai* [Textbook on Land Law], Nha Xuat Ban Cong An Nhan Dan, Hanoi:47–76.

——, 2001c. 'Che Do Quan Ly Nha Nuoc Doi Voi Dat Dai [The Regime of State Management with Respect to Land]' in Hanoi Law University (ed.), *Giao Trinh Luat Dat Dai* [Textbook on Land Law], Nha Xuat Ban Cong An Nhan Dan, Hanoi:77–110.

Vo Dinh Toan, 2002. 'Nhung Van De Ly Luan [Major Theoretical Issues about Vietnamese Banking Law]', in Hanoi Law University (ed.), *Giao Trinh Luat Ngan Hang* [Textbook on Banking Law], Nha Xuat Ban Cong An Nhan Dan, Hanoi:5–24.

Zamboni, M., 2001. '"Rechtsstaat": just what is being exported by Swedish development organisations?', *Law, Social Justice & Global Development Journal*, 2001(2):n.p. Available online at <http://elj.warwick.ac.uk/global/issue/2001-2/zamboni.html>.

8

Vietnamese jurisprudence: informing court reform

Pip Nicholson

In April 2002 the Communist Party of Vietnam (CPV) finalised its Resolution of the Political Bureau on Forthcoming Principal Judiciary Tasks ('Resolution 8'), a policy paper identifying priorities for Vietnamese legal reform. Subsequently, the Vietnamese Party–state issued laws to reform the courts, responding specifically to the needs identified in Resolution 8.[1] The question emerging from this policy paper and the subsequent reforms is whether, or to what extent, this latest round of court reforms reflects contemporary Vietnamese theorising on the role and function of law and the courts.

At the heart of this question hovers a larger question. In its transition from a planned economy to a socialist-oriented market economy, the Vietnamese Party–state appears relatively certain about the nature of mixed market economy it envisions and seeks. While not abandoning the role of the state, the Vietnamese Party–state seeks to enable a mixed market–public sector economy (Van Arkadie and Mallon 2003). This requires a radical reduction in the role of the state in terms of market planning, production and employment and the take-up of production and employment by the private sector (Fforde and Vylder 1996; Beresford 1997).

It is not clear that the same vision exists with regard to the shape and form of the Vietnamese legal system, which is apparently radically changing to accommodate the changing economic conditions. While the economic base changes, it is suggested that the Party–state has not yet articulated an equivalently detailed vision for the form or shape of the transitional legal system. This chapter aims to explore whether a role for the courts has been articulated and whether the reforms reflect this.

This chapter does not consider the question of whether transitional legal systems will inevitably emerge as systems committed to the Anglo-European US liberal legal

159

order. The story of Vietnamese legal reform in the context of global harmonisation debates is another tale. Instead, it focuses on the question of what, if any, role and place has been ascribed to the courts in the transitional Vietnamese state. In particular, is it that the courts will be theorised as continuing instruments of the Party–state or will they be increasingly positioned as independent of Party and/or state mechanisms?

Finally, in discussing legal reform and legal theory it is important to note that they are not causally connected; that is, legal theory does not necessarily inform legal reform or vice versa. Instead, it is perhaps better to understand the exchange between legal theory and legal reform as a dialogue. Further, legal reform may anticipate change and document past changes. By analogy, Vietnamese constitutional reform is thought often to reflect underlying changes already given effect and to foreshadow changes not yet implemented (Vu Dinh Hoe 1995).

RESOLUTION 8

Resolution 8 of the Central Executive Committee of the Communist Party of Vietnam released on 2 January 2002 needs to be understood, not as the blueprint for law reform, but as the first step in the process of developing a blueprint for law reforms across Vietnamese legal institutions.[2] Resolution 8 provides insight into the direction of legal reform and how challenges are to be addressed. It should, however, be read as a work in progress rather than firmly establishing the trajectory of law reforms.

Further, it is very important to clarify terminology. Resolution 8 reflects upon and prescribes changes for '*cong tac tu phap*', usually translated as 'judicial work'. In the Vietnamese context a reference to 'judicial work' is a reference not only to the work of judges and court staff, but also to the work of all organs that feed into the courts. Therefore, for example, the work of the procuracy (*kiem sat*), police (*cong an*) and investigators (*canh sat*) all falls within the Vietnamese term 'judicial work'. It could perhaps be better translated as 'justice work', but that is not the term ordinarily used. To avoid confusion, where the term '*cong tac tu phap*' is used, it will be translated as 'court-related work'. This distinction is adopted to identify when a reform targets the courts and when it is pitched more generally to court-related bodies.[3]

Resolution 8 commences with a sustained critique of court-related work.[4] It argues that court-related institutions have historically failed the community by making 'unfair judgments' (particularly of innocent people), failing to convict criminals, and generally reducing the trust of the people in courts and the Party. Further, it is implicit that the courts have also, at least partly, failed the Party, where they fail to implement the Party line. Following this frank general condemnation of the courts and court-related institutions, the Resolution proceeds to make five particular criticisms of the Vietnamese legal system. Briefly, these criticisms are that

- there are insufficient judges. Further, the judiciary is morally weak, lacks courage and is technically poorly trained

- there remains a lack of uniformity in the organisation and perceptions of the function and responsibilities within court-related agencies and institutions are unclear (although this has somewhat improved recently)
- the working conditions (including salaries) within court-related agencies and institutions are very poor. In particular, District Court judges have poor working conditions[5]
- the laws relating to the court-related agencies and institutions are fragmented, inconsistent and incomplete and need to be reworked. Further, dissemination and education concerning relevant laws needs to be improved
- The government and the Party remain insufficiently involved in the theoretical research and practical performance of the court-related agencies and institutions.

Following this robust self-criticism by the Party–state of its court-related agencies and institutions, including the court system, the policy paper establishes a 'Directions' (*quan diem chi dao*) section, providing a framework or paradigm within which more detailed reforms are to be made.

The first comment made in Part A of the 'Directions' section of Resolution 8 explains that it is the role of the courts (and other agencies) to follow and implement Party policy. In particular, the court-related agencies must give effect to political tasks in the relevant period (*cac nhiem vu chinh tri trong tung giai*) and ensure the power of the state is united (*bao dam quyen luc nha nuoc la thong nhat doan*). In addition to being charged to give effect to the Party line, all court-related institutions are required to implement legislative, executive and judicial instructions. This section concludes by reminding the reader that Vietnam is a socialist law-based state of the people, from the people and for the people (*nha nuoc phap quyen xa hoi chu nghia cua nhan dan, do nhan dan va vi nhan dan*). Subsequently, this section calls for society to participate in court-related work. This appears to be an implicit restatement of a commitment to popular justice: a concept to which the Party officially committed in the mid 1950s when it embraced Soviet-style reforms to the existing 'bourgeois' legal system (Nicholson 2000).

The remainder of the 'Directions' section is less preoccupied with the broader role of court-related institutions and focuses on aspects of courts that need to be developed. For example, courts are to settle cases in a timely fashion, especially where serious criminal matters or offences against the state are involved, and there is a call for modernised, 'transparent', stable and 'strong' legal institutions.

Having set the framework for reform of court-related institutions, Resolution 8 proceeds to set out the mission or operational plan for these bodies (*nhiem vu trong tam*). This is the longest section of the policy, comprising eight parts, each of which proposes a specific reform. The proposed reforms reflect the critique of court-related agencies made at the outset of Resolution 8 and the general tenor of reforms set out in the 'Directions' section.

The eight reforms to court-related work set out in Resolution 8, Part B, are[6]
- to enhance the quality and increase the responsibilities of those charged with implementing court-related work
- to give effect to Party policy on the reform (*cu the hoa*), organisation and renovation (*doi moi*) of court-related work
- to develop a transparent (*trong sach*), strong and stable (*vung manh*) court-related system
- to invest in the facilities necessary to enable completion of assigned tasks
- to enhance the ability of political organisations to oversee court-related work
- to increase the explanation of, instruction in, propaganda about, dissemination of, education in, and research about, law
- to strengthen international cooperation concerning court-related work
- to strengthen the leadership of the Party over court-related work.

Having set out the general parameters of Resolution 8, this chapter now identifies the extent to which each of the reforms affects the Vietnamese court system.

Enhancing quality and responsibility for court-related work

Section B(1)(C) of Resolution 8 charges the courts to guarantee citizens equal treatment before the law (*deu binh dang truoc phap luat*), real democracy (*thuc su dan chu*)[7] and objective treatment (*khac quan*) (Resolution 8, section B(1)(C)). Further, it notes that judges and people's assessors must be independent and need only obey the law (Resolution 8, section B(1)(C)). Following this statement of the role and function of the courts, court personnel are instructed to determine cases on their merits in a timely manner after testing the evidence (Resolution 8, section B(1)(C)). To this end, the courts are instructed to enable the full participation of lawyers before trial, during collection of the evidence, and during hearings (Resolution 8, section B(1)(Dz)). Further, courts are instructed to cooperate with other agencies to enhance the enforcement of judgments (Resolution 8, section B(1)(E)).

Section B(1)(dz) of Resolution 8, addressing the hearing and determination of cases, is a request to court-related agencies to 'reconsider' the death penalty. In particular, the institutions are asked to investigate the possibility of restricting its use (Resolution 8, section B(1)(Dz)).

Party policy on the reform, organisation and renovation of court-related work

Section B(2) addresses concerns relating to the implementation of prior Party resolutions on court-related reform by targeting specific courts. In particular, the District Courts (Vietnam's lowest courts) are to be strengthened, an investigation into whether it is appropriate to expand the jurisdiction of the Administrative Court is proposed, and the possibility of establishing a family court is mooted (Resolution 8, section B(2)(C)).

Further, many reforms are directed at the Supreme People's Court, Vietnam's highest court. In particular, the Supreme People's Court is to manage the organisation of local courts and to supervise the professional development and the provision of guidelines to lower courts. Further, it is empowered to comment on the duties of court staff. The president is to appoint judges to the Supreme People's Court. By implication, the Supreme People's Court is to be given the power to appoint all judges of lower courts (Resolution 8, section B(2)(C)). This package of reforms suggests the repositioning of the courts to be less influenced and managed by the Ministry of Justice and president. Before the reforms giving effect to Resolution 8 were introduced, the Ministry of Justice determined the budget for the courts and the number of judges, and was at least partly responsible for judicial training.[8] I have argued elsewhere that, when read together, the subsequent reforms implemented to give effect to Resolution 8 indicate a 'self-managing' court system (Nicholson and Nguyen Hung Quang, 2005).

Developing a transparent, strong and stable legal system

The third reform objective, set out in section B(3), calls for the development of 'transparent, strong and stable judicial personnel'. Also, all court-related agencies are called upon to increase the educational qualifications and political, moral and professional standards of their staff (Resolution 8, section B(2)(C)). This section particularly seeks the promotion of candidates with appropriate political and moral fibre and seeks more transparent, timely and democratic appointment procedures (Resolution 8, section B(2)(C)).

This same section makes clear that the position of people's assessors (*hoi tham nhan dan*) or jurors should be investigated. In particular, Resolution 8 seeks review of the selection, role in court, training and management of jurors (Resolution 8, section B(2)(C)). In effect, jurors' function is not to be taken for granted and is to be reappraised.

As a result of the generic nature of this document, in that it targets all court-related institutions and personnel, it is hard at times to be sure that the reforms apply to courts. Section B(3) is particularly ambiguous because courts are never specifically identified in association with any of the posited reforms. For example, it is not clear whether the proposal for the rotation of staff applies to courts, nor is it clear that the call for the annual review of the work performance of court-related personnel applies to judges.

Enhancing infrastructure

Likewise, there is no particular mention of judges or courts in section B(4), which advocates the improvement of facilities and wages for court-related personnel (Resolution 8, section B(2)(C)). It appears implicit that the general call for the completion of building works and the reappraisal of salaries and allowances applies to judges as much as other agencies such as the police but, again, they are not specifically mentioned.

Enhance participation in and oversight of court-related work

Section 5 of Resolution 8 commences with a statement of the need to attract community support for reform. It then urges the National Assembly and local People's Councils to oversee the work of courts. In particular, the National Assembly and local People's Councils are to monitor the decision-making and enforcement of judgments and to supervise the development of normative legal documents by court-related agencies (Resolution 8, section B(2)(C)). It is not made clear to what extent these bodies would oversee the development of case notes and jurisprudence affecting courts (Luu Tien Dung 2003).[9]

In addition, section B(5) recommends development of the existing alternative dispute resolution mechanisms. In particular, it advocates that mediation and arbitration be adopted in the hope that fostering these alternatives will reduce the burden on courts and promote the prompt resolution of disputes.

Increase the explanation of, instruction in, propaganda about, dissemination of, education in and research about law

Section B(6) identifies the need to reform the laws on procedure and enforcement of judgments, recommending research, explanation and education relevant to court-related services. The Party urges an increase in the number of mobile hearings to maximise the flow of information concerning courts (Resolution 8, section B(6)). There is little else in this section that directly touches on the role of courts. However, it is again implicit that the courts would be caught by a general policy preference for greater legal propaganda and that they would be expected to contribute to this.

Strengthen international cooperation

The penultimate section B(7) of the policy paper seeks the strengthening of international cooperation by all court-related bodies, and various issues are identified for additional research. Of particular interest is the Party's request for comparative research that considers the question of the sovereignty and security of Vietnam and, by implication, its court system. The Resolution also advocates comparative research on training and crime prevention.

Strengthen the leadership of the Party

The final section of the operational plan (section B(8)) restates that the Party 'shall lead' (*lanh dao*) all court-related agencies. In particular, three main areas are identified for Party leadership: politics, organisation and personnel. The posited aim in this regard is to ensure compliance with the Party's policies and state laws. It is also noted that Party membership should be increased and that courts should 'use the correct employees'. It appears that the Party is here urging the maximum use of Party members in court-related agencies, including courts.

Reading the reforms together

It is hard to know whether any significance should be attached to the order of these reforms. They appear to move from the legally-specific to the contextual. I do not think they should be read as indicating a lesser role for Party leadership simply because comments about this ongoing feature of Vietnamese court culture appear at the end. Rather, this may fall at the end of the section on reforms as it is merely a restatement of the points made in the prior 'Directions' section of the Policy Paper.

Implementation

Part III of Resolution 8 provides an implementation plan. In broad terms, this seeks to centralise the implementation of this Resolution and to enable various stakeholders to contribute. In particular, the leadership of Communist Party committees in each of the Supreme People's Procuracy, Supreme People's Court, Ministry of Justice, Police, Military and Commission on Internal Affairs of the CPV are called upon to assist.

The policy summarised

In summary, Resolution 8 reiterates the leading role of the Party in court-related work. This is stressed both at the beginning of the policy paper and at its conclusion. Yet within this overarching statement, it is also said that citizens should be treated equally by courts and judges and that people's assessors are to be independent and subject only to law. The Resolution also requires the National Assembly and People's Councils to oversee the work of court-related agencies. In this way, the policy seeks to balance the role of the Party, the state and its laws, and the public or society.

Moving from the general to the particular, the policy paper canvasses various specific reforms. It requires that the lowest and highest courts within the Vietnamese court hierarchy, the District and Supreme People's Court respectively, be strengthened. It urges legal institutions to circulate information about their work more widely and, in particular, to make greater use of mobile courts. It also calls for the greater use of mediation and arbitration to resolve disputes.

In terms of personnel, Resolution 8 calls for the appointment of better-educated staff with good ethical and political credentials. By implication, these appointees are also to be Party members or, at the very least, endorsed by the Party. The policy paper also seeks greater transparency in the appointments process and an increased role for the Supreme People's Court in court appointments and management. Following the Resolution, the president is only to appoint judges to the Supreme People's Court, with the Chief Justice of the Supreme People's Court now appointing all other judges, albeit with local agencies playing a large consultative role. Salaries and working conditions are also to be enhanced.

Finally, the Resolution seeks investigation of
* the role of the people's assessors
* the possibility of a family court

- the possibility of expanding the jurisdiction of the Administrative Court
- the possibility of limiting the death penalty
- comparative research on the role and place of courts in terms of state sovereignty.

INTERPRETING RESOLUTION 8

As noted above, not all reforms outlined in Resolution 8 necessarily target the courts.[10] Therefore, to assist with interpreting Resolution 8 in this context, it is necessary to see where those reforms targetting courts have been implemented in the subsequent legislative package introducing court reforms.[11] A brief consideration of the key features of the legislation affecting courts is set out below to give some insight into how the Party–state has interpreted its own policy recommendations.

The core features of legislation affecting people's courts introduced in the 2002 Law on the Organisation of People's Courts are that

- judges must have a Bachelor of Laws Degree, have attended adjudication training, and have had legal experience (Article 37).
- with the exception of the Chief Justice and judges of the Supreme People's Court, all appointments, removals and dismissals of judges to provincial and district courts will be made by the Chief Justice of the Supreme People's Court on the advice of especially constituted Judicial Selection Councils. Appointment, removal and dismissal of Chief Justices and Deputy-Chief Justices of provincial and district courts will be by the Chief Justice of the Supreme People's Court, acting on the advice of the relevant People's Council (Articles 25 and 40).
- there will no longer be a Supreme People's Court Justice Committee (Article 24).
- people's assessors will be elected by local People's Councils on the recommendation of the relevant Fatherland Front organisation (Article 41).
- people's assessors can be dismissed by the Chief Justice of the court to which they have been elected with the agreement of the relevant Fatherland Front committee (Article 41).
- the Standing Committee of the National Assembly will determine court budgets acting on the advice of the Chief Justice of the Supreme People's Court (Article 44).
- the number of judges and people's assessors will be determined by the Standing Committee of the National Assembly on the advice of the Chief Justice (Article 42(1)).
- the Supreme People's Court, in conjunction with local people's councils, will be responsible for the management of local People's Courts (Article 17).
- the need to develop information technology to help the courts do their work is explicitly recognised (Article 46).

The specific recommendations made in Resolution 8 have been taken up by the 2002 Law on the Organisation of People's Courts.[12] While the list of amendments looks very impressive, I have argued elsewhere that in some respects the changes are more apparent than real.[13] For example, the Chief Justice's new powers to appoint judges to lower courts do not decrease the Party's grip on judicial appointments (Nicholson and Nguyen Hung Quang, 2005). In particular, candidates for judgeships still have to produce a letter in support from the Chief Judge and the Head of Organisation and Personnel of the Provincial People's Court of the province to which they apply.[14] If they apply to a district court, support for the appointment needs to be supplied by the relevant Provincial People's Court. Further, candidates need to demonstrate that they have a political theory diploma.[15]

This, however, is not a story of court reform but a story of the intersections and conflicts between the role and place ascribed to law and the role of the courts in transitional Vietnam. It is therefore not necessary here to examine in detail the features of the recently legislated reforms (Nicholson 2003). The question remaining for this part of the chapter is to characterise the nature of the court's role as it is set out in Resolution 8 and then see to what extent this diverges from, or is reflective of, the role ascribed to law in contemporary Vietnam.

One of the most interesting aspects of Resolution 8 is the tension around the Party–court relationship. On the one hand, the courts are explicitly under the Party's leadership including by virtue of the fact that appointments to the courts ought to be Party members with demonstrated political credentials (Nicholson and Nguyen Hung Quang, 2005).[16] On the other hand, courts are to be independent and obey only the law. How can these apparently contradictory statements be reconciled?

If one reads this from a Western perspective imbued with notions of judicial independence, it is not possible to reconcile the policies. The courts as described are intended to enable Party policy, with the judiciary and court personnel being members of the Party. Concurrently, these political functionaries are to be officers of the court, whose role is to enforce only the law. To those schooled in the requirement that judges have no allegiance other than to the law and the fair determination of disputes before them, free from interference from any other party, body or individual, this dual loyalty required of Vietnamese judges is not tenable.

This raises the question 'what is "law" in Vietnam?' In socialist states, law is traditionally seen instrumentally—it is the force that gives effect to Party policy, whether that be through a legal instrument or policy. One of the best characterisations of Vietnamese law offered by a Western researcher describes it as follows

the underlying notion of law is not so much that of an immutable order to which all should bow, but rather that of an important element of the way in which the Party line is implemented (Fforde 1986:62).

This matter is taken up in greater detail below, but for present purposes, law has to be seen as the Party line which may be (and today, more often is) enacted via legal instruments passed by those with state legislative authority.

One reconciliation of this apparent conflict is to see courts as independent of Party interference, but not of Party influence (Gillespie 2003). Put another way, courts are to be guided by Party policy and to see its implementation as one of their objectives, but Party members ought not influence particular proceedings.

Under this approach, courts can concurrently be bound by law and receive Party guidance, particularly if it is accepted that guidance from the Party assists with the interpretation of laws. Many Vietnamese laws are expressed in general terms only and their interpretation is open. The Party can then illuminate and explain how laws are to be implemented. For example, Article 37 of the Law on the Organisation of People's Courts sets out that

> Vietnamese citizens who are loyal to the Fatherland and the Constitution of the Socialist Republic of Vietnam, who have good qualities and virtue, are incorrupt and honest, determined to protect the socialist legislation, have the Bachelor of Laws Degree and have been trained in adjudicating operations, have engaged in practical work for a period of time prescribed by law, have adjudicating capability and have good health to ensure the fulfilment of assigned tasks may be selected and appointed to work as judges.[17]

In this list of attributes required of judges, there are various undefined and imprecise terms. Just to take two examples, it is not clear how 'loyalty to the Fatherland and the Constitution' is to be interpreted, nor how 'adjudicating capability' is to be construed.

Various commentators have suggested how they ought to be read. For example, in relation to 'adjudicating capability', the Chief Justice of the Hanoi People's Court has written that those who have completed a course at the Legal Professional Training School have the requisite judicial capacity. Further, he has also suggested that judicial capacity should be interpreted to mean a preference for mature or older candidates (Nguyen Van Hien 2001). We see that a senior judicial officer explains how these criteria are to be interpreted; presumably because he is empowered, as a senior judge, to speak both on behalf of the court and also on behalf of the Party. Yet this is not the final word on this point. The Party retains the right to clarify this at any time in a variety of ways—for example, by policy statement endorsing a circular between courts, or more informally through consultation with senior Party figures from the courts, the National Assembly or the Party itself.

A further tension evident in Resolution 8 surrounds the balancing of individual and collective rights. Resolution 8 exhorts the courts to treat all persons equally (Resolution 8, section B(1)(C)).On the face of it, this is a call for equal treatment by the courts of all people before it and could form the basis of an argument that individual litigants have rights equal to those of the state or the collective. This echoes the 1992 Constitution, which provides that 'all Vietnamese citizens are equal before the law' (Article 7). Concurrently the judiciary is instructed to follow Party leadership and is reminded that it is subject to the 'supervision' of local democratic institutions such as People's Committees and, in the case of the Supreme People's Court, the National Assembly. Accountability to the National Assembly is also constitutionally enshrined (Article 135, 1992 Constitution).

Again this tension needs to be contextualised. In practice, this reference to equal treatment can not be read as a statement of the individual rights of claimants or defendants, but a statement that all those before the courts ought to be judged by the same policies and laws.[18] That is, this statement cannot be read as abandoning the value placed on the collective interest in the Vietnamese context, but must be interpreted to say that those in proceedings before a court must be equally subject to the same sets of values, policies and laws. Again, what is being set out is not that courts will only be bound by law, but that courts should be consistent in their evaluation of cases which in turn requires consistency in understanding laws and the direction of Party leadership.

Resolution 8 also calls for greater community knowledge of court work. To this end, one concrete proposal is that courts should increase the number of mobile hearings (Resolution 8, section B(6)).[19] While this may increase the public scrutiny of hearings, it will not enable the public to understand how cases are decided. Although Resolution 8 calls for the formation of normative legal documents, it does not make any specific recommendation with respect to that process.

Court judgments have not to date been a great source of normative legal principles. As with many civil law systems, why it is that a particular case is determined in a particular way is not evident from the written record. Further, judgments are not publicly available. For example, in criminal cases, judgments record the names and background of the parties, the charges and whether they have been found guilty.[20] The evidentiary basis for the conviction is not recorded.[21] When explaining sentencing, the judgments include an analysis of the moral and political credentials of those being tried, explicitly linking these to the imposition of lenient or harsh penalties.[22] It is not clear from Resolution 8 how the balance between increasing the role of law and maintaining popular justice is to be achieved.[23]

Finally, Resolution 8 appears to promote the role of lawyers (both advocates and prosecutors). It instructs judges to enable lawyers to participate fully in pre-trial and trial work (Resolution 8, section B(1)(C)). How this would affect the outcome in a trial is not clear. It has been common practice in Vietnam for the procuracy to meet with the judges and determine the outcome of cases before trial. Enhancing the role of lawyers raises the possibility of the judge allowing more adversarial-style advocacy in court (ordinarily associated with the common law tradition). Further, it could indicate a shift from predetermined resolution of cases to testing the evidence before deciding the case.[24]

Promoting the work of lawyers may suggest that the state seeks to foster public trust in the emerging court system by way of empowering the advocate. Just as Mark Sidel has noted that it is too simplistic to talk of Party instrumentalism in the context of Vietnam's constitutional reforms, it may be the case that the relatively greater role accorded to lawyers in court could produce tensions (even contests) about the proper resolution of cases and enable explicit or implicit criticism of Party policy in court (Sidel 2002). Thus the court (the Party–state) may eventually negotiate the outcome of cases with lawyers (many of whom are privately employed and not Party–state functionaries).[25] This appears highly experimental in a state where the control of courts has, until recent times, been absolute.

It appears, therefore, that Resolution 8 opens up the possibility of quite radical legal change. Although it appears significant, the principle of court independence, mediated by Party leadership, is perhaps the least radical feature of this policy. The potentially more fundamental changes lie in the enhancement of the role of law and of the legal profession, including prosecutors. The Party–state may conceive that by retaining Party leadership of the institution, and particularly by reinforcing its tight control over the selection of personnel, changes to the primacy of law and the profession can be incrementally implemented. Alternatively these potentially radical changes might reflect either a new vision giving law a more central and stronger role in regulating social relations (but perhaps not state–society relations?) or simply an experimental phase exploring such possibilities.

CONTEMPORARY VIETNAMESE DEBATES ABOUT THE ROLE AND PLACE OF LAW

The question is then to what extent the changes introduced in Resolution 8 reflect a theorised understanding of law within Vietnam. This involves some exploration of the role and place of law in Vietnam generally and, more particularly, the role the courts play within any general conception of the role of law.

This part of the chapter will outline the key concepts used to describe the political and legal theories underpinning the Democratic Republic of Vietnam (1945–76) and the Socialist Republic of Vietnam (1976 to the present day). The core concepts introduced are 'democratic centralism', 'collective mastery', 'socialist legality' and 'rule-based state' (sometimes erroneously translated as rule of law). The role and place of socialist and revolutionary morality and how valuing moral precepts affects or interacts with the role and place of law is also briefly discussed. It will then be possible to revisit Resolution 8 and see how it reflects or diverges from established Vietnamese legal thinking.

The discussion is organised chronologically to reflect the emergence of Vietnamese legal theory and divided into the time periods: 1945–59, 1960–76 and 1986–2003. The period 1976–86 is not a particular focus as it can largely be viewed as a period of consolidation rather than change, with the North exporting its views and practices to the South of the country in post-unification Vietnam (Gillespie 2004).[26]

The role and place of Vietnamese law has been dynamic over time. Initially the communist state had a fairly instrumentalist view of law. Theorising was mainly political, looking at the role of 'democratic centralism' (*tap trung dan chu*) and the role of law as an administrative mechanism, coexisting with, but not binding, political leaders and policymakers. In the DRVN over the period 1960–76, socialist legality (*nguyen tac phap che xa hoi chu nghia*) gained increasing currency. In more recent times, and particularly since the 1991 Seventh Party Congress, the Party–state arguably has endorsed, while not clearly identifying the features of, a law-based state (*nha nuoc phap quyen*) and a socialist law-based state (*nha nuoc phap quyen xa hoi chu nghia*). The role of collective mastery (*lam chu tap te*) in the contemporary period is harder to isolate.

In the Vietnamese context it is not possible to talk of the state without talking about the Communist Party of Vietnam (Fall 1956; Huynh Kim Khanh 1982). The Party is at the epicentre of Vietnamese politics and remains responsible for the official enunciation and implementation of all policy changes. The Party dates back to the early 1930s, although it was officially disbanded between 1945–51 and renamed on several occasions, ultimately carrying the name the Communist Party of Vietnam (*Dang Cong San Viet Nam*) from 1976 (Weggel 1986).[27] Between the 1930s and 1976 the personnel at meetings and congresses essentially remained the same, indicating that, whatever the appellation, the core group of leaders who identified with the original Indochinese Communist Party continued at the helm until unification (Klein and Weiner 1959). Thayer has commented on the increasing trend of younger and better-educated Party members in the National Assembly, but while new figures are emerging within state institutions, continuity with the past remains (Thayer 2002).

Through its extensive *nomenklatura* system, the contemporary Communist Party of Vietnam continues to ensure that all significant office holders of the state are Party members (Gillespie 2002). For example, 90 per cent of judges are said to be Party members (Nicholson and Nguyen Hung Quang, 2005). Similarly, Thayer estimates that the current National Assembly comprises around 90 per cent Party members (Thayer 2002). It is not possible to separate the Party from the state. State functionaries are Party members, and as a consequence bear all the obligations that membership of the Party involves.[28] It is for this reason that the term Party–state is used.

Although the Party–state is the dominant political force in Vietnam, it is an organisation where various political views are expressed and debated. For example, it is widely known that Party members have preferences ranging from transition to a multi-party state to retaining strong one-Party leadership.[29]

While Vietnamese jurisprudence is closely linked to that of the old Soviet Union and arguably not isolated from that of the People's Republic of China, it is not a replica of either.[30] From 1945 to the early 1970s, Vietnam was most influenced by Soviet jurisprudence (Nicholson 2000). In more recent times, while the extent to which the Chinese and Vietnamese converse about legal theory remains unclear, it is known that exchanges occur (Sidel 1998).

Morality and law

Much has been written about the marginal role of law in Vietnam (Sidel 1997; Gillespie 2001a; Nicholson 2000). Broadly speaking the argument is that custom and morality (Confucian and Socialist)[31] played a major role in shaping Vietnamese social mores and that law existed largely as a punitive instrument of the state, rather than as the basis for social interaction. This chapter does not address the question of whether law is more relevant in contemporary Vietnam. This is a subject for another study. Yet the fundamental significance of morality is raised to protect against any misconception that the role of law has changed to such an extent that morality is no longer relevant. Without significant studies of legal consciousness this matter cannot be resolved, but studies among local Vietnamese businesses indicate that the relevance of law remains marginal (Bergling 1999; McMillan and Woodruff 1999).

Early days: war and legal instrumentalism

Between 1945 and the late 1950s, during which period the DRVN defeated the French and the country was partitioned, the role and place of law was contested.[32] Arguably, Ho Chi Minh never anticipated governing without the assistance of law.[33] He wrote of the excesses of colonial court systems (Ho Chi Minh 1961:96–102), but did not foreshadow a society without law or legal institutions (Nguyen Ngoc Minh 1985). Ho Chi Minh argued convincingly that the French were able to maintain one law for the Vietnamese and another for their own subjects (Hooker 1978). Ho's trenchant criticisms of the French administration of justice, which describe the scales of justice being permanently skewed against the local population of Vietnam, was not a critique of law in general (Ho Chi Minh 1961).[34]

Lawyers debated the uses to which the new DRVN government put law and legal institutions (Sidel 1997a). These discussions were at their most divided and outspoken during the publication and then banning of the *Nhan Van* (*Humanity*) and *Giai Pham* (*Beautiful Literary Work/Masterpiece*) periodicals. These two publications were circulated in 1956 and contained some extremely direct critiques of the uses to which law had been put by the Viet Minh leadership. For example, three categories of critique were undertaken by *Nhan Van*: freedom and democracy; legality, human rights and the strengthening of institutions; and opening up all legal thought and research (Boudarel 1990). Those that spoke out on these issues did so without circumlocution or delicacy, as demonstrated by the following passage.

> It is the absence of legislation that favours abuse of power and authoritarianism (Boudarel 1990:165–6).[35]

This extract is taken from an article dealing with the errors of the land reform campaign[36] and the 'contempt for legality' prevailing, so it was argued, in Vietnam at this time (Boudarel 1990).

The government was exhorted to put a stop to these expressions of dissent; the request that the publications be closed down was printed in the official newspaper.

> We demand that the authorities take definite measures against *Nhan Van*. The souls of the young students are still as pure as a white page inscribed with beautifully bright pictures of our regime, our future and our happiness. We want to be given healthy thoughts and are determined to oppose anything which stands in the way of our advancing steps.[37]

By 1960, the Party had closed down the publications and a series of trials ensured that the major players were incarcerated (Boudarel 1990).[38]

The organisational basis of the DRVN shortly after the revolution is perhaps best described by the term 'democratic centralism'.[39] When describing the features of the newly introduced Vietnam Workers' Party in 1951, Ho Chi Minh wrote 'As regards its organisation, it adopts the system of democratic centralism' (Ho Chi Minh 1994:127). In short, democratic centralism in Vietnam meant that all office holders and Party representatives were elected and each organisation was accountable to the higher equivalent body.[40] For example, a District People's Committee was responsible to a Provincial People's Committee and a local court was accountable to the next highest court. Ultimately most organisations were accountable to the Party via the National Assembly, Ministries or the Party committees at local and regional levels.[41] It was only through such accountability and central control (also referred to as 'iron discipline') (Ho Chi Minh 1994:127)[42] that the Party could hope to enforce its policies effectively. This approach was justified on the basis that it enabled grassroots involvement (through election) in the democratic process,[43] but also that once the 'correct' policy had been determined (one that benefited the 'masses')[44] implementation would be centrally coordinated. Failure to implement according to instruction carried with it censure (Truong Chinh 1994). In relation to the courts, this basic principle was an ideal to which the courts aspired, but implementation was problematic. As we shall see, democratic centralism has been retained as an organising principle to the present day.

The regime's supporters during the period 1945 to 1959 propounded an instrumentalist view of law without explicitly theorising about socialist legality (see below; and Sidel 1997a).[45] No separate narrative emerges from the available sources for the period that explicitly relies on socialist legality to connect law, socialism and the new nation.[46]

The perception that law was more commonly viewed instrumentally rather than theoretically (except by its detractors) rests on several commentaries on Vietnamese legal development and the nature of the debates between intellectuals and Party figures over this period. For example, Nguyen Nhu Phat, a theorist with the Institute of State and Law, writes

> The Communist Party of Vietnam is a political party which gained society's almost absolute confidence and is able to call on the support of all people. Moreover, in the first years of the people's democratic system, the distinction between the leadership of the Party and the administration of the state was out of the question because the state could not be present everywhere in the country and secret Party cells had to play the role of the state (Nguyen Nhu Phat 1997:398).

Nguyen Nhu Phat portrays Vietnamese law in the early period of the revolution as reflecting the domination of political expediency and practical considerations. In effect, the State Plan (or policies) was the law. Legal jurisprudence was relegated to a critique of practice (Nguyen Nhu Phat 1997). The *Nhan Van/Giai Pham* experience reinforces this perception. Not surprisingly, the socialist legal debates did not immediately take hold in war-torn Vietnam.

A unified DRVN: the policy–law dichotomy

There was not one view of law between the defeat of the French in 1954 and unification of the country in 1976, but the outspokenness of the *Nhan Van/Giai Pham* period did not resurface (Nicholson 2000). The publications of the Supreme People's Court explicitly condemned it.[47] Instead, this period witnessed the development of a legal studies group (*to luat hoc*) debating law. The legal studies group originally convened under the auspices of the Social Sciences Division of the State Sciences Committee, later forming the genesis of the Institute of State and Law (Sidel 1997a). According to Mark Sidel, this group, comprising scholars and non-communist intellectuals, included 'leading voices for legal reform' (Sidel 1997a:16).[48]

One of the key tensions for the emerging system of administration was the relationship between law and policy. All too often, policy was not enacted as law and yet Party–state officials were expected to implement both. Policy was at least as significant as *luat* (law) (Sidel 1997a). For example, law could be used interchangeably with policy (Le Duan 1994).[49] As a result, the importance of policy (or the State Plan, as it was also referred to) cannot be underestimated. As we saw above, Fforde aptly characterises law as 'an important element' of the Party line, but it was not authoritative at this time (Fforde 1986:62).

Nguyen Nhu Phat expresses the view, in the context of economic contracts, that the State Plan operated as law when he writes

> [i]n the old regime, planning was the main instrument used by the state to administer the national economy. That is to say that planning but not law was the main and most important factor. Planning would always prevail over law. Any conflict between the law and the planning would be resolved in 'favour' of the planning. Generally speaking the law was only a subsidiary instrument while the policy and resolutions passed by the Party, administrative commands and planning documents were the main instruments in governing economic activities (1997:398).

Yet there was debate about the application of policy that was intended to be law, but was not yet enacted. A Vietnamese lawyer writing in 1964 talked of the need to enforce laws, distinguishing them from policies.

> The policies of the Party must go through a process of explanation and elucidation so that the people will understand them clearly, support them and by their self-awareness carry them out. These policies must also pass the National Assembly, the government Council and other government organs before being enacted into law and before being backed by the authority of the government (Truong Tan Phat 1964:2).

This more legalistic approach, requiring that policy be enacted as law in order to be enforceable, is rarely so clearly stated in major public speeches.[50] More commonly, the terms 'policy' and 'law' are used interchangeably or ambiguously (Sidel 1997a).[51] For example, in this period the role of the Party was developed and entrenched via active promotion of its work and by training its members—a strengthening of the Party, as Truong Chinh (1994:605) described it when he wrote that '[i]n Party building we stress both ideological and organisational aspects'. In short, the Party aimed to raise the calibre of members through training. In 1968, all cadres were to be schooled in the 'four-good' principles. The second of the four tenets was

[g]ood at helping the people in obeying the law and in the implementation of Party and state policies (Truong Chinh 1994:606).[52]

This statement suggests that policy, after it became law, was what the people had to obey. Yet both law and policy must be 'implemented'. Truong Chinh did not address the issue of whether policy and law were interchangeable or what happened if they differed.

Le Duan (1994:452) writes that

> [f]ormerly the Party line and policies penetrated the masses and were implemented through propaganda and agitation work with regard to each person or each group. Today besides these methods which we must apply even more effectively, broadly and adequately, we must also use large-scale organised measures...This can be done only through state laws which reflect the interests and the will of the working people.

This statement, made in 1973, advocates the passage of policy into law. This approach is echoed in contemporary Vietnam. One typical call for a law-based state refers to earlier times when 'it seems that for a while we emphasised building a society by means of the "rule of morality" and thus somehow neglected the law' (Nguyen Nham 1997:3).

Despite a clearer articulation of how the emerging socialist state would be administered (democratic centralism with the Party at the epicentre of politics), the state's policy priorities were variously implemented via laws or policies or both. In effect, the debate about the role of law and policy continued, but law was not necessary to state-sanctioned decision-making (Sidel 1997a).

It is relevant here to consider how the Vietnamese courts themselves conceived their role.[53] The Chief Judge, in an article summarising the Supreme People's Court's Five-Year Plan 1961–65, commenced by referring to the Third Communist Party Congress, held in September 1960. He noted the comments made at that Congress on the relationship between Party and state 'in the transitional stage towards socialism in the North' (Pham Van Bach 1961b:1). He argued that the Party's role in the leadership of the state was paramount

> [t]o unite the entire people, bring into full play our people's ardent country-loving spirit, traditions of brave fighting and hard work, at the same time to reinforce the solidarity among the socialist countries headed by the Soviet Union, to create favourable conditions for the North to march speedily, strongly and firmly towards socialism, build a comfortable and happy life in the North and consolidate the North as a steady base for the struggle for the country's unification, thus making a contribution to strengthening the socialist camp and the defence of peace in Southeast Asia and the world (Pham Van Bach 1961b:1).

The Chief Judge reiterated the Third Party Congress' view that the People's Democratic Administration, of which the court was a part, must 'fulfil the historic task of the proletariat's dictatorship' and to that end implement socialist reformation in the areas of agriculture, industry, economic policy and cultural change (Pham Van Bach 1961b:1). Chief Judge Pham Van Bach pointed out that the 'position, role and political responsibilities of the People's Court are not separable from position, role and political and economic responsibilities of the People's Democratic State'. In turn the state's responsibilities were 'pointed out clearly in the political report of the Party Central Committee' (Pham Van Bach 1961b:2). Here the connection between

Party and court is at its most clear. The Chief Judge has drawn the connections so that no reader could doubt that the role of the courts was, ultimately, to implement state policy.

Having outlined the court's political role the Chief Judge proceeded to connect the court's work with the five-year plan (Pham Van Bach 1961b). He urged the work of the court to assist the revolution; to defend the social order (which included economic policies); to educate the masses to fight against acts violating the law, policy and disciplines of the state; and to promote the people's democratic legality. This call to arms also stipulated that the role for the courts was to implement state policies as well as state laws (Pham Van Bach 1961b).

To implement the Party's policies effectively, court officials were told

> [w]e must be fully aware of the role and effectiveness of the People's Court in contributing to the furtherance of the entire revolutionary work...apply properly the line and policy of the Party and state, always heighten the People's Court characteristic of true democracy, apply strict basic principles guiding the work of adjudication, organise trials according to the *Law on the Organisation of People's Courts* and ensure careful, correct and lawful adjudication which always enjoy sympathy and support of the people (Pham Van Bach 1961b:6).

Judges and assessors were thus instructed not only to apply state and Party policies, but also the Law on the Organisation of People's Courts when organising trials. This law set out the basic elements of a fair trial, the role of assessors and judges, and the meaning of an open court. The statement suggested that careful and correct adjudication required the judge and people's assessors to apply policies to produce lawful adjudication acceptable to the masses.

In summary, this publication explained to court officials that they had to implement state policies and rely on senior courts and training as the basis for understanding those policies. Pham Van Bach reiterated that officials must understand that their work was political and that both the Party and the community must endorse it. He sought to inspire pride in the work of the courts as institutions linked to the fortunes of the war-dominated country. The role of the Supreme People's Court was to show leadership, and in so doing, reflect the Party's policies.

Throughout the 1960s, a judicial conference was held annually to reinforce the duties and responsibilities of judges. The Supreme People's Court issued a report on the conference's conclusions. The issues raised in the Chief Judge's first Five-Year Plan for the courts, outlined above, were echoed over the years. The central political role of the courts was reiterated.[54] It was the duty of the Supreme People's Court to foster the upholding of socialist legality by lower courts.[55] However, it was pointed out that there was not always agreement among senior judges about what the law ought to say or, where it existed, how it ought to be interpreted.[56]

This exploration of the policy–law dichotomy in Vietnam is one way of unpacking what is meant by socialist legality. It demonstrates that law is not binding or immutable, but rather a support to, and manifestation of, the Party line. In particular, law does not override policy, but exists to give it effect. As an element of the Party line, law is therefore not binding on Party members who would have a better appreciation of the Party's intentions and how they should be implemented in particular settings. For example, a judge writing about how law and policy interacted explained,

> At present the people's courts only apply the new laws of the people's power. In the event of there being no legislative text they follow the principle of analogy or simply the general political line of the revolution (Le Kim Que 1974:99).

In a similar vein, Gillespie explains that socialist legality characterises policy as the 'soul and spirit (*linh hon*) of the law' (Gillespie 2004:150). Further, Gillespie argues that socialist legality conflated legalism and 'state discipline (*ky luat nha nuoc*)' with the result that 'violations of the law were considered revolutionary betrayals' (Gillespie 2004:150).

From 1959 to 1976, a subtle change emerged. In effect, socialist conceptions of law were introduced and promoted. In particular, the Supreme People's Court articulated a clear commitment to socialism and socialist legality, which saw law as a vehicle for Party–state policies, inferior to the Party line where conflicts occurred. The press and the leadership criticised capitalist legal systems for working only to the advantage of the bourgeois classes.[57] In Vietnam a socialist legal system was endorsed where law was neither independent of, nor binding on, the Party–state.

Legal theory in the contemporary period

Thus far we have seen the Party–state construct theories concerning the interaction of the Party and its laws and legal institutions (socialist legality) and the mechanism by which all organisations are to be held accountable to, and led by, central Party institutions (democratic centralism). What remains unexplored is theory indicating the Party's relationship with the people.[58]

Through the revolutionary period the Party–state positioned itself as giving effect to the 'mass' line.[59] Its leadership was 'of the people, from the people and for the people' (*nha nuoc phap quyen xa hoi chu nghia cua nhan dan, do nhan dan va vi nhan dan*). This principle of Party leadership giving effect to the will of the people is captured in the two DRVN constitutions of 1945 and 1959 and their two SRVN successors of 1980 and 1992.[60] However, the principle of 'collective mastery' (*lam chu tap the*) was not articulated as a concept until the 'euphoria surrounding reunification in 1975'.[61] Gillespie argues that at this time the state explicitly acknowledged the 'mastery' of the working peoples, and posited the interests of the state and individual as one—the political leadership existing to reflect and enable the worker–peasant alliance.[62]

As Gillespie notes, the classless society envisioned by Vietnamese collective mastery is predicated upon social harmony and group effort. In presenting it this way, the doctrine removes private 'space' for talk and debate outside the state-sanctioned domains of collectives and state bureaucracies. Further, Gillespie notes that the doctrine was 'hostile to private legal rights' (Gillespie, Chapter 3). How the doctrine accommodates the transition from socialist legality to law-based state (set out below) remains unclear.

In 1991, the Seventh Party Congress of the Communist Party of Vietnam adopted *'nha nuoc phap quyen'*, variously translated as 'state-legal-rights' or 'law-based state'. As Gillespie points out, this is a Vietnamese adoption of the Russian concept *'pravovoe gosudarstvo'*, in turn reflecting the German principle of *'Rechtsstaat'* (Gillespie, Chapter 3). In each case, the principle has the 'state posited as the highest, if not the only source of law' (Gillespie, Chapter 3). In the Vietnamese context, *nha nuoc phap quyen* means that the state will not only be the source of law but also be bound by law. This was the basis of the very fundamental constitutional changes made in 1992, which saw the introduction of an amended Article 4 to include a statement requiring Party members to be bound by the law.[63]

The introduction of 'law-based state' as a conceptual basis for the place and role of law in contemporary Vietnam has not replaced socialist legality as the current orthodoxy. Instead, the two concepts of law coexist and fuse to produce 'socialist law-based state' (*nha nuoc phap quyen xa hoi chu nghia*) (Gillespie 2004:152). Two issues emerge. What is meant by the state in this context? Further, to what does the term 'law-based' refer?

As we have seen, it was not possible to conceive of the Vietnamese state without admitting the leadership of the Party, which remains the situation today. For example, the most recent round of constitutional amendments did not change the leadership role ascribed to the Party in 1992.[64] Resolution 8 also restates the Party's leadership role.

The extent and limits of the term 'law-based' are less clear. One view is that the Vietnamese Party–state has repositioned law as the 'highest', if not ultimately the sole source of, binding instrument. This view is supported by the fact that the Party, through the Constitution, is said to be bound by law.[65] More particularly, it envisions law ultimately becoming superior to policy.[66] Yet as a matter of practice law remains subordinate to Party policy, particularly given the reliance on policy to interpret law.

Socialist legality and law-based state compared

Table 8.1 summarises, albeit briefly, the similarities and differences between socialist legality and the law-based state at a broad conceptual level. In an attempt not to confine the comparison to Western liberal notions of law, a range of indicators have been listed to tease out what each of the concepts reflects. This categorisation generalises change across jurisdictions, institutions, localities and experiences. It is therefore vulnerable to critique as it might misrepresent changes in particular sites.

This analysis demonstrates that, whereas socialist legality sees law and legal institutions existing to give effect to a socialist conception of a Party-led state, the law-based state (or at least its socialist variant) envisages a shift from an instrumental role for law (and courts) to a situation where law exists to regulate social relations and where legal institutions are increasingly self-managed, although within the auspices of Party leadership. The law-based state does not posit state institutions as autonomous of Party influence, rather it reconfigures Party influence. The Party remains the dominant influence, mediated by an ancillary set of duties to the law. Yet, as we shall see, this remains more fluent in the abstract than it does in practice.

RESOLUTION 8 AND LEGAL THEORY

Returning to Resolution 8, we see that the reforms affecting courts can be summarised as follows
- increasing the role of the Supreme People's Court in the management of lower courts
- giving the Supreme People's Court power to appoint judges
- increasing the technical competency of judges
- increasing the public's knowledge of the work of courts
- increasing the role of lawyers/prosecution in court advocacy
- investigating the role and function of the administrative court, family court, people's assessors, as well as of the death penalty, state sovereignty, legal practice and international cooperation.

The central tenet of Vietnamese jurisprudence (or political-legal theory) has moved from socialist legality to the emerging conception of the law-based state. The core feature of the law-based state is its attempt to characterise the law as a phenomenon that binds the state. The law, however, is always subject to interpretation and thus what is drawn upon to determine its meaning might be law or policy that has not yet been, or may never be, enacted.

In Vietnam, the notion of a law-based state does not sit alone, but is accompanied by other legal doctrines, in particular, collective mastery and democratic centralism, each of which, while dynamic, also affords continuity with Vietnam's legal history. Yet neither of these doctrines has been fundamentally revisited or rejected since the reconceptualising of the state as 'law-based'.

COMMENT IN CLOSING

Resolution 8 appears largely to give practical effect to recent Vietnamese theorising. Its most significant changes potentially enable the courts to manage their own staff, professional development and guidelines (Nicholson 2003). In other words, as a legal institution, the courts are uncoupled from the executive arm of the state and given autonomy to implement Party direction. This is evident in the Supreme People's Court's greater control over budgets and staff selection and the project of developing a trained, technically competent judiciary.

As noted in both Resolution 8 and the shift to law-based state, the Vietnamese leadership does not countenance a diminishing role for the Party. The Party retains a very tight grip on who will be appointed by the Supreme People's Court to lower courts (Nicholson and Nguyen Hung Quang, 2005). The requirements ensure that local and central branches of the Party vet all judicial candidates. Further, every

Table 8.1

Feature	Socialist legality	Law-based state or socialist law-based state
Policy–law dichotomy	Law supports and where possible gives effect to Party policy. Law does not override policy (DRVN Constitutions of 1959, 1980), but is a means by which the Party line can be instituted (Fforde 1986:63).	All state organs and the Party are to be bound by law (Article 4, SRVN Constitution 1992). Policy remains central as a guide to the interpretation of law. What is left unclear is whether, in cases of conflict, law would override policy.[a]
Role of morality	Socialist legality is a valid mechanism to give effect to Party policy because it reflects appropriate sentiment, specifically revolutionary or socialist morality (Gillespie 2004). That is, the correct revolutionary mores/morality infuse the law and assist with its interpretation. Characterised in this way Vietnamese law is a moral force.	Vietnamese commentators note that Vietnamese culture has a long tradition of valuing moral precepts over legal ones (Giebel 2001; Sidel 1997; Nicholson 2000; Gillespie 2004). Where does this leave law? In theory, law regulates and morality is relevant to the extent that it is used as a lens through which to interpret and apply laws. In reality, the legitimacy of law rests on its connection to the wider moral framework. It is perhaps for this reason that we witness the neo-traditionalism of a classic good governance paradigm being reappropriated in Vietnam today so as to enable the conflation of nationalism, moralism and legalism.[b]
Democratic centralism	A concept that accompanies socialist political thought and socialist legality requiring that all representative functionaries be elected and accountable to the next highest equivalent authority.	In theory, retained as a political doctrine to deliver accountability and consistency to Vietnamese laws and institutions and enabling Party leadership of the socialist law-based state.
Role of state institutions: courts	The Party leads, the state administers or manages and the people represent. In this formulation the courts exist to give effect to Party leadership whether the relevant doctrine is in policy or law. There is no separation of powers. The courts are instruments of the Party–state.	The Party leads, the state administers and the people represent is retained as an operational plan. However, the administrative function is linked explicitly to the legal function and ideally policy is not implemented until it is law, except to the extent that it is drawn upon to explain and interpret law. While there is no separation of powers, there is to be greater separation of functions among the

		management organs of the state. The courts are an increasingly self-managed institution while continuing under the leadership of the Party-state and implementing the law. Due process is characterised as a significant feature of the newly emerging law-based state (Gillespie 2004).
Role of the Party—implicit in many of the categories above	The Party is the sole force leading the country and legal institutions exist to give effect to its political leadership of the people, for the people and by the people. The Party exists effectively to represent the masses.c	The Party retains its leading role in political affairs, but the administrative arm of the state is to have more autonomy to implement Party leadership.
Collective rights	Best captured in the doctrine of collective mastery. Collective mastery does not strain socialist legality. It preserves the dominance of the Party–state over the individual, by doctrinally positioning the Party–state as working on behalf of the worker-peasant alliance.	It is unclear how collective mastery and socialist law-based state can be reconciled. However, collective rights retain their prominent place in socialist-law based state by virtue of the continued leadership of the Party to give effect to the collective will.d
Individual rights	Individual rights will always be subservient to the collective interest (Constitution 1992).66	Individual rights remain secondary to the collective interest (Constitution 1992). However, it is officially recognised that individuals have rights to trade and profit not previously held and that the collective interest must be exercised in a more transparent manner.

Notes: aFor example, in 2003, a Ho Chi Minh City prosecutor refused to be bound by principles enunciated in Resolution 8 as it had no legal force until it was implemented by way of the relevant procedure law. Unknown Author 2003, located on www.vnexpress.net [accessed 5 June 2003].b Giebel (2001:91-5) writes persuasively of the repositioning of good governance within contemporary Vietnam through a reclaiming of earlier 'proper rule' theories propounded by Nguyen Trai (1380 – 1442). c As Gillespie explains this predicates the authority of the Party on class-theory: the Party exists to lead on behalf of the worker peasant alliance. Ibid.d Constitution of 1992. Sidel (2002:42–89) argues that the conception of the contemporary Vietnamese constitution as instrumentalist no longer holds, if it ever did.

appointment is revisited every five years. Without security of tenure it is very unlikely that judges will ignore Party direction generally or in particular cases.

The areas that Resolution 8 nominates for further investigation indicate that the Party–state either does not have a comprehensive blueprint for legal change or wishes to see legal changes introduced incrementally.[67] In particular, it is currently too difficult to reformulate the role of people's assessors and the Administrative Court in a state where the mass line and Party leadership have not been abandoned. In other words, the Party leadership is not prepared to remove lay representatives from trials (although they have disappeared from the Supreme People's Court) and radically expand the review of administrative decisions. Each of these reforms could potentially see the Party's leadership diminished.

By avoiding reforms to the system of people's assessors and administrative review, the leadership of the Party and its claims of representing the 'masses' via democratic centralism and collective mastery are left largely intact. This arguably reflects their connection with the socialist/collective and popular notions of justice. For example, the socialist state, having introduced people's assessors to democratise and popularise the law and the courts, may find it difficult to remove them. Therefore potential people's assessors reforms (such as better training or even abolition) have not yet been implemented despite criticism of the lack of technical competence by lawyers. Instead, their role is to be 'investigated'. In a similar vein, widening the scope of administrative review could threaten the leadership of the Party as it could enable challenges to the Party–bureaucracy's discretionary decision-making. Again, rather than challenge the leadership of the Party by expanding review of administrative action, it is left for future debate.

While the notion of law-based state is not entirely consistent with either democratic centralism or collective mastery, precisely because it envisages the Party–state being bound by law and not able to respond as directly as now to pressures and policies from the Party and state, this conflict has not been taken up by Resolution 8. Yet again, Resolution 8 appears consistent with Vietnamese theoretical understandings of law where this tension is not widely debated.

Finally, as we have seen, Resolution 8 specifically promotes the role of the lawyer in the emerging law-based state. The socialist law-based state implicitly requires a repositioning of lawyers as it is consistent with a move from political discretion to law-based decision-making. It appears on the face of it, however, that an active private legal profession could challenge the Party–state's hold on the synergies between Vietnamese legal theory and policy review. An activist group of lawyers could potentially push for legalisation of institutions and practices in Vietnam, which could fracture the delicate balance between socialist conceptions of law and justice and institutional renovation currently in place. Only time will tell whether the nascent Vietnamese legal profession will act as a catalyst for more dramatic legal change or whether they will work closely with the Party–state to reshape Vietnam's legal system further. The policy should be read as an ideological endorsement of incremental and cautious change.

This chapter commenced by asking whether the latest Party policy statement on 'judicial reform' reflected contemporary Vietnamese legal theory. As we have seen, in the main it does. The orientation of Resolution 8 accords with the emerging doctrine of a law-based state. More particularly, we have seen that the policy direction for courts—that they be self-managed, bound by law and also implementing law— echoes the notion of a Vietnamese state based on law. At the same time, both the policy paper and the doctrine of 'law-based state' assume the continuing supremacy and leadership of the Communist Party of Vietnam. In conclusion, Resolution 8 appears largely consistent with Vietnamese jurisprudence. It reflects Vietnam's adoption of the socialist law-based state while containing the same ambiguities evident in legal theory about the role and place of the masses and Party-state leadership.

This chapter also raised a larger question at the outset; namely, the extent to which Vietnam has conceived of the role and place of law in post-*doi moi* Vietnam. While it is harder to answer this question solely on the basis of an analysis of one, albeit major, recent policy, it appears that the Party–state has adopted cautious incrementalism and experimentalism in its reshaping of law and legal institutions. Vietnamese pragmatism is once again evident.

ACKNOWLEDGMENT

The author gratefully acknowledges translation assistance by Nguyen Thi Ngoc Quynh, Masters Student in Applied Linguistics at the University of Melbourne in 2003.

NOTES

[1] Law on Organisation of People's Courts, 2 April 2002 and Ordinance on Judges and Jurors of People's Courts, 11 October 2002. See also Inter-circular No. 05/TTLN of the Ministry of Justice and SPC, dated 15 October 1993, Providing Guidelines on Ordinance on People's Judges and Jurors 1993 and Resolution 131/2002/NQ- UBTVQH11 On Judges, People's Assessors and Prosecutors, dated 3 November 2002.

[2] Comment made by conference participant Nguyen Chi Dung, at the Law and Governance: Socialist Transforming Vietnam conference, Melbourne, 13 June 2003.

[3] This chapter will not follow the reforms affecting other court-related agencies such as the police or the procuracy.

[4] The settlement of CPV policy would have involved circulation of drafts of the policy to relevant organs, including the heads of Party cells in law-related institutions. Once the document was settled, it would have been circulated to all relevant agencies and the membership of Party cells within these. This policy can also be purchased from the Party publisher and bookstalls.

[5] Not only are the working conditions poor (for example, offices are too small) but the facilities are old.

[6] As set out earlier, this chapter looks only at the policy's effect on court work, and not at its implications for other legal institutions such as the police, the investigators or the procuracy.

[7] Real democracy is the literal translation of *thuc su dan chu*. In the Vietnamese context it connotes equal rights for individuals.

[8] For a general discussion of the Vietnamese court system in the 1990s, see Quinn (2002) and Nicholson (2001).

[9] Dung reminds us that Article 6 of the 1992 Socialist Republic of Vietnam (SRVN) Constitution gives the National Assembly and its Standing Committee supremacy. Further, Dung (2003)

argues that this entails a reporting function to the National Assembly and the relevant People's Council.

[10] See Directive No 10/2002/CT on the implementation of the Political Bureau's Resolution No. 8 for a general implementation plan.

[11] Law on Organization of People's Courts, 2 April 2002; and Ordinance on Judges and Jurors of People's Courts, 11 October 2002. See also Inter-circular No. 05/TTLN of Ministry of Justice and SPC, dated 15 October 1993, Providing Guidelines on Ordinance on People's Judges and Jurors 1993; and Resolution 131/2002/NQ- UBTVQH11 On Judges, People's Assessors and Prosecutors, dated 3 November 2002.

[12] See also Ordinance on Judges and Jurors of People's Courts, 11 October 2002; Inter-circular No. 05/TTLN of Ministry of Justice and SPC, dated 15 October 1993, Providing Guidelines on Ordinance on People's Judges and Jurors 1993; and Resolution 131/2002/NQ- UBTVQH11 On Judges, People's Assessors and Prosecutors, dated 3 November 2002.

[13] In particular, implementing legislation has waived the requirement that judges have a Bachelor of Laws Degree.

[14] Circular No. 01/2003/TTLT/TANDTC-BOP-BMV/UBTWMTTQVN Guiding the Implementation of a Number of Provisions of the Ordinance on Judges and Jurors of the Supreme People's Court, The Ministry of Defence, The Ministry of Justice, The Ministry of the Interior and The Vietnam Fatherland Front Central Committee, dated 1 April 2003 ('Circular 01'), Chapter III, Article 2, Step 3.

[15] Step 4, Article 2, Chapter III, Circular 01.

[16] This position is clear in the legislation passed to give effect to this policy. In particular, judges seeking appointment need a letter of support from the Party Cell of the court to which they seek appointment and a Political Knowledge Certificate from the Central Political Training Institution.

[17] Translation from *Cong Bao*, the Official Gazette, No. 25, of 5 June 2002.

[18] Many parties bemoan the lack of equal treatment. For example, it has been explained to the author by a Ministry of Justice official that the great challenge to the enforcement of foreign arbitral awards in Vietnam is usually they are to be enforced against state-owned enterprises. Thus, courts charged with establishing the 'legality' of foreign awards do not treat the interests of the parties' 'equally'. State policy to protect state-owned enterprises (and the stability they bring through employment) is given priority by the courts. Interview by author, Hanoi, 11 October 2003.

[19] Since 1959, when the Democratic Republic of Vietnam (DRVN) as it then was established its official court systems, mobile hearings have been a feature of court work (Nicholson 2000).

[20] For example, the judgment resulting from the 1997 trial of Tran Thi Chieu and Bui Van Tham for corruption does not indicate the basis upon which either Chieu or Tham were found to have breached the Criminal Code. Judgment No. 233/HSST 22 February 1997 of the Hanoi People's Court.

[21] Neither do jury trials in common law systems record the evidentiary basis of the conviction.

[22] See Judgment No. 233/HSST of the Hanoi People's Court, 22 February 1997.

[23] The lack of reasons has several consequences. First, it is very hard for courts and lawyers to appeal or review cases when they are not able to understand the reasons behind judgments and particularly if they do not have access to the prosecution documents. Second, it is hard for higher courts to instruct lower courts on the basis of judgments alone. This then provokes a need for case summaries to be written and circulated, a need which has traditionally been met through publications in the Court's Journal and more recently by case summaries prepared for the sole purpose of transmitting how to adjudge cases. See Nicholson (2000) on the use of the court journal. On the use of case summaries in civil and economic cases, see Gillespie (2003).

[24] Both lawyer Nguyen Hung Quang and legal journalist Nguyen Hien Quan (currently a doctoral student at the University of Melbourne) have pointed out to me that lawyers have played an adversarial role in the Nam Cam trial, reflecting an experiment by the state to allow advocates to test the evidence publicly in open court.

[25] Changes to the regulation of lawyers are in fact reinforcing this distinction by requiring state lawyers not to work in private practice. Discussion with Pham Duy Nghia and Bui Bich Thi Lien in Canada, April 2003.

[26] Gillespie notes that whether revolutionary thinking should dominate legal thinking was on the agenda in conferences before 1986, but that no decision was made to change the *status quo* during these earlier debates.

27   It is commonly asserted that the Party continued to operate even after its official dissolution in 1945. This position is supported when Tran Thi Tuyet (1997:25) writes 'in fact it withdrew into secret'.

28   Statute of the Communist Party of Vietnam, 2001.

29   Conversation with lawyers in Hanoi over the period 1992–2002.

30   For example, the Supreme People's Court Journal over the period 1960–76 draws very little on Chinese jurisprudence while it borrows heavily from the USSR, devoting sections to translation of Soviet jurisprudential terms (Nicholson 2000). With the collapse of the Chinese legal system during the anti-Rightist campaign launched in 1957 and the Cultural Revolution (1966–76), Vietnam received little Chinese leadership on law and legal development during this period (see Leng 1967).

31   Shaun Malarney (1997) traces the continuities between Confucian and socialist ethics.

32   This discussion of the role and place of law after the Declaration of Independence in Vietnam until unification of the country in 1976 is drawn from Nicholson (2000).

33   This contrasts with the position in the USSR where during the early days of the revolution legal philosophers conceived of law withering away (Nicholson 2000).

34   Truong Trong Nghia similarly characterises Ho Chi Minh's attitude to law in 'The Rule of Law in Vietnam: Theory and Practice' available at http://www.mcpa.org. He argues Uncle Ho was committed to the Rule of Law. Laws were passed early in the life of the new regime. For example, in 1946 they passed laws to establish the Military Court with powers to try civilians and military figures for treason.

35   Here Boudarel is quoting from an editorial written by Nguyen Huu Dang (1956) in the fourth issue of *Nhan Van*.

36   Between 1953 and 1956 Vietnam introduced a land reform policy closely modelled on the land redistribution policies of China. See generally White (1981).

37   *Nhan dan*, 1956, Hanoi, 13 December; reprinted in Hoa Mai (ed) *The Nhan Van Affair*, pp. 161–162. This material is cited by Turner (1975:158–9). Turner notes that the article was written by students of the Hanoi–based Nguyen Trai School at the instigation of the Vietnam Workers' Party.

38   Boudarel notes that five main players (Nguyen Huu Dang, Luu Thi Yen, Tran Thien Bao, Phan Tai and Le Nguyen Chi) were tried and that all received periods of imprisonment followed by a period of national indignity when they were not permitted to leave their homes.

39   This organising principle is also reflected in the 1959 Constitution and its inclusion in Article 4 was specifically referred to by Ho Chi Minh (1961:416) in his 'Report on the Draft Amended Constitution' to the National Assembly in 1959. Ginsbergs (1963:209) points out that the DRVN was the first communist state to include democratic centralism in its constitution. For a discussion of Soviet democratic centralism, see Butler (1983); Hazard (1969); Gryzbowski (1962); Ioffe (1985); Ioffe and Maggs (1983).

40   Article 10, Statute of the Vietnam Workers' Party, 1960. This legislation is referred to here, although it was not introduced until 1960, because it reflects the practices that emerged in the preceding years of the administration. In many cases, as we shall see, formal laws were introduced after a period in which that which was introduced had already been operative. See also Gainsborough (2003).

41   The Party ceased to exist between 1945 and 1951, but once reformed its membership comprised major office holders such as the president and prime minister (Ho Chi Minh) and ministers. For example, the Ministers of Defence and Foreign Affairs and the Commander in Chief of the Armed Forces were all Party members. See Fall (1956).

42   Ho Chi Minh (1994:119) also refers to Stalin's leading role in this regard citing Stalin's argument that 'close control' can help the Party to 'avoid many grave mistakes'.

43   Gillespie (2003) notes that this is the foundation of socialist democracy: where, borrowing from Lenin, the working class have to 'centralise power in their hands'.

44   Preamble, Statute of the Vietnam Workers' Party, 1960. Here the word 'masses' is used because of its use in the Statute. However, it will also be used throughout this chapter when a reference is made to Vietnamese people who were members of the agricultural or labouring classes. It is an overtly political word used throughout Vietnamese writing to refer to the previously oppressed, but soon to be liberated, classes of Vietnamese society. Use of the word assists the reader to understand the militant political milieu in which this story was unfolding.

[45] The understanding that law had a role to play in the revolution seems to have been spoken about by lawyers and politicians, but it is hard to ascertain how it was more generally debated.

[46] Compare this with the situation in the Soviet Union, Nicholson (2000).

[47] Editors, *Justice Journal*, Vol. 1, 1964, pp. 1–4 (in Vietnamese).

[48] In particular, Sidel cites Vu Dinh Hoe (previously Minister for Justice, a non-communist lawyer) and Tran Cong Truong as leading figures campaigning for legal reform.

[49] Here law is used to refer to economic principles ('objective economic laws').

[50] The tone of the article is legalistic rather than critical. This distinguishes it from the articles published in *Nhan Van* (*Humanity*) discussed previously.

[51] As mentioned previously, Sidel describes the activities of the Legal Studies Group in the 1960s and early 1970s, pointing out that legal scholars debated the role of law throughout the period.

[52] The other three tenets were 'good at guiding production work and fighting'; 'good at caring for the masses and integration with them'; and 'good at strengthening the work of the Party'.

[53] The ensuing discussion is drawn from Nicholson (2000). The DRVN officially established a 'court system', as opposed to a system of regionally administered courts, in 1959.

[54] Chief Judge of the Supreme People's Court (1967) Editors, *Conference Summary*, p. 3 [in Vietnamese].

[55] Chief Judge of the Supreme People's Court (1967) Editors, *Conference Summary*, p. 3 [in Vietnamese].

[56] Chief Judge of the Supreme People's Court (1968), *Conference Summary*, p. 25 [in Vietnamese].

[57] For example: Unsigned Article (1961:4). See also comments made by Ho Chi Minh (1924:772), as cited in Turner (1975:137).

[58] Before proceeding, I wish to acknowledge the work of John Gillespie in mapping contemporary Vietnamese socialist legal thinking. Much of the Vietnamese legal theory relied upon in this section is directly drawn from his more recent, and as yet unpublished, work.

[59] Gillespie (2003) notes that this is the foundation of socialist democracy—according to Lenin's thought, the working class have to 'centralise power in their hands'.

[60] For analysis of the Northern Vietnamese Constitutions, see Duiker (1992); Marr (1995); Nicholson (1999).

[61] The 1976 unification Constitution is the most explicitly socialist of all Vietnam's Constitutions, as evidenced by its preamble. See also Nicholson (1999); and John Gillespie's chapter in this publication.

[62] John Gillespie's chapter in this publication.

[63] Article 4, SRVN Constitution 1992.

[64] Article 4, SRVN Constitution 1992, as amended in 2001.

[65] Article 4, SRVN Constitution 1992, as amended in 2001.

[66] Certainly this is suggested by Resolution 8.

[67] This comment is not intended to detract from the very great pace of legal change in Vietnam since the adoption of the renovation (*doi moi*) policy. In interviews by the author in June 2005, it was suggested that the Politburo has approved the legal reform strategy. It is yet to be made public.

REFERENCES

Beresford, M., 1997. 'Vietnam: the transition from central planning', in G. Rodan, K. Hewison and R. Robison (eds), *The Political Economy of South-East Asia: conflicts, crises and change*, Oxford University Press, Melbourne:206–32.

Bergling, P., 1999. *Legal Reform and Private Enterprise: the Vietnamese experience*, Volume 1, Umea Studies In Law, Department of Law, Umea University, Sweden.

Bo Tu Phap (Justice Ministry), 1957. *Tap Luat Le ve Tu-Phap* [Collection of Laws about Justice], Ministry of Justice Publishing House, Hanoi.

Boudarel, G., 1990. 'Intellectual dissidence in the 1950s: the *Nhan Van Giai Pham* affair', *The Vietnam Forum*, 13:154–74.

Butler, W.E., 1983. *Soviet Law*, Butterworths, London.

Chao-chuan Leng, 1967. *Justice in Communist China*, Oceana Publications Inc., New York.

Clark, D., 1999. 'The many meanings of the rule of law', in K. Jayasuriya (ed.), *Law, Capitalism and Power in Asia*, Routledge, London:28–44.

Dang Quang Phuong, 1996. 'Vai net ve qua trinh hinh thanh va phat trien cua Toa an nhan dan, [Some sketches of the establishment and development of the People's Court]', *Thuat Chung Ket Qua Chinh Nghien Cuu De Tai (Final Abstract about Principal Research)*, Unpublished work of the Supreme People's Court, Hanoi.

Duiker, W., 1992. 'The constitutional system of the Socialist Republic of Vietnam', in L.W. Beer (ed.), *Constitutional Systems of Late Twentieth Century Asia*, University of Washington Press, Seattle:331–61.

Fall, B., 1956. *The Viet Minh Regime Government Administration in the Democratic Republic of Vietnam*, Greenwood Press Publishers, Connecticut.

Fforde, A., 1986. 'The unimplementability of policy and the notion of law in Vietnamese communist thought', *Southeast Asian Journal of Social Science*, 62(1):60–70.

—— and de Vylder, S., 1996. *From Plan to Market: the economic transition in Vietnam*, Westview Press, Colorado.

Gainsborough, M., 2003. *Changing Political Economy of Vietnam: the case of Ho Chi Minh City*, Routledge Curzon, London and New York.

Giebel, C., 2001. 'Museum-shrine: revolution and its tutelary spirit in the village of My Hoa Hung', in Hue-Tam Ho Tai (ed.), *The Country of Memory: remaking the past in late Socialist Vietnam*, University of California Press, Berkeley:77–105.

Gillespie, J., 2001a. 'Self-interest and ideology: bureaucratic corruption in Vietnam', *Australian Journal of Asian Law*, 3(1):1–36.

——, 2001b. 'Globalisation and legal transplantation: lessons from the past', *Deakin Law Review*, 6(2):286–311.

——, 2002. 'The political-legal culture of anti-corruption reforms in Vietnam', in T. Lindsey (ed.), *Corruption in Asia: rethinking the governance paradigm*, The Federation Press, Sydney:167–200.

——, 2003. Extra-constitutional Law-making: Vietnam's unacknowledged legislators, Paper presented at the conference Mapping Vietnam's Legal Culture: where is Vietnam going to?, University of Victoria, Victoria, Canada, 27–29 March.

——, 2004. 'Concept of law in Vietnam: transforming statist socialism', in R. Peerenboom (ed.), *Asian Discourses of Rule of Law*, Routledge, London:146–82.

Ginsbergs, G., 1963. 'Local government and administration in the DRVN since 1954 (Part 2)', *The China Quarterly*, 14:195–210.

Gryzbowski, K., 1962. *Soviet Legal Institutions, Doctrines and Social Functions*, University of Michigan Press, Ann Arbor.

Hazard, J.N., 1969. *Communist and Their Law*, University of Chicago Press, Chicago.

Ho Chi Minh, 1924. 'The martyrdom of the negro, American lynch-justice', *International Press Correspondence* (Moscow), 4(60):772, in R.F. Turner, 1975. *Vietnamese Communism: its origins and development*, Hoover Institution Press, Stanford:136–37.

——, 1961. *Selected Works*, Volume II, Foreign Languages Publishing House, Hanoi.

——, 1994. 'Political report at the second national congress of the Vietnam workers' party', in *Ho Chi Minh Selected Writings*, Revised Edition, Gioi Publishers, Hanoi:101–29.

Hooker, M.B., 1978. *A Concise Legal History of South-East Asia*, Butterworths, Singapore.

Huynh Kim Khanh, 1982. *Vietnamese Communism 1925–1945*, Cornell University Press, Ithaca, New York.

Ioffe, O.S., 1985. *Soviet Law and Soviet Reality*, Martinus Nijhoff, Dordrecht.

—— and Maggs, P.B., 1983. *Soviet Law in Theory and Practice*, Oceana Publications Inc, Dobbs Ferry, New York.

Klein, W.C. and Weiner, M., 1959. 'North Vietnam' in G. McTurnan Kahin (ed.), *Governments and Politics of Southeast Asia*, Cornell University Press, Ithaca, New York.

Le Duan, 1994. 'Some problems of cadres and organization in socialist revolution in 1973', in *Le Duan Selected Writings*, Gioi Publishers, Hanoi:410–76.

Le Kim Que, 1974. 'The People's Courts', in anonymous, *An Outline of the Institutions of the Democratic Republic of Vietnam*, Gioi Publishers, Hanoi.

Leng, Chao-chuan, 1967. *Justice in Communist China*, Oceana Publications Inc., New York.

Luu Tien Dung, 2003. *Judicial Independence in Transitional Countries*, Governance Centre, Oslo.

Malarney, S.K., 1997. 'Culture, virtue and political transformation in contemporary Northern Viet Nam', *The Journal of Asian Studies*, 54(4):899–920.

Marr, D., 1995. 'Ho Chi Minh's independence declaration', in K.W. Taylor and J.K. Whitmore (eds), *Essays Into Vietnamese Pasts*, Studies on Southeast Asia, Cornell University, Ithaca, New York:221–31.

McMillan, J. and Woodruff, C., 1999. 'Dispute prevention without courts in Vietnam', *Journal of Law, Economics and Organization*, 15(3):637–58.

Ngo Van Thanh, 1996. 'Chuyen de Chuc Nang va vai tro cua toa an quan su trong cac thoi ky cua cach mang Viet Nam [The role and function of the Military Courts in the stages of the Vietnamese revolution]', *Tong Thuat Chung Ket Qua Chinh Nghien Cuu De Tai* [Final Abstract about Principal Research], Unpublished work of the Supreme People's Court, Hanoi.

Nguyen Ngoc Minh, 1985. 'Building a new type state in Vietnam', *Vietnam Social Sciences*, 1:51–65.

Nguyen Nhu Phat, 1997. 'The role of law during the formation of a market-driven mechanism in Vietnam', in J. Gillespie (ed.), *Commercial Legal Development in Vietnam: Vietnamese and foreign commentaries*, Butterworths, Singapore:397–412.

Nguyen Nham, 1997. Foreign Broadcast Information Service East Asia, 97-203, 23 June:3.

Nguyen Van Hien, 2001. 'Tieu chuan tham phan-thuc trang va nhung yeu cau dat ra trong thoi ky moi [Judicial criteria—current situation and requirements for new era]', *People's Court Journal*, 4:2–6.

Nicholson, P., 1999. 'Vietnamese legal institutions in comparative perspective: contemporary constitutions and courts considered', in K. Jayasuriya (ed.), *Law, Capitalism and Power in Asia*, Routledge, London:300–29.

——, 2000. Borrowing Court Systems: the experience of the DRVN 1945–76, PhD thesis, University of Melbourne, Melbourne.

——, 2001. 'Judicial independence and the rule of law: the Vietnam court experience', *Australian Journal of Asian Law*, 3(1):37–58.

——, 2003. Vietnamese Court Reform: constancy and change in the contemporary period, Conference paper presented at Mapping Vietnam's Legal Culture, University of Victoria, Canada, 28 March

—— and Nguyen Hung Quang, 2005. 'The Vietnamese judiciary: the politics of appointment and promotion', *Pacific Rim Law and Policy Journal*, 14(1):1–34.

Pham Van Bach, 1961a. 'Bao Cao cua Toa an nhan dan toi cao tai ky hop thu hai cua Quoc hoi Khoa II [The report of the Supreme People's Court to the second session of the National Assembly's second legislature]', *Tap San Tu Phap*, 6:1–12.

——, 1961b. 'Vai nhan thuc ve nhiem vu cua Toa An Nhan Dan trong Ke Hoach Nha Nuoc 5 Nam: 1961–1965 [Several points about the responsibilities of the People's Courts in the state five-year plan 1961–1965]', *Tap San Tu Phap*, 1:1–8.

——, 1964. 'Bao Cao ve su tich cuc cho nam 1963 va chieu phua cho nam 1964 [Report on the activities of the year 1963 and directions for the year 1964 of the People's Courts]', Annex to *Tap San Tu Phap*, Annexure to No. 5.

Quinn, B.J.M., 2002. 'Legal reform and its context in Vietnam', *Columbia Journal of Asian Law*, 15(2):219–91.

Sidel, M., 1997a. 'Some preliminary thoughts in contending approaches to law in Vietnam, 1954–1975', paper presented at the Association for Asian Studies Conference, March (unpublished).

——, 1997b. 'Vietnam', in P-L Tan (ed.), *Asian Legal Systems*, Butterworths, Sydney:356–89.

——, 1998. Chinese Legal Influences on Vietnamese Legal Development since 1986, Paper presented at the Law and the Chinese Outside Asia Conference, Canberra, 5–6 July.

——, 2002. 'Analytical models for understanding constitutions and constitutional dialogue in socialist transitional states: re-interpreting constitutional dialogue in Vietnam', *Singapore Journal of International & Comparative Law*, 6(1):42–89.

Thayer, C., 2002. Recent Political Developments: Vietnam in 2002, paper presented at the Vietnam Update, The Australian National University, Canberra, 28–29 November.

Tran Thi Tuyet, 1997. 'Vietnamese state structures and law during the anti-French colonialist war', *Vietnam Legal Forum*, 25(1):25–26.

Truong Chinh, 1994. *Truong Chinh Selected Writings, Hanoi,* Revised Edition, Gioi Publishers, Hanoi.

Truong Tan Phat, 1964. *Nhan dan,* 26 March:2.

Truong Trong Nghia 'The Rule of Law in Vietnam: theory and practice'. Available online at http://www.idlo.int/texts/IDLI/mis6094.pdf.

Turner, R.F. (ed.), 1975. *Vietnamese Communism: its origins and development,* Hoover Institution Press, Stanford.

Unnamed Editors, 1996. 'Dat van De [Presentation]', *Thuat Chung Ket Qua Chinh Nghien Cuu De Tai* [Final Abstract about Principal Research], Unpublished work of the Supreme People's Court, Hanoi.

Unknown Author, 2003. '2 cong to vien tranh luan voi hon 70 luat su [2 Prosecutors Argue with More than 70 Lawyers]', *Nguoi Lao Dong* [Labour Men], 16 February.

Unsigned Article, 1961. *Nhan dan,* 18 May:4.

Van Arkadie, B. and Mallon, R., 2003. *Viet Nam: a transition tiger?,* Asia Pacific Press, Canberra.

Vu Dinh Hoe, 1995. 'Les quatres constitutions du Viet Nam', *Vietnamese Law Journal,* 2:24–28.

Weggel, O., 1986. 'The Vietnamese Communist Party and its status under law', in D.A. Loeber, D.D. Barry, J.M. Feldbrugge, G. Ginsbergs and P.B. Maggs (eds), *Ruling Communist Parties and their Status under Law,* M. Nijhoff, Dordrecht, Boston:411–19.

White, C., 1981. Agrarian Reform and National Liberation in the Vietnamese Revolution: 1920–1957, PhD thesis, Faculty of the Graduate School, Cornell University, Ithaca, New York.

9

Ideology and professionalism: the resurgence of the Vietnamese bar

Nguyen Hung Quang and Kerstin Steiner

The legal profession is crucial to a democratic society and is one of speciality. The legal profession is, primarily, necessary to ensure the constitutional rights of the citizen, the right to be protected, and the right to defense counsel where rights and interests are violated.

Nguyen Dinh Loc (2001)
Minister of Justice

In the cause of building a socialist state based on rule of law, the Communist Party of Vietnam and the Government of Vietnam have issued a number of resolutions, directives and legal normative documents to improve the state apparatus and laws (Hoang The Lien 2002). In early 2001, as part of the legal reform process, the Politburo of the Party Central Committee issued a resolution on future reforms to the judicial branch,[1] laying the foundation for legal reform in Vietnam and resulting in a number of legal normative documents being passed. These documents regulated judicial activities and generally supported the aim of building a law-based socialist state in Vietnam.

This chapter seeks to analyse how individual lawyers and their organisations can be strengthened and consolidated as part of Vietnam's legal reform. In order to address this issue, the chapter will first explore the history of lawyers in Vietnam. It examines the different points of view and attitudes of governmental organisations and judicial organs towards legal practitioners. It then continues with a case study of the Nam Cam case—the largest and most infamous criminal case in Vietnamese legal history—to illustrate the shortcomings of the current legal reforms. The chapter concludes by arguing for further changes to secure the role of lawyers in judicial reform.

THE HISTORY OF LAWYERS IN VIETNAM

Prior to the August Revolution

Lawyers, also known as *thay cai* ('defence counsel'), appeared in Vietnam with the French introduction of the court system (Nguyen Van Tuan 2001; Le Kim Que 2003). Before then, people only hoped for justice *den gioi soi xet* ('God willing')[2] in feudal courts (Le Kim Que 2003). The feudal system did not recognise the role of defence counsel, especially under a Confucian social order which views the King as the son of God and the Mandarin as the parent—kings and mandarins did not accept the protestations of their people, their servants, or their children. In some dynasties, however, those who possessed certain legal knowledge occasionally helped people draft claims or advised them on petition or court procedures. Recent scholarship sees this as a preliminary form of the 'lawyer' profession (Tan Van Tai 2002), but it really only occurred on an *ad hoc* and unprofessional basis.

After the French colonial government conquered southern Vietnam in 1862, it established a French court to adjudicate French citizens (Le Kim Que 2003). Initially, lawyers had to be naturalised as French, but this restriction was gradually lifted to include Vietnamese who held French citizenship (Le Kim Que 2003). By 1884, when the French had colonised southern Vietnam completely and asserted their dominance over Central and North Vietnam, Vietnamese who held a Bachelor of Laws degree were permitted to practise as lawyers (Phan Huu Thu 2001). On 25 May 1930, the French colonial government issued an Order on the Establishment of the Bar Association that permitted bar associations in Hanoi and Saigon for the first time. This order officially recognised the existence of lawyers in Vietnam and provided that Vietnamese lawyers could appear before court if they

- held a Bachelor of Law degree
- had served at least five years' apprenticeship in a lawyers' office
- had passed the exam and been admitted to the bar association
- taken an oath to abide fully by the law and be loyal to the French government (Phan Huu Thu 2001).

Once accepted, these lawyers were allowed to open their own practice and receive clients.

It is self-evident that lawyers during the French colonial period had to respect the colonial government, as it was nothing but a replica of the homeland government. The laws implemented in southern Vietnam were transplanted French laws while those implemented in Central and North Vietnam were strongly influenced by French law (Durand 2002; Tran Thi Tuyet 2003; Nguyen Phan Quang and Phan Van Hoang 1995; Pham Hung 2000). This also explains the success of some lawyers in defending Vietnamese revolutionaries in the colonial courts (D.T. 2002).

After the August Revolution (1945–87)

Immediately after occupying Northern Vietnam, the revolutionary government started to reorganise the judicial system. In October 1945, President Ho Chi Minh issued the Order on the Lawyer Organization.[3] This order was the first document of the revolutionary government to recognise the existence and role of lawyers in the judicial system, representing a significant move towards compliance with the real situation in Vietnam at the time. Restrictions placed by the colonial government on the admission of lawyers to practise were loosened (Nguyen Van Tuan 2001; Phan Huu Thu 2001; Nguyen Dinh Loc 2001). The right of the defendant and the accused to present their case was established immediately after the first Order on Establishment of the Revolutionary Government Court was issued.[4] These were important documents in the initial stage of the revolutionary government as they recognised the existence and necessity of lawyers in the revolutionary state apparatus.

The first Constitution of Vietnam reinforced this right by stating that it was an 'important democratic right of the accused' to be legally represented in criminal proceedings.[5] Hence, it assumed the existence of a legal profession capable of fulfilling this task. Since Vietnam was a revolutionary state at that time, the safeguarding of this right proved to be a challenge for the new revolutionary government. Trained lawyers were mostly educated in the French legal system and had sworn allegiance to the French colonial government. However, some lawyers remained in Vietnam or returned from France and became members of the new Vietnamese government (Nguyen Phan Quang and Phan Van Hoang 1995; Pham Hung 2000). These lawyers made significant contributions to the rebuilding of Vietnam and also ensured that the legal profession continued to exist during the transition period. Still, there were not enough trained lawyers to ensure that all accused were legally represented and defended at trial, prompting President Ho Chi Minh to issue an order in 1949 that allowed those accused to nominate a citizen who was not a lawyer as defence counsel subject to approval by the chief judge.[6] This led to the development of the new concept of *bao chua vien nhan dan* ('people's advocate'), very similar to that of *certificat de citoyennet* ('citizen certificate') during the 1798 French bourgeois revolution. At that time, the French Revolution abolished bar associations, arguing that citizens had the right to defence. In order to defend others, they only needed a *certificat de citoyennet* (see Le Kim Que 2003).

On 12 January 1950, the Ministry of Justice issued a decree providing details to President Ho Chi Minh's Order stating the conditions by which a citizen could become a people's advocate (Nguyen Van Tuan 2001): the person had to be a Vietnamese citizen, at least 21 years old, of good morality, with no prior criminal convictions.

At the beginning of every year, the provincial resistance and administrative committees, together with the provincial chief judge, would develop a list—which the chief judge could alter at his discretion—of the qualified citizens who had agreed to appear as people's advocates before the court. This list would then be posted at the local court offices (Nguyen Van Tuan 2001). The incomes of lawyers and people's advocates differed—the people's advocate received an allowance from the court budget while lawyers received fees from the defendant or the defendant's relatives.[7] Furthermore, people's advocates, unlike lawyers, had no obligation to pay personal income tax.[8] Together these conditions ensured that poor people could access representation by defence counsel during court trials. This is possibly the most outstanding achievement of the revolutionary government in the initial stage.

People's advocates continued to exist and were further asserted through Circular No. 101/HCTP of the Ministry of Justice, 29 August 1957. Circular No. 101 clearly stated that 'While there are no adjustments to the "people's advocate" institution, the Order No. 69 dated 18 June 1949 and Decree 01/ND-NY dated 12 January 1950 on the "People's Advocate Organization" shall continue to be implemented' (Nguyen Van Tuan 2001:74).

After North Vietnam was liberated in 1955, the Vietnam Lawyers' Association (VLA) was established to encompass everyone working in the legal field.[9] The association's membership therefore comprised not only lawyers but also people working within the legal sector at state institutions (Pham Hung 2000). Since the VLA's main purpose was to serve state policies (Pham Hung 2000) and to provide defence counsel if requested by the court, it cannot be regarded as comparable with a professional organisation like the bar association in Western legal systems.

The 1959 Constitution established the court and prosecutorial systems, and the Ministry of Justice was eliminated. The administrative judicial work, including the advocate's work, was assigned to the Supreme People's Court (Pham Hung 2000). A pilot law office, the *Van phong Luat su Ha noi* [Hanoi Lawyer Office], was established in 1963[10] to ensure the constitutional right to defence. In its early years, the Hanoi Lawyer Office

- defended the accused in criminal cases and protected the legitimate rights of the parties in civil cases before the courts
- provided legal advice to the people and the cadres
- helped people draft petitions and other legal documents such as contracts and covenants
- contributed to legal propaganda through the court proceedings (Pham Hung 2000).

Despite the name 'Law Office', however, the organisation in fact comprised only people's advocates and operated as an administrative body under the direct administration of the Supreme People's Court (Phan Huu Thu 2001). The people's advocates were civil servants and received their salaries out of the state budget (Hanoi Bar Association 2002). It can, therefore, be said that in the period between 1960 and 1980, the legal profession virtually did not exist as it had been replaced by that of the people's advocates (Nguyen Van Thao 2001). Furthermore, people's advocates acted only in cases dealt with by the courts. In cases conducted by the Resistance, Administrative and Land Reform Committees, adjudicating matters where people protested against the revolution or were carrying out land reform, participation of the people's advocates was not necessary. The operations of those committees were indeed far more forceful than the courts (White 1981; Nicholson 2000). This caused Vietnamese society to perceive lawyers as limited only to criminal defence in court proceedings (Phan Huu Thu 2001).

The 1980 Constitution provided for the establishment of an organisation for lawyers, the first such provision since the revolution (Phan Huu Thu 2001; Nguyen Dinh Loc 2001). It was set up after the reunification of Vietnam and, taking into account the different habits of the people in the south of Vietnam—where people had long used lawyers to protect their rights in court—reaffirmed the defendant's right to defence as stated in the previous constitution.[11] The new constitution thus formed the legal foundation to pass more laws with respect to the organisation of lawyers in Vietnam (Nguyen Van Tuan 2001; Hanoi Bar Association 2002:19) and harmonised the two systems of using lawyers' services.

After the Ministry of Justice was re-established, the management of lawyers was transferred from the government's Legal Committee back to the Ministry of Justice.[12] The need to promulgate a legal document on the organisation of the legal profession began to take shape. Before issuing a legal document on the organisation of lawyers and defence work, the Ministry of Justice had to consult with the Supreme People's Court, the Supreme People's Procuracy as well as some other state authorities (Nguyen Van Tuan 2001). This legal document served as the legal foundation establishing a number of local *doan bao chua vien nhan dan* ('people's advocate organisations'). By the end of 1987, over 30 provinces and cities in Vietnam launched their own people's advocate organisations consisting of over 400 people's advocates. These continued to operate until the 1987 Ordinance on Lawyer Organisation was passed (Nguyen Van Tuan 2001).

Following promulgation of the Ordinance on Lawyer Organisation (1987–2001)

The Ordinance on Lawyer Organisation was enacted on 18 December 1987 and provided further details on lawyers' organisations. This ordinance was sought to revitalise careers as lawyers in preparation for the socioeconomic reform process in Vietnam (Nguyen Van Tuan 2001; Phan Huu Thu 2001). By 1989, 16 bar associations had been established, replacing the former people's advocate organisations (Nguyen Van Tuan 2001). To boost the establishment of local bar associations, the Ministers' Council (now called the 'government') issued on 21 February 1989 Decree No. 15/ HDBT on the Regulations of Bar Associations. The Ministry of Justice issued a document detailing this decree.[13] Under these regulations, 61 bar associations with 82 branches had been set up by 30 September 2001, covering all provinces and cities in Vietnam. These bar associations comprise approximately 2100 practising lawyers (Nguyen Dinh Loc 2001; Nguyen Van Tuan 2001).

Increasing professionalism is also reflected in the number of lawyers currently holding a university law degree. The figure increased from 60 per cent in 1989 to 85 per cent in 2001 (Nguyen Van Tuan 2001). The number of qualified judges and prosecutors, however, trails the figure for lawyers (Nicholson and Nguyen Hung Quang, forthcoming).[14]

The 1987 Ordinance on Lawyer Organisation has had limited success in changing people's attitudes towards the legal profession (Nguyen Van Thao 2001). In fact, the ordinance hindered lawyers' careers by stipulating governmental administrative control over lawyers (Nguyen Van Thao 2001). This control encompassed all aspects of lawyers' practice such as opening a legal practice and forming partnerships, thus denying activity, independence and freedom to practising lawyers (Nguyen Van Thao 2001; Nguyen Van Bon 2001). The practice of assigning cases and setting fees through the bar association's management serves further to restrict lawyers in their practice. The bar association charged an amount for the service depending on internal regulations (Nguyen Van Tuan 2001; Nguyen Van Bon 2001); and the practice essentially infringed citizens' right to choose their own lawyer, thus damaging public perceptions of lawyers (Nguyen Van Bon 2001).

In 1997, the Communist Party released a policy consolidating and strengthening the judicial assistance agencies, strongly emphasising the role of lawyers, legal consultancy and forensic examination.[15] These reforms were taken one step further in the 2001 Ordinance on Lawyers.

From 2001 to the present

The 2001 Ordinance on Lawyers has played an important role in the reform process of building a socialist state based on the rule of law. These reforms were meant to be implemented in depth and to include judicial reforms (Nguyen Dinh Loc 2001). This ordinance has considerably expanded lawyers' rights, addressing some of the shortcomings of the 1987 Ordinance. The 2001 Ordinance stipulates in more detail the scope of lawyers' practice, allowing them, for example, to practice independently or form partnerships with any number of members.[16] Lawyers now may also establish joint ventures with foreign law firms under certain prescribed conditions.[17] Moving beyond litigation, the ordinance is more attentive to the legal consultation of lawyers, particularly legal consultations on investment and business. To some extent, the 2001 Ordinance has enhanced lawyers' position, but in order to improve the social acceptance of lawyer's services it will be necessary to amend a number of procedural legal normative documents (Nguyen Dinh Loc 2001). The most significant change in the 2001 Ordinance was the recognition of the career as a lawyer as a professional career. Beside the provisions on organisation and professional practice, the 2001 Ordinance provides a mechanism to protect clients.[18] All these changes have helped build public confidence in lawyers.

This is reflected in some statistics. Throughout the country, 2,360 lawyers have registered so far in 61 bar associations, practising in 680 legal offices, 45 branches and four law partnership companies.[19] As of 30 September 2004, under the 2001

Ordinance on Lawyers, approximately 26 per cent of these lawyers will be ineligible to practise law as they are civil servants, and 5 per cent will be rendered ineligible beyond the next five years because of their age.[20] However, taking into consideration the number of trainees enrolled in legal professional training schools—over 1,835 trainees in two years (2002–03)[21] alone—it seems that the professional lawyer career is developing.

ATTITUDE OF THE STATE AND THE PUBLIC TOWARDS LAWYERS

Several factors shape how lawyers are perceived by society, such as certain characteristics of the state organisation, social features and legal institutions.

Structure of the state

Based on the comment of the former Minister of Justice Nguyen Dinh Loc that the 'lawyer career is a profession crucial to a democratic society', it would appear evident that lawyers can only function well in a democratic society. Resolution 8 mentioned the concept *tranh tung dan chu* ('democratic adversarial proceeding'), but no definition of this concept has yet been given. Nor has the question of whether this 'democratic' concept might be governed by the principle of 'democratic centralism' yet been answered. State agencies seem puzzled in implementing the principle in democratic adversarial proceedings; one document by the Ministry of Police states that lawyers, who are Communist Party members, must respect the adjudication directions of the Party in the adjudicating proceedings.[22] This almost reflects the attitude of state agencies and officers towards the lawyers.

Lawyers are still not on equal footing with prosecutors in the democratic litigation process and administrative agencies are still not recognised appropriately in administrative procedures. This diminishes lawyers' role, confining it to the position of a sub-actor needed to perform a complete *vo kich* ('play').

Structure of the society

Agricultural society. Perhaps the primary reason for the lack of recognition of professional lawyers might be attributed to the fact that Vietnam is an agricultural country, with more than 80 per cent of its population living in rural areas. In these areas, perceptions of social order are still heavily influenced by Confucian ideology. Efforts to change that perception have been unsuccessful. The revolution of August 1945 dismantled the feudal regime, and the revolutionary government attempted to explain the new concept that state officers are *day to cua nhan dan* ('servants of the people'). Involvement of state officers is still avoided; instead, the guidance of decision-making bodies is followed.

In cases of dispute, recourse to alternative dispute resolution mechanisms is preferred. These mechanisms include amicable settlements, *to hoa giai* ('conciliation groups'), *luat rung* ('lynch law or self-justice'), or approaching senior officers in the administrative system. Courts are seen as the last resort to resolve a dispute.

Feudal ideology. Even though the August 1945 Revolution overthrew the feudal regime, the ideology upon which this regime had been based was much harder to eliminate from the people's thinking. State agencies and officers often refused to work with lawyers. In fact, many state officers were still influenced by feudal ideology (Nguyen Thanh Binh 2002). The mandarin-like behaviour of *mal du siècle* ('disease of the century'), or as it was popularly called, *quan tinh,* was considered appropriate under Confucian thought.[23] This practice was often criticised by the Party. Although the Communist Party of Vietnam criticised feudal norms, in practice the principle of democratic centralism enabled a continuation of feudal thinking and relationships. Therefore, the attitude of revolutionary state officials, who considered lawyers as *thay cai* ('master of arguing', which did not facilitate an environment of mutual respect).

Legal history. Judicial inexperience also contributed to the population's general resentment of lawyers. The military and political influences affected not only lawyers but also the judicial system. This continued even after the revolutionary government took power.

The court was immediately considered one of the agencies serving the political agenda of the new government. From 1946 to 1954, the major task for the revolutionary government was to drive out the French colonisers. The Revolutionary Court was primarily a military-style court to adjudicate over soldiers who did not fully perform their duties, anti-revolutionary gangs, capitalists, feudalists and landlords. Quite often the judges had already made their decision before the hearing and the trial was only held for political purposes, which may explain the popular concept in Vietnam of *an bo tu* ('judgment already in the pocket') (Pham Hong Hai 2003). The defence counsel was often a cadre, a soldier of the Resistance Committee or the Administrative Committee, assigned by the court. The defence counsel's function guided by the higher officials and/or the judge.[24] The role of the defence counsel was simply to demonstrate that the judgment of the Revolutionary Court reflected principles of democracy and fairness, while in fact they were only an integral constituent of the revolutionary adjudication system. Furthermore, the fear of being stigmatised for defending anti-revolutionary activists prevented defence lawyers from voicing dissenting opinions. The principle of *tap trung dan chu* ('democratic centralism') guided the operation of all agencies in the socio-political system. Therefore, defence counsel could not, or dared not, break this rule. Some defence counsel even refused to take up a case when the other party was a state agency (which often happened in the administrative cases). Even so, several lawyers accepted the role of defence subject to 'guidance' of a state agency or a court body.[25]

Contemporary experience with lawyers. Until the enactment of the Civil Code in 1996, contemporary laws had no provisions permitting lawyers to act as representatives of their clients before the administrative agencies. After the Civil Code was enacted, however, the state officers were still permitted only to work directly with the concerned parties. To be involved in the process, therefore, lawyers had to establish a relationship with the state officers. These relationships were called *moi quan he tot dep* ('good relationships') and included bribing state officers, and gave rise to the perception of lawyers as *nguoi moi gioi* ('the broker or middle man') or *nguoi song ky sinh* ('parasites').[26]

Judicial proceedings

Lawyers' role in judicial proceedings is more clearly defined than their role before the executive agencies—their appearance demonstrating the new government's democratic characteristics but their actions ultimately serving revolutionary aims. In theory, decisions and judgments were considered to express the righteousness of the revolutionaries, represent the people's will, and were objectively and democratically rendered according to the principle of democratic centralism. Therefore, as a matter of practice, any act against the people's will would not be tolerated.

The role of lawyers in criminal proceedings illustrates this point. Their participation was confined to presenting their clients' case at court since they were not allowed to be involved in the investigation stages.[27] The current Criminal Procedure Code allows lawyers to participate from the time the suspect is accused, except in special cases of extremely serious offences endangering national security where it is necessary to keep the investigation secret.[28] In reality, however, the investigative agency, the court and the prosecution have often denied lawyers the right to participate in the investigative stage, and there is no record so far of any cases where lawyers were allowed to participate in the investigative process, except for juvenile cases where it was essential that a lawyer was involved in order to provide a signature for completion of the case file.[29] If a lawyer wants to participate in the investigation process, a good relationship with the prosecution is vital. The absence of lawyers in most cases creates opportunities for the investigative body and the prosecution to handle the file alone, and this lack of oversight opens the potential for investigators and prosecutors to become 'subjective, or even sometimes, negative enough to distort the case file'.[30] In many cases defendants have declared during court hearings that they were 'induced or coerced to give testimonies',[31] placing the court in the difficult position of deciding whether these claims were true. This seems to be one of the reasons for many 'wrongfully decided' cases in Vietnam.

There are several practical restrictions on lawyers when a case comes to trial. First, a lawyer needs an introductory letter from the bar to gain access to the criminal file. Second, access to the file is only granted when it is not needed by a panel member. Third, a lawyer is not allowed to photocopy the case file, but is permitted only to take notes of the important points. In complicated criminal cases, it can often take days for a lawyer to go through the file. Finally, if a lawyer wants to meet the client in a detention camp, another introductory letter, this time from the court or the bar, is required. All these aspects form a part of the *xin cho* ('beg and give') practice in criminal proceedings.

At the hearing, the lawyer has the right to express his opinions to defend his client. However, such opinions are rarely respected by the trial panel or recorded in the judgment. In reality, the conclusion of the judgment, or sometimes the entire judgment, is often written beforehand and contains only the opinions of the prosecutor as expressed in the indictment and offered to the trial panel. The defence lawyer's opinions are summarised in one or two lines in the judgment[32] or only with the phrase 'after hearing the lawyer's opinions'.

This contributed to the development of a particular style for the speeches of the defence counsel

- admitting that the prosecutor's accusation is correct
- analysing the causes to show that the defendant committed the crime
- presenting some mitigating elements on behalf of the defendant
- suggesting that the trial panel mitigate punishment of the defendant.

This structure is widespread, especially among older lawyers.[33]

The factors discussed above meant that the majority of citizens did not fully understand what the functions of lawyers were in criminal proceedings. Some viewed lawyers as government officials and therefore believed that they were of limited help since they would adopt a similar attitude to that displayed by governmental agencies. People who possessed some legal knowledge, or who were involved in court cases, knew that lawyers only had a limited function as a *nguoi moi gioi* ('broker'). Thus, before seeking a lawyer's services, many people resorted to their *quan he* ('relationships') to settle the case. Many business entities, especially state-run enterprises, rarely used lawyers in their business affairs, preferring instead to take advantage of administrative interrelationships among the line agencies, or the privileges of a state agency, to support or defend their case. Moreover, lawyers were seen to complicate the case unnecessarily and annoy state officials.

Law graduates also prefer not to become lawyers directly after graduation. Most graduates want to work in secure jobs in governmental institutions. This is the common attitude among graduates in the *bao cap* ('government subsidy') period of a centrally planned economy. Only those graduates who could not find jobs in government institutions would reluctantly accept a position as a lawyer.[34] Even then, acting as a lawyer is regarded as a temporary job while waiting for a position in a government institution.

Since the education of lawyers falls short in the area of practical experience—no training courses in professional skills existed until a pilot one-week course was held by the Ministry of Justice in 1996—a lawyer has to develop these skills alone.[35] This is a significant difference from other legal professionals where training courses were held and funded countrywide. Two years after the pilot course, the Asian Development Bank provided funds for the Ministry of Justice to establish a 3-month comprehensive professional training courses for lawyers. The newly-established Legal Professional Training School[36] has held three professional skills training courses for lawyers in the last two years (2002–03). The training courses run for six months and are expected to equip the trainees with good theoretical knowledge. However, they fail to reflect or address the difficulties and challenges that lawyers may face in practice.

According to the Legal Needs Assessment Report for Vietnam for 2002–10, Viet Nam needs 17,000 to 18,000 lawyers by 2010.[37] Unfortunately, the basis for this assessment is not known, but if these numbers are correct it is vital that the attitude towards the role and activities of lawyers in the judicial system is changed in order to attract lawyers to a career as practicing lawyers.

Resolution No. 08-NQ/TW of the Politburo on Forthcoming Principal Judicial Tasks has laid foundations for judicial reforms. In particular, for the first time, an important document of the Central Communist Party and the state requires the legal systems 'to ensure democratic pleading with the barristers and the people's advocate'.[38]

It can bee seen that some important improvements have been made during the law reform process, at least on paper.

THE 'NAM CAM' CASE[39]

The Nam Cam trial tested the recent law reforms. This case study illustrates the shortcomings and improvements of the recent legal reforms, highlighting the discrepancies between the official Party line and the perception of the population with respect to the effectiveness of the legal system.

The case of Truong Van Cam is considered the biggest case in the history of criminal procedures in Vietnam.[40] This is not only because of the high number of defendants involved in the case—about 155, compared to the 77 defendants in Tang Minh Phung's criminal case in 1999 and 74 defendants in Tan Truong Sanh's case in 1999[41]—but also because of its far-reaching implications.

The trial tested the judicial system in two ways. First, it tested the seriousness and commitment of the Party to crack down on corruption within the Party and police. Therefore, if the Party was seriously committed to changes, it should have interfered less with the prosecution of officials. Crime and graft are two of the major problems investors are facing in Vietnam. The vicious circle of corruption is spurred on by civil servants' low wages and a bureaucratic legal system that encourages businesses 'to cut corners by offering bribes' (Maria 2003:n.p.).

Second, the trial tested the recent reforms with respect to the close nexus between the state and the Party. The question was whether the judges would utilise the changes in the legal system and thus withstand political pressure. According to the presiding judge Bui Hoang Danh, 'it was a public and democratic trial, in line with legal reforms' (Judge Bui Hoang Danh, cited in Cohen 2003b:A4). The trial has been further praised for the improvement of the rights of the defendant. Among other things,[42] the court showed an unprecedented willingness to grant defence lawyers the right to express their opinion and the right to have access to their clients before the trial (Cohen 2003b).

In general, the criminal case against Nam Cam contains all the elements of a good Mafia criminal story and reads like Mario Puzo's novel 'The Godfather'.[43] When Nam Cam was arrested in December 2001, the charges brought against him did not foreshadow the ultimate scandal. One of Nam Cam's gang members had incurred an illegal gambling debt and left a car as collateral. The car's licence plate, however, was fake, and the resulting search for the owner pointed to Nam Cam (Vasavakul 2003). The subsequent investigation resulted in a mass arrest of 155 accomplices.

Criminal history of Nam Cam

Truong Van Cam has a long-standing criminal record. Owing to the intervention of corrupt state officials such as police, prosecutors and Party members, however, he had persistently been able to avoid arrest and prosecution (Quinn 2003).

According to his police file, he was sentenced to a 3-year prison term for stabbing a man to death when he was 15 years old (Rowse 2003a).[44] His career path afterwards included working at the docks and joining the South Vietnamese army, but after the reunification he started to rise through the criminal ranks to become a feared Mafia boss.[45] The three arrests for gambling charges between 1978 and 1982 appeared trivial compared with what was to come. In 1995, army intelligence was alarmed by Nam Cam's criminal activities and a report was given to Prime Minister Vo Van Kiet.[46] He was sentenced to a 3-year prison term in a re-education camp for his connections to the so-called *xa hoi den* ('black societies') and his money-lending practice.[47] By then, however, Nam Cam had already established a close network with Party officials[48] and was able to secure an early release eight months ahead of schedule (Thayer 2002).

The trial

In December 2001, Nam Cam was arrested along with 155 associates. The trial proved to be an unprecendented logistical exercise. In preparing for the trial, the Ho Chi Minh City People's Court spent billions of dong (VND) to upgrade trial facilities.[49] In order to reflect the recent law reforms, the Ho Chi Minh City People's Court established an adjudication group of six judges (four principal judges and two on standby), five people's assessors, and three court secretaries (two principal and one standby).[50] The paperwork of the trial was immense; the case dossier consisted of 118 volumes (20,000 pages in all), a 600-page indictment (colour-printed for the first time) distributed to all the lawyers and defendants, and a 400-page prosecutorial conclusion (The Gia 2003).[51]

The hearing of the Nam Cam case took 57 working days, with 83 lawyers participating for the defence, and 238 summoned individuals.[52] Over 300 police officers were mobilised to preserve order at the court proceedings.

Experience of lawyers during the trial

Lawyers experienced several improvements in their working conditions in preparation for and during the trial. With respect to preparation for the trial, the meetings between clients and their lawyers were less restricted. The lawyers had access to the files and were given copies of the indictment free of charge.[53]

The most significant improvements, however, were during the trial. Defence counsels were allowed to express their opinions without any interruption. Other activities allowed for the first time in a Vietnamese court hearing were that

- defence lawyers were allowed to use secretaries in the court hearing
- defence lawyers were allowed to use pictures and tape recorders to illustrate evidence before the court
- defence lawyers were given the opportunity to present their case with more freedom and without the typical interruption or silencing by judges
- defence lawyers asked for adversarial opinions of the prosecutor at the hearing in order to determine the objective facts.[54]

The question of whether the defence counsel really had a position equal to the prosecutor during the proceedings can only be answered by studying the experience of Dang Van Luan.

Dang Van Luan was the defence lawyer for Tran Mai Hanh, a former member of the Central Communist Party and former state radio chief who was accused of receiving bribes and disclosing state secrets. In the first days of the hearing, the proceedings were conducted without any startling events, but during the pleading procedure the defence counsel boldly stated that his client was innocent, that the charges brought against Tran Mai Hanh were 'vague, unsubstantiated and unpersuasive' and that the 'police had orchestrated gangsters' testimony in prison rehearsals' (Cohen 2003a:22). The prosecutor's case indeed included some contradictions and gaps, the witnesses could not remember the location of Hanh's office nor specify when and where Tran Mai Hanh was allegedly bribed. Defence Attorney Luan requested clarification of these points by the prosecution office but the prosecutor refused.[55]

Dang Van Luan's comments in court sparked a public debate about the appropriate behaviour in court of defence attorneys. The press was divided in its opinion about Luan's comments, either finding it *lam dung quyen dan chu* (an 'abuse of the democratic right') or supporting the lawyer's freedom of speech.[56] It also showed the far-reaching consequences such behaviour could generate. The prosecutor of Tran Mai Hanh's case commented that Dang Van Luan's behaviour 'offended the agencies conducting the proceedings' and referred to a provision of the Criminal Procedure Code, asking the presiding judge to prosecute the defence counsel at the hearing.[57] The Ministry of Police asked several official bodies[58] to initiate disciplinary proceedings against Dang Van Luan.[59]

Dang Van Luan protested against these accusations, saying that he had not deliberately offended or slandered the judicial agencies; he had just performed the *thien chuc* ('heavenly mandate') and the *su menh* ('mission') of a barrister[60] and condemned the actions by the prosecution office as *gay ap luc* ('applying pressure').[61] He was supported by the chairman of the Hanoi Bar Association Nguyen Trong Ty who said that 'lawyers have the right to argue, to defend their clients' and that there was 'no reason to have a police investigation [of Luan]' (Cohen 2003a:23).

However, the judgment did not take Luan's arguments into consideration. Instead, they were regarded as *suy luan chu quan* ('subjectively deduced')[62] and thus irrelevant.[63] The imposed sentence was therefore close to the sentence sought by the prosecutor.

Thus, lawyers were willing to utilise recent law reforms and establish a more involved and active role in criminal proceedings, but these attempts fell short since the prosecution and the court rejected these efforts and resumed their 'old ways'.

Dang Van Luan's experience in particular shaped public opinion of the Nam Cam trial. It was noted that defence lawyers had more freedom to conduct their defence, and was read as a sign that less political restriction was placed on lawyers than in the past. But the case also raised questions as to whether the current reforms went far enough (Tran Dinh Thanh Lam 2003).

Public response to the case

Daily press conferences, extensive press coverage in the newspapers and live television broadcast throughout the trial brought public attention to the trial. People from all social classes attended the public hearings. This exposure affected the way the public viewed the recent reforms to the legal system and the anti-corruption campaign. While the state and Party aimed to show their commitment to these changes, the public's perception of the Nam Cam affair was split. The trial initiated the recent law reforms and pointed out the urgency for law reforms (Quinn 2003). It also secured Party commitment, albeit circumscribed, to crack down on corruption.

The public, however, questioned this commitment during the trial. Neither foreign nor local observers were satisfied with the depth of the investigation. While speculation about the guilt of the charged Party officials was limited, most people saw them as just scapegoats to a very widespread problem, sacrificed in a trial that appeared '...more to do with competing factions and power bases among senior party members than anything else' (Rowse 2003e).

A television talk show broadcast the night before the verdict was delivered featured a discussion about a new anti-corruption movie, *Luoi Troi* ('Heavens Net'), that confirmed this impression. Apparently reflecting reality, the movie showed Party officials and business linked in a web of corruption, only its lesser criminal characters being convicted while the mastermind, a Party official, walks free. This caused one talk show participant to raise the question of whether the recent anti-corruption campaign targeted the 'tigers' or the 'cats' (Cohen 2003a:23).

Evidence given during the trial supports this speculation. Party officials appeared to have been bought by minimal bribes, even by Vietnamese standards,[64] probably in order to avoid the harsh punishments of the new anti-corruption law (Cohen 2003c). It is not surprising, therefore, that none of the government-linked defendants received death sentences (*Chicago Tribune*, 15 September 2003).

CONCLUSION

The Nam Cam trial illustrates the contradictions of the recent law reforms. On the one hand, improvements have been made with respect to the rights of the defendant and the participation of defence lawyers in the course of the trial. These recent changes have not yet been adopted and incorporated by other legal parties such as the judges and the prosecution. In fact their attitude and behaviour towards lawyers has not undergone significant changes. This is reflected in the public's perception of the criminal justice system, which has not significantly improved. The public still views the legal system as unequipped to address the criminal activities of Party officials and views lawyers as still restricted by political constraints.

In order for reforms to be more effective, significant changes in the judicial system are necessary; not only the position of lawyers but all parts of the judicial system need to be strengthened. This would enhance the effectiveness of judicial activities and reduce the phenomenon of *may moc, don thuan, vo chinh tri* ('mechanical and simple legalism, non politics') in the judiciary (Nguyen Van Hien 2001).

The motive behind such improvements is not only internal as Vietnam is preparing for accession to the WTO. Lawyers are especially equipped to inspire and strengthen judicial reforms and contribute to an independent and transparent justice system.

NOTES

[1] Resolution 8, On Forthcoming Principal Judiciary Tasks, Communist Party Politburo, 2 January 2002.
[2] *Den gioi* or *den troi* means 'God's light'; *Soi xet* means 'considering'; *Den gioi soi xet* means 'God will consider the case' or 'God willing'. Perhaps this idiom appeared as a reflection of people's expectations of the human courts in the past.
[3] Order No. 46/SL of President Ho Chi Minh on Lawyer Organisation, 10 October 1945. Available from the law database of the National Assembly Office.
[4] Order on Army Court Organisation, 15 September 1945, law database of National Assembly Office. See also Nguyen Van Tuan (2001).
[5] Article 67, Constitution of Vietnam 1946. See also Nguyen Van Tuan (2001).
[6] Order No. 69-SL of President Ho Chi Minh on Permission of Accused Requesting a Citizen who is not a Lawyer to Defend before Ordinary Courts and Special Courts, 18 June 1949.
[7] Article 3, Order No. 69-SL (1949).
[8] Part B, Order No. 49-SL on Direct Tax, 18 June 1949.
[9] The Vietnam Lawyers' Association was established on 4 April 1955.
[10] According to Nguyen Van Tuan (2001), the 'Law Office' was established in 1963, but the Hanoi Bar Association (2002) claims that it was established in 1965.
[11] Article 133, Constitution of Vietnam 1980.
[12] The Legal Committee was established in 1972, and the Supreme People's Court transferred the Lawyer Office to this committee in 1974. Decree 143/HDBT of the Government on Functions, Tasks and Powers of Ministry of Justice, 22 November 1981.
[13] Circular 313/TT/LS of Ministry of Justice, 21 February 1989, providing guidelines for Decree 15/HDBT on Regulations of Bar Associations.

[14] *Ho Chi Minh City Legal Newspaper* (No. 52/2003, 17 July 2003) disclosed that only 48 per cent of prosecutors have a Bachelor of Laws degree. See also Pham Hong Hai (2003).

[15] Nghi quyet Hoi nghi lan thu ba Ban chap hanh Trung uong Dang Cong san Vietnam [Resolution of the Third Meeting of Vietnam Communist Party Central Committee], Communist Party Central Committee, September 1997.

[16] Article 15, Ordinance on Lawyers 2001.

[17] Article 22, Ordinance on Lawyers 2001.

[18] Articles 16, 23, 25, 29 and 41, Ordinance on Lawyers 2001.

[19] Pers. comm. with various lawyers and the Legal Consultancy Department, Ministry of Justice.

[20] Pers. comm. with various lawyers and the Legal Consultancy Department, Ministry of Justice.

[21] Content from the Legal Professional Training School Update, October 2003.

[22] Official letter 071/C16, Ministry of Police, 14 May 2003.

[23] *Quan tinh* is also translated as 'red tape' by the *Legislative Studies Magazine* (No. 5/2002, English summary, p 83); English Index of Article Published in 2002, Special Issue No. 2, January 2003. The author, Nguyen Hung Quang, prefers the translation of 'mandarin-like behaviour' because it is more comprehensive.

[24] Order 217/SL of President Ho Chi Minh dated 22 November 1946 on laying down mechanism of judges becoming lawyers.

[25] See, for example, the article 'Luat su voi nhung ap luc "vo hinh" [Lawyers with invisible pressures]', *Sunday Legal Newspaper*, No. 166, 13 June 2003:7.

[26] The author, Nguyen Hung Quang, heard this description in 2000 from a client when discussing the role of lawyers in society.

[27] 'Luat su chua duoc tao dieu kien de thuc hien quyen bao chua [Lawyers have not created adequate conditions for performing defence work]', *Vnexpress*, 18 August 2001. Available online at http://vnexpress/vietnam/phapluat. The 2003 Criminal Procedures Code passed by the National Assembly in November 2003, however, accepted lawyers' participation in the investigation stage but had not come into force when this chapter was completed.

[28] Article 36, Criminal Proceedings Code.

[29] 'Luat su chua duoc tao dieu kien de thuc hien quyen bao chua' [Lawyers have not created adequate conditions for performing defence work]', *Vnexpress*, 18 August 2001. Available online at http://vnexpress/vietnam/phapluat.

[30] 'Luat su chua duoc tao dieu kien de thuc hien quyen bao chua [Lawyers have not created adequate conditions for performing defence work]', *Vnexpress*, 18 August 2001. Available online at http://vnexpress/vietnam/phapluat. See also Pham Hong Hai (2003:34, 38).

[31] 'Luat su chua duoc tao dieu kien de thuc hien quyen bao chua [Lawyers have not created adequate conditions for performing defence work]', *Vnexpress*, 18 August 2001. Available online at http://vnexpress/vietnam/phapluat.

[32] 'Bai bao chua-dau phai kieu gi cung duoc', ('Argument Speech-Not Any Form Is Acceptable?'), *Ho Chi Minh City Legal Newspaper* No 65/2003, 1 September 2003, p. 7.

[33] This claim is based on anecdotal evidence noted by Nguyen Hung Quang, a barrister in Hanoi, after he participated in numerous hearings where the old barristers provided arguments of this structure.

[34] I base this opinion on my time studying at the Hanoi Law University. Of the 700 graduates in 1996 from the Hanoi Law University, only about 40–50 work as private lawyers.

[35] In 20–25 November 1996, the Ministry of Justice organised a training course for lawyers in the Northern area. A similar course was also organised in the Southern area in December 1996 for about 100 lawyers.

[36] The Legal Professional Training School was established by Decision 34/1998/QD-TTg of the Prime Minister, 11 February 1998.

[37] Legal Needs Assessment on Vietnam Legal System 2001-2010, Item 6.6.

[38] Item b, section 1, Part B, *Resolution No. 08-NQ/TW* of the Politburo on Forthcoming Principal Judicial Tasks, dated 2 January 2002.

[39] The popular name of the case 'Nam Cam' derives from the nickname of Truong Van Cam, the defendant, which is 'Nam Cam' or 'Fifth Orange'.

[40] This heading was the title of many articles about Nam Cam case in Phap Luat newspaper.

[41] See http://www.laodong.com.vn/sodara/0599/24/thoisu/blsk.htm [accessed 16 September 2003]; and http://www.laodong.com.vn/sodara/1199/17/thoisu/ct.htm [accessed 16 September 2003].

42   For further details on the improvements, compare the section 'The experience of lawyers during the trial' below.

43   The association of Truong Van Cam with 'The Godfather' has been made by several authors such as Cohen (2002:56); Mills (2003); and 'Appeal for Vietnam Mafia boss and Party cadres set for September 15', *Agence France Press*, 13 August 2003.

44   See also Indictment of Truong Van Cam and Associates, p. 377.

45   Indictment of Truong Van Cam and Associates, p. 24. See also Cohen (2002).

46   Indictment of Truong Van Cam and Associates, p. 10; see also Rowse (2003a).

47   Indictment of Truong Van Cam and Associates, p. 24; see also Vasavakul (2003).

48   In the wake of the 'Nam Cam' case, the two senior Party members, Tran Mai Hanh and Pham Sy Chien, were found guilty of securing Nam Cam's early release in return for cash and gifts (Rowse 2003c).

49   *Nhan Dan Newspaper* website, http://www.nhandan.org.vn, visited 13 June 2003.

50   Quang Chung (2003); and 'Khai mac phien toa xet xu vu an hinh su lon nhat tu truoc toi nay [Opening of biggest criminal trial from the time before to now]', *VnExpress*. Available online at www.vnexpress.net [accessed 25 February 2003].

51   'Nam Cam trial flags state's fight against serious crime', *The Vietnam Investment Review*, 10 March 2003

52   Stories conflict on how many people were summoned. According to http//vnexpress.net/legal.html, there were 238 related persons, but the *Nhan Dan Newspaper* website, http://www.nhandan.org.vn, reported that there were 253 related persons.

53   This was a significant difference because, as noted earlier, lawyers previously had to take notes in court office.

54   See 'Phong cach bao chua cua luat su Luan va luat su Tri [Defending the methods of lawyer Luan and lawyer Tri]', *Ho Chi Minh City Legal Newspaper*, 15 May 2003:10; 'Nay sinh cac van de phap ly [Arising Legal Issues]', *Sunday Legal Newspaper*, No. 118, 18 May 2003:11; 'Khac nhau ve ap dung luat? [Different application of law?]', *Sunday Legal Newspaper* No. 124, 25 May 2003:11; 'Minh hoa tai toa, duoc khong? [Demonstrating and illustrating in the hearing, can be done?]', *Ho Chi Minh City Legal Newspaper*, 8 May 2003:7.

55   'Tranh luan voi cac luat su, cong to vien phat bieu "bao chua xuc pham co quan to tung la to ra bat luc truoc viec chung minh than chu cua minh vo toi"' [Argument with defence counsels, the prosecutor's speech on defence aiming to offend the judiciary bodies that manifests itself as helpless in the face of the demonstration of innocence of the clients]', *Phap Luat Newspaper*, 21 May 2003:11. Several defence attorneys were faced with a similar problem but in most cases these concerns were not addressed by the prosecution office ('Nhung cau noi an tuong trong tranh luan [Some impressive words in the pleading section]', *Phap Luat Newspaper*, No. 124, 25 May 2003:11; 'Vien kiem sat khong tranh luan co nghia la dong y [Procuracy refused to argue the meaning of "consent"]', *Vnexpress*, 22 May 2003.

56   'Phong cach bao chua cua luat su Luan va luat su Tri' [Defending methods of lawyer Luan and lawyer Tri]', *Ho Chi Minh City Legal Newspaper*, 15 May 2003:10; 'Tran Mai Hanh khong pham toi [Tran Mai Hanh has not been found guilty]', *Ho Chi Minh City Legal Newspaper*, 13 May 2003:11.

57   'Vien kiem sat de nghi khoi to luat su Dang Van Luan' [The procuracy requests to bring barrister Dang Van Luan To Trial]', *Vnexpress*, 20 May 2003.

58   Official letters were send to the Ho Chi Minh City People's Court, the People's Procuracy, The Ministry of Justice, the trial panel and the Communist Party Committee, since Dang Van Luan was a Party member.

59   'Luat su Dang Van Luan da vu khong co quan dieu tra [Barrister Dang Van Luan has slandered the investigation body]', *Vnexpress*, 16 May 2003; Official Letter 071/C16 of Ministry of Police, 14 May 2003; Official Letter No 071/C16 of Ministry of Police, 14 May 2003.

60   'Luat su Luan bao luu toan bo y kien cua minh [Barrister Luan sticks to his argument]', *Vnexpress*, 22 May 2003; 'Toi khong mat sat co quan dieu tra ma chi lam dung thien chuc luat su' [I did not slander the investigation body, only perform heaven mandate of lawyers]', *Vietnam News Agency*; 'Luat su Dang Van Luan: "Vai nam nua du luan se phan quyet chuyen nay" [Barrister Dang Van Luan said: some years later public opinions will judge this issue]', *Ho Chi Minh City Legal Newspaper*, No 46/2003, 26 June 2003:7; 'Luat su va co quan to tung phai ton trong nhau, Doan Luat su Thai Binh rut kinh nghiem sau vu an Nam Cam [Lawyers and judicial bodies should respect each other]', 'Thai Binh Bar Association holds a meeting to study the experience of the Nam Cam Case]', *Phap Luat Newspaper*, 21 July 2003:5.

[61]   'Luat su Luan bao luu toan bo y kien cua minh [Barrister Luan sticks to his argument]', *Vnexpress*, 22 May 2003.

[62]   In the wake of the Nam Cam trial, the Ministry of Justice requested that all bar associations with members participating in the trials conduct further training of the defence lawyers in order to develop their skills and avoid the accusation of 'subjective deduction'. However, most bar associations took the opportunity to request from state agencies as well as the courts that their independence and professionalism should be respected. This is clear evidence of the professional pride and attitude of these associations ('Luat su va co quan to tung phai ton trong nhau, Doan Luat su Thai Binh rut kinh nghiem sau vu an Nam Cam' [Lawyers and judicial bodies should respect each other, Thai Binh Bar Association holds a meeting to study the experience of the Nam Cam case], *Phap Luat Newspaper*, 21 July 2003:5).

[63]   'Hau het cac lap luan cua luat su trong vu an Nam Cam bi bac bo [Most arguments of defence counsels in Nam Cam hearing were rejected]', *Vnexpress*, 4 June 2003.

[64]   Former radio chief Tran Mai Hanh, who assisted Nam Cam's criminal career, particularly by securing his early release from re-education camp in 1997, allegedly received US$6,000 and an Omega watch (Cohen 2003b).

REFERENCES

Cohen, M., 2002. 'Murder and mystery', *Far Eastern Economic Review*, **165**(56):56–58.

——, 2003a. 'Crime fighting for the masses', *Far Eastern Economic Review*, 19 June, 166(24):22–23.

——, 2003b. 'Rare move targets gangs, protectors in government', *The Asian Wall Street Journal*, 6 June:A4.

——, 2003c. 'Vietnam crime figures receive death penalty', *Asian Wall Street Journal*, 6 June:A4.

D.T., 2002. 'Khi luat su vung tay [When the lawyer swings his arm]', *Laodong Newspaper*, 189:n.p. Available online at http://www.laodong.com.vn [accessed 8 June 2003].

Duc Uy-Duc Dung, 2002. *Bi an tam ly nguoi Vietnam* [Secrets of the Mental Habits of the Vietnamese People], People's Police Publishing House, Hanoi.

Durand, B., 2002. 'Cac luat gia Phap va van de phap dien hoa o Vietnam—vi du ve luat to tung dan su nam 1918 [French lawyers and law development in Vietnam]', *Foreign Researchers Discussing Vietnam*, Volume 1, The Gioi Publishing House:91–105.

Hanoi Bar Association, 2002. *Lich su Doan Luat su thanh pho Ha Noi (1984–2002)* [History of the Hanoi Bar Association from 1984–2002], Hanoi Bar Association, Hanoi.

Hoang The Lien, 2002. Quan diem cua Dang va Nha nuoc ve cai cach tu phap tu nam 1986 cho toi nay [The Point of View of the Communist Party and State on Judicial Reform from 1986 until Now], conference paper presented at 'The Points of View on Judicial Reform in Circumstance of Building Up Socialist Law-based State of the People, by the People and for the People' Conference, Ministry of Justice, Hanoi.

Kazim, A., 2003. 'Vietnam's top gangster found guilty of murder and bribery', *Financial Times*, 5 June:12.

Le Kim Que, 2003. 'Nguon goc nghe luat su [Origin of the lawyer career]', *Lawyer Today Magazine*, 11 September.

Lindsey, T., 2002. 'History always repeats? Corruption, culture and "Asian values"', in T. Lindsey and H. Dick (eds), *Corruption in Asia: rethinking the governance paradigm*, Federation Press, Sydney:1–23.

Maria, K., 2003. 'Vietnam: death sentence upheld for "Nam Kam"', *Voice of America News*, 30 October 2003. Available online at http://www.voanews.com/english/Archive/a-2003-10-30-40-Vietnam.cfm [accessed 10 January 2005].

Marr, D., 2000. 'Concepts of 'Individual' and 'Self' in Twentieth-Century Vietnam', *Modern Asia Studies*, 34(4):769–96.

Mills, E., 2003. 'Crime boss faces execution as Vietnam's government tries to resurrect its legitimacy', World Markets Research Centre Daily Analysis, 30 October

Nguyen Dang Thuc, 1992. *Lich su tu tuong Vietnam* [History of Vietnamese Ideologies], Ho Chi Minh City Publishing House, Ho Chi Minh City.

Nguyen Dinh Loc, 2001. 'Ve Phap lenh luat su 2001 [Comments on the Ordinance on Lawyers 2001]', *Legal and Democratic Magazine*, Special Issue for the Ordinance on Lawyers 2001:6–17.

Nguyen Ngoc Huy and Ta Van Tai, 1986. 'The Vietnamese text', in M.B. Hooker (ed.), *Laws of South-East Asia*, Volume 1, Butterworths, Singapore:435–96.

Nguyen Phan Quang and Phan Van Hoang, 1995. *Luat su Phan Van Truong* [Lawyer Phan Van Truong], Ho Chi Minh City Publishing House, Ho Chi Minh City.

Nguyen Thanh Binh, 2002. 'Quan tinh va xoa bo quan tinh [About "red tape" and how to kill it]', *Legislative Studies Magazine*, 5:6.

Nguyen Van Bon, 2001. 'Hinh thuc to chuc hanh nghe luat su theo Phap lenh Luat su 2001 [Forms of legal practising organizations according to the Ordinance on Lawyers 2001]', *Legal and Democratic Magazine*, Special Issue for Ordinance on Lawyers 2001:61.

Nguyen Van Hien, 2001. 'Thuc trang doi ngu tham phan o Vietnam va phuong huong doi moi trong thoi ky moi [Judicial criteria: current situation and requirements for new era]', *People's Court Journal*, 4:2–6.

Nguyen Van Thao, 2001. 'Mot so van de can quan tam khi thi hanh Phap lenh Luat su [Several concerns when the Ordinance on Lawyers is implemented]', *Legal and Democratic Magazine*, Special Issue for the Ordinance on Lawyers 2001:26–37.

Nguyen Van Tuan, 2001. 'Su hinh thanh va phat trien nghe luat su o Vietnam [Formation and development of the lawyer career in Vietnam]', *Legal and Democratic Magazine*, Special Issue for the Ordinance on Lawyers:38–46.

Nicholson, P., 2000. Borrowing Court Systems: the experience of the Democratic Republic of Vietnam, 1945–1976, PhD thesis, University of Melbourne, Melbourne.

——, 2002. 'The Vietnamese court and corruption', in T. Lindsey and H. Dick (eds), *Corruption in Asia: rethinking the governance paradigm*, Federation Press, Sydney:201–18.

—— and Nguyen Hung Quang, 2005. 'The Vietnamese judiciary: the politics of appointment and promotion', *Pacific Rim Policy Journal*, 14(1):1–32.

Pham Hong Hai, 2003. *Mo hinh ly luan Bo luat to tung hinh su Vietnam* [Theoretical Model of the Criminal Procedures Code of Vietnam], People's Police Publishing House, Hanoi.

Pham Tri Thuc, 2002. 'Ve Du an Luat To chuc Vien Kiem sat nhan dan sua doi [About the Project of Amendment of Law on the Procuracy Organization]', *Legislative Magazine*, No.2

Pham Hung, 2000. Speech at 45 Year Establishment Anniversary of the Vietnam Lawyers Association, The Summary Record of 45 Year Anniversary, Vietnam Lawyers Association, Hanoi.

Phan Huu Thu, 2001. 'Dao tao, boi duong luat su trong thoi ky doi moi [Training and professionally improving the lawyer career in the Doi Moi period]', *Legal and Democratic Magazine*, Special Issue for the Ordinance on Lawyers 2001:92–102.

Quang Chung, 2003. 'Giant criminal ring to stand trial on February 25', *The Saigon Times Daily*, 20 February.

Quinn, B., 2003. 'Vietnam's continuing legal reform: gaining control over the courts', Asian Pacific Law and Policy Journal, 4(12):431–68.

Rowse, B., 2003a. 'Game over for defiant Vietnam crime boss', *Agence France Presse*, 5 June.

——, 2003b. 'Vietnam crime boss fighting for his life', *Agence France Presse*, 4 June.

——, 2003c. 'Vietnam Mafia boss found guilty as Communist Party corruption exposed', *Agence France Presse*, 4 June.

——, 2003d. 'Vietnam ousts top Communist Party cadres over Mafia scandal', *Agence France Presse*, 15 July.

——, 2003e. 'Vietnam's explosive corruption showtrial reaches scripted climax', *Agence France Presse*, 5 June.

Tan Van Tai, 2002. 'Phap quyen trong phap luat truyen thong cua Vietnam va Trung quoc co—tap tuc phap ly Dong A truyen thong duoi anh sang cua cac chuan muc phap quyen hien dai [Rule of law in traditional legislation of ancient Vietnam and China: traditional legal customs of East Asia in the light of modern rule of law standards]', *Foreign Researchers Discussing Vietnam*, Volume 2, The Gioi Publishing House, Hanoi:424–46.

Thayer, C.A., 2002. Recent Political Developments: Vietnam in 2002, Paper presented at the Vietnam Update Conference, The Australian National University, Canberra.

The Gia, 2003. 'Phien toa xet xu Nam Cam va Dong bon, Doi Moi Theo Tinh Than Cai Cach Tu Phap' [Nam Cam and associates trial, a renovation in judicial reform]', *Nhan Dan Newspaper* website, 23 June.

Tran Dinh Thanh Lam, 2003. 'Vietnam: crackdown on corruption must go further, citizens say', *Inter Press Service*, 7 June.

Tran Thi Tuyet, 2003. 'Dac diem chu yeu ve to chuc va hoat dong tu phap nuoc ta thoi ky truoc nam 1945 [Characteristics of judicial organization and operation of our country before 1945]', *State and Law Reviews*, No. 8, (184)/2003:13–19.

Tran Trong Kim, 2001. *Viet Nam Su luoc* [Vietnamese Historical Summary], Dang Nang Publishing House, Da Nang.

White, C., 1981. Agrarian Reform and National Liberation in the Vietnamese Revolution: 1920-1957, PhD Thesis, Cornell University, Ithaca, New York

Vasavakul, T., 2003. Mapping Vietnam's Legal Culture: reflections on corruption, organized crime, and state building in the post-Socialist era, Conference Paper presented at Vietnam Legal Culture Symposium, Centre for Asia Pacific Initiatives, University of Victoria, Victoria, Canada, 27–29 March.

10

Mapping legal change in the context of reforms to Chinese police powers

Sarah Biddulph

In 1978, the Central Committee of the Communist Party of China (CPC) began a program of economic modernisation and reform,[1] a core aim of which was rebuilding the Chinese legal system.[2] The importance of this aim increased further in 1996, when the Party approved the program of 'ruling the country according to law' (*yifa zhiguo*). In a speech in 1996 and in his subsequent keynote address to the Fifteenth National Congress of the CPC in September 1997, Jiang Zemin advocated 'Us(ing) law to rule the country, protect the long-term peace and good order of the state (*yifa zhiguo, baozhan guojia changzhi jiu'an)'*.[3] Subsequently, the Party adopted the slogan that 'ruling the country on the basis of law is the basic program by which the Party leads the people in ruling the country' (Zhu Rongji 1999:2). An increasingly important component of 'ruling the country according to law' has been a requirement that law provide the foundation on which state power is defined and exercised. That is, implementation of a system of law-based governance. The desire for formal legal legitimation of the exercise of the state's administrative power is captured in the slogan 'administration according to law' (*yifa xingzheng*).[4]

The process of constructing the legal system has, accurately, been described as 'an event of epic historic proportions' (Alford 1999:193). While reforms to the legal regulation of economic relations have taken place at a phenomenal rate, this chapter focuses on the slower, and arguably more complex, process of reforming state administrative powers, specifically one of the administrative detention powers of the Chinese public security organs (*gong'an jiguan*, also referred to in this chapter as the 'police')[5]—detention for investigation (*shourong shencha*).[6] This power is particularly interesting because it was ostensibly abolished by amendments to the *Criminal Procedure Law* in 1996.

DESCRIBING THE PROCESSES OF LEGAL REFORM: THE PROBLEM STATED

Why choose to examine this power? My concern with the police and their detention powers in particular, lies in the slowness, complexity and unevenness of the legal reforms in this area. Scholars and human rights organisations agree that the reforms to the sanctioning system, including criminal and administrative sanctions, have not been as effective as in other areas of Chinese law.[7] One scholar has commented that legal reforms in different sectors may 'be out of synchrony and in conflict with each other' (Winkler 1999:3). In attempting to describe the story of China's legal modernisation in areas such as police power, we must find a way to engage with the internal diversity, even inconsistency, in the ways in which legal reform is given substance and implemented across different sectors.

There are many different ways to approach a study of legal reform. The analytical framework brought to bear will influence not only the questions posed, but also our understanding of the answers to those questions. Even if we are content with a purely descriptive framework, the very act of selecting what to describe involves a choice about what we consider to be relevant or important. Arguably, pure description thus also reflects some paradigm, even if that paradigm is not articulated.

One influential paradigm for evaluating legal reform since the beginning of the reform era[8] has been to trace the strengthening and entrenchment of formal, bureaucratic, or judicial modes of justice under the rubric of socialist legality against a weakening of the informal modes of justice that predominated in revolutionary periods (Baum 1986; Brugger and Reglar 1994; Dreyer 1996). When plotted against the criteria of formal and informal modes of justice, the ongoing use of administrative forms of detention suggests that informal administration of justice persists.

As legal reform has progressed, many studies have focused on whether reforms to China's legal system indicate a transition from an instrumentalist vision of rule by law toward some version of the rule of law.[9] Randall Peerenboom, for example, concludes that the Chinese legal system is moving towards, but has not yet achieved, a formalist rule of law. Nonetheless, he argues it is no longer apposite to characterise the Chinese legal system as rule by law.[10] He argues that many areas of the Chinese legal system, including the administrative law system, have, over the last 20 years, shown signs of convergence with Western legal systems (Peerenboom 2002a). As this trend continues, it is likely that the Chinese system will develop traits in common with the legal systems of industrial countries (Peerenboom 1999, 2002b). Seen in this way, legal reform of the state's coercive powers for crime control and social order appears to have 'lagged' behind that of other sectors. Many scholars argue that, despite legal reforms, the state's sanctioning system remains an instrument of social and political control (Potter 1999; Lubman 1999).[11] Viewed within the paradigm of transition towards a system of the rule of law, the continuing use of administrative forms of detention and hard strikes against crime has been characterised as a form of 'pernicious instrumentalism' (Peerenboom 1999:327–8).

Closely aligned to this model of the transition to the rule of law is consideration of the extent to which China's legal system is becoming 'modern'. The work of Weber[12] is considered by many as the yardstick of whether a 'modern' criminal justice system is being created (Tanner 1999). Scholars such as Ma and Wong have noted that reforms in the structure and powers of the Chinese police have been the catalyst for the creation of a professional and 'modern' police force.[13] Others conclude that the Chinese police have become an 'institutional hybrid', pointing to the coexistence of Maoist strategies of mass campaigns and the retention of 'such mainstream Stalinist institutions as labour camps', with a 'groping toward more modern forms of police work...based on legal institutions and professional training' (Winkler 1999:16–7).

These models for understanding legal change focus our attention on the extent to which reforms have progressed towards embracing either a formal system of justice, the rule of law, or modernity. They highlight the continuing influence of earlier, revolutionary modes of justice on current reform processes by focusing our attention on the outcomes of current reform measured against some standard.[14]

In this chapter, I will outline an alternative approach that focuses more on the processes of change than on its outcomes. This approach adopts the hypothesis that legal change is a structured yet contested process with an unknown endpoint. To do this, I will draw on a version of Bourdieu's concept of the legal field, applied in the context of rapid change currently taking place in China.

THE ANALYTICAL FRAMEWORK INTRODUCED: THE LEGAL FIELD

According to Bourdieu, a society comprises a 'series of interrelated yet semi-autonomous fields, each of which has a distinct structure' (Trubek et al. 1994:414). Each field may be divided into subfields, each of which has its own particular logic and rules (Bourdieu and Wacquant 1992).

A field is described as 'an area of structured, socially patterned activity or "practice" in this case (that is, the legal field) disciplinarily and professionally defined' (Terdiman 1987:805–6) and a 'network...of objective relations between positions' (Bourdieu and Wacquant 1992:97). The legal field is 'organised around a body of internal protocols and assumptions, characteristic behaviours and self sustaining values'.[15] Each field has its own logic that is 'specific and irreducible to those that regulate other fields' (Bourdieu and Wacquant 1992:97).[16]

Bourdieu draws an analogy between the legal field and a 'game', such as a game of tennis (Bourdieu and Wacquant 1992). The legal field is constituted by the ongoing struggle or competition between different legal actors to 'appropriate the specific products' (Bourdieu 1987:818; Bourdieu and Wacquant 1992), or stakes, of the field—money, status, power (Trubek et al. 1994)[17] and what Bourdieu describes as the 'right to determine the law' (Bourdieu 1987:816, 817).[18]

Whilst the players compete with each other for the stakes of the game, they all concur in their belief that both the game itself and the stakes of the game are worth competing for and vie with each other on the basis of the 'rules of the game' (Bourdieu and Wacquant 1992:98).[19] Using the analogy of a tennis game, the net and the lines on the tennis court mark out the parameters within which these contests take place. Legal actors share a legal '*habitus*', which is the shared practices, views, values and dispositions of actors, and what Terdiman describes as the 'habitual ways of understanding, judging and acting'.[20]

In China, the process of reconstructing the legal system is just over twenty years old. During the revolutionary era of CPC governance prior to 1978, efforts were made to obliterate the distinctive vocabulary and logic of the law and to displace legal institutions and actors in favour of political ones. The CPC's decision to rebuild the legal system has created conditions conducive to the emergence of a distinctive legal field. Rather than assume the existence of an established, relatively autonomous legal field, the search in China is to trace the emergence of a legal field—that is, to identify legal actors, a distinctly legal *habitus*, rules of the game and stakes over which actors compete.

The basic requirement that administration be carried out according to law has placed the Party's authority behind the process of legalisation of the administrative agencies' powers, requiring that powers now be justified in legal, rather than political terms. While the impetus for the emergence of the legal field derives from Party policy and Party leadership, it is not inevitable that the Party controls all the contests that take place within the field. Arguably, the policies of rule according to law and administration according to law are sufficiently flexible to permit adoption of a range of legitimate positions about the meaning and scope of these policies.[21]

The boundaries of the field, according to Bourdieu, are themselves porous and constantly being negotiated—the 'stakes of the struggles' that take place within the field itself (Bourdieu and Wacquant 1992; Trubek et al. 1994). The competition between legal actors helps to define the scope of the legal field itself (Terdiman 1987). The logic and rules of the legal field are created as a result of this competition and not because of some immutable development toward a pre-ordained point (Bourdieu and Wacquant 1992).

The building of law in China has promoted the emergence of a range of legal actors, whose professional qualifications now distinguish them from lay people. This has been facilitated by the program of legal institution building in China, which has imposed increasingly onerous qualification criteria on admission to be, for example, a lawyer or a judge.

The use of specialised legal language and reasoning help define the legal field's boundaries and degree of autonomy by requiring that disputes be reconstructed in legal terms and that they be resolved in accordance with the 'rules and conventions of the field itself' (Bourdieu 1987:831). Thus, for conflicts between parties to be resolved legally, they must first be redefined or, as Bourdieu (1987) puts it, retranslated, in legal terms before being submitted for resolution in accordance with legal rules and procedures. The expansion of the field takes place as matters previously defined and exercised in a non-legal way are redefined in legal terms and brought within the legal field ('appropriative constitution') (Bourdieu 1987).

The ongoing conflict over competence and status between legal actors results in the creation of a hierarchy amongst legal actors (Bourdieu 1987; Terdiman 1987), which is itself susceptible to change over time (Bourdieu 1987). This conflict, according to Bourdieu, determines which actors are authorised to make legitimate interpretations of legal texts and legal practice (Bourdieu 1987; Terdiman 1987). Changes in this hierarchy of privilege and authority reflect the changing political status of groups (Bourdieu 1987). Although some actors may dominate the field and 'are in a position to make it function to their own advantage...they must always contend with the resistance, the claims, the contention, political or otherwise, of the dominated' (Bourdieu and Wacquant 1992:102). Law is produced as an outcome of this competition.

An examination of the reforms to the administrative power of detention for investigation carried out in terms of the legal field raises a number of questions. Is there an emerging legal space in which a range of actors may adopt diverging positions, while at the same time agreeing on the basic parameters within which these positions are to be contested? Are the terms of the debate identifiably legal, using specialist legal vocabulary and legal reasoning? Is there sufficient force or attraction of this field, in terms of legitimation or some other stakes, to reconfigure a debate, which might otherwise have been conceived in political terms, into one framed in terms of legality?

THE POLICE AS LEGAL ACTORS

Of relevance to a discussion about police powers is the role of the police in legal debates. I argue that it is possible to define the police as legal actors and to see the police force itself as constituting a semi-autonomous social field[22] that intersects with the legal field. The police are both influenced by, and influence, debates in the legal field and the state's legal order.

Alongside the reconstruction of the legal system, since 1978, the police have been required to transform themselves from a revolutionary force into a security force responsible for the management of public order and control of crime (Dutton 2000; Fu Hualing 1994). Prior to 1979, their primary task was the violent suppression of class enemies. During what was seen as the revolutionary stage of establishment of the PRC, the police constituted one of the main politico-legal organs of the state, responsible for development and protection of the people's democratic dictatorship (Cui Ming 1993a; Zhengci Falu Jiaoyanshi 1983). In their own words, the public security organs were a 'sharpened weapon for suppression of class enemies' (von Senger 1985:172; see also Wang Fang 1993).[23]

The task of reconstructing the public security organs began with decisions to revive the criminal investigation division to strengthen local-level public order work (Xi Guoguang and Yu Lei 1996) and revive the local-level organisations involved in that work, including residents' committees, mediation committees and security defence committees (Peng Zhen 1982). In April 1983, the Central Committee of CPC approved a decision of its Central Political–Legal Committee to undertake a systematic and comprehensive reform of the public security organs, including strengthening the legal basis of police organisation and powers.[24]

Since then, police reforms have gradually created a more professional force (Dutton 2000; Ward and Bracey 1985), with greater emphasis placed on the education and specialist technical training of police officers[25] and the legalisation of police powers (Shen Zhongmin and Xu Zhenqiang 1997). Although the process of legalisation of police powers is incomplete in many respects,[26] scholars such as Ma point to laws such as the 1995 People's Police Law (PPL) as being significant in 'China's efforts to create a more professional and modern police force' (Ma Yue 1997:113). Kam Wong (2002:294) asserts that the introduction of a system of police ranks has 'regularised, rationalised and legalised the police along Weberian lines'.

Fu Hualing's work also suggests that it is no longer appropriate to assume that the police are an unreflexive enforcement arm of the Party; instead, the police have their own distinct institutional interests. Fu (1994) suggests that, along with their transformation to a more regular security force, the police have lost their privileged position with the CPC *vis-à-vis* other government departments.

Viewed as a semi-autonomous social field, the police can be seen as having a multifaceted relationship with law. They have a vested interest in participating in the contests in which their powers are legally defined, most notably in areas where the principles of law enforcement are established and systems of accountability for the exercise of police power are set up.

THE EXAMPLE OF ABOLITION OF DETENTION FOR INVESTIGATION

Development of detention for investigation from the 1950s

Detention for investigation (*shourong shencha*) developed out of the CPC's efforts to restore social order after it took power in 1949. The power of detention for investigation was adopted by the CPC Central Committee (the 'Central Committee'), and the State Council, at the end of 1957, to deal with the problem of unauthorised rural migration (Central Committee 1957; Zhang Qingwu 1990). It was used initially primarily to detain and repatriate rural migrants, as well as to investigate suspected criminal activities (Zhang Qingwu 1990). In response to the social upheaval caused by the famine resulting from the Great Leap Forward (Spence 1990), in 1961, the Central Committee approved the creation of 'detention for repatriation stations'.

These stations were used for the detention and repatriation of rural migrants who had floated to the cities and for the investigation of those suspected of criminal or counter-revolutionary offences (Central Committee 1961; Fan Chongyi and Xiao Shengxi 1991; Cui Ming 1993b). At this time, the official purpose of the power was 'primarily to rescue, educate and help settle down people who had floated to the city as beggars and to protect social order' (Wang Jiancheng 1992:179).

Towards the end of the Cultural Revolution in 1975, the use of detention for investigation of suspected criminal conduct by transients was separated from the detention for repatriation of unauthorised rural migrants (Fan Chongyi and Xiao Shengxi 1991). The police were given responsibility for managing the detention and investigation of those suspected of criminal conduct, while the civil administration organs ran the stations responsible for repatriation of rural migrants (Fan Chongyi and Xiao Shengxi 1991). In 1980, at the beginning of the reform era, the Central Committee and the State Council jointly issued a report prepared by the Ministry of Public Security which provided for the gradual absorption of detention for investigation into Re-education Through Labour (RETL), where investigations of suspected criminal activity were to be carried out.[27] At that time, legislative drafters declined to include detention for investigation within the scope of the Criminal Procedure Law. Instead, the Criminal Procedure Law provided the police with a more restrictive power to detain for interrogation a person suspected of committing a crime, which was limited to 10 days.[28]

Before detention for investigation could be incorporated within RETL, in August 1983 the Party launched the first campaign of the Hard Strike Against Serious Crime (Fan Chongyi and Xiao Shengxi 1991; Cui Ming 1993b). Not only was the work of integrating detention for investigation with RETL halted, but the use of detention for investigation expanded dramatically.[29] As one senior academic noted at the time, 'detention for investigation centres became large storehouses for detaining all types of offenders' (Cui Ming 1993b:92).

After this time, detention for investigation became a tool used by the police to detain for interrogation a wide range of people suspected of committing crimes. The time limits imposed for detention for investigation were considerably longer than the criminal detention power authorised under the Criminal Procedure Law (CPL).[30] Not surprisingly, the power was used as a substitute for criminal detention and investigation and for a range of other purposes (Liu Huayin and Liu Baiyang 1992; Zhang Shanyu and Zhang Shuyi 1991).[31]

The problems with detention for investigation

Detention for investigation was described as the 'longstanding difficult problem' (*laodanan wenti*) between construction of a socialist legal system and enforcement practice (Liu Shipu 1990:22). It was a power essentially without any formal legal basis. From 1985, the Ministry of Public Security (MPS) issued a range of official documents that sought to define the targets, time limits, and procedures for imposing detention as a means of curbing the rampant abuse of this power.[32]

In 1987 the MPS described the power as

> ...a type of coercive administrative investigation measure used by public security organs in accordance with State Council regulations against those who are suspected of roaming around committing offences, or have committed a criminal act and do not tell their correct name and address and whose background is not clear. It is not a type of criminal punishment, nor is it a public order administrative punishment.[33]

By 1987, local public security organs had been repeatedly criticised by the MPS for abusing their powers of detention for investigation.[34] The MPS continued to exhort local public security organs to curb abuse of the power, and even suggested that the power itself might be lost should the abuses continue unabated.[35]

In 1987, the MPS issued a notice that criticised the continuing abusive practices under this power but at the same time sought to limit the public outcry against abuse of the power by restricting disclosure or public discussion of the power. It was argued that public and media discussions of the use of detention for investigation in handling criminal investigations had led to 'misunderstandings' and 'bad impressions'.[36]

The continuing problems of serious abuse led to increasing public dissatisfaction and concern at senior political levels (Wong 1996), in turn prompting increased scrutiny by state organs outside the public security sector. Amongst the numerous notices demanding that abuses of the power be curbed,[37] the MPS indicated that abuses of detention for investigation had been the subject of complaints and investigation by people's congresses at both local and national levels.[38]

Finding a legal basis for detention for investigation

While seeking to curb abuse and deal with the growing criticism of police misconduct, the MPS was also trying to address the criticisms that there remained no clear legal basis for the power. The clearest legal basis of the power had been provided by the Notice issued by the State Council on 29 February 1980 titled On Supporting the Unification of the Two Measures of Forced Labour and Detention for Investigation with RETL. Although this notice sets out the scope of targets for detention for investigation,[39] it was unsatisfactory as a legal basis for the power in several respects,[40] most notably because the main purpose of the notice—to merge detention for investigation with RETL—was never carried out.[41] Further, this notice did not clarify the relationship between detention for investigation and other police powers to detain and interrogate criminal suspects set out in the Criminal Procedure Law, nor did it clarify its relationship to administrative sanctions for minor public order infringements that could be punished under the Security Administrative Punishment Regulations (SAPR).[42] The MPS sought to supplement this document by providing a more detailed directive setting out targets and procedures for exercising the power in the 1985 MPS Notice on Strictly Controlling the Use of Detention for Investigation Measures.

By requiring the MPS to draft a Detention for Investigation Law (Shourong Shencha Fa) in May 1983, the Central Committee of the CPC made it clear that detention for investigation required a legislative basis and that it be subject to strengthened legal supervision (Central Committee 1983; Gao Xianduan 1990). However, the MPS failed in its bid to have its draft legislation placed on the legislative plan of the National People's Congress Standing Committee and enacted as legislation because of its inability to obtain consensus on the major issues (Gao Xianduan 1990; Guo Dawei 1990).

Passage of the Administrative Litigation Law (ALL), which came into effect on 1 October 1990, increased the urgency of finding a legislative basis for detention for investigation.[43] The Administrative Litigation Law empowered the courts to determine the legality of certain categories of administrative decision-making, including those dealing with the imposition of detention[44] and coercive measures against the person and property.[45] Under the Administrative Litigation Law, the administrative agency was obliged to prove the lawfulness of the conduct, at least requiring the police to point to conformity of the detention with laws and regulations which, together, constituted the 'legal basis' of the power.[46] There was some ambiguity about whether detention for investigation should be seen as an administrative act and so whether it fell within the scope of the Administrative Litigation Law. That question was resolved in the Opinion of the Supreme People's Court Concerning Several Questions on the Implementation of the 'PRC Administrative Litigation Law' (for trial implementation), issued on 29 May 1991,[47] which stated that

> [t]he scope of accepting cases at Article 11 of the ALL…citizens who are dissatisfied with the decision of a public security organ for coercive detention for investigation, can commence litigation in the people's courts.[48]

The MPS then outlined criteria on which the lawfulness of detention for investigation would be determined in the Notice on Several Questions about the Implementation by Public Security Organs of the 'Administrative Litigation Law'.[49] The question of whether the MPS was authorised at all to specify the documents constituting the legal basis of the powers it exercised was ignored.

DEBATES ABOUT REFORM OR ABOLITION OF DETENTION FOR INVESTIGATION

Despite the MPS's efforts to stifle public discussion of detention for investigation, in the late 1980s[50] and early 1990s, debate about the possible reform of detention for investigation began appearing in law and police journals, and became incorporated in broader discussions about reform of the Criminal Procedure Law (Zhongguo Faxue Hui Susong Fa Yanjiu Hui 1992; Fan Chongyi and Xiao Shengxi 1991; Wang Jiancheng 1992).[51] A number of proposals for reform of detention for investigation emerged. These included passing *sui generis* legislation either by the NPC or administrative regulations by the State Council, incorporating the substance of the power into the revised Criminal Procedure Law, or merging the power with RETL (Gao Xianduan 1990; Fan Chongyi and Xiao Shengxi 1991).

Many legal academics and some representatives of people's congresses, and one legal academic in the public security system in particular, argued that the power should be abolished as it was both arbitrary and illegal (Cui Ming 1993b).[52] The arguments were framed in both legal and practical terms. There were a number of aspects to the legal arguments, with the overarching premise resting on assertions that the power's existence was unconstitutional. First, it was argued that the power was contrary to the spirit of Article 37 of the Constitution, which guarantees freedom of the person unless lawfully arrested (Cui Ming 1993b; Wang Xixin 1993). A second argument was that the State Council was not competent to pass laws authorising detention.[53] Third, it was noted that the power to detain administratively undermined the integrity of the criminal procedure system as it was, in practice, a substitute for criminal detention, but was outside the Criminal Procedure Law (Cui Ming 1993b).

On a practical level, it was argued that the power was ineffective in the investigation of crimes (Zhang Jianwei and Li Zhongcheng 1994), and that reform would not solve the problem of abuse (Cui Ming 1993b). There was common recognition that the power was used as a substitute for criminal detention and other criminal coercive powers (Li Huayin and Liu Baiyang 1992; Zhang Shanyu and Zhang Shuyi 1991; Gu Haiwen 1992).

Police, government officials[54] and academics who argued for retention of the power agreed that reform was needed to rectify its inadequate legal and regulatory basis, but they also noted that it was very effective in practice (Li Huayin and Liu Baiyang 1992; Gao Chuanli 1990; Fan Chongyi and Xiao Shengyi 1991; Chen Weidong and Zhang Tao 1992b; Wang Jiangcheng 1992; Jiang Bo and Zhan Zhongle 1994) and accorded with the 'national spirit' (Chen Weidong and Zhang Tao 1992b:172). Views differed amongst academics discussing revisions to the Criminal Procedure Law about whether detention for investigation should be included as a criminal coercive measure.[55]

Central to the debates about reform or abolition of detention for investigation was the question of whether the power should be characterised as administrative or criminal in nature.[56] On one hand, the question had already been answered by the Supreme People's Court's interpretation of the scope of the Administrative Litigation Law.[57] This was subsequently acted upon by the MPS in its specification of the documents constituting the legal basis for judging the lawfulness of any act of detention under the Administrative Litigation Law.[58] Nonetheless, as part of the debate about reform or abolition of the power, its proper legal characterisation remained an important issue.

The discussions about the fate of detention for investigation became subsumed within the debates about reform of the Criminal Procedure Law after a group of legal academics was appointed to prepare a discussion draft, published in 1995, of amendments to the Criminal Procedure Law (Chen and Yan 1995). The paper advocated the abolition of detention for investigation (Chen and Yan 1995), despite the obvious inconvenience to the police this would cause (Chen and Yan 1995:205–6).

As compensation, they suggested that the standard of evidence required to approve arrest be lowered to 'where there is evidence to support a strong suspicion that a crime has been committed where the criminal suspect could be sentenced to punishment of no less than imprisonment' (Chen and Yan 1995:22).[59] The drafting group considered that, even though detention for investigation was to be abolished, it was inappropriate to lengthen the time limit for detention of a maximum of 10 days set out under the 1979 Criminal Procedure Law.[60]

In the meetings that were held after publication of the draft discussion paper, attended by interested state organs, the MPS turned its attention to negotiating inclusion of substantive elements of the power of detention for investigation into the amended Criminal Procedure Law.[61] Proposals included decreasing the standard of evidence required for arrest[62] and expanding the scope of targets and time permitted for detention to include those who previously fell within the scope of detention for investigation.[63] It was further suggested that, in cases where suspects withheld their real names and addresses, the calculation of time in detention would not commence until the suspect's name, address and background had been clarified.[64]

Incorporation of detention for investigation into the amended Criminal Procedure Law and ongoing interpretations

In his explanatory speech on the draft amended Criminal Procedure Law to the Fourth National Peoples' Congress Meeting on 12 March 1996, Gu Angran proclaimed the abolition of detention for investigation, stating

> [d]etention for investigation is a type of administrative coercive measure that has been of positive use for clarifying and investigating crime, especially for investigating those who float from place to place-committing crime and whose identity is not clear. But, the time of detention in detention for investigation is comparatively long. Moreover, because it doesn't involve any other judicial organ and the decision is made by the public security alone, it lacks a system for supervision and restriction and does not conform to the relevant requirements of the CPL.

> In order gradually to strengthen socialist democracy and legal system construction, better to protect the rights and interests of citizens, we have absorbed the contents of detention for investigation needed in practice for the struggle against crime into the CPL by supplementing and amending the relevant criminal coercive measures and have not retained the administrative coercive measure of detention for investigation.

In the final version of the Criminal Procedure Law passed by the National People's Congress, the public security organs had managed to claw back more power than the discussion draft would have allowed, in effect to incorporate many aspects of detention for investigation into the Criminal Procedure Law. The standard for approval of arrest had been further reduced to where 'the principal facts of the crimes have been clarified and [the criminal suspect] could be sentenced to a term of not less than imprisonment'.[65] The scope of targets for detention was expanded to include targets of the former detention for investigation where 'there is a strong suspicion that the person goes from place to place committing crimes, who repeatedly commits crimes, or who gangs up with others to commit crime'.[66] The time limits for requesting arrest of certain categories of detainees, including some previous targets of detention for investigation,[67] was increased from a maximum of seven days to 37 days.[68]

After passage of the amended Criminal Procedure Law, a police commentator suggested that, in theory, the broadening of coercive powers in that law provided the public security organs with sufficient power to perform their criminal investigation functions and to compensate for their loss of detention for investigation (Cui Xin 1996). The amendments, this author suggested, required the public security organs to 'change their traditional work style' from an emphasis on obtaining evidence through interrogation of detained suspects to a broader range of investigation techniques and competencies (Cui Xin 1996:36–7). Changing the police work style and improving their technical investigation skills may be difficult.[69]

Of course, passage of the amended Criminal Procedure Law did not end the ongoing process of construction and reconstruction of police detention powers. After passage of the Criminal Procedure Law, the MPS issued a notice interpreting police-related provisions of the Criminal Procedure Law, which further expanded the calculation of the time limits for detention of criminal suspects who were targets of the former detention for investigation.[70] In particular, the interpretation asserted the requirement that the time limits for detention not commence until there was clarification of the name, address and background of the detainee. Article 28 of the Criminal Procedure Law permits the 'investigation and detention period' (*zhencha jiya qixian*) for those 'who do not tell their true name and address or whose identity is unclear' to commence from the date their identity is clarified. Article 112 of the MPS's interpretation document explained the scope of Article 128 of the Criminal Procedure Law as follows

> Criminal suspects who do not tell their true name and address, whose identity is not clear, if it has not been possible to clarify these matters and to apply for arrest within thirty days, after receipt of approval from the responsible person in the public security bureau at county level or above, the time period for detention will commence from the date on which the identity of the person is clarified, but it is not permitted to halt the investigation into their criminal actions.

One academic claims the original intent of Article 128 of the Criminal Procedure Law was to permit extension of the period of detention after, rather than prior to, the arrest, and that in no circumstances could the period of pre-arrest criminal detention be extended past a total of 37 days (Wang Jiancheng 2000). The commentator suggests that such an interpretation should be abolished, otherwise 'it would be easy for the previous detention for investigation to remain unchanged' (Wang Jiancheng 2000:95).

Law as the forum for debates about administrative coercive powers

What does the story of abolition of detention for investigation tell us about the process of legal reform? This story suggests that the legal forum provides an important framework within which debate about reform of the state's coercive powers may be conducted. Although police administrative detention powers were developed in the politically dominated context of social order policy, their reform and restructuring is now being debated in legal terms.

This illustrates the importance of legally-grounded arguments relating to the organisation and justification of police administrative powers. The debate surrounding reform of detention for investigation was fuelled by concerns about its serious and endemic abuse, but also by the inability of the MPS to justify the power in legal terms. The terms of the debate and the ultimate fate of the power were legally framed in terms of the lawfulness of the power, its proper legal characterisation and its place in the legislative regime governing criminal justice. These debates could be seen as implementing the Party's program of administration according to law.

This case illustrates the active engagement of the MPS in the legal debates to define and justify its powers and how such debates can accommodate a range of different voices and positions to a greater extent than would be possible in a more overtly political context, such as the formulation of social order policy. The outcome—abolition of detention for investigation—shows that when the debate about the fate of the power was conducted in legal terms, the police were unable to assert their preferred option. Academics, congress members and permanent employees of the congress were more influential.

Viewed in terms of the emergence of a legal field, these debates about the fate of detention for investigation indicate the development of a specialist language and logic which framed the debate about detention for investigation. It also revealed that the different actors adopted and advocated different positions, though strictly within the boundaries of, and arguably in furtherance of, Party policies favouring administration according to law and the preservation of social order. In contrast to the pre-reform era, with its focus on class struggle, the Party's programs in the reform era are framed in terms that accommodate legitimate disagreement over how Party policy should be interpreted and implemented. The scope of these policies themselves enables the emergence of a field, and permits it a degree of autonomy consistent with the Party's overall agenda for reform. We might argue that the policies of the reform era have permitted a pluralisation of interests and positions that remain consistent with, and in furtherance of, the Party's overall reform agenda.

The emergence of a legitimate sphere within which differing positions may be taken, and a specialist vocabulary in which they are debated, does not guarantee an outcome that better protects citizens' rights. In the case of detention for investigation, though the power was abolished, the power of the public security organs to detain and interrogate criminal suspects was not dramatically reduced, just re-organised.

CONCLUSION

The process described above may be seen as one of the outcomes of economic reform and modernisation. Party policy has facilitated the emergence of a legal field in which actors, within the constraints of policy, compete to determine the law and hence a space in which a proliferation of positions and views can take place. The self-interested nature of these debates facilitates the expansion of legal norms into areas and in relation to powers not previously framed in legal terms, as was the case with detention for investigation. The debates about detention for investigation reveal the emergence of not only a legal vocabulary but also a form of legal logic. Efforts to reform the power reveal the concern of academics at least to improve the internal coherence of the legal system.

It is harder, however, to characterise the reform of this power as part of a transition towards a system of rule of law, as the power of the police to detain has not been substantially constrained, nor, arguably, even made more accountable. By the same token, it is no longer accurate to characterise the law as simply a tool of policy as the scope of policy itself is now susceptible to a range of differing interpretations which are not all necessarily directly controlled by the Party. From this, we might discern that the policy of governance on the basis of law is acquiring a force of its own, not in opposition to Party leadership, but out of it and, at present at least, as a way of implementing Party policies.

NOTES

[1]   See Benshu Bianxie Zu (2001); Baum (1994); and Potter (1995), who discuss the state's central role in economic reform.

[2]   Deng Xiaoping argued that socialist democracy must be 'institutionalised and written into law'. In this speech, Deng set out the blueprint for subsequent legal reform by asserting that the program required that 'there must be laws to go by, laws must be observed and strictly enforced and breaches of the law must be pursued' (Deng 1978:157). See also Central Committee (1978:14).

[3]   Jiang Zemin's speech, extracted in Liu Hainian (1996:1).

[4]   Ying Songnian (1992:415) defines *yifa xingzheng* in formalist terms as follows
    1. The administrative department must be established and its powers conferred by law. If the organ or any official acts outside the scope of organisational laws, acts where there is no delegated power, or acts in excess of delegated powers, the act will be void.
    2. Administrative acts must not be in conflict with the law and discretionary powers and must be exercised within the scope permitted by law
    3. Any act not carried out within the legally specified procedure will be in excess of power and so void.

[5]   The categories of forces falling within the definition of the people's police (*renmin jingcha*) are set out in Article 2 of the PRC People's Police Law 1995 (PPL). They include the public security organs (*gong'an jiguan*), the state security organs (*guojia anquan jiguan*), the police in prisons (*jianyu*), RETL management organs (*laodong jiaoyang guanli jiguan*) and the judicial police (*sifa jingcha*) of the people's courts and people's procuracy. In this study, all references to 'the police' are to the public security organs.

[6]   Also translated as 'sheltering for investigation' by Hsia and Zeldin (1992); 'shelter and investigation' by Hecht (1996:21–2), Epstein and Wong (1996:480), Chen Jianfu (1999:201–5) and 'sheltering for examination' by Wong (1996:367).

[7]   See, for example, Lubman (1995, 1999); Clarke (1985, 1995); Chiu Hongdah (1992); Leng Schaochuan and Chiu Hongdah (1985); Amnesty International (1991, 1992, 1996); Dobinson (2002); Hecht (1996); Turack (1999); Human Rights in China (2001b).

[8]   In this chapter, the 'reform era' refers to the period after December 1978 when the CPC Central Committee resolved to embark on a program of economic reform and modernisation.

[9]   These include Lubman (1999); Epstein (1994); Peerenboom (1999, 2002a); Keith (1994); Keith and Lin Zhiqiu (2001); Li (2000); Orts (2001). Peerenboom (1999) draws a distinction between

'thick' (substantive) and 'thin' (formalist) versions of the rule of law and discusses different versions of the thick theories of the rule of law. Craig (1997:467) distinguishes formalist from substantive versions of the rule of law on the basis that the former is concerned with the manner in which law is promulgated, clarity of the norm and the 'temporal' aspects of the law, whilst the latter is concerned in addition with the content of the law, whether it protects rights and whether the law is considered 'good'.

[10] For the purposes of this discussion, I adopt the distinction drawn by Peerenboom (2002b:510), when he distinguishes a 'thin', or formalist version of the rule of law from rule by law on the grounds that the 'former entails meaningful legal limits on the government actors'. This distinction is drawn differently, however, by other scholars such as Orts (2001:94) who defines rule by law in a manner equating to Peerenboom's 'thin' rule of law as 'the use of legal rules in order to assure the uniformity and regularity of an existing legal system'. Orts (2001:94) defines the rule of law as referring 'to a normative and political theory of the relationship of legal institutions and the political state that includes, but is not limited to, a theory of limited government through some form of constitutional separation between the judiciary and other state powers', equating to Peerenboom's 'thick' theory of the rule of law.

[11] For a similar analysis, see Lubman (1995); Clarke and Feinerman (1995); H. Tanner (1999); Dobinson (2002); Chen Jianfu (1999). Keith and Lin (2001) on the other hand, argue that amendments to the Criminal Procedure Law and the Criminal Law reflect a changing balance between the instrumental role of law as a tool for social control and law as a mechanism to protect the rights and freedoms of citizens. They subsequently revised this view in light of the state's handling of the 'Falun gong problem' (see Keith and Lin Zhiqiu 2003).

[12] More particularly, interpretations of Weber by US sociologists, such as Talcott Parsons, that give universal application to Weber's consideration of the conditions for the emergence of modern capitalism. Parsons argues that societal evolution and modernisation depends on the development of a general legal system that comprises an 'integrated system of universalistic norms' (Parsons 1964:351, 357). Parsons' expanded application of Weber's work is also discussed in Friedman (1969).

[13] Ma Yue (1997:113) argues that passage of the People's Police Law in 1995 represented 'the most significant event in China's efforts to create a more professional and modern police force'. Wong (2002:294) asserted that the introduction of a system of police ranks 'regularised, rationalised and legalised the police along Weberian lines', and continued to argue that 'a modern Weberian bureaucracy was in the making, the public security being restructured according to the functional needs of and based on a rational division of labour principle.'

[14] Not all scholars are in full agreement with the use of such models to evaluate legal reform. Clarke (2001), for example, criticises as teleological analyses that view the development of the Chinese legal system in terms of how far away it is from a rule of law ideal.

[15] Terdiman (1987:806) suggests that this might informally be referred to as a 'legal culture'. I prefer not to adopt this characterisation as it fails to address the extensive literature and divergent views on what constitutes legal culture.

[16] Emphasis in original.

[17] These are described by Bourdieu (1987:816–17) as economic, social, cultural, symbolic and juridical capital. Juridical capital is the capacity to define the language in which conflicts are expressed. Bourdieu and Wacquant (1992:98–9) and Johnston and Percy-Smith (2003:323) describe social capital as encompassing personal relationships and the benefits available to individuals as a result of participation in social groups.

[18] Although these actors are self interested, this definition suggests that the self-interest is not necessarily narrowly defined. Bourdieu (1990) argues it should not be understood as rational and conscious self-interest.

[19] Bourdieu uses the term 'illusio', to designate that each of the actors has their own 'interest' in the game and that they accept the stakes as valuable (Bourdieu and Wacquant 1992:116–7).

[20] More specifically, Terdiman (1987:811) explains the term habitus as 'the habitual, patterned ways of understanding, judging and acting which arise from our particular position as members of one or several social "fields", and from our particular trajectory in the social structure'.

[21] See general discussions on this point for example in Potter (2003) and Pei (1995).

[22] Goldsmith (1990) also discusses the Australian police as a semi-autonomous social field.

[23] Zhengci Falu Jiaoyanshi (1983:4) cites Lenin in support of their proposition that, as an instrument of class rule, the police are an instrument of violence to carry out the dictatorship of the proletariat.

24 Xi Guoguang and Yu Lei (1996:395–6) refer to the Several Questions Concerning Strengthening and Reform of the Public Security Work adopted at that meeting. Decisions at this meeting included transfer of responsibility for management of Re-education Through Labour (RETL) Camps to the Ministry of Justice (MOJ) and creation of a separate armed police force, the People's Armed Police.

25 In 2002, for example, 50,000 police officers studied for college diplomas; 35,000 studied for tertiary qualifications; 520,000 participated in new recruit training, professional or promotions training; 16,000 economic criminal investigation police sat proficiency tests; and 280,000 police attended skills training programs (Gong'an Bu 2002:65).

26 See, for example, Winkler (1999).

27 State Council Notice Supporting the Unification of the Two Measures of Forced Labour and Detention for Investigation with Re-education through Labour, 29 February 1980.

28 Article 41, Criminal Procedure Law 1979.

29 The Ministry of Public Security's Temporary Regulations on the Management work of Detention for Investigation Centres, 15 February 1984, were passed to 'strengthen and improve the work of detention for investigation centres'. Article 2 states that 'Detention for investigation centres are specialised organs for managing detention for investigation personnel, co-ordinate investigation and protect security'.

30 Under the 1979 Criminal Procedure Law, Article 48, the police could only detain a person for three days prior to making an application for arrest to the procuracy, with a possible extension of up to four days. The procuracy was required to respond within three days. The total possible time for criminal detention was thus ten days. The initial period of detention for investigation, on the other hand, was one month, with possible extensions approved by higher level public security organs of up to a total of three months. Article 3, Ministry of Public Security, Notice on Strictly Controlling the Use of Detention for Investigation Measures, 31 July 1985.

31 Zhang Yu (1993:20) suggests that between 80–90 per cent of people convicted of criminal offences were first detained under this power. Ministry of Public Security, Notice Strictly Prohibiting Public Security Organs from Interfering in Economic Disputes and Illegally Seizing People, 25 April 1992, criticised and prohibited detention by the police of one party to a contract dispute and demanding payment of the amount in dispute to secure their release.

32 The first of which is Ministry of Public Security, Notice on Strictly Controlling the Use of Detention for Investigation, 31 July 1985.

33 Ministry of Public Security, Notice on the Inappropriateness of Publicly Reporting Detention for Investigation, 27 January 1987.

34 These notices included: Ministry of Public Security, Notice on Strengthening the Management Work of Detention Centres and Detention for Investigation Centres, 23 November 1983; Ministry of Public Security, Notice on Strictly Controlling the Use of Detention for Investigation Measures, 31 July 1985; Ministry of Public Security, Notice on Immediately and Conscientiously Rectifying Detention for Investigation Work, 31 July 1986.

35 Ministry of Public Security, Notice on Immediately and Conscientiously Rectifying Detention for Investigation Work, 31 July 1986:381–2.

36 Ministry of Public Security, Notice on the Inappropriateness of Publicly Reporting Detention for Investigation, 27 January 1987.

37 Ministry of Public Security, Notice on Further Controlling the Use of Detention for Investigation Measures, 11 June 1991; Ministry of Public Security, Notice on Urgently Rectifying the Abuse of Detention for Investigation Measures, 15 February 1992; Ministry of Public Security, Notice on Strengthening the Work of Management of the Three Detention [Centres] and Putting an End to Situations where Detainees get Beaten to Death, 22 April 1993; Ministry of Public Security, Notice Strictly Prohibiting Public Security Organs from Interfering in Economic Disputes and Illegally Seizing People, 25 April 1992.

38 Ministry of Public Security, Notice on Further Controlling the Use of Detention for Investigation Measures, 11 June 1991. Yang Xinhua (1991) reports on an inquiry into enforcement practices made by the Internal Affairs and Judicial Work Committee in 1990, which noted systematic abuse of detention for investigation. Ministry of Public Security, Notice on Urgently Rectifying the Abuse of Detention for Investigation Measures, 15 February 1992, refers to an investigation carried out by the Office of the Law Committee of the NPC and the Legislative Affairs Committee of the Standing Committee in December 1991 into abuses of detention for investigation.

[39]   Article 2 provides that
[t]hose people who have committed minor criminal offences and do not tell their name and address and whose background is not clear, or they have committed a minor criminal offence and are suspected of floating from place to place committing crime, committing multiple crimes or forming a group to commit crime, who need to be taken in to investigate their criminal acts, should be sent to a specially formed unit in RETL camps to carry out investigation...In general where the danger would not be great if they were placed in society, can be placed under house arrest, or released on bail etc in accordance with the provisions of the CPL whilst carrying out investigation.

[40]   One argument was that it was beyond the power of the State Council to regulate detention powers, discussed below.

[41]   The process was commenced but never completed because it was overshadowed by the hard strike law and order campaign that started in August 1983 (Gao Xianduan 1990) and the transfer in May 1983 of responsibility for management of RETL camps from the Ministry of Public Security to the Ministry of Justice (Luo Feng 1992; Xia Chongsu 2001).

[42]   Passed by the NPC Standing Committee on 5 September 1986 and amended 12 May 1994.

[43]   Guo Dawei (1990:28) argues that the 'only way out' to preserve the existence of the power was for the NPC to pass legislation, to use legal means to regularise its existence. The Ministry of Public Security's Notice on Several Questions about the Implementation of the 'Administrative Litigation Law' by Public Security Organs, 30 October 1990, set out the rules that were to constitute the legal basis of the power.

[44]   Article 11(1)(i) enables those who are dissatisfied with an administrative punishment such as detention, imposition of a fine, revocation of a permit or licence, an order to suspend production of business activities or the confiscation of property to commence an action. This paragraph includes punishments such as administrative detention under the Security Administrative Punishment Regulations.

[45]   Article 11(1)(ii) of the Administrative Litigation Law enables the court to accept complaints about, among other things, the lawfulness of measures taken to restrict or deprive freedom of the person.

[46]   Articles 32, 52 and 53, Administrative Litigation Law.

[47]   Discussed and passed at the 499th meeting of the Adjudication Committee of the Supreme People's Court on 29 May 1991, reproduced in Huang Jie (1993:659).

[48]   Article 2, Opinion of the Supreme People's Court Concerning Several Questions on the Implementation of the 'PRC Administrative Litigation Law'.

[49]   Reproduced in Huang (1993:668). Point 3 of the Notice provides that
[u]ntil the new detention for investigation legislation is published, the targets of detention for investigation can be determined according to the provisions of the 1980 *Notice of the State Council on the Unification of the Two Measures of Forced Labour and Detention for Investigation with Reeducation through Labour*, which was promulgated in the (1980) No.2 Gazette of the State Council. Investigation and approval procedures and the time limits for detention for investigation must be implemented according to the provisions of the 1985 Ministry of Public Security *Notice on Strictly Controlling the Use of Detention for Investigation Measures*. In handling specific detention for investigation cases you must incorporate the Ministry of Public Security *Notice Printing and Distributing the 'Summary of the Minutes of Meeting of National Public Security Legal System Work'* of May this year, know it well and handle matters strictly according to its spirit. Each level public security organ must strictly eliminate the wanton expansion the scope of detention for investigation, exceeding the time limits, taking people into detention etc, such illegal phenomena.

[50]   Hsia and Zeldin (1992) list articles published between 1987 and 1991.

[51]   Hecht (1996) suggests that organised academic discussions on revision of the Criminal Procedure Law commenced in late 1991.

[52]   Cui is professor in the Chinese People's Public Security University. See also Wang Xixin (1993); Zhang Jianwei and Li Zhongcheng (1994).

[53]   Cui Ming (1993b) cited arguments that the power to pass laws authorising detention was outside the scope of Article 89 of the Constitution, which sets out the powers of the State

Council. Cai Dingjian (1991) asserts that only the NPC or its Standing Committee has the power to pass laws that restrict personal freedom.

54   Cui Ming (1993b) cites leadership of public security organs and government at different levels as the main proponents of its retention

55   Fan Chongyi and Xiao Shengxi (1991) argued the power should be incorporated into the revised Criminal Procedure Law. Song Qian (1992) and Chen Weidong and Zhang Tao (1992b) argued it should not.

56   Mao Zhibin (1991); Zhang Shanyu and Zhang Shuyi (1991); Chen Weidong and Zhang Tao (1992a, 1993) argue that the power is administrative and should not be abolished. Wang Xixin (1993), however, argues that the power is substantively criminal in nature and should be abolished.

57   Passed by the National People's Congress on 4 April 1989.

58   Ministry of Public Security, Notice on Several Questions on the Implementation of the Administrative Litigation Law by Public Security Organs, 30 October 1990, at point 3 discusses the documents that are to form the normative legal basis for reviewing the legality of determinations to impose detention for investigation.

59   The requirement for arrest in Article 40 of the 1979 Criminal Procedure Law was that 'the principal facts of the crime have been clarified and [the defendant] could be sentenced to a punishment of not less than imprisonment'.

60   Article 48, Criminal Procedure Law 1979. The maximum time for detention was three days, with a possible extension of up to four days. The procuracy was required to approve or reject the application within three days of receipt of the application. Article 96, Draft Criminal Procedure Law; Chen and Yan (1995).

61   The unpublished Ministry of Public Security document is entitled Plan for Specific Revision of Provisions of the CPL Relevant to the Public Security Organs (Draft Soliciting Opinions).

62   Proposed amendment to Criminal Procedure Law 1979 Article 40 to enable arrest where 'there is evidence to show a criminal acts or suspicion of a crime, where it is necessary to pursue criminal responsibility...', Plan for Specific Revision of Provisions of the CPL Relevant to the Public Security Organs (Draft Soliciting Opinions).

63   Specifically, amendments to Criminal Procedure Law 1979 Article 41 to include those suspected of committing crime, who do not tell their true name and address and whose status is unclear, those who have committed a minor crime, who are suspected of going from place to place committing crime, and those who have committed a minor crime who are strongly suspected of committing many crimes or committing crimes in a gang. Plan for Specific Revision of Provisions of the CPL Relevant to the Public Security Organs (Draft Soliciting Opinions). See also the proposal that Article 48 of the Criminal Procedure Law 1979 be revised to extend the time limits for applying for arrest to seven days and for a possible extension of between five and 10 days 'where there is a serious suspicion that they have gone from place to place committing crimes, committed many crimes or committed crimes in a gang, where the facts are complicated'.

64   The proposal would amend Article 48 of the Criminal Procedure Law 1979. See Plan for Specific Revision of Provisions of the CPL Relevant to the Public Security Organs (Draft Soliciting Opinions).

65   Article 60, Criminal Procedure Law.

66   Article 61(7), Criminal Procedure Law.

67   Article 69(2), Criminal Procedure Law refers to 'Major suspects who are on the run, who repeatedly commit crime, or who gang up with others to commit crime.'

68   Article 69, Criminal Procedure Law. This category of person can be held for 30 days before the public security organ is required to apply for arrest. The people's procuracy is required either to approve or reject the request for arrest within seven days of receipt.

69   See Hecht (1996) and Human Rights in China (2001a) on the difficulties in reforming the Criminal Procedure Law. Fu Hualing (1998) discusses access of an accused person in detention to a lawyer. H. Tanner (1999) considers that in the 1980s many enforcement problems were due in part to problems of poor payment and lack of training.

70   Ministry of Public Security, Regulations on the Procedures for Handling Criminal Cases, passed on 20 April 1998.

REFERENCES

Alford, W., 1999. 'A second Great Wall? China's post-Cultural Revolution project of legal construction', *Cultural Dynamics*, 11(3):193–212.

Amnesty International, 1991. *China: punishment without crime*, Amnesty International, London.

——, 1992. *Detention Without Trial: a system for extra-judicial punishment*, Amnesty International, London:10–13.

——, 1996. *China: no-one is safe—political repression and abuse of power in the 1990s*, Amnesty International, London.

Bakken, B., 1993. 'Crime, juvenile delinquency and deterrence policy in China', *Australian Journal of Chinese Affairs*, 30(3):29–58.

——, 2000. *The Exemplary Society, Human Improvement, Social Control and the Dangers of Modernity in China*, Oxford University Press, New York.

Baum, R., 1986. 'Modernization and legal reform in post-Mao China: the rebirth of socialist legality', *Studies in Comparative Communism*, 19(2):69–103.

——, 1994. *Burying Mao: Chinese politics in the age of Deng Xiaoping*, Princeton University Press, Princeton.

Benshu Bianxie Zu, (Book Editorial Committee) (ed.), 2001. *Zhongguo Gongchandang Bashi Nian Xuexi Duben* [Reader on 80 Years of the Chinese Communist Party], Zhonggong Zhongyang Dangxiao Chubanshe [Central Party School Press], Beijing.

Bourdieu, P., 1987. 'The force of law: toward a sociology of the juridical field', *Hastings Law Journal*, 38(5):814–54 [tr. R. Terdiman].

——, 1990. *In Other Words: essays towards a reflexive sociology*, Polity Press, Cambridge.

—— and Wacquant, L., 1992. *An Invitation to Reflexive Sociology*, University of Chicago Press, Chicago.

Boxer, J.T., 1999. 'China's death penalty: undermining legal reform and threatening the national economic interest', *Suffolk Transnational Law Review*, Summer:593–618.

Brugger, B. and Reglar, S., 1994. *Politics, Economy and Society in Contemporary China*, MacMillan Press, Hong Kong.

Cai, Dingjian, 1991. 'Guojia Quanli Jiexian Lun [Discussion of the limits of state power]', *Zhongguo Faxue* [Chinese Legal Science], 2:54–61.

Central Committee, 1961. *Report on Urgently Preventing the Free Movement of the Population*, Central Committee of the Communist Party of China, Beijing, 7 November.

——, 1957. *Instruction on Preventing the Blind Outflowing of People from Rural Areas*, Central Committee of the State Council, Beijing, 18 December.

——, 1978. Communique of the Third Plenary Session of the 11th Central Committee of the Communist Party of China, 22 December, Central Committee, Beijing:6–16.

——, 1983. *Notice Approving and Issuing the Two Documents of the National Public Security Work Meeting*, Central Committee, Communist Party or China, Beijing, 28 May.

Chen, Guangzhong and Yan, Duan (eds), 1995. Zhonghua Renmin Gongheguo Xingshi Susong Fa Xiugai Jianyi yu Lunzheng [Preliminary Version for Revision of the 'Criminal Procedure Law of the People's Republic of China' and its Annotations], Zhongguo Fangzheng Chubanshe, Beijing.

Chen, Jianfu, 1999. *Chinese Law: towards an understanding of Chinese law, its nature and development*, Kluwer Law International, The Hague.

Chen, Weidong and Zhang, Tao, 1993. 'Zai Tan Shourong Shencha Buyi Feichu [Another discussion of why detention for investigation should not be abolished]', *Zhongguo Faxue* [Chinese Legal Science], 3:113–14.

——, 1992a. 'Shourong Shencha de Ruogan Wenti Yanjiu [An examination of several questions about detention for investigation]', *Zhongguo Faxue* [Chinese Legal Science], 13:82–87.

——, 1992b. "Shourong Shencha Ruogan Wenti Yanjiu [Research on several questions about detention for investigation]' in Zhongguo Faxue Hui Susong Fa Yanjiu Hui [Procedure Law Association of the China Law Society] (eds), *Xingshi Susong Fa de Xuigai yu Wanshan* [Revision and perfection of the Criminal Procedure Law], Zhongguo Zhengfa Daxue Chubanshe [China University of Politics and Law Press], Beijing:170–78.

Chiu, Hongdah, 1992. 'China's criminal justice system and the trial of pro-democracy dissidents', *New York University Journal of International Law and Politics*, 24(3):1181–201.

Chu, M., 2001. 'Criminal procedure reform in the People's Republic of China: the dilemma of crime control and regime legitimacy', *UCLA Pacific Basin Law Journal*, 18(2):157–208.

Clarke, D.C., 2001. 'Puzzling observations in Chinese law: when is a riddle just a mistake?', Social Science Research Network, available online at http://ssrn.com/abstract=293627.

Clarke, D., 1985. 'Concepts of law in the Chinese anti-crime campaign', *Harvard Law Review*, 98(8):1890–908.

——, 1995. 'Justice and the legal system in China' in R. Benewick and P. Wingrove (eds), *China in the 1990s*, Macmillan, London:83–93.

—— and Feinerman, J., 1995. 'Antagonistic contradictions: criminal law and human rights in China', *The China Quarterly*, 141:135–54.

Conner, A., 2000. 'True confessions? Chinese confessions then and now' in K.G. Turner, J.V. Feinerman and R.K. Guy (eds), *The Limits of the Rule of Law in China*, University of Washington Press, Seattle:132–62.

Craig, P., 1997. 'Formal and substantive conceptions of the rule of law: an analytical framework', *Public Law*:467–87.

Cui, Ming, 1993a. 'Shehui Zhuyi Chuji Jieduan yu Gong'an Jianshe [Preliminary stages of socialism and public security construction]' in Cui Ming (ed.), *Zhongguo Dangdai Xing yu Fa* [China's Contemporary Crime and Law], Qunzhong Chubanshe, Beijing:353–57.

——, 1993b. 'Shourong Shencha de Lishi, Xianzhuang Yu Chulu [The history, present situation and prospects of detention for investigation]' in Cui Ming (ed.), *Zhongguo Dangdai Xing Yu Fa* [China's Contemporary Crime and Law], Qunzhong Chubanshe, Bejing:90–98.

Cui, Xin, 1996. 'Xingshi Susong Fa Xiugai Hou Gong'an Gongzuo Mianling de Xingshi Ji Renwu [The situation and tasks of public security work after revision of the Criminal Procedure Law]', *Gong'an Yanjiu* [Public Security Studies], 3:31, 36–38.

Curran, D. and Cook, S., 1993. 'Growing fears, rising crime: juveniles and China's justice system', *Crime and Delinquency, Special Issue: crime and justice in China and Japan*, 39(3):296–315.

Deng, Xiaoping, 1978. 'Emancipate the mind, seek truth from facts and unite as one in looking to the future' in Bureau for the Compilation and Translation of Works of Marx, Lenin, Engels and Stalin under the Central Committee of the Communist Party of China (ed.), *Selected Works of Deng Xiaoping (1975–1982)*, Volume 2, Foreign Languages Press, Beijing:151–65.

Dobinson, I., 2002. 'The Criminal Law of the People's Republic of China (1997): real change or rhetoric?', *Pacific Rim Law and Policy Journal*, 11(January):1–62.

Dowdle, M., 1997. 'The constitutional development and operations of the National People's Congress', *Columbia Journal of Asian Law*, 11(1):1–125.

——, 1999. 'Heretical laments: China and the fallacies of "rule of law"', *Cultural Dynamics*, 11(3):287–314.

Dreyer, J., 1996. *China's political system: modernization and tradition*, Allyn and Bacon, Boston.

Dutton, M., 1992a. 'Disciplinary projects and carceral spread: Foucauldian theory and Chinese practice', *Economy and Society*, 21(2):276–94.

——, 1992b. 'A mass line without politics, community policing and economic reform' in A. Watson (ed.), *Economic Reform and Social Change in China*, Routledge, London:200–27.

——, 1995. 'Dreaming of better times: "repetition with a difference" and community policing in China', *Positions: East Asia Cultures Critique*, 3:415–47.

——, 2000. 'The end of the (mass) line? Chinese policing in the era of contract', *Social Justice*, 27(2):61–105.

—— and Lee, Tianfu, 1993. 'Missing the target? Policing strategies in the period of economic reform', *Crime and Delinquency, Special Issue: Crime and Justice in China and Japan*, 39(3):316–36.

Epstein, E., 1994. 'Law and legitimation in post-Mao China' in P. Potter (ed.), *Domestic Law Reforms in Post-Mao China*, M.E. Sharpe, Armonk:19–55.

—— and Wong, S. Hing-Yan, 1996. 'The concept of "dangerousness" in the People's Republic of China and its impact on the treatment of prisoners', *British Journal of Criminology*, 36(4):472–97.

Fan, Chongyi and Xiao, Shengxi (eds), 1991. *Xingshi Susong Fa Yanjiu Zongshu Yu Pingjia* [Summary and Appraisal of Criminal Procedure Law Study], Zhongguo Zhengfa Daxue Chubanshe, Beijing.

Feinerman, J., 1994. 'Legal institution, administrative device, or foreign import: the roles of contract in the People's Republic of China' in P. Potter (ed.), *Domestic Law Reforms in Post-Mao China*, M.E.Sharpe, New York:225–44.

Forster, K., 1985. 'The 1982 campaign against economic crime in China', *Australian Journal of Chinese Affairs*, 14:1–19.

Friedman, L., 1969. 'On legal development', *Rutgers Law Review*, 24(1):11–64.

Fu, Hualing, 1994. 'A bird in the cage: police and political leadership in post-Mao China', *Policing and Society*, 4:277–91.

——,1998. 'Criminal defence in China: the possible impact of the 1996 Criminal Procedure Law reform', *China Quarterly*, 153(March):31–48.

Gai, Jun (ed.), 2001. *Zhongguo Gongchandang 80 Nian Lishi Jianbian* [A Short History of the 80 Years of the Chinese Communist Party], Zhonggong Zhongyang Dangxiao Chubanshe, Beijing.

Gao, Chuanli, 1998. 'Xuexi Yifa Zhiguo Jianshe Shihui Zhuyi Fazhi Guojia Jiben Fanglue: Tuidong Shiwu Da Jingshen de Guanche Luoshi [Study ruling the country by law to construct the basic plan for ruling the country by law: promote implementation of the spirit of the Fifteenth Central Committee]' in Sifabu Sifa Yanjiu Suo [Judicial Research Office of the Bureau of Justice] (ed.), *Yifa Zhiguo Jiben Fanlue Lunwenji* [Collection of Essays on the Basic Plan for Ruling the Country by Law], Falu Chubanshe, Beijing:1–16.

Gao, Xianduan, 1990. 'Shourong Shencha de Wenti yu Chulu [The Problem and Prospects for Detention for Investigation]' *Gong'an Yanjiu* [Public Security Studies], 3:18–21.

Ge, Fei, 1998. 'Second class citizen: a record of China's first "severe strike" campaign' in M. Dutton (ed.), *Streetlife China*, Cambridge University Press, Cambridge:65–69.

Goldsmith, A., 1990. 'Taking police culture seriously: police discretion and the limits of law', *Policing and Society*, 1:91–114.

Gong'an Bu [Ministry of Public Security], 2002. *Zhongguo Gong'an Gongzuo* [Policing in China], Gong'an Bu, Beijing:1–90.

Gu, Haiwen, 1992. 'Gong'an Jiguan dui Bupi Bo de Dangshiren you Xingju zhuan Shoushen Chuyi [My humble opinion on public security organs transferring criminal detainees to shelter and investigation when arrest has not been approved]', *Fanzui yu Duice* [Crime and Countermeasures], 4:56–7.

Guo, Dawei, 1990. 'Zuohao Shishi Xingzheng Susong Fa de Zhunbei Baozheng Gong'an Jiguan Yifa Xingzheng [Do a Good Job of Preparation for Implementation of the Administrative Litigation Law to Ensure Public Security Organs Carry out Administration according to Law]', *Gong'an Yanjiu* [Public Security Studies], 1:27–29.

Hecht, J., 1996. *Opening to Reform? An analysis of China's revised Criminal Procedure Law*, Lawyers' Committee for Human Rights, New York,

Hsia, Tao Tai and Zeldin, W., 1992. 'Sheltering for examination [Shourong Shencha] in the legal system of the People's Republic of China', *China Law Reporter*, 7(2):97–128.

Huang, Jie (ed.), 1993. *Xingzheng Susong Shiyong Daquan* [Encyclopedia of Administrative Litigation], Hebei Renmin Chubanshe, Heibei.

Human Rights in China, 2001a. *Empty Promises: human rights protection and China's Criminal Procedure Law in practice*, Human Rights in China, New York:1–94.

——, 2001b. *Re-education through labour (RTL): a summary of regulatory issues and concerns*, Human Rights in China, Hong Kong.

Jiang, Bo and Zhan, Zhongle, 1994. Gong'an Xingzheng Fa [Public Security Administrative Law], Zhongguo Renshi Chubanshe [China Personnel Press], Beijing.

Johnston, G. and Percy-Smith, J., 2003. 'In search of social capital', *Policy and Politics*, 31:321–34.

Jones, W., 1979. 'On the campaign trail in China', *Review of Socialist Law*, 5(4):457–62.

Keith, R., 1994. *China's Struggle for the Rule of Law*, St Martin's Press, New York.

—— and Lin, Zhiqiu, 2001. *Law and Justice in China's Marketplace*, Palgrave, New York.

——, 2003. 'The "Falungong Problem": politics and the struggle for the rule of law in China', *China Quarterly*, 175:623–42.

Leng, Shaochuan and Chiu, Hongdah, 1985. *Criminal Justice in Post-Mao China: analysis and documents*, University of New York Press, Albany.

Li, Huayin and Liu, Baiyang (eds), 1992. *Gong'an Xingzheng Chengxu Yu Zingzheng Susong* [Public Security Administrative Procedure and Administrative Litigation], Qunzhong Chubanshe, Beijing.

Li, Linda Chelan, 2000. 'The "rule of law" policy in Guangdong: continuity or departure? Meaning, significance and processes", *China Quarterly*, 161:199–220.

Lieberthal, K., 1995. *Governing China From Revolution Through Reform*, W.W. Norton and Company, New York.

Liu, Hainian, 1996. 'Qian Yan [Forward]' in Wang Jiafu, Liu Hainian, Li Buyun and Li Lin (eds), *Yifa Zhiguo Jianshe Shehui Zhuyi Fazhi Guojia* [Ruling the Country According to Law, Establishing a Socialist Nation Ruled according to Law], China Legal System Press, Beijing:1–4.

—— and Liu, Baiyang (eds), 1992. *Gong'an Xingzheng Chengxu yu Xingzheng Susong* [Public Security Administrative Procedure and Administrative Litigation], Qunzhong Chubanshe, Beijing.

Liu, Shipu, 1990. 'Guanyu Shourong Shencha de Sikao [Reflections on detention for investigation]', *Gong'an Yanjiu* [Public Security Studies], 5:22–26.

Lo, Carlos Wing-Hung, 1997. 'Socialist legal theory in Deng Xiaoping's China', *Columbia Journal of Asian Law*, 11(2):469–486.

Lubman, S., 1995. 'Introduction: the future of Chinese law', *China Quarterly*, 141:1–21.

——, 1999. *Bird in a Cage: legal reform in China after Mao*, Stanford University Press, Stanford.

Luo, Feng, 1992. 'Laodong Jiaoyang Shenpi Gongzuo de Huigu yu Sikao [Retrospect and thoughts on investigation and approval of re-education through labour]', *Gong'an Yanjiu* [Public Security Studies], 5:33–37.

Ma, Yue, 1997. 'The Police Law 1995: organization, functions powers and accountability of the Chinese Police', *Policing: an international journal of police strategies and management*, 20(1):113–35.

Mao, Zhibin, 1991. 'Shourong Shencha shi Xingzheng Qiangzhi Cuoshi [Shelter and investigation is an administrative coercive measure]', *Gong'an Daxue Xuebao* [Journal of the Public Security University], 5:13–14.

Munro, R., 2000. 'Judicial psychiatry in China and its political abuses', *Columbia Journal of Asian Law*, 14(1):1–128.

Orts, E., 2001. 'The rule of law in China', *Vanderbilt Journal of Transnational Law*, 34(1):43–115.

Parsons, T., 1964. 'Evolutionary universals in society', *American Sociological Review*, 29:339–57.

Peerenboom, R., 1999. 'Ruling the country in accordance with law: reflection on the rule and role of law in contemporary China', *Cultural Dynamics*, 11(3):315–51.

——, 2002a. *China's Long March toward Rule of Law*, Cambridge University Press, Cambridge.

——, 2002b. 'Let one hundred flowers bloom, one hundred schools contend: debating rule of law in China', *Michigan Journal of International Law*, 23(3):471–544.

Pei, Minxin, 1995. '"Creeping democratisation" in China', *Journal of Democracy*, 6(4):65–79.

Peng, Zhen, 1982. 'Xin Shiqi de Zhengfa Gongzuo [Political-legal work in the new era)' in *Lun Xin Zhongguo de Zhengfa Gongzuo* [Discussion of the Political Legal Work in New China], Zhongyang Wenzhai Chubanshe, Beijing:282–91.

Potter, P., 1995. 'Foreign investment law in the People's Republic of China: dilemmas of state control', *China Quarterly*, 141(March):155–85.

——, 1999. 'The Chinese legal system: continuing commitment to the primacy of state power', *China Quarterly*, 159(September):673–83.

——, 2003. 'Globalization and economic regulation in China: selective adaptation of globalized norms and practices', *Washington University Global Studies Law Review*, 2(1):119–50.

Shen, Yuan Yuan, 2000. 'Conceptions and receptions of legality: understanding the complexity of law reform in modern China' in K.G. Turner, J.V. Feinerman and R.K. Guy (eds), *The Limits of the Rule of Law in China*, University of Washington Press, Seattle:20–44.

Shen, Zhongmin and Xu, Zhenqiang, 1997. 'Lun Zhongguo Jingcha Jiaoyu de Fazhan Zouxiang [Discussing trends in the development of China's police education]' in Kang Damin (ed.), *Lun Zhongguo Tese de Gong'an* [Discussion of Public Security with Chinese Characteristics], Qunzhong Chubanshe, Beijing:138–56.

Shih, Chih-yu, 1999. *Collective Democracy, Political and Legal Reform in China*, The Chinese University Press, Hong Kong.

Situ, Yingyi and Liu, Weizhang, 1996. 'Comprehensive treatment to social order: a Chinese approach against crime', *International Journal of Comparative and Applied Criminal Justice*, 20(1):95–115.

Song, Qiang, 1992. 'Lun Woguo Xingshi Qiangzhi Cuoshi Xin Tixi [Discussing the new system of China's criminal coercive measures]' in Zhongguo Faxue Hui Susong Fa Yanjiu Hui [Procedure Law Association of the China Law Society] (ed.), *Xingshi Susong Fa de Xuigai yu Wanshan* [Revision and Perfection of the Criminal Procedure Law], Zhongguo Zhengfa Daxue Chubanshe, Beijing:136–45.

Spence, J., 1990. *The Search for Modern China*, W.W. Norton and Company, New York and London.

State Council, 1975a. Report of the National Meeting on the work of Public Order on Railways, State Council, Communist Party or China, Beijing.

——, 1975b. Notice on doing a good job of Ferreting out Floating Criminals during the New Year and Spring Festival Period, State Council, Communist Party of China, Beijing.

Tanner, H., 1994. Crime and Punishment in China, 1979–89, PhD Thesis, Columbia University, New York.

——, 1995. 'Policing, punishment and the individual: criminal justice in China', *Law and Social Inquiry*, 20(1):277–303.

——, 1999. *Strike Hard! Anti-crime campaigns and Chinese criminal justice, 1979–85*, Cornell University, Ithaca.

Tanner, M.S., 1999. 'Ideological struggle over police reform, 1988–1993' in E.A. Winkler (ed.), *Transition from Communism in China: institutional and comparative analyses*, Lynne Rienner, London:111–28.

——, 2000. 'State coercion and the balance of awe: the 1983–1986 "Stern Blows" anti-crime campaign', *China Journal*, 44(July):93–125.

Terdiman, R., 1987. 'Translator's Introduction: the force of law—Toward a sociology of the juridical field', *Hastings Law Journal*, 38(5):805–13.

Trubek, D., Dezalay, Y., Buchanan, R. and Davis, J., 1994. 'Global restructuring and the law: studies of the internationalization of legal fields and the creation of transnational arenas', *Case Western Reserve Law Review*, 44(2):407–98.

Turack, D., 1999. 'The new Chinese criminal justice system', *Cardozo Journal of International and Comparative Law*, 7(1):49–72.

von Senger, H., 1985. 'Recent developments in the relations between state and party norms in the People's Republic of China' in S.R. Schram (ed.), *The Scope of Power in China*, The Chinese University Press, Hong Kong:171–207.

Wang, Fang (ed.), 1993. *Mao Zedong Gong'an Gongzuo Lilun* [Mao Zedong Public Security Work Theory], Qunzhong Chubanshe, Beijing.

Wang, Jiancheng, 1992. 'Shourong Shencha Chulu Hezai [Where lies the way out for detention for investigation?]' in Zhongguo Faxue Hui Susong Fa Yanjiu Hui, [Procedure Law Association of the China Law Society] (ed.), *Xingshi Susong Fa de Xuigai yu Wanshan* [Revision and Perfection of the Criminal Procedure Law], Zhongguo Zhengfa Daxue Chubanshe, Beijing:179–86.

——, 2000. 'Qiangzhi Cuoshi [Coercive Measures]' in Chen Guangzhong (ed.), *Xingshi Susongfa Shishe Wenti Yanjiu* [Research on the Issues in Implementation of the Criminal Procedure Law], Zhongguo Falu Chubanshe, Beijing:78–99.

Wang, Xixin, 1993. 'Shourong Shencha Zhidu Ying yu Feichu [The System of detention for investigation should be abolished]', *Zhongguo Faxue*, 3:110–12.

Ward, R. and Bracey, D., 1985. 'Police training and professionalism in the People's Republic of China', *The Police Chief*, 5(52):36–38.

Webb, J., Schirato, T. and Danaher, G., 2002. *Understanding Bourdieu*, Sage Publications, London.

White, L.T., 1999. *Unstately Power: Local Causes of China's Intellectual, Legal and Governmental Reforms*, M.E. Sharpe, London.

Winkler, E.A., 1999. 'Describing Leninist Transitions' in E.A. Winkler (ed.), *Transition from Communism in China: institutional and comparative analyses*, Lynne Rienner, London:3–48.

Wong, Kam, 1996. 'Police Powers and Control in the People's Republic of China: The History of Shoushen', *Columbia Journal of Asian Law*, 10(2):367-390.

——, 2002. 'Policing in the People's Republic of China: the road to reform in the 1990s', *British Journal of Criminology*, 42(2):281–316.

Xi, Guoguang and Yu, Lei (eds), 1996. *Zhongguo Renmin Shigao* [Draft History of the Chinese People's Public Security], Jingguan Jiaoyu Chubanshe, Beijing.

Xia, Chongsu (ed.), 2001. *Laodong Jiaoyang Zhidu Gaige Wenti Yanjiu* [Research on the Reform of Re-education Through Labour], Falu Chubanshe, Beijing.

Yang, Xinhua, 1991. 'Shourong Shencha Cunzai de Wenti Ji Duice [Problems and strategies of the existence of detention for investigation]', *Jiangxi Faxue* [Jiangxi Legal Studies], 4:42.

Ying, Songnian (ed.), 1992. *Xingzheng Fa yu Xingzheng Susong Fa Cidian* [Dictionary of Administrative Law and Administrative Litigation Law], Zhongguo Zhengfa Daxue Chubanshe, Beijing.

Zhang, Jianwei and Li, Zhongcheng, 1994. 'Lun Feichu Shourong Shencha [Discussing the abolition of detention for investigation]', *Zhongwai Faxue*, 3:55–59.

Zhang, Qingwu, 1990. 'Hukou Qianyi Zhengce Yanjiu [Study of Household Registration Migration Policy]', *Gong'an Yanjiu* [Public Security Studies], 1:35–37.

Zhang, Shanyu and Zhang, Shuyi (eds.), 1991. *Zouchu Digu de Zhongguo Xingzheng Faxue -Zhongguo Xingzheng Faxue Zongshu Yu Pingjia* [The Under-estimated Chinese Administrative Law Studies: summary and review of China's Administrative Law Studies], Zhongguo Zhengfa Daxue Chubanshe, Beijing.

Zhang, Xu, 1993. 'Lun Shoushen de Chulu yu Daibu de Gaige [Discussing the way out for Detention for Investigation and Reform of Arrest]', *Xiandai Faxue* [Modern Legal Science], 2:20.

Zhengci Falu Jiaoyanshi [Politics and Law Teaching and Research Office] (ed.), 1983. *Gong'an Gongzuo Gailun* [Introduction to Public Security Work], Zhongguo Xingshi Jingcha Xueyuan Chubanshe, Beijing.

Zhongguo Faxue Hui Susong Fa Yanjiu Hui [Procedure Law Association of the China Law Society] (ed.), 1992. *Xingshi Susongfa de Xiugai yu Wanshan* [Revision and Perfection of the Criminal Procedure Law], Zhongguo Zhengfa Daxue Chubanshe, Beijing.

Zhu, Rongji, 1999. 'Renzhen Guanche Yifa Zhiguo Fanglue Qieshi Quanmian Tuijin Yifa Xingzheng [Diligently implementing the General Plan of Ruling the Country According to Law is to conscientiously and comprehensively advance administration according to law]' in Guowuyuan Yifaxingzheng Gongzuo Huiyi [State Council Administration According to the Law Working Committee] (ed.), *Yifa Xingzheng, Congyan Zhizheng, Jianshi Lianjie, Qinzheng, Wushi, Gaoxiao Zhengfu* [Administration According to Law, Strictly Establish an Honest, Industrious, Pragmatic and Highly Efficient Government], Zhongguo Fazhi Chuanshe, Beijing:1–12.

11

SOEs, law and a decade of market-oriented socialist development in Vietnam

Adam Fforde

THE BACKGROUND: SOEs IN CLASSIC AND REFORMED SOCIALIST THINKING, AND THE VIETNAMESE CASE

Three questions are common to the chapters in this book. The first is whether and how socialism shapes law and law-related institutions; the second is the role of external and internal factors in explaining legal change; the third is whether 'socialist' doctrine inhibits legal change. This chapter will look at these issues in the context of state-owned enterprises (SOEs).

For obvious reasons, the meaning of 'Socialist' in 'Socialist Republic of Vietnam' is not often discussed in academic fora. I think this is a pity, for, as Tony Benn remarked when interviewed shortly after the fall of the Soviet Union, this is the best thing to have happened to socialism in ages. Granted that the emerging labour regime in Vietnam appears relatively favourable to workers (Chan and Norlund 1999), at least compared with China, and granted that Vietnam's focus on the state sector positions Vietnam in a highly unorthodox position in terms of standard policy prescriptions, I welcome the chance to explore.

In the longer term, we need to address the 'Vietnam paradox' of the surprisingly positive developmental role played by that part of the economy labelled as 'state'. This was clear in the 1990s, when GDP data showed a rising share produced by the state sector, accompanied by rapid growth and macroeconomic stability—an outcome almost unthinkable in other developing countries though visible historically elsewhere, such as France after the Second World War. But here I want simply to look at law, the 1990s and SOEs.[1]

Beresford and Fforde (1997) provides one introduction to a possible definition of the changing notions of Vietnamese socialism. It argues that the basic ideas of socialism permit a division into necessary and unnecessary elements, and that the crucial partial reforms of the early 1980s saw a shift away from the latter but not the former. The first and most fundamental set, related to the traditional *definition* of socialism, comprised three principles: public ownership of the means of production, central planning, and distribution according to labour. The second set was of secondary importance and was in essence *operational* principles. It included central monopoly of foreign trade, state monopoly of the domestic circulation of goods, cooperative production in the agriculture and handicraft industries, planning of industrial production, state control of finance and credit, state determination of virtually all prices (including wages) and planned allocation of labour. It will be clear that this distinction permits the coexistence of central planning (suitably defined) and public ownership of the means of production with market-based domestic circulation of goods and market-based determination of industrial production.

This distinction is, in essence, to argue that the 'Law of Value' is not antipathetic to socialism, so long as the definitional (rather than the operational) elements of socialism are maintained.[2] This is, of course, the same position as that taken by Stalin in his 'The Economic Problems of Socialism in the USSR', and much addressed by important Left intellectuals such as Bettelheim.[3] It seems quite obvious that the basic issue here is that the progressive aspects of capitalism, perhaps expressed in terms of the operation of the 'Law of Value', had to be contained within and by the power of the socialist regime.

It is clear that this intellectual distinction is consistent in many ways with what happened in Vietnam during the 1980s and 1990s, and opens the way to a working definition of the difference between 'classic' and 'reformed' socialism in Vietnam. I argue that (as we put it in Beresford and Fforde (1997)) the difference can be found in the distinction made above: whilst reform socialism abandoned the 'operational' aspects, it retained from 'classic' socialism the traditional defining elements of public ownership of the means of production, central planning and distribution according to labour, necessarily, however, losing the old content of 'central planning' but replacing it with a pervasive utilisation of state authority to regulate the internal workings of the state economy. This can be seen as not amounting to much of a change, especially if we recall the basic political thrust of these ideas, which is to subordinate the progressive elements of a development of the forces of production to a political power based on various structures, including those associated with the SOEs.

It follows, then, that I will need to make the argument that little has essentially changed during the 1990s, a period when the state sector increased its share of total economic output, and, in the 'Vietnam paradox', it was sufficiently well-regulated for this not to be accompanied by macroeconomic instability. I will base this argument on the following

- comparison of the writings in the quality Vietnamese press that addressed SOEs and state business in the two periods 1992 and 2002
- an examination of the legislation in force during these two periods that related to SOEs
- a discussion of the contexts, and so a characterisation of how the SOE issue was conceived and how law and state activities sought to address this.

Before going into these matters, though, it is worth saying something about other values and concepts related to these issues, not entirely the property of the Communist Party of Vietnam.

DEVELOPMENT THINKING AND THE VIETNAMESE CASE

Discussions of the role of the state in development have a long history, derived from attempts both to create development and to cope with the consequences of rapid change. Attempts to influence the flow of events often come down to discussions about the suitable role of the state, with opinions polarised between viewing the state as part of the problem, associated with the dominant Washington Consensus of the 1980s and 1990s, and views that treat the state as the most appropriate source of solutions.

There are fundamental critiques of both tendencies, to do with their evidential basis. A good starting point for reflection, for example, is the literature on the empirics of the relationships between policy settings and economic performance, where respectable authorities argue that there are almost no robust examples of such relationships.[4] It is hardly exceptional to point out that views of the correct role of the state in development not only vary, but orthodox opinion has shifted from a generally pessimistic view of markets after the Second World War and up to the late 1970s, through a generally optimistic position, to what is now a somewhat confused situation, according to some.[5]

Certainly, the increasing interest in the conditions leading to 'market failure', and growing belief that they are likely to be extremely common, has supported far greater interest in institutions amongst students of development, especially economists.[6] Crucially, however, throughout much of the literature we find a combination of great certainty with questionable empirical evidence, accompanied by profound revisions to established positions. It is possible that what is going on here is what has been described, by Cowen and Shenton (1996) in their *Doctrines of Development*, as a resolution of the inherent nonsense of robust belief in a predictable future through a 'logical sleight of hand' that *defines* correct development as what authority says it is.

Although I am no expert, a quick examination of the literature on 'law and development' would seem to show similar characteristics to those of the general development literature. Thus, Pistor and Wellons (1998:34) posit three 'core theories' in 'the current thinking about law and socioeconomic development in their tendency to converge both with each other and between economies and cultures'. This evolutionary theory they trace to Weber and Durkheim, linking the emergence of capitalism to actors such as law: here, 'theory [predicts] that law develops over time and in interaction with changes in the socio-economic environment' (1998:34). Cultural theory is said to be a defining feature of theories that view cultural factors as the major determinants for legal systems—law is essentially local in its character. Finally, utilitarian theorists reportedly see law as 'an instrument to be used to promote economic development' (Pistor and Wellons 1998:35). Pistor and Wellons' position is that 'law made an important contribution to Asia's economic development and was most effective when it was congruent with economic policies' (1998:1). Clearly, this assumes that economic policies were knowably 'correct', here situated in knowable cause–effect relations with economic performance, and that 'law' can be treated as a similar 'independent variable' to economic policy. Arguably, this simply reflects the 'statism' that is so common in thinking about development and change: the view that 'policy' can be construed as a category 'external' to, and so a cause that operates upon, 'society'.[7] A survey of recent articles shows that this position is common, as it must be given the general view of development as something that can be caused through correct state actions, construed as 'policies'.[8]

From this perspective, as hinted at by Almond in 1988, the use of state power in the Soviet Union to accelerate change through the methods that emerged under Stalin, and thus called 'Stalinism' can be seen as simply an extreme example of 'statism', amplified in north Vietnam before 1975 by wartime social mobilisation and the particular certainties of Marxist social science. In my own opinion, it is unwise to take a dogmatic position for or against the importance of particular 'causes' of change; indeed, given the dominant view that 'policy matters', it is often hard to isolate from much academic output empirics that permit a reasonable guess at the question 'OK, but how much?', which involves at least the possibility that policies do not matter at all.

This chapter takes seriously the possibility that 'law' tends to reflect underlying socioeconomic processes and states. Such a 'policy pessimism' is contentious, assuming as it does that legal change has little active role to play in important change processes. It is not easy to situate within the simple typology presented by Pistor et al. (2003), but derives from a sense that formal law need not be important to economic life: markets can function efficiently enough, and accumulation processes can be robust enough, without identifiable and certain legal formality.[9] In this sense the relationship between 'law' and outcome is likely to be complicated if not remote.

Woodside, in his *Community and Revolution* (1976), is a rare example of scholarship that attempts to link more specific Vietnamese concerns to these wider sets of views. He argued that the combination of Vietnamese cultural and philosophical concerns with the particular historical circumstances of the destruction of community and invalidation of ideas caused by the French conquest 'suited' the 'proletarian mandarins' of the Communist movement. The argument could be taken further, to the view that a suitable economic system would be one that brought accumulating capital (beyond the peasant household) under 'public' regulation through the state economy, with its relationship with the farming economy mediated through exchange, perhaps market-based, perhaps through a plan, but not something that was 'spontaneous'. 'Law', then, would be associated with this project.

It follows that it would be unwise to view Vietnamese 'socialism' as being driven ideologically by imported texts. Rather, there is much in local conditions and circumstances to drive change and adaptation. Yet, we can see that defining the state and the state sector, and, more importantly for this chapter, the sources of its order, is central not only to Vietnamese concerns, but to those of many others.

THE SITUATION IN THE EARLY 1990s

Overview

In the early 1990s, Vietnam was recovering from the major shocks associated with the emergence of an economy that no longer had as one of its major activities the use of the central planning apparatus to allocate Soviet bloc assistance to the state sector. Through the 1980s, SOEs had become increasingly market-focused.[10]

After the loss of Chinese and most Western assistance in the late 1970s, assistance from the Soviet bloc had risen to around US$20 per capita, which is relatively high. The complicated economic events of 1988–90 had seen SOEs cut loose from these supports, and major job losses threatened social stability at a time when a 'Yeltsin' solution to the political problems of a 'reformist' Communist Party posed major obstacles.[11] The sacking of Tran Xuan Bach appeared to mark the end of these trends.

Examination of the detailed policy record, however, shows no clear shift away from the legislation and decrees of the late 1980s. Rather, people found that SOEs could and did find ways of generating cash flow and earnings that allowed them to survive, and this could be placed under a heading of 'state-led rationalisation'.[12] Parallel to this, the balance of payments was brought under control, inflationary tendencies were curbed after the successful anti-inflationary measures of 1989, and a tax base was recreated that could secure resources for the government from what was now in many ways an 'unplanned' economy. But the economy was only 'unplanned' in the sense that the planning methods of the classic neo-Stalinist system no longer existed.[13] Through a range of mechanisms, the government continued to influence the pattern of economic growth, which, by the middle of the decade, was increasingly seen as regime-threatening in its stress on urban areas and SOEs.

Compared with what was to come, and compared for example with China, however, the economic situation was one where SOEs had mainly to compete with each other and with imports. There was only a very negligible private sector, and almost no foreign direct investment to speak of. The 'rationalisation' forced upon SOEs was therefore coming from imports and the effects of the major economic changes accompanying the reforms and the loss of the large Soviet bloc aid program.

The 'Law of Value', therefore, allowed market forces to play themselves out *within* the state sector, giving the state, as Beresford (1997) has pointed out, a particularly subtle role in mediating interests. Interestingly, signs of a collapse of monetary and fiscal order marked by the impotency of central government in its relations with local authorities (a clear problem in China), seem to have been lacking; *ad hoc* decisions to delay tax payments, ease loan conditions and so forth, all with national systemic potential, tended to be mediated through Vietnamese national state structures.

Law and policy towards SOEs needs to be seen in this light. It can be argued that the context, requiring a political and fiscal tightening, required strong attempts to bring SOEs under greater state control—a 'conservative' push in terms of the liberalising trends of the 1980s (Fforde, in progress).

Law and policy towards SOEs

A search of the Official Gazette for laws and decrees relating to SOEs for the period shows rather little innovation in the early years of the decade. The most interesting pointer is towards greater regulation of market-oriented activities, and a reduction of SOE property rights compared with the state.

The thrust of legislation was still coming from the reforms of the late 1980s, specifically 217-HDBT, which was a strong attack on the central planning system, and other guiding documents that, it is clear (see Table 11.1), were to do with four areas.

- Regulation. Matters such as No. 13 (business accounting) and No. 26 (on the role of the Chief Accountant), also No. 144 (financial management—also No. 408).
- Addressing particular issues of the moment, specifically dealing with shed labour (No. 2), and the continuing program of equitisation.
- Matters to do with profit shares and the nature of the property relations between the state and the SOE (No. 93 on depreciation and No. 316 on 'capital allocation', as well as decree No. 27 on Enterprise Unions).
- Matters to do with the creation and dissolution of SOEs (No. 315), especially the program of re-establishment of SOEs (No. 388).

The process of negotiation and renegotiation of matters to do with state property—profit sharing (though often not called by that name), and relations between SOEs and the state (importantly No. 217, but also the Decree on Enterprise Unions)—show a continuity of focus that went back to the start of the 1980s and, as we will see, on into the 2000s. As is usual, much of this can appear arcane to the uninitiated, but an apparently dry decree on depreciation needs to be understood beside the reality that depreciation payments were, in essence, part of what value the SOE could retain from its commercial activities. And this was negotiable, regulated through these documents and decisions (a tendency that would also continue into the 2000s).

Here, there are already the beginnings of an apparent *reversal* in direction, so that, whereas law of the late 1980s had reduced the power of formal state property rights over SOEs, this was reversed in the very early 1990s (probably influenced by the context—see above). To gloss the preamble to No. 93, earlier decrees (No. 217 and No. 50) had stipulated that 100 per cent of 'basic depreciation' (a category from the formal accounting system) was to be left to the enterprise—only for a small number of large projects was some to be given to the state budget. No. 93, however, bearing in mind the state's need for revenue to carry out key investments, stipulated that

- new projects must pay 70 per cent of basic depreciation to the state for the first three years, the remainder goes to 'own-capital' for use in the enterprise's own investments
- for existing base units, depreciation on assets paid for out of state budgetary funds will be left to the units at an average rate of 50 per cent for all branches—the rest will be paid to the state budget. The Minister of Finance will fix concretely the percentage retention for each enterprise in accordance with demand and requirements for replacement of the enterprise's assets
- The decision came into effect on 1 July 1989.

This survey suggests that the details of SOE rationalisation, to cope with the problems of the moment and secure greater competitiveness, were not expressed in decrees at a level worthy of being published in the Official Gazette. Rather, decisions were taken on an *ad hoc* basis, and reported and disseminated through media such as the press.

Local views of SOEs and their problems

This discussion, and the next, rests simply on a reading of articles related to SOEs in the quality Vietnamese press. A search of my databases for 1992 and early 1993 revealed over 100 articles relating to SOEs. Perhaps the most telling one was a 'Tin ngan' [Short News] in No. 4 (p.9) 1993 of KTVN 'SOEs: holding to their key role but still loss-making'. This reported the results of a piece of research and a survey, showing that SOEs held two-thirds of economic assets and received 90 per cent of invested capital. That competition at this stage was mainly coming from imports and other SOEs is relatively clear (for example, Vu Manh Cuong 1992).

These public discussions focused to a great extent on the problems of particular SOEs. This was an approach going back many years, for example to the early 1980s, before *doi moi*, when the official press carried many articles discussing the pros and cons of early steps to the commercialisation of SOEs. There is less concern, especially compared with the perceptions a decade later, with the details of systemic change; rather, the 'market economy'—the 'new system'—was largely taken as given.[14] The concern of many articles was to show how SOEs had, through positive exploitation of the market mechanism, done well in terms of survival, maintenance of employment, payments to the state, and increased economic activity. These micro experiences show much about how law fitted into the local meaning of state commerce.

Regulation. Regulations were not widely discussed. It is clear from the texts that there was widespread illegality (see the discussion of kickbacks in the construction industry in Nguyen Toan Thang and Trong Dat (1992)). Law itself was not an active element in regulating the important changes of the moment. This is not so surprising, as central to change was the push to secure 'return on capital' as the gauge of enterprise performance, in a situation where SOEs' formal structure did not permit this core element of the 'Law of Value' to be clearly realised. The shift to state business status, with the importance of treating SOEs as sites for the use of capital, marks this clearly. Thus, for example, Pham Bang Ngan notes

> the most specific characteristic of commercial performance for a business is the budgetary contribution target. High contributions, on the basis of high turnover, and high and rational employee incomes…are the most accurate way of establishing the commercial results of a business from the point of view of state management (1993:4).

Particular issues of the moment. The overriding issue of the moment, which comes through very strongly from these articles, was to ensure that SOEs survived and were capable of competing, holding markets and employees, under the often very difficult economic conditions. Pro-SOE positions saw their main duties as often weakening their competitive position. Thus, for example, Dam Minh Thuy (1992) argued that four factors tended to push up their costs
- preserving and developing state investments
- high depreciation payments (see above)
- positive real interest rates at the banks
- the cost of electricity (this had recently been raised by the government).

This article, however, respecting realities and the need to reduce inflationary pressures, ended up calling for import controls.

Profit shares and the nature of property relations. As we have seen, law was pushing for a further redefinition of the relationships between SOEs and the state, and towards a formation of state interests that was more to do with return on capital and investments. An important element of this was the treatment of SOE's 'own' capital. For example, the success story of the Hung Yen garments export factory (Tran Ta Uyen 1993) claimed that 4 billion dong of new investment had been made, of which 3 billion was from the SOE's 'own capital' (*von tu co*).

This, interestingly, coincided with a wide range of accepted, but apparently extra-legal, arrangements that involved effective joint ventures. On the surface, these were usually reported in terms of deals done with the SOE's workers. One example is 'share groups'. These were essentially groups of workers who gave high fixed-interest loans to their SOE (Hoang Lan 1993). There is no mention in the article of any regulation.

Creation and dissolution of SOEs. There were extensive reports of the re-establishment of SOEs as 'state businesses' (that is, from *Xi nghiep quoc doanh*, to *Doanh nghiep nha nuoc*), in accordance with Decision No. 388 (20/11/91). However, this was not a topic that generated much detailed discussion in the press, suggesting, as is probably the case, that the shift was largely nominal. To quote Trong Nghia

(1992a:1) 'this is just the first step, the problem is how, through categorising SOEs and reorganising production, the city and the ministries can rapidly concentrate capital in stable and progressive enterprises that are short of capital'. The effects of No. 388 could include dissolution of SOEs (Trong Nghia 1992d) and were clearly part of the ongoing process of rationalisation.

An interesting aspect of these references, which provides continuity through to the discussions a decade later, was the use of local terminology to refer to various forms of business cooperation. This was treated separately from the formal legal aspects of the creation and dissolution of SOEs (suggesting that law was derivative rather than proactive in relation to the direction of commercial change). For example

- the distinction between *lien ket* and *lien doanh* (Trong Nghia 1992c); *lien ket* referred to cooperation that contained a technical basis, and was covered by the notion of 'contract'; *lien doanh* was understood to involve a pooling of capital. That the distinction was locally significant points simply to the characteristics of the capital market at the time.
- that of 'share groups' (see above).

One can conclude that the market in institutions was rather free —people could try out various arrangements extra-legally to test their efficacy.

Another example of this institutional variety was is the privatisation of the HCM City refrigerator factory (Tran Trung 1993), reportedly the second SOE to be privatised in the city. There were very few details of how this had been done, but by the late 1990s its shares were being actively traded.

Ideological issues. The articles in the Party press organ, *Nhan dan*, largely present stories about how individual SOEs had coped with what was called the 'shift to a market economy'. Consistent with the overall ideological acceptance of a push to a market economy, we see greater stress upon acceptance of the role of return on capital, though subject to 'social' and political issues—the 'Law of Value' was to operate only subject to the political power of the socialist regime.

Conclusion

Examination of the legislation and the articles from the quality Vietnamese press seems to lead to the conclusion that, at this time, there is no significant difference between the position taken by Stalin and that of the Communist Party of Vietnam. Whilst the 'Law of Value' was to be allowed to operate, and clearly did in Vietnam in the early 1990s to a far greater extent than in early 1950s Soviet Russia, law and other elements of state activities are part of a conscious attempt to subject it to the priorities of the socialist regime. Further, the apparent willingness to permit extra-legal activities that clearly could have a strong effect on state control suggests that law was perhaps not the most important part of how the Communist Party of Vietnam governed SOEs.

The argument here goes beyond the one, common in Vietnam studies, that it was the local market and players that were central to the dynamic of SOE change. Rather, viewed in terms of the overall political dynamic, and bearing in mind Beresford's

(1997) stress on the importance of the state as a *mediator* between interests, for the overall political goals of regime survival and order in relationships between higher and local levels, SOEs appear to have maintained an important political function. Their existence, and the possibility of mediating interest group conflicts through such levers as the mass organisations and Party organisations within them, the allocation of state credits, deliberations over access to foreign direct investment, to participation in development plans, export marketing exercises, and so on, all reflect Beresford's thesis. And, since this political project seems to have been successful, it follows, granted the widespread illegality, that law was not an important element of the 'techniques of rule'. Another way of putting this is that, if one focuses on the 'rule' in 'rule by law', then law was not very important to this, at least as far as SOEs were concerned. Little real effort was put into dealing with the widespread illegality, and this reflected political realities and priorities.

THE SITUATION IN THE EARLY 2000s

Overview

In the early 2000s, the Vietnamese economy was, compared with the early 1990s, also showing somewhat unexpected signs of resilience and rapid growth after a period of shocks and difficulties. In this case the shocks were associated with the Asian financial crisis and the steep reductions in inward foreign investment at the close of the decade. The confidence of major aid donors was again high, however, marked by large loan arrangements made with the World Bank. One major trend was the apparent rapid emergence of a corporate private sector, and fast growth of labour-intensive exports, often coming from foreign-invested factories. The 'Law of Value' could, therefore, operate through a more complex field of commercial competition, where the private and foreign sectors both eased systemic issues by their contributions to exports and employment, whilst also offering sources of market-driven rationalisation that were not coming from within the state sector.

It is important to realise also that after a decade of rapid growth the Vietnamese population, especially that associated with SOEs, was far richer, in terms of both assets and real incomes. It can be argued that the mid and late 1990s saw a build up in savings amongst the emerging middle classes that, combined with experience gained in business, amounted to a strong force pushing for the emergence of more strictly private forms of business than that which was entrenched in SOEs. In other words, the emerging middle classes sought property rights that could more easily be transferred, inherited and merged with others in various forms of joint venture.

It is important to stress how important the state sector was to the rapid growth in the 1990s, and how much support it had been obtaining from the state. Even by the early 2000s, 85 per cent of subsidised credits were going to SOEs (Bac Hai 2002b).

Further, it is useful not to assume that changes affecting SOEs reflect a metaphor of policy and policy implementability. I have argued elsewhere (Fforde 2002) that the apparently random pattern of SOE equitisation[15] and reform, when viewed as a policy-driven process, could as easily reflect a process where the key element of equitisation is the *de facto* and (now) *de jure* recapitalisation of an existing joint venture (rather than a Weberian bureaucratic entity). Further, since the apparent net flow of capital at equitisation is *inwards* (Fforde 2002), a more persuasive metaphor may well be the need for equitisation to compete with other opportunities for increasingly important and mobile capital.

Law and policy towards SOEs

The most significant element of policy towards SOEs in this later period was marked strongly at the Third Plenum of the Party Central Committee, which stressed the need to accelerate equitisation of SOEs. But this, of course, was simply a variation on the earlier theme of rationalisation and regulation of the nature of property relations.

Reviewing the laws and decrees in the Official Gazette for the approximate 18 months from mid 2000 to the end of 2002, we see a range of concerns that is very similar to those a decade earlier (see Table 11.2). There are, however, rather more legislative instruments than a decade earlier. The overall impression is one of far greater sophistication and textured awareness of the nature of the state sector: a 'fine tuning' of various elements already present a decade earlier. Thus, a rather large number of regulations deal with the particular event of equitisation of individual SOEs.

Local views of SOEs and their problems

The literature of the early 2000s is far richer and more detailed. Whereas the literature of the early 1990s offers a picture of individual SOEs, a decade later 'SOEs' are treated far more generally. This in part reflects the particular context: whilst in the early 1990s the major changes of 1989–90 were still being digested, in the early 2000s there was much discussion of the 'SOE problem' and the advantages and disadvantages of 'SOE reform', including the central issue of why 'equitisation' was happening at the speed observed—for many, too slowly and clearly below the legislative targets.

One can note, though, that the 'formal reform' aspects of what was happening were reflected in detailed regulation of the various 'forms' of SOE. Typologies were set by state decision rather than by the market. Thus, in one example amongst many, Doan Kim (2002:5) refers to decree No. 58 as defining the following 'types' of SOE

- those with 100 per cent state capital
- those that have been 'transmogrified' (*da dang hoa*)—equitised, dissolved, bankrupted. According to another source (P.V. 2002a) these other types were in fact clearly defined in 'law' as (a) Type 1, with 100 per cent state holdings and/or state holdings of 20 billion dong or more; (b) Type 2, with state holdings of over 50 per cent, or state holdings of under 50 per cent, but state control maintained through special legal decisions; and

SOEs with less than 5 billion dong in assets, which could not be equitised and which would be more directly handed over to other agents (see below); (c) Type 3, including SOEs not of Type 1, suffering long-term losses, which would be dissolved.

Doan Kim (2002) argues that the basic reason for the slow pace of SOE reform is that ministries and localities are afraid of 'losing' them. Le Dang Doanh contends that equitisation is essentially the transfer of the business to a new investor [sic— *'nha dau tu'*, not 'owner'—'*chu*'] to increase the efficiency of the business (Le Dang Doanh, in Bac Hai 2002c).

Regulation. By this stage the 'new regulations' section of the leading newspaper, the *Vietnam Economic Times*, was producing regular and high-quality glosses of new decrees, on topics such as the treatment of financial aspects of SOE dissolution (for example, No. 66 in *Thoi bao Kinh te Viet Nam* [*Vietnam Economic Times*], 30 August 2002:2).

Particular issues of the moment. The dominant issue of the moment was the effort to improve competitive performance nationally, of which rationalisation of SOEs was a central part. In particular, where rationalisation was focused on property relations, understood essentially as a further extension of the 'Law of Value' through equitisation and the accelerated divestment of smaller SOEs.[16]

As part of this, we see legal decisions to manage and deal with the old problem of the unpaid debts among many SOEs (No. 69). In a way familiar from the early 1990s, if not far earlier, this decree stated (to gloss P.V. 2002b) that 'the SOE must itself deal with the problem, acting with the debtor to share burdens and solve the issue…'.

Profit shares and the nature of property relations. A wide range of stories considers the implications of the shift to equity companies, such as the granting of permission for businesses to sell shares to foreign investors (Chan Hung 2002), discussed in the context of a draft decree from the Ministry of Finance. This was earlier said to be required to occur through a financial intermediary. Priority was to be given to sales 'within' the SOE, including sales to poor workers.

There was also much discussion of how SOEs were to be valued, with officials such as Tran Van Ta, a Deputy Minister of Finance, arguing that market valuation was needed (Quy Hao 2002a).

Showing the process-nature of change, and the role of law in underpinning state projects, we see ideas floated that would have removed the power of line for ministries over SOEs (called 'abolishing the 'lead management role'') and vesting delegated state power in the hands of the Ministry of Finance as holder of the state's shares (Quy Hao 2002b).

Perhaps the clearest reflection of the nature of property relations can be seen in the reported differences between two decisions on equitisation—No. 44 (1998) and No. 64 (2002). These were reported (Kim Dan 2002) as follows

- it was no longer obligatory to use all the workers in the SOE at equitisation, only as many as possible
- earlier, a corporate entity could buy a maximum of 10–20 per cent of the shares (sic), and an individual 5–10 per cent. Now there were no limits

- SOE management staff, from deputy section heads upwards, were no longer limited in the numbers of shares sold at 'favourable prices'. All employees could buy, and allocation would be based upon period in state employment [sic—not specifically at the SOE] prior to equitisation
- it was now compulsory to sell a minimum of 30 per cent of the shares outside the SOE at equitisation. Priority should be given to producers and suppliers of agricultural, forestry and marine products inputs to the SOE, and all sales had to go through financial intermediaries
- the establishing shareholders had to have at least 20 per cent of the equity
- the form of shares would be based on the Ministry of Finance's model, but did not have to follow it exactly
- a variety of measures could be used to value the SOE being equitised
- land-use rights could only be part of the deal for SOEs involved in housing and infrastructure; all others would still have to rent their land from the state
- employees would receive a maximum of 10 shares per year of employment at the favourable price (defined as 30 per cent below the general price of 100,000 dong per share)
- the value of the SOE would be set by the Minister or the Chairman of the relevant People's Committee
- the prime minister would no longer directly approve all equitisations, but only the general plan of each ministry and locality.

We can see from this the way in which the Communist Party of Vietnam had gradually shifted its position on SOEs, and even at this relatively late stage in the process was still using a range of powers to involve itself in the issue of who would have formal ownership of these businesses. The underlying power and position of the Party and mass organisations within these bodies, which remain powerful, was not discussed.

Another area that offered great scope for confusion was the position of the general companies. A general company is a formal legal entity, essentially a sort of holding company. Their history is complex, but dates back well into the 1970s and a flirtation with the apparent success of the East German *kombinaten* in easing the problems of central planning. Here, planning of SOEs had been reformed by shifting them into large holding companies, which were then planned by central government: thus the number of units planners had to deal with was reduced, and the holding companies were often vertically and horizontally integrated. For example, inputs suppliers and groups of inputs users were brought within the one holding company, hopefully reducing transactions and coordination costs.

In Vietnam, these *Lien hiep* also grouped SOEs, initially taking into their management officials from the line ministries. In the early 1990s, however, these were reformed through their transformation into general companies, for reasons that are not well understood. These existed at central and local level, and also as groups (*Tap Doan*, rather than the *Tong Cong Ty*, which I translate as 'general company').

Central to the discussion here of the role of law, and its continued irrationalities, is that the question of the power of general companies over their constituent SOEs once the latter had been equitised appears to have been left open. Thus whilst the shareholders would appoint, in some arguments, the management board of such an SOE, the general company would appoint the General Manager.[17] Here, legislation to shift to a 'Mother Company–Child Company' model emerged (Minh An 2002a). Again, though, there were 'experiments' with four models (B.H. 2002). An Order in early 2002 apparently stated that an equitised SOE would remain a member of any general company it had belonged to (D.T. 2002).

In a further extension of the experiments with legal forms seen in the early 1990s, we see general companies shifting to a situation where they have 'no state supplied capital' (Minh An 2002b). This apparently meant that they would shift to basing their activities on collateralised bank loans (90 per cent) and likely their capital. This was reportedly viewed by many as a rational model.

Another example of this flexibility of form was the emergence of 'single member Limited Companies'—that is, equitised SOEs with 100 per cent state ownership. This was addressed in a circular letter of the Ministry of Planning and Investment (M.G. 2002).

Creation and dissolution of SOEs. The legislation clearly has much to do with the re-establishment of SOEs, as it did a decade earlier. Apart from details already mentioned, the treatment of small SOEs is very interesting.

Decree No. 49 follows a series of decrees going back to the 1980s on relatively simple methods for handing small SOEs over to other agents, through 'allocation, sale, business contracting (*khoan kinh doanh*) or renting (*thue*). According to Hoanh Anh (2002), many of these were loss-making, but sales would be possibile if conditions were eased further.

Ideological issues. It is important to note how the legislation required a 'typology' of SOEs, and how this reflected a range of interests, above all the need to balance limited economic goals with the need to maintain capacity to deal with likely adverse political consequences. There was considerable political 'push' to secure the economic goals, with the combination of legislation to accelerate equitisation, overt commitment by the Communist Party of Vietnam, and sweeteners to possible new investors.

Conclusion

The sources reveal a different but essentially similar treatment of relations between SOEs and the state as a decade previously. In 1992, SOEs were commercialised entities participating in a range of joint ventures and seeking to meet a variety of goals suited to the position in which they were placed by the Party and state—a priority role in securing the general goals of national development and the specific political goals of securing the regime. At the time, conceptions were very much focused on the need for individual SOEs to survive the greatly increased pressures caused by the loss of Soviet aid and the need to tighten state support so as to maintain macroeconomic stability that had only recently been re-established. Law played a role in regulating and ordering SOEs, but was ignored by both SOEs and the Party–state as necessary.

By 2002, law was still essentially a fluid instrument of a ruling Communist Party, used to confront the progressive opportunities offered to them (as to Stalin) by an expanded role of the 'Law of Value'; it was not something that governed and determined the activities of either SOEs or the Party–state, for, as we have seen, confusion in important areas remained, and the law was ignored by both sides when it suited.

What is different about the early 2000s, however, is the presence of a dynamic private domestic sector and the foreign investment sector. The literature rarely refers to this, but considerable resources are devoted to maintaining the state sector. In fact, the intense focus of legislation on regulating the state sector can be interpreted as reflecting a pressing need to secure its position against the trend to a private market in the later years of the decade.

The equitisation process itself, legally expressed, preserved considerable opportunity for hemming the operation of the 'Law of Value' in many ways, consistent with the continuing socialist direction. We can point to the residual powers to control SOEs when the state's share was below 50 per cent, the commitment to use of the general companies as a channel of influence, not at all clearly defined, and the ongoing negotiated relationship between the managers and workers in SOEs and the wider world of the state and Party, still mediated by the Party's local organisations and the mass organisations, whose attention could be increased and diminished as required. Law was not politically important to this. Other forces existed to support and order the emergence of markets.

CONCLUSION: LAW AND THE NATURE OF MARKET-ORIENTED DEVELOPMENT IN VIETNAM

This chapter contends that there has been no fundamental change in the basic structures of state–SOE relations during the decade from around 1992. The decade did not start with a SOE sector that was a-legal in the sense that pure Stalinism could be said to ignore the need to regulate 'outside' activities, of which those aimed at the market, and in a Marxian sense accepting of the 'Law Of Value', appear the most likely candidate. Rather, SOEs immediately after the crisis of 1989–91 were legally viewed as objects of regulation rather than control, or, rather, both, but certainly not subject to a definitive plan. As Beresford (1997) has stressed, planners had grown long accustomed to negotiating with SOEs, and from this it was not a long step to treating their commercial activities as such, relatively autonomous from the state's wider goals—the plan—and driven as much by profit as other goals. Nor did the decade end with a clear program of 'privatisation'; rather, SOEs, even the equitised ones, continued to operate in an environment where rationalisation and regulation went hand in hand, and where their activities were clearly subject to the wider political and social intentions of government and Party.

If we trace Vietnamese socialism back to Stalin's great surprise of the early 1950s, when he re-admitted economics to formal discussion, and the 'Law of Value' to an acceptable 'existence' within what Brezhnev was later to call 'existing socialism', then clearly so long as the Communist Party of Vietnam and its government continue to hold to definitions of the defining elements of socialism as 'public ownership of the means of production, central planning and distribution according to labour', and consider that the relations they have with the economy provide the political and developmental results that central planning promised and failed to deliver, then they have much room for manoeuvre. Central to this is the 'public' nature of the various business forms pertaining. In Vietnam it is said that 'the private is not entirely private and the public not entirely public',[18] then clearly much will turn, not on the private nature of SOEs, but the public nature of private companies.

If we now return to the three questions set out at the beginning, some hesitant answers can be attempted. Does socialism shape law and law-related institutions, and, if so, how? It is clear from the discussion above that you need to know quite a lot about 'socialism' in order to understand the dynamics of SOEs and their political position. It is, however, the *real* rather than doctrinal aspects of socialism that are important; the politics of a 'conservative' transition were deeply influenced by neo-Stalinism and its local reality. Socialism, then, shapes law and law-related institutions through its influence over the local dynamic, and does so in contingent ways: for example, it turned out that illegality in matters to do with SOEs was not inconsistent with local political priorities during the 1990s.

What is the balance between external and internal factors in explaining legal change? Since it appears that formal legal change was largely irrelevant, this question may appear moot. The forces that maintained illegality, however, were clearly domestic in origin.

Finally, does 'socialist' doctrine inhibit legal change? The answer to this goes beyond the scope of the chapter. This is because the central position of SOEs in the 1990s accompanied the relative absence from the scene of more private forms, which only started to emerge fast in the late 1990s. The work by McMillan and Woodruff (1999a, 1999b) argues that formal legal institutions were not necessary to the development of good inter-firm relations; the market did not need the state. But whether and to what extent the failure of private firms to emerge in the 1990s was due to 'socialist' doctrine is not something that can easily be answered. What the argument does suggest, however, is that the state (and Party) could effectively mediate between social groups without use of legality *per se*, and that it was, perhaps, this political success rather than doctrine that was central. After all, the great effort, reported above in terms of the decrees and other legal documents, did go into developing the outward forms of law.

NOTES

[1]   In other ongoing work, I am examining the nature of SOEs in terms of 'real property', and also the longer-term history of SOEs, going back to before 1975.

2   The 'Law of Value' is a term used by Marx, and more importantly by Stalin, to refer to the economic and social effects of the exchange of commodities; that is, production for the market—for profit. Stalin's 'Economic Problems of Socialism in the USSR' surprised many at the time (the early 1950s) by arguing that the Law of Value operated within the Soviet economy, specifically in areas such as trade with the peasantry on their private plots. That such an obscure terminology should mean this can be understood by reference to Marx's theory of surplus value, whereby separation of workers from the means of production allowed capitalists to pay them less than the value of their work, with value understood here in terms of the embodied labour in commodities, rather than the market price. The point in the discussion here is that profit-oriented exchange was doctrinally accepted within Stalinist thinking, which may come as a surprise to some readers.

3   It was of course Stalin's famous U-turn in the Bolshevik position on collectivisation that saw the retention of private plots and output from them disposable on markets, that defined what was, in the future, to be a critical difference between Stalinist and neo-Stalinist thinking and the 'pure' position of Maoism, reflected in the extinction of differences between 'state' and 'economic' structures in the People's Communes—a position never accepted by the Communist Party of Vietnam.

4   See Levine and Zervos (1993), which looks at the evidence from cross-country regression work, reporting almost no robust relationships between economic policy settings and economic performance, Also, Kenny and Williams (2001) who discuss the significance of the assumptions of ontological and epistemological universality inherent in the use of terms such as 'law' and 'development' in many contexts. See also Brock and Durlauf (2000) for further and later work than Levine and Zervos (1993); Rodriguez and Rodrik (1999) for an examination of the evidential basis for blanket policies that advocate trade liberalisation; and Prasad et al. (2003) for an example of a clear reversal in established orthodoxy, in this case arguing that capital market liberalisation is not necessarily associated with good economic performance.

5   For a neat argument about the current state of affairs, see Lindauer and Pritchett (2002).

6   See North (1995) for what I read as an open and non-doctrinaire approach. Greenwald and Stiglitz (1986) was a major push to exploration of these issues within economics. If market failure is pervasive then there are strong a priori arguments for an active state.

7   Cowen and Shenton (1996) discuss issues to do with the historical origins of this view in the longer term, and Almond (1988) looks at how, and perhaps why, mainstream political science, having largely abandoned state–society metaphors, eventually re-adopted them.

8   For example, Pistor et al. (2003:89) remarks that the 'importance of law and economic development has been long acknowledged', but then appears to argue in a more 'evolutionary' vein, that, based upon the evidence from transitionary economies, simple transplanting of law does not cause the desired effects; rather, what is sought are the conditions for the creation of endogenous processes of legal evolution suited to rapid economic growth, a more subtle cause-effect logic. Berkowitz et al. (2003) argue similarly, for the importance of successful localisation. Botero et al. (2003) reflect modern scepticism about the arguments over the implications of simple economic theory and the links between policy and performance, and can be read as suggesting that any particular causal links posited are not likely to be robust.

9   Compare with McMillan and Woodruff (1999a, 1999b) for studies of how such order can be based upon things like trust, with empirical reference to Vietnam, and so economic success be attained *without* apparent formal legal support.

10   See de Vylder and Fforde (1996) and Fforde (in progress). Micro level data show this uneven process clearly. For example, the 10-10 Hanoi textile mill had (according to Trong Quyen 1992) stopped being subject to any central planning in 1985 (that is, *before* the announcement of *doi moi* at the 1986 Sixth Party Congress) and had been the first SOE in the city to be allocated capital upon which a return had to be made (as part of the shift to state businesses), in 1990. For a contrary example, of rather slow adaptation to the market, see for example Vu Phong Tao (1992) on the Viet-Tiep local factory, which only really started to diversify in 1992.

11   By a Yeltsin solution, I mean one where somebody from within the apparat presents to the population for proper election, thus perhaps (and in Yeltsin's case with success) acquiring enough political legitimacy to crash the system when and if circumstances permit. Perhaps the Vietnamese conservatives saw this coming, or perhaps Tran Xuan Bach's activities were simply a stalking horse, to flush out possible adherents to such a strategy.

12   See Johnson (1982) for the importance of 'rationalisation' within the economic development support activities of MITI in Japan.

[13]   Whilst the basic ideas of central planning emerged during the Soviet Five Year Plans of the late 1920s and 1930s, there is enough *prima facie* reason to suppose the possibility of local adaptation of these in other countries for the term 'neo-Stalinist' to be useful. For example, whilst Uncle Jo (Stalin) simultaneously held the top positions in the Party, state and security structures in the USSR, thus permitting a certain pattern of 'mediation' (to apply such a term to his appalling practices), once Ho Chi Minh had lost influence, power at the top in Vietnam tended to be shared between competing groups, leading to characteristic problems for a country used to a monarchy, that used a system effectively monarchical/dictatorial in character (Stalinism), but had a number of competing offices. A wide range of books explain the peculiarities of central planning, where most goods and services were sold, but in quantities and at prices set by the plan, so that the meaning of 'sell' is quite different from that in market economies. Typically, in such economies planners ensured that prices were set at levels where SOEs enjoyed large profits, which were then used to finance large levels if investment. For a while, thanks to the high levels of investment, growth was very fast, but then slowed as constraints such as primary inputs and the low efficiency of the system started to bite. For a fascinating account of the collapse of this system in the USSR see Ellman and Kontorovich (1998), which collects writings by insiders after the event.

[14]   For example, in discussions of the Hai Phong refrigerator works (Trong Nghia 1992b) and the garments industry (Phan Huy Hien 1992).

[15]   Occasional confusion continues about the significance of this term. Literally translated as 'equitisation', it seems as often to be used to refer to the re-establishment of an SOE as an equity company, with some ownership rights expressed through that form, as it refers to an avowed process of privatisation.

[16]   As discussed below, these smaller SOEs were not treated as subject to equitisation, but rather to simpler and more radical (in terms of the 'Law of Value') measures.

[17]   The original legislation on the new-style general companies was extremely opaque on their rights and powers. On the situation in the early 2000s, see for example Bac Hai (2002a).

[18]   Dao Xuan Sam, personal communication—'Tu khong han la tu, cong khong han la cong'.

REFERENCES

Almond, G.A., 1988. 'The return to the state', *American Political Science Review*, 82(4):853–74.

B.H., 2002. 'Thi diem 4 loai hinh cong ty me—con [Experimenting with four types of 'mother–child' companies]', *Vietnam Economic Times* (Vietnamese edition), 27 February:2

Bac Hai, 2002a. 'Co cau lai TCTy Nha nuoc [Restructuring of State General Companies]', *Vietnam Economic Times* (Vietnamese edition), 20 May:5

——, 2002b. 'DNNN vay 85 per cent von tin dung uu dai [State businesses borrow 85 per cent of soft credits]', *Vietnam Economic Times* (Vietnamese edition), 15 May:3.

——, 2002c. 'Hau co phan hoa DNNN [The consequences of SOE equitisation]', *Vietnam Economic Times* (Vietnamese edition), 27 September:5.

Beresford, M., 1997. 'Vietnam: the transition from central planning', in G. Rodan, K. Hewison, and R. Robison (eds), *The Political Economy of South-East Asia*, Oxford University Press, Oxford.

—— and Fforde, A., 1997. 'A methodology for analysing the process of economic reform in Vietnam: the case of domestic trade', *Journal of Communist Studies and Transition Politics*, 13(4):99–128.

Berkowitz, D., Pistor, K. and Richard, J-F., 2003. 'Economic development, legality and the transplant effect', *European Economic Review*, 47(1):165–95.

Botero, J.C., La Porta, R., López-de-Silanes, F., Shleifer, A. and Volokh, A., 2003. 'Judicial reform', *World Bank Research Observer*, 18(1):61–88.

Brock, W.A., and Durlauf, S.N., 2000. *Growth Economics and Reality*, NBER Working Paper 8041, National Bureau of Economic Research, Cambridge, Massachusetts.

Chan Hung, 2002. 'Mo rong dau tu gian tiep [Expansion of indirect investment]', *Investment* (Vietnamese edition), 18 September:5

Chan, A. and Norlund, I., 1999. 'Vietnamese and Chinese labour regimes: on the road to divergence', in B. Kerkvliet, A. Chan and J. Unger (eds), *Transforming Asian Socialism: China and Vietnam compared*, Allen and Unwin, St Leonards and Department of International Relations, The Australian National University, Canberra.

Cowen, M. and Shenton, R., 1996. *Doctrines of Development*, London, Routledge

D.T., Van la, 2002. 'DNNN neu Nha nuoc giu 51 per cent co phan [Problems of SOEs if the state keeps 15 per cent of the shares]', *Investment* (Vietnamese edition), 20 February:3.

Dam Minh Thuy, 1992. 'Doanh nghiep nha nuoc truoc nhung thach do nghiet nga [SOEs face severe trails]', *Labour* (Vietnamese edition), 13 August:1,2.

Dang Phong and Beresford, M., 1998. *Authority Relations and Economic Decision-making in Vietnam: an historical perspective*, NIAS, Copenhagen.

de Vylder, S., and Fforde, A., 1996. *From Plan to Market: the economic transition in Vietnam*, Westview, Boulder.

Doan Kim, 2002. 'Cai cach DNNN vuong...phuong an [SOE reform blocked—project?]', *Vietnam Economic Times* (Vietnamese edition), 30 September:5.

Investment (Vietnamese edition), 2002. 'Phat hanh co phieu ra ben ngoai phai thong qua to chuc tai chinh trung gian [Issuing shares to the public must go through intermediary financial organisations]', *Investment* (Vietnamese edition), 16 September 2002:3.

Ellman, M. and Kontorovich, V., 1998. *The Destruction of the Soviet Economic System: an insiders' history*, ME Sharpe, Armonk, New York.

Fforde, A., 2002. 'Light within the ASEAN gloom? The Vietnamese economy since the first Asian Economic Crisis and in the light of the 2001 downturn', in ISEAS (ed.), *Southeast Asian Affairs 2002*, Institute for Southeast Asian Studies, Singapore.

——, A., in progress. 'Dragon's tooth or curate's egg? Reform and reaction in Vietnamese Industrial Organisation'.

Greenwald, B.C. and Stiglitz, J.E., 1986. 'Externalities in economies with imperfect information and incomplete markets', *Quarterly Journal of Economics*, 101(2):229–64.

Hoang Anh, 2002. 'Nghi dinh ve giao, ban, khoan, cho thue doanh nghiep nha nuoc. Se sua gi va can sua gi? [Decrees on allocating, selling, contracting and renting out SOEs. How will they be addressed and what needs addressing?]', *Business* (Vietnamese edition) 3 April:6

Hoang Lan, 1993. 'To hop co phan: diem moi cua mot xi nghiep quoc doanh [Share groups: a new element of SOEs]', *Vietnamese Economy*, 4:3.

Hai Phong (Vietnamese edition), 1992. 'Hoan chinh ho so thanh lap lai 24 doanh nghiep nha nuoc doc lap, giai the 2 doanh nghiep [Finishing the files for the re-establishment of 24 independent SOEs, and the dissolution of 2]', *Hai Phong* (Vietnamese edition), 7 August:1, 4.

Johnson, C., 1982. *MITI and the Japanese Miracle: the growth of industrial policy 1925—1975*, Stanford University Press, Stanford.

Kenny, C. and Williams, D., 2001. 'What do we know about economic growth? Or, why don't we know very much?', *World Development*, 29(1):1–22.

Kim Dan, 2002. 'Day manh hon co phan hoa [Stimulating equitisation]', *Vietnam Economic Times* (Vietnamese edition), 21 June:1.

Levine, R. and Zervos, S.J., 1993. 'What have we learnt about policy and growth from cross-country regressions?', *American Economic Review*, 82(2):426–30.

Lindauer, D.L. and Pritchett, L., 2002. 'What's the big idea? The third generation of policies for economic growth', *Economia*, 3(1):1–39.

M.G., 2002. '3 dieu kien de doanh nghiep Nha nuoc chuyen doi thanh cong ty, TNHH mot thanh vien [Three conditions for SOEs to become companies, single member limited liability companies]', *Saigon* (Vietnamese edition), 2 February:2.

McMillan, J. and Woodruff, C., 1999a. 'Dispute resolution without courts', *Journal of Law and Economic Organisation*, 15(3):637–58.

——, C., 1999b. 'Interfirm relations and informal credit in Vietnam', *Quarterly Journal of Economics*, 114(4):1285–320.

Minh An, 2002a. '"Xe rao" cho doanh nghiep ["Fence breaking" for businesses]', *Investment* (Vietnamese edition), 13 March:1.

——, 2002b. 'Tang tai luc cho doanh nghiep [Strengthening businesses]', *Investment* (Vietnamese edition) 3 April:4.

Nguyen Toan Thang and Trong Dat, 1992. 'Xi nghiep xay dung thuy loi tien giang: gop suc lam nen mot trieu tan thoc [The Loi Tien irrigation construction SOE: pooling strength to produce a million tonnes of paddy]', *The People* (Vietnamese edition), 21 December:2.

North, D.C., 1995. 'The New Institutional Economics and Third World development', in J. Harriss, J. Hunter and C.M. Lewis (eds), *The New Institutional Economics and Third World Development*, London, Routledge.

P.V., 2002a. 'Ba tieu chi phan loai DNNN [Three criteria for differentiating SOEs]', *Vietnam Economic Times* (Vietnamese edition), 3 May:2.

——, 2002b. 'Nghi dinh cua CP ve quan ly va xu ly no ton dong [Government decision on managing and dealing with unpaid debts]', *Vietnam Economic Times* (Vietnamese edition), 15 July:1.

Pham Bang Ngan, 1993. 'Xi nghiep ruou nuoc giai khat Thang Long—hieu qua kinh doanh thuoc do phong trao "Nguoi tot, viec tot" [The Thang Long Alcohol and Beverages Enterprise—business results as the measure of the movement "Good people, good work"]', *Commerce* (Vietnamese edition), 40:4.

Phan Huy Hien, 1992. 'Xi nghiep may son tay: mo huong lam an moi [The Son Tay Garment SOE: opening up a new business strategy]', *The People* (Vietnamese edition), 3 November:2.

Pistor, K. and Wellons, P.A., 1998. *The Role of Law and Legal Institutions in Asian Economic Development 1960–95*, Oxford University Press, Oxford.

Pistor, K., Keinan, Y., Kleinheisterkamp, J. and West, M.D., 2003. 'Evolution of corporate law and the transplant effect: lessons from six countries', *World Bank Research Observer*, 18(1):89–112.

Prasad, E., Rogoff, K., Shang-Jin Wei and Kose, M.A., 2003. *Effects of Financial Market Liberalisation on Developing Countries: some empirical evidence*, International Monetary Fund, Washington, DC.

Quy Hao, 2002a. 'De day nhanh co phan hoa [To speed up equitisation]', *Vietnam Economic Times* (Vietnamese edition), 13 September:3.

——, 2002b. 'Xoa chu quan doi voi doanh nghiep Nha nuoc [Getting rid of the 'line ministry or department' for SOEs]', *Vietnam Economic Times* (Vietnamese edition), 31 July:5.

Rodriguez, F. and Rodrik, D., 1999. *Trade Policy and Economic Growth: a skeptic's guide to the cross-national evidence*, NBER Working Paper 7081, National Bureau of Economic Research, Cambridge, Massachusetts.

Stalin, J., 1952. *Economic Problems of Socialism in the USSR*, Foreign Languages Publishing House, Moscow.

'Tin Ngan' (no author), 1993, 'Doanh nghiep nha nuoc: giu vai tro then chot nhung thua lo' (SOEs: keeping their leading role but loss making), Tin Ngan [Short news] *Vietnam Economic Times* (Vietnamese edition), 4:9.

Tran Ta Uyen,1993, 'Xi nghiep may xuat khau hung yen: tung buoc tu khang dinh minh' (The Hung Yen garment export factory: step by step defining itself), 27 *Commerce* (Vietnamese edition), 7-14/1993:10.

Tran Trung, 1993. 'Xi nghiep dien lanh tphcm duoc tu nhan hoa [The Ho Chi Minh City Refrigerator Enterprise is privatised]', *Investment* (Vietnamese edition), 16–31 October:12.

Trong Nghia, 1992a. 'Thieu von, tro ngai lon nhat hien nay cua cac doanh nghiep nha nuoc [Capital shortage, now the biggest obstacle of SOEs]', *Hai Phong* (Vietnamese edition), 14 December:1.

——, 1992b. 'Xi nghiep dien co hai phong hoan thanh ke hoach 1992 truoc thoi han [The Hai Phong electricity enterprise fulfils its plan for 1992 before schedule]', *Hai Phong* (Vietnamese edition), 8 December:2.

——, 1992c. 'Xi nghiep giay dep so 2 mo huong san xuat moi phat trien [The No. 2 shoe and sandal factory expands new production development], *Hai Phong* (Vietnamese edition), 5 November:1

——, 1992d. 'Ket qua buoc dau va nhung van de dat ra trong viec thuc hien Nghi dinh 388/HDBT [Initial results and problems arising from implementation of Decree # 388/HDBT]', *Hai Phong* (Vietnamese edition), 19 November:2.

Trong Quyen, 1992. 'Mot xi nghiep det man tuyn co uy tin [A tuile net textile factory that has prestige]', *Quan doi Nhan dan* (Vietnamese edition), 6 November:2.

Vu Manh Cuong, 1992. 'Xi nghiep lien hop pham dam va hoa chat habald sau van tan ure: ky luc tu su hoi sinh [Best ever: the HABALD Associated Enterprise fertiliser and chemical factory produces 60,000 tones of Urea]', *Labour* (Vietnamese edition), 22 October:1, 3.

Vu Phong Tao, 1992. 'Xi nghiep khoa viet tiep: dau tu hon 1 ti dong de phat trien san xuat [The Viet-Czech lock factory: investing more than a billion dong in the development of production]', *People's Army* (Vietnamese edition), 17 September:3

Woodside, A.B., 1976. *Community and Revolution in Vietnam*, Houghton Mifflin Company, Boston.

APPENDIX

Table 11.1   Legislation and decrees relating directly to SOEs immediately prior to 1992 (chronological order)

Quyet dinh so 217-HDBT ban hanh cac chinh sach doi moi ke hoach hoa va hach toan kinh doanh xa hoi chu nghia doi voi cac xi nghiep quoc doanh [Resolution # 217-HDBT Promulgating Policies for the Reform of Planning and Socialist Accounting for SOEs]; Authority: HDBT; Date:14/11/87; Source: CB 10/12/87

Chi thi so 13-CT ve viec trien khai thuc hien Quyet dinh so 217-HDBT ngay 14/11/87 ban hanh cac chinh sach doi moi ke hoach hoa va hach toan kinh doanh xa hoi chu nghia doi voi cac xi nghiep quoc doanh [Order # 13-CT on Implementation of Resolution # 217-HDBT 14/11/87...]; Authority: HDBT; Date: 7/1/88; Source: CB 31/1/88

Quyet dinh so 98-HDBT ve viec ban hanh ban Quy dinh ve quyen lam chu cua tap the lao dong tai xi nghiep quoc doanh [Decision # 98-HDBT on the Promulgation of Regulations on the Rights to Collective Mastery of the Collective of Labour in SOEs]; Authority: HDBT; Date: 2/6/88; Source: CB 30/6/88

Nghi dinh so 26-HDBT ban hanh Dieu le ke toan truong xi nghiep quoc doanh - Dieu le ke toan truong xi nghiep quoc doanh [Decision # 26-HDBT Promulgating the Statute on the Chief Accountant of an SOE—The Statute...]; Authority: HDBT; Date:18/3/89; Source: CB 31/3/89

Nghi dinh so 27-HDBT ban hanh Dieu le Lien hiep xi nghiep quoc doanh - Dieu le Lien hiep xi nghiep quoc doanh [Decision # 27-HDBT Promulgating the Statute on Enterprise Associations—the Statute...]; Authority: HDBT; Date: 22/3/89; Source: CB 15/4/89

Quyet dinh so 93-HDBT ngay 24/7/89 cua Hoi Dong Bo Truong ve viec sua doi che do nop khau hao co ban cua cac don vi xi nghiep kinh te quoc doanh [Resolution No. 93-HDBT of Council of Ministers on Revising the System of Depreciation Contributions of State Economic Enterprises].

Quyet dinh so 144-HDBT ngay 10/5/90 cua Hoi Dong Bo Truong ve chan chinh quan ly tai chinh xi nghiep quoc doanh [Resolution No. 144-HDBT of the Council of Ministers on Improving the Financial Management of State Enterprises].

Quyet dinh so 143-HDBT ngay 10/5/1990 cua Hoi Dong Bo Truong ve viec tong ket thuc hien Quyet dinh so 217-HDBT ngay 14/11/87, cac nghi dinh 50-HDBT ngay 22/3/88 va 98-HDBT ngay 2/6/88 va lam thu viec tiep tuc doi moi quan ly xi nghiep quoc doanh [Resolution No. 143-HDBT of the Council of Ministers on Summarising the Results of Implementing the Decision No. 217-HDBT dated 14/11/87, as well as the Decisions No. 50-HDBT dated 22/3/88 and No. 98-HDBT dated 2/6/88 and on Experimental Continuation of State Enterprise Management Reform].

Quyet dinh so 315-HDBT ngay 1/9/90 cua Hoi dong Bo truong ve chan chinh va to chuc lai san xuat va kinh doanh trong khu vuc kinh te quoc doanh. - Qui dinh mot so diem co ban ve thu tuc giai the xi nghiep quoc doanh bi thua lo nghiem trong (Resolution No. 315-HDBT of the Council of Ministers on Improving and Reorganising Production and Business in the State Sector. Regulations on Some Basic Points Regarding the Dissolution of State Enterprises Suffering Serious Losses].

Chi thi so 316-CT ngay 1/9/90 cua Chu tich Hoi dong Bo truong ve viec thi diem trao quyen su dung va trach nhiem bao toan von san xuat kinh doanh cho don vi co so quoc doanh. Qui dinh tam thoi ve nhung nguyen tac va noi dung trao quyen su dung trach nhiem bao toan va phat trien von cho cac xi nghiep quoc doanh [Order No. 316-CTHDBT of the President of the Council of Ministers on Experimentation with Allocating the Rights and Responsibility to Use Capital to State Production Units. Temporary Regulations Thereon].

Chi thi so 408-CT ngay 20/11/90 cua Chu tich Hoi dong Bo truong ve viec tiep tuc chan chinh cong tac tai vu ke toan va hach toan kinh te cua cac xi nghiep quoc doanh; [Order No. 408-CT of the President of the Council of Ministers on Continuation of the Strengthening of Financial Work in Accounting and Economic Accounting in State Enterprises].

Thong tu lien bo so 2-TT/LB ngay 5/3/91 huong dan viec giai quyet chinh sach doi voi lao dong khi giai the xi nghiep quoc doanh [Inter-Ministerial Circular Letter No. 2-TT/LB Guiding Implementation of the Labour Policy on Dissolution of State Enterprises].

Table 11.2   Legislation and decrees relating directly to SOEs, second half of 2001 and 2002 (chronological order)

Quyet dinh so 153/2001/QD-TTg ngay 9/10/2001 cua Thu Tuong Chinh Phu phe duyet doanh nghiep Nha nuoc hang dac biet [Decision No. 153/2001/QD-TTg of the Prime Minister on the Approval of Special State-Own Enterprises].

Quyet dinh so 172/2001/QD-TTg ngay 5/11/2001 cua Thu Tuong Chinh Phu ve viec xu ly gian no, khoanh no, xoa no thue va cac khoan phai nop ngan sach nha nuoc doi voi nhung doanh nghiep, co so san xuat kinh doanh co kho khan do nguyen nhan khach quan [Decision No. 172/2001/QD-TTg of the Prime Minister on the Reduction, Deferral, and Forfeit of Overdue Taxes and Other Payments to the State Budget Due to Objective Difficulties].

Quyet dinh so 182/2001/QD-TTg ngay 20/11/2001 cua Thu Tuong Chinh Phu ve viec sua doi, bo sung Quy che cong khai tai chinh doi voi ngan sach nha nuoc cac cap, cac don vi du toan ngan sach, cac doanh nghiep nha nuoc va cac quy co nguon thu tu cac khoan dong gop cua nhan dan ban hanh kem theo Quyet dinh so 225/1998/QD-TTg ngay 20/11/1998 cua Thu tuong Chinh phu [Decision No. 182/2001/QD-TTg of the Prime Minister on the Amendment of, and Supplement to, the Protocal on the Disclosure of Budget of Local Governments, Public Entities, SOEs, and Funds from Public Contributions According to Decision No. 225/1998/QD-TTg].

Quyet dinh so 1489/2001/QD-TTg ngay 21/11/2001 cua Thu Tuong Chinh Phu ve viec thanh lap to cong tac trien khai thuc hien chuyen doi doanh nghiep nha nuoc, doanh nghiep cua to chuc chinh tri, to chuc chinh tri - xa hoi thanh cong ty trach nhiem huu han mot thanh vien [Decision No. 1489/2001/QD-TTg of the Prime Minister on the Commission of a Specialist Group to Change SOEs, Economic Enterprises of Political and Socio-Political Bodies into Single-Owner Limited Liability Companies].

Chi thi so 27/2001/CT-TTg ngay 22/11/2001 cua Thu Tuong Chinh Phu ve viec trien khai thuc hien chuyen doi doanh nghiep Nha nuoc, doanh nghiep cua cac chuc chinh tri, to chuc chinh tri - xa hoi thanh cong ty trach nhiem huu han mot thanh vien [Directive No. 27/2001/CT-TTg of the Prime Minister on Changing SOEs, Economic Enterprises of Political and Socio-Political Bodies into Single-Owner Limited Liability Companies].

Thong tu lien tich so 89/2001/TTLT-BTC-BCA ngay 8/11/2001 cua Bo Tai Chinh va Bo Cong An huong dan viec nop, su dung va quyet toan tien thu thue doi voi cac doanh nghiep nha nuoc hoat dong cong ich thuoc Bo Cong an [Inter-Circular No. 89/2001/TTLT-BTC-BCA of the Ministry of Finance and the Ministry of Police on the Collection, Use and Report of Tax Payments of Non-Profit Enterprises of the Ministry of Police].

Thong tu so 94/2001/TT-BTC ngay 22/11/2001 cua Bo Tai Chinh huong dan bo sung quy dinh tai Thong tu so 121/2000/TT-BTC ngay 29/12/2000 cua Bo Tai chinh huong dan thuc hien dau thau mua sam do dung, vat tu, trang thiet bi, phuong tien lam viec doi voi cac co quan Nha nuoc, luc luong vu trang, doan the va doanh nghiep nha nuoc su dung nguon ngan sach Nha nuoc [Circular No. 94/2001/TT-BTC of the Ministry of Finance to Supplement Circular 121/2000/TT-BTC of the Ministry of Finance on Auction for the Purchase of Facilities and Equipments for Public Bodies, the Arm Force, Associations and State Enterprises Funded by the State Budget].

Quyet dinh so 1627/2001/QD-TTg ngay 27/12/2001 cua Thu Tuong Chinh Phu ve viec chuyen doanh nghiep Nha nuoc cong ty xuat nhap khau hang tieu thu cong nghiep TP HCM thanh cong ty co phan [Decision No. 1672/2001/QD-TTg of the Prime Minister on Changing the HCMC's Import–Export Company of Industrial Consumption Products into a Public Company].

Quyet dinh so 53/2002/QD-TTg ngay 11/1/2002 cua Thu Tuong Chinh Phu ve viec chuyen doanh nghiep Nha nuoc Cong ty xuat nhap khau thuy dac san tanh cong ty co phan [Decision No. 53/2002/QD-TTg of the Prime Minister on Changing the Import–Export Company of Marine Special Products into a Public Company].

Quyet dinh so 55/2002/QD-TTg ngay 14/1/2002 cua Thu Tuong Chinh Phu ve viec chuyen doanh nghiep nha nuoc cong ty kinh doanh xuat nhap khau thuy san Minh Hai thanh cong ty co phan [Decision No. 55/2002/QD-TTg of the Prime Minister on Changing Minh Hai Import–Export Company of Marine Products into a Public Company].

Quyet dinh so 110/2002/QD-TTg ngay 4/2/2002 cua Thu Tuong Chinh Phu ve viec chyen doanh nghiep Nha nuoc cong ty Noi hoi VN thanh cong ty co phan [Decision No. 110/2002/QD-TTg of the Prime Minister on Changing Vietnam Hydraulic Pumping Company into a Public Company].

Quyet dinh so 111/2002/QD-TTg ngay 4/2/2002 cua Thu Tuong Chinh Phu ve viec chyen doanh nghiep Nha nuoc cong ty xay dung thuoc TCTy cao su VN thanh cong ty co phan [Decision No. 111/2002/QD-TTg of the Prime Minister on Changing Construction Company of the Vietnam General Rubber Company into a Public Company].

Chi thi so 04/2002/CT-TTg ngay 8/2/2002 cua Thu Tuong Chinh Phu ve viec tiep tuc sap xep, doi moi, phat trien va nang cao hieu qua doanh nghiep Nha nuoc [Directive No. 04/2002/CT-TTg of the Prime Minister on Continuation of Rearrangement, Reform, Development and Improvement of Efficiency of SOEs].

Quyet dinh so 178/2002/QD-TTg ngay 28/2/2002 cua Thu Tuong Chinh Phu ve viec chuyen doanh nghiep nha nuoc Cong ty phat trien dau tu cong nghe (FPT) thanh cong ty co phan [Decision No. 178/2002/QD-TTg of the Prime Minister on Changing FPT Company into a Public Company].

Thong tu so 03/2002/TT-BLDTBXH ngay 9/1/2002 cua Bo Lao Dong-Thuong Binh-Xa Hoi huong dan thuc hien Nghi dinh so 28/CP ngay 28/3/1997 va Nghi dinh so 03/2001/ND-CP ngay 11/1/2001 cua Chinh phu ve doi moi quan ly tien luong va thu nhap trong doanh nghiep xay dung Nha nuoc [Circular No. 03/2002/TT-BLDTBXH of the Ministry of Labor–Invalid–Social Affairs to Implement Decree No. 28/CP and Decree No. 03/2001/ND-CP of the Government on Reform in Salary and Income in State Construction Companies].

Thong tu so 04/2002/TT-BLDTBXH ngay 9/1/2002 cua Bo Lao Dong-Thuong Binh-Xa Hoi huong dan thuc hien quan ly tien luong va thu nhap doi voi doanh nghiep Nha nuoc hoat dong cong ich [Circular No. 04/2002/TT-BLDTBXH of the Ministry of Labor–Invalid–Social Affairs on Reform in Salary and Income in Non-Profit Public Entities].

Quyet dinh so 213/2002/QD-TTg ngay 25/3/2002 cua Thu Tuong Chinh Phu ve viec chuyen doanh nghiep Nha nuoc Cong ty giong cay trong mien Nam thanh con ty co phan [Decision No. 213/2002/QD-TTg of the Prime Minister on Changing FPT Company into a Public Company].

Thong tu so 22/2002/TT-BTC ngay 21/3/2002 cua Bo Tai Chinh huong dan xu ly tai chinh va hach toan doi voi doanh nghiep Nha nuoc co gop von thanh lap doanh nghiep lien doanh theo Luat Dau tu nuoc ngoai tai VN khi doanh nghiep lien doanh cham dut hoat dong (Nghi dinh so

41/2002/ND-CP ngay 11/4/2002 cua Chinh Phu ve chinh sach doi voi lao dong doi du do sap xep lai doanh nghiep Nha nuoc [Circular No. 22/2002/TT-BTC of the Ministry of Finance on Financial Works and Report in State Enterprises Investing in Joint-Venture According to the Law on Foreign Investment in Vietnam When the Joint-Venture is Dissolved].

Thong tu so 26/2002/TT-BTC ngay 22/3/2002 cua Bo Tai Chinh huong dan xu ly tai chinh khi chuyen doi doanh nghiep nha nuoc, doanh nghiep cua to chuc chinh tri, to chuc chinh tri - xa hoi thanh cong ty trach nhiem huu han mot thanh vien [Circular No. 26/2002/TT-BTC of the Ministry of Finance on Financial Works When SOEs, Enterprises of Political and Socio-Political Bodies are Changed into Single-Owner Limited Liability Company].

Nghi dinh so 49/2002/ND-CP ngay 24/4/2002 cua Chinh Phu sua doi, bo sung mot so dieu cua Nghi dinh so 103/1999/ND-CP ngay 10/9/1999 cua Chinh phu ve giao, ban, khoan kinh doanh, cho thue doanh nghiep Nha nuoc [Decree No. 49/2002/ND-CP of the Government to Amendment of, and Supplement to Decree No. 103/1999/ND-CP on Assignment, Sale, Lease, Rent SOEs].

Quyet dinh so 58/2002/QD-TTg ngay 26/4/2002 cua Thu Tuong Chinh Phu ve ban hanh tieu chi, danh muc phan loai doanh nghiep Nha nuoc va TCTy nha nuoc [Decision No. 58/2002/QD-TTg of the Prime Minister on the List and Criteria to Classify SOEs and State-Owned General Companies].

Thong tu so 30/2002/TT-BTC ngay 27/3/2002 cua Bo Tai Chinh huong dan tam thoi su dung khoan tien su dung von nha nuoc tai doanh nghiep [Circular No. 30/2002/TT-BTC of the Ministry of Finance on Temporary Guidelines on the Use of State Investment in SOEs].

Thong tu so 32/2002/TT-BTC ngay 10/4/2002 cua Bo Tai Chinh huong dan thuc hien Quyet dinh so 172/2001/QD-TTg ngay 5/11/2001 cua Thu tuong Chinh phu ve xu ly hoan no, khoanh no, xoa no thue va cac khoan phai nop ngan sach nha nuoc doi voi nhung doanh nghiep co so san xuat kinh doanh co kho khan do nguyen nhan khach quan [Circular No. 32/2002/TT-BTC of the Ministry of Finance on the Implementation of Decision 172/2001/QD-TTg on the Reduction, Deferral, and Forfeit of Overdue Taxes and Other Payments to the State Budget Due to Objective Difficulties].

Thong tu so 22/2002/TT-BTCCBCP ngay 23/4/2002 cua Ban To Chuc Can Bo Chinh Phu huong dan viec xu ly can bo, cong chuc, can bo trong doanh nghiep nha nuoc vi pham cap phat, su dung van bang, chung chi khong hop phap [Circular No. 22/2002/TT-BTCCBCP on Guidelines for Sanctions against SOEs' Cadre Who use Fake Education Certificates].

Nghi dinh so 64/2002/ND-CP ngay 19/6/2002 cua Chinh Phu ve viec chuyen doanh nghiep Nha nuoc thanh cong ty co phan [Decree No. 64/2002/ND-CP of the Government on Changing SOEs into Public Companies].

Thong tu so 11/2002/TT-BLDTBXH ngay 12/6/2002 cua Bo Lao Dong-Thuong Binh-Xa Hoi huong dan thuc hien mot so dieu cua Nghi dinh so 41 2002 ND CP ngay 11/4/2002 cua Chinh phu ve chinh sach doi voi lao dong doi du do sap xep lai doanh nghiep Nha nuoc [Circular No. 11/2002/TT-BLDTBXH of the Ministry of of Labor–Invalid–Social Affairs on Policies for Surplus Workforce as a Result of Reform of SOEs].

Nghi dinh so 69/2002/ND-CP ngay 12/7/2002 cua Chinh Phu ve quan ly va xu ly no ton dong doi voi doanh nghiep nha nuoc [Decree No. 69/2002/ND-CP of the Government on Management of Overdue Debts in SOEs].

Quyet dinh so 85/2002/QD-BTC ngay 1/7/2002 cua Bo Tai Chinh ban hanh quy che quan ly va su dung quy ho tro lao dong doi du do sap xep lai doanh nghiep nha nuoc [Decision No. 85/2002/QD-BTC of the Ministry of Finance on the Protocol on the Management and Use of Funds for Surplus Workforce of Reformed SOEs].

Thong tu so 66/2002/TT-BTC ngay 6/8/2002 cua Bo Tai Chinh huong dan trinh tu, thu tuc xu ly tai chinh khi giai the doanh nghiep Nha nuoc [Circular No. 66/2002/TT-BTC of the Ministry of Finance Guiding the Procedure for Financial Settlement of Dissolved SOEs].

Thong tu so 76/2002/TT-BTC ngay 9/9/2002 cua Bo Tai Chinh huong dan nhung van de ve tai chinh khi chuyen doanh nghiep nha nuoc thanh cong ty co phanb [Circular No. 76/2002/TT-BTC of the Ministry of Finance on Changing SOEs into Public Companies].

Quyet dinh so 895/2002/QD-TTg ngay 4/10/2002 cua Thu Tuong Chinh Phu ve viec phe duyet Phuong an tong the sap xep, doi moi doanh nghiep nha nuoc thuoc TCTy luong thuc mien Bac giai doan 2002–2005 [Decision No. 895/2002/QD-CP of the Government on Reform of the Northern General Food Company during 2002–2005].

Thong tu so 75/2002/TT-BTC ngay 9/9/2002 cua Bo Tai Chinh huong dan thuc hien phuong an tai chinh co cau, sap xep lai doanh nghiep nha nuoc va ngan hang thuong mai 2001–2003 [Circular No. 75/2002/TT-BTC of the Ministry of Finance on Guidelines on the Implementation of Financial Outlines for Reform of SOEs and Commercial Banks During 2001–2003].

Thong tu so 79/2002/TT-BTC ngay 12/9/2002 cua Bo Tai Chinh huong dan xac dinh gia tri doanh nghiep khi chuyen doanh nghiep nha nuoc thanh cong ty co phan [Circular No. 79/2002/TT-BTC of the Ministry of Finance on Guidelines on Evaluating SOEs for privatization].

Thong tu so 80/2002/TT-BTC ngay 12/9/2002 cua Bo Tai Chinh huong dan bao lanh phat hanh dau gia ban co phan ra ben ngoai cua cac doanh nghiep nha nuoc thuc hien co phan hoa [Circular No. 80/2002/TT-BTC of the Ministry of Finance on Guidelines for Guarantee of Auction of Shares of Privatized SOEs].

Thong tu so 85/2002/TT-BTC ngay 26/9/2002 cua Bo Tai Chinh huong dan thuc hien Nghi dinh so 69/2002/ND-CP ngay 12/7/2002 cua Chinh phu ve quan ly va xu ly no ton dong doi voi doanh nghiep nha nuoc [Circular No. 85/2002/TT-BTC of the Ministry of Finance on Implementing Decree 69/2002/ND-CP].

Quyet dinh so 1015/2002/QD-NHNN ngay 19/9/2002 cua Ngan Hang Nha Nuoc ve viec ban giao ho so dang ky khoan vay nuoc ngoai cua doanh nghiep [Decision No. 1015/2002/QD-NHNN of the State Bank on the Registration of Borrowing from Foreign Creditors].

Thong tu so 05/2002/TT-NHNN ngay 27/9/2002 cua Ngan Hang Nha Nuoc huong dan viec cho vay von doi voi nguoi san xuat, doanh nghiep ky ket hop dong tieu thu nong san hang hoa theo Quyet dinh so 80/2002/QD-TTg ngay 24/6/2002 cua Thu tuong Chinh phu [Circular No. 05/2002/TT-NHNN of the State Bank on Lending Producers and Enterprises Buying Agricultural Products According to Decision 80/2002/QD-TTg].

Thong tu so 94/2002/TT-BTC ngay 21/10/2002 cua Bo Tai Chinh huong dan xac dinh chi tieu von nha nuoc va thu nop ngan sach de phan loai doanh nghiep theo Quyet dinh so 58/2002/QD-TTg ngay 26/4/2002 cua Thu tuong Chinh phu [Circular No. 94/2002/TT-BTC of the Ministry of Finance Guiding Criteria on State Investment and Payments to the State Budget to Classify SOEs According to Decision No. 58/2002/QD-TTg].

Quyet dinh so 1101/2002/QD-BCN ngay 22/10/2002 ve viec to chuc lai cong ty xay lap 3, doanh nghiep thanh vien hach toan doc lap cua TCTy xay dung cong nghiep VN thanh cong ty me nha nuoc truc thuoc Bo Cong nghiep thi diem hoat dong theo mo hinh Cong ty me - cong ty con [Decision No. 1101/2002/QD-BCN of the Ministry of Industry on Restructure of the Construction Company No. 3, a Subsidiary of the General Industrial Construction Company of the Ministry of Industry].

Thong tu so 15/2002/TT-BLDTBXH ngay 23/10/2002 cua Bo Lao Dong-Thuong Binh-Xa Hoi huong dan ve chinh sach doi voi nguoi lao dong khi chuyen doanh nghiep Nha nuoc thanh cong ty co phan theo Nghi dinh so 64/2002/ND-CP ngay 19/6/2002 cua Chinh Phu [Circular No. 15/2002/TT-BLDTBXH of the Ministry of Labor–Invalid–Social Affairs on Policies for Labor in Privatized SOEs According to Decree 64/2002/ND-CP].

Quyet dinh so 15/2002/QD-TTg ngay 7/11/2002 cua Thu Tuong Chinh Phu ve viec phe duyet phuong an tong thu sap xep, doi moi doanh nghiep nha nuoc truc thuoc tinh VinhLong giai doan 2002–2005 [Decision No. 15/2002/QD-TTg of the Prime Minister on Approval of the Policy for Overall Restructure of SOEs in Vinh Long during 2002–2005].

Quyet dinh so 152/2002/QD-TTg ngay 7/11/2002 cua Thu Tuong Chinh Phu ve viec phe duyet phuong an tong the sap xep, doi moi doanh nghiep nha nuoc truc thuoc Bo Thuong mai giai doan 2002–2005 [Decision No. 152/2002/QD-TTg of the Prime Minister on Restructure of SOEs of the Ministry of Finance during 2002–2005].

Quyet dinh so 11/2003/QD-TTg ngay 2/1/2003 cua Thu Tuong Chinh Phu phe duyet phuong an tong the sap xep doi moi doanh nghiep Nha nuoc truc thuoc Uy ban nhan tinh Phu Yen giai doan 2002–2005 [Decision No. 11/2003/QD-TTg of the Prime Minister on the Restructure of SOEs of the People's Committee of Phu Yen Province during 2002–2005)

Quyet dinh so 12/2003/QD-TTg ngay 2/1/2003 cua Thu Tuong Chinh Phu phe duyet phuong an tong the sap xep doi moi doanh nghiep Nha nuoc truc thuoc Uy ban nhan tinh TuyenQuang giai doan 2002–2005 [Decision No. 12/2003/QD-TTg of the Prime Minister on Restructure of SOEs of the People's Committee of Phu Yen Province during 2002–2005].

Quyet dinh so 13/2003/QD-TTg ngay 2/1/2003 cua Thu Tuong Chinh Phu phe duyet phuong an tong the sap xep doi moi doanh nghiep Nha nuoc truc thuoc Uy ban nhan tinh Thai Nguyen giai doan 2002–2005 [Decision No. 13/2003/QD-TTg of the Prime Minister on Restructure of SOEs of the People's Committee of Thai Nguyen Province during 2002–2005].

Quyet dinh so 39/2003/QD-TTg ngay 8/1/2003 cua Thu Tuong Chinh Phu ve viec phe duyet Phuong an tong the sap xep, doi moi doanh nghiep Nha nuoc truc thuoc tinh VinhPhuc den nam 2005 [Decision No. 39/2003/QD-TTg of the Prime Minister on Restructure of SOEs of the People's Committee of Vinh Phuc Province until 2005].

Quyet dinh so 60/2002/QD-TTg ngay 13/1/2002 cua Thu Tuong Chinh Phu ve viec phe duyet phuong an tong the sap xep, doi moi doanh nghiep Nha nuoc tinh CanTho giai doan 2002–2005 [Decision No. 60/2003/QD-TTg of the Prime Minister on Restructure of SOEs of the People's Committee of Can Tho Province during 2002–2005].

Quyet dinh so 64/2002/QD-TTg ngay 14/1/2003 cua Thu Tuong Chinh Phu ve viec phe duyet de an tong the sap xep, doi moi doanh nghiep Nha nuoc thuoc Uy ban nha dan tinh ThuaThien - Hue den nam 2005 [Decision No. 12/2003/QD-TTg of the Prime Minister on Restructure of SOEs of the People's Committee of Thua Thien–Hue Province until 2005].

Chi thi co 01/2003/CT-TTg ngay 16/1/2003 cua Thu Tuong Chinh Phu tiep tuc day manh sap xep, doi moi phat trien va nang cao hieu qua doanh nghiep Nha nuoc [Directive No. 01/2003/CT-TTg of the Prime Minister on Accelerating the Restructure and Improving Efficiency of SOEs].

Quyet dinh so 14/2003/QD-TTg ngay 20/1/2003 cua Thu Tuong Chinh Phu phe duyet phuong an tong the sap xep, doi moi doanh nghiep Nha nuoc truc thuoc TCTy thuoc la VN giai doan 2003–2005 [Decision No. 14/2003/QD-TTg of the Prime Minister on Restructure of Subsidiaries of the General Tobaco Company during 2003–2005].

Quyet dinh so 109/2003/QD-TTg ngay 24/1/2003 cua Thu Tuong Chinh Phu ve viec phe duyet phuong an tong the sap xep doi moi doanh nghiep Nha nuoc truc thuoc Uy ban nhan dan tinh Hung Yen giai doan 2002–2005 [Decision No. 109/2003/QD-TTg of the Prime Minister on Restructure of SOEs of the People's Committee of Hung Yen Province during 2002–2005].

Quyet dinh so 115/2003/QD-TTg ngay 27/1/2003 cua Thu Tuong Chinh Phu ve viec phe duyet Phuong an tong the sap xep, doi moi doanh nghiep Nha nuoc truc thuoc UBND tinh Ca Mau giai doan 2002–2005 [Decision No. 115/2003/QD-TTg of the Prime Minister on Restructure of SOEs of the People's Committee of Ca Mau Province during 2002–2005].

Quyet dinh so 125/2003/QD-TTg ngay 28/1/2003 cua Thu Tuong Chinh Phu ve viec phe duyet de an tong the sap xep, doi moi TCTy nha nuoc va doanh nghiep Nha nuoc thuoc bo Cong nghiep giai doan 2003–2005 [Decision No. 125/2003/QD-TTg of the Prime Minister to Approve the Masterplan on Restructure of SOEs of the Ministry of Industry during 2003–2005].

Quyet dinh so 132/2003/QD-TTg ngay 30/1/2003 cua Thu Tuong Chinh Phu ve viec phe duyet phuong an tong the sap xep, doi moi doanh nghiep Nha nuoc truc thuoc UBND tinh Ha Tay giai doan 2002–2005 [Decision No. 12/2003/QD-TTg of the Prime Minister on Restructure of SOEs of the People's Committee of Ha Tay Province during 2002–2005].

Quyet dinh so 133/2003/QD-TTg ngay 30/1/2003 cua Thu Tuong Chinh Phu ve viec phe duyet phuong an tong the sap xep, doi moi doanh nghiep Nha nuoc truc thuoc UBND tinh SocTrang giai doan 2003–2005 [Decision No. 12/2003/QD-TTg of the Prime Minister on Restructure of SOEs of the People's Committee of Soc Trang Province during 2002–2005].

Quyet dinh so 134/2003/QD-TTg ngay 30/1/2003 cua Thu Tuong Chinh Phu ve viec phe duyet phuong an tong the sap xep, doi moi doanh nghiep Nha nuoc truc thuoc UBND tinh BacGiang giai doan 2003–2005 [Decision No. 12/2003/QD-TTg of the Prime Minister on Restructure of SOEs of the People's Committee of Bac Giang Province during 2002–2005].

12

Public Administration Reform in Vietnam: foreign transplants or local hybrids?

Martin Painter

> [Reform]…must be started from the practices of Vietnam, of its characteristics, its national traditions; concurrently it must consult and learn from the international achievements and experience. But it must not absolutely copy them and apply them exactly, as this would be harmful for the interest of the nation (Do Muoi 1995).

> …[G]lobal capitalism, far from simply threatening the Vietnamese state, is supplying an arsenal of techniques by which state-directed cultural borrowing will salvage and refine a managerial regime whose previous policies had seriously tarnished it (Woodside 1997:74)

Vietnam is in the midst of a process of fundamental state restructuring prompted by the abandonment of the command economy and the adoption of a long-term strategy of *doi moi* ('renovation') that essentially entails market reform and integration with the world economy. In the process, the Vietnamese government has embarked on a substantial public administration reform (PAR) program. The public administration reform program was basically initiated with the launch of *doi moi* at the Sixth Party Congress of 1986, but it was formally given the status of a coordinated national program at the Eighth Plenum of the Seventh Party Congress in January 1995. Following a major review in 2000, the government decided in September 2001 to set out a Master Program on Public Administration Reform for the Period 2001–2010, with four key reform areas (institutional reform, organisational structures, civil service reform and public finance). Different government agencies were responsible for seven programs within these four areas, and implementation plans and sub-programs were drawn up and fleshed out (UNDP 2001, 2002).

The Master Program summarises the problems and makes proposals for reform within the broad framework of a move towards 'a market-oriented economy with a socialist orientation'. The program identifies the Soviet-style 'centralized and subsidized bureaucratic management system' as a major cause of many problems (Government of Vietnam 2001:2), with pre-existing procedures, structures and habits continuing to hold back the adaptation of public administration to the new environment. Administrative structures are 'overlapping...inconsistent... centralized and compartmentalized', while 'administrative procedures are cumbersome and complex' and 'administrative order and discipline are loose'. '[A]ppropriate financial mechanisms', it finds, do not exist for the operation of public service and administrative agencies. Cadres and civil servants lack skills, professionalism and ethical standards, and corruption and 'harassment for bribes' remain a 'rather serious' problem.

The main focus of this chapter is on the origins of, and reasons for, the selection and adoption of reform ideas and proposals as a solution to these problems. Here, we consider two sources of reform ideas in particular: first, Party doctrine as it has evolved within the context of recent Vietnamese development; and second, external, 'global' models of administrative reform.[1] The Master Program is quite explicit about the significance of both these sources, stressing, first, the Party's role in articulating theories and practical issues and, second, that public administration reform 'must benefit from appropriate application of international knowledge and experience of organization and management operations' (Government of Vietnam 2001:3).

Thus, on the one hand, parts of the document bear the stamp of contemporary critical 'insider' reviews of the role of the Party, including the manner in which it should 'renovate' itself consistent with its socialist traditions, and current reflections on the developing role of the state under the doctrine of democratic centralism.

- The reform and perfection of public administration will be closely linked to the building and rectification of the Party, the renovation of the contents and leading modalities of the Party over the state in general and public administration in particular...(Government of Vietnam 2001:7)
- Administrative agencies and civil servants should place themselves under close supervision by people. There must be effective measures to curb acts which violate democracy and freedom and which indulge in arbitrariness, red tape, corruption, harassment for bribes and trouble-making to people (Government of Vietnam 2001:7)
- PAR policies...should encourage...the maintenance of order and discipline in economic activities to promote the economic growth and improve the people's life (Government of Vietnam 2001:7)
- ...implement the grassroots democracy regulation...whereby leading officials...at the various levels will be required to periodically and directly meet and talk with people and businesses (Government of Vietnam 2001:9)
- The state will develop policies, mechanisms to enable social organisations, mass organisations and the people themselves to deliver directly services which serve production and living requirements (Government of Vietnam 2001:16)

On the other hand, Vietnam is hungry for ideas, and in the world of administrative reform there is no shortage. Armies of consultants hired by aid donors promote apparently consensual 'best practice' global models (Larmour 2002).[2] To add to their weight and authority, international agencies such as the OECD and World Bank give these ideas their seal of approval (Common 2001). This global exchange of reform ideas increases policy diffusion and 'transfer' (Bennett 1991; Dolowitz and Marsh 1996; Halligan 1996). Not surprisingly then, the 'menu' of proposals and solutions shows a strong trace of conventional global public administration reform discourse.[3]

- Functions and duties of heads of institutions will be clearly established whereby they will be responsible and accountable for the performance and results of the institutions which they head (Government of Vietnam 2001:12).
- The mechanism for decentralising financial and budgetary management will be reformed to ensure unity of the national financial management system...(and) promote localities' and sectors' proactiveness, dynamism, creativity and accountability...a mechanism for calculating budget requirements on the basis of outputs and quality of operations, ensuring the monitoring of outputs, quality of targets and objectives (Government of Vietnam 2001:16).
- The salary system will be reformed in line with a new concept...fully monetising salaries...a salary-related allowance scheme...a system of bonuses for excellent services (Government of Vietnam 2001:14).
- A number of activities and public services, which are not necessarily handled by government agencies, should be transferred to enterprises, social organisations, private...and non-government organisations (Government of Vietnam 2001:5–6).
- ...encourage investors to invest in the development of...education institutions and...high quality hospitals...Contracting out mechanism will be applied to some...services (Government of Vietnam 2001:17).

Since the reform proposals in the public administration program stem from different sources, several important questions remain. First, is this all rhetoric, or 'reform talk', governed by the need to pay lip-service to one or more sets of doctrine? Second, in so far as the substance of the 'talk' relates to proposals for action, what factors lie behind the appropriateness and attractiveness of particular proposals? Third, are 'foreign ideas' carefully and systematically filtered through a prism of Communist Party doctrine? Is consistency or coherence required? And finally, how are solutions adapted to a local set of problems when taken 'out of context'?

Here, we have two quite distinct issues to address. The first is the fate of solutions with origins in Communist Party doctrine in a context of reform proposals that address problems of 'marketisation'; and the second is the fate of solutions drawn from the wider global discourse when they are applied in the specific context of development and transition being experienced in Vietnam. If parts of the menu are familiar, are the dishes the same? And what sort of meal do they produce?

GARBAGE CANS AND TRANSPLANTS

A useful starting point is John Kingdon's (1984) application of 'garbage can' theories of organisation (Cohen, March and Olsen 1972). In this view, the reform process can be considered as three separate streams of action: a 'problem stream', a 'policy stream' and a 'politics stream'. Reform is not so much a rational decision-making process in which problems are first identified and solutions then sought, but a more disjointed set of events in which the nature and significance of problems are contested in the 'problem stream', and solutions currently found in the policy stream become attached to some of them as a result of events in the politics stream. In the policy stream, ideologues, policy experts and advocates explore and contest ideas and proposals. The separate streams have a life of their own, and solutions look for problems as much as problems give rise to a search for solutions. Ideas and doctrines about administrative improvement emerge in the policy stream independently of administrative problems, and the way they are connected is somewhat random. An important part of this process of attaching solutions to problems is rationalisation of the 'choice', meaning that the process of justification is as much retrospective and rhetorical as it is prospective and analytical. Means–end rationality—whether it is in the form of Party doctrine or management theory—is suborned to the purpose of justifying a particular, convenient attachment of solution to problem.

This depiction of the meeting of solutions and problems shares similarities with Alan Watson's (2001) analysis of the transplantation and borrowing of legal ideas. Watson also suggests that a somewhat serendipitous process is at work in this process: fashions come and go, local reformers pick and choose what seems like a 'good idea' from the contemporary scene for reasons that are none too systematic, and much of what is transplanted (often for reasons of political convenience) subsequently lies on the surface of a set of social processes from which it can remain disconnected. The 'substance' of what is borrowed is not necessarily linked to the reason for its adoption (Watson 2001). Similarly, the manner in which contemporary administrative reform ideas and recipes are picked up in different jurisdictions seems by most accounts to be a somewhat haphazard affair. Nils Brunsson (1998:264), for example, calls the phenomenon of simultaneous adoption of contemporary reform proposals 'cropping up'. As he describes it, the adoption of new organisational forms in a number of places simultaneously is as much in the realm of 'talk' as in the realm of instrumental problem-solving and action (in Brunsson's 'garbage can' view of organisational life, 'talk' and 'action' are frequently 'de-coupled'). Rationalisation through expounding a reform discourse is a very large part of reform activity, which is principally about future intentions and hopes. How the adopted solutions actually affect local practices is another story (Brunsson 1998)—whatever is borrowed is also 'transformed' as it is adapted to a local political or administrative culture (Christensen and Laegreid 2001). The result of the transplants is a set of new hybrids.

One objection to this approach is that it seems to trivialise the importance of reform as 'problem solving'. In Vietnam, reform is a central political priority because the regime's survival depends on its success. The process brings to the surface a long list of deep and urgent policy problems. On the one hand, these imbue the reform agenda with an especial urgency, which may seem to offer a stern test of the approach outlined above, in particular the proposition that the process is best understood as a somewhat haphazard connection of solutions with problems. On the other hand, the heightened need for successful problem solving is precisely the condition under which the somewhat random and serendipitous attachment of ready-made solutions—including foreign transplants—might become more common. The intensity of solution advocacy as an independent stream of activity in such a situation also increases. Similarly, the Party's production lines of doctrinal affirmation and renovation shift rapidly through the gears as the lengthening list of problems pose new puzzles. As the pressure to adopt solutions becomes more urgent, this urgency may prompt the Party to lower its ideological resistance to particular solutions and subsequently to find new forms of rationalisation.

The analysis presented here begins with a broad historical overview of the evolution of the public administration reform program as interconnected streams of problems and solutions. This draws on official accounts given by Vietnamese public officials about the nature, aims and achievements of the reform process, both when the reforms were announced and retrospectively. These accounts reflect on both the nature of the problems—the diagnosis—and the justifications for the solutions. The data are drawn to a large degree from an official comprehensive review undertaken in 2000, with the close involvement of senior officials in the central agency concerned most with public administration reform, namely the Government Committee for Organization and Personnel (now the Ministry for Home Affairs).[4] This approach has its limitations, of course: any text has its own purposes and cannot be treated simply as a piece of 'objective evidence', and every text has an inner history that can rarely be recounted. With these limitations in mind, the analysis also pursues a case study strategy, looking at a range of interconnected issues underlying and associated with salary reform, one of the seven public administration reform programs. This brief case study draws on additional sources, including media reports, documents released by the government and other sources, and discussions with officials and government advisors.

What is presented here, however, is only one 'take' on the reform process. Separate attention needs also to be given to the political factors that are at play in giving priority to one set of problems and, at the same time, to a parallel set of solutions. Observing some of the products of these political struggles—official statements of intent, government decisions and announced programs of particular administrative reform—the discussion and analysis in this chapter seek to provide some glimpses of the subtle interplay of local agendas and foreign transplants in administrative reform in Vietnam. The account stops short of looking at the implementation and outcome of reforms.

UNDERLYING THEMES OF PUBLIC ADMINISTRATION REFORM IN VIETNAM

The underlying purposes of public administration reform in Vietnam are derived from a set of quite particular local circumstances and problems. The core of the issue, according to most public officials, is the transformation of the state from one that managed a command economy to one that seeks to regulate a 'multi-sector' economy. Public administration reform is officially perceived as one of the core elements of *doi moi*, and is traced back to the same origins. The Sixth Party Congress of 1986, when the *doi moi* program was launched, stated the need to 'carry out a major reform of the organizational structure of the state machinery' by (among other things) creating a 'unified system, with clear definition/separation of jurisdictions...according to the principle of democratic centralism; distinguishing between functions of economic-administration management and production-business management' and 'a lean apparatus with...a contingent of officials and civil servants who are politically qualified and competent in state management and socio-economic management' (quoted in Government Steering Committee 2000b:8). The Sixth Party Plenum in March 1989 newly emphasised that 'the state has to...manage all activities in social life by laws and in accordance with the Party's direction and policies'.

In the early 1990s, a number of measures were implemented, including a reduction in the number of administrative units at central and local levels, the introduction of a Civil Service Ordinance in 1993 and re-drafting of legal documents. Further important changes to the structure of government were brought in under the new 1992 Constitution, such as setting out a clearer distinction between the executive, legislative and judicial arms of the state machinery, defining the powers and responsibilities of state offices such as that of prime minister, and specifying more clearly the relationships between them. This marked a clearer delineation of authority, replacing a tradition of diffuse power sharing and collective leadership. At the same time, the leadership role of the Party was clearly re-affirmed, albeit within the context of a 'state ruled by law'. A report to the Second Session of the Ninth National Assembly in December 1992 highlighted this second element

> In principle, the national administration must be *institutionalized and regulated by the system of administrative laws to govern the relations arising in the process of state management* [emphasis in original] (Government Steering Committee 2000b:14).

This growing formalisation and rule-governed nature of administrative practices was a broad umbrella under which a number of specific administrative measures advanced, for example anti-corruption efforts, simplification of overlapping administrative jurisdictions, monetisation of *ad hoc* reward systems, and 'bringing to account' off-budget fees and charges. The underlying agenda, however, was tempered by recognition of a set of cross-cutting concerns. As stated in the 1992 report to the National Assembly quoted above

> In order to accomplish the objective of PAR, which is to develop an *effective and efficient* administration and prevent any sign of devolution, and localism, it is important to move towards the *democratic administration which is close to the people and responsive to people's needs* (Government Steering Committee 2000b:14).

A clear expression of this link between 'democratic' administrative reform and political stabilisation was provided in the resolution of the mid-term Party plenum in January 1994, which set out a set of principles underlining the 'gradual perfection of the State of Vietnam based on rule-of-law' (sic)—

- the state of the people, by the people and for the people, governing all social activities by laws, develops the country under the socialist orientation
- practising socialist democracy
- protecting human rights and basic civil liberties
- mobilising people to the cause of the country's development
- installing orders and rules (Government Steering Committee 2000b:15).

In sum, public administration reform was only in part about efficiency and effectiveness. Of equal, if not greater, concern were order and stability under the Party's political guidance. Development, requiring rationally ordered and efficient state machinery, would also require the mobilisation of consent and of closely monitored group and individual contributions. The prominent references to 'grassroots democracy' and 'close supervision by the people' in the 2001 Master Program continue to reflect this political priority.

The first official recognition of public administration reform as a coherent program came at the Eighth Party Plenum of the Seventh Congress in January 1995. The resolution on public administration reform had three 'fundamental themes'.

- Public administration reform is considered a pressing need and central task in developing and improving the Socialist Republic of Vietnam
- The main objective of public administration reform is to develop a competent, clean and transparent administration that does not abuse its power and is moving towards modernisation effectively and efficiently, to manage the affairs of the state, to promote the healthy development of society in the right direction, to serve the people better, and to develop a rule-of-law routine.
- Public administration reform is…composed of the following three components: institutional reform, re-engineering of the organisational structures…and the development of a contingent of administrative civil servants (Government Steering Committee 2000b:16).

The agenda of administrative reform has continued to be dominated by these responses to the initial 'transition problem', but it has also been affected by a set of issues arising from the course of the reform process itself. The importance of these second-order issues is reflected in the problems created by dismantling the old administrative control and command mechanisms over production units, which created a vacuum that was filled by more informal systems of control and ownership. The grant of commercial freedoms resulted in a virtual appropriation of state property by managers, bureaucrats and Party officials. On the one hand, this may have succeeded in releasing productive potential but, on the other hand, the dispersed centres of wealth and power that resulted challenged the authority of the state and the legitimacy of the Party, particularly where they were associated with corruption and other abuses (Beresford 2001; Fforde 1993; Gainsborough 2003; Vasavakul 1996). Similar authority gaps and loss of control were seen in relations between central and provincial governments and within the control and coordination systems of ministries and departments. Thus, the public administration reform agenda as it evolved gained new political significance and reinforcement as a set of measures through which the central Party–state could reassert authority (Vasavakul 1996).

In sum, by 1995 the substance of the public administration reform agenda had been set out and many of the dilemmas and obstacles identified. A series of remedies adapted to the Party's needs and local circumstances were being identified. As second-order issues such as growing corruption came to the fore, the stream of problems grew in volume. Moreover, the interconnectedness of the problems became increasingly apparent. For example, the problem of transition from a state that managed production to a state that managed a 'multi-sectoral economy' and regulated private economic activity was seen in terms of the need to disentangle the state simultaneously from economic micro-management and from some pre-existing forms of social protection and dependency. A conception of the role of the state as manager/funder, but not provider/producer, evolved in a manner that did not distinguish between economic and social policy sectors.

> There has been a clear distinction between state management functions pertaining to public power organs and business administration and production pertaining to enterprises and businesses and public services provision pertaining to public professional agencies and units; thus every and each one of them can perform their own right given authority, functions and responsibilities within the overall public administration system. Those functions that do not belong to state management agencies will be transferred to SOEs and professional agencies, especially those functions of direct productive and business administration and management and the provision of public services (Government Steering Committee 2000c:8).

In addition, the reform agenda spoke in one breath of 'equitisation' and 'socialisation' (the word 'privatisation' was quite deliberately not appropriated to the local discourse) and of self-help, or co-production.

> The stance and viewpoint of Vietnam is that socialisation of some activities in the public sector, as well as equitisation of a proportion of SOEs, can be by no means considered as privatisation. Socialisation will be conducted under the principle that 'the work is shared between the State and the people, and the State will take the principal role, exercising State management functions (Government Steering Committee 2000b:18).

Thus, 'socialisation' was conceived as 'the transfer of government work to non-government agencies' (Vasavakul 2002:10). As against the traditional style of 'begging and giving' and state subsidy, the 'people's resources' needed to be mobilised for public service delivery, along with 'associations, non-government organisations and private sector organisations' (Government Steering Committee 2000a:15). This manner of framing the issue appears as a product of socialist doctrinal traditions that put collective above individual effort and contributions. The 'people's resources', however, were to be both collective and individual—local communities would meet to contribute labour and funds to local road maintenance, and families would pay user fees and charges to support local schools and health centres. Vietnam's burgeoning NGO sector, which was subject to increasing regulation and political oversight in the 1990s, was viewed as a potential participant in this process of socialisation (Vasavakul 2002).

The distinction between the functions of 'state management' on the one hand, and 'production' or 'public service delivery' on the other, received greater attention during the 1990s as demands for public services grew. In the process, 'socialisation' and 'equitisation' as solutions became attached to one cross-cutting problem: the effects of 'state subsidy'. The characterisation of state budgetary support for both economic and social protection as 'subsidy' served to derogate both kinds of public expenditure. Ways were sought to restrain demands for subsidy, and many social expenditures came to be viewed in that light. As discussed later in more detail, the solution was to increase user fees and charges. An overriding 'driver' of this agenda was a strict budget constraint, which was partly a deliberate policy of fiscal prudence that had been adopted as part of the stabilisation strategies in the late 1980s, when Vietnam experienced rampant inflation. The need for restraint was also dictated by weaknesses in a tax system that was only slowly being adapted to the realities of a market economy. Tight fiscal policy was maintained by effective central control over disbursements to spending units, one result of which was increased pressure on local governments to make up the shortfall.

Local governments' share of state expenditure grew from 26 per cent in 1993 to over 43 per cent in 1998 (World Bank 2002a). Local governments increasingly relied on a variety of *ad hoc* revenue sources, particularly service charges and fees, over which there was quite loose central oversight (probably deliberately so), with local units operating many accounts and activities 'off-budget'. This situation solved problems for the central Party–state by easing some of the burden of service delivery or regulatory functions, and also created problems, by increasing local autonomy. Reformers worried about the ills of 'devolution and localism', as the idea of 'decentralisation' was tainted by a conventional Party–state centralist predisposition. As we see in the next section, however, certain sorts of decentralisation were increasingly both legitimate and convenient.

THE CASE OF SALARY REFORM

'Salary reform' was identified from the beginning of *doi moi* as a key area for action. In 1993, a set of simplified salary scales was drawn up and new rates applied to provide for a greater degree of uniformity across types of job and to take account of movements in prices. This new system of steps, based on multiples of a base salary, provided the pegs on which to hang a system of grades and ranks in the public service under the Civil Service Code, also promulgated in 1993. Uniform salary scales pegged to length of service and differentiated by job types were a necessary component. In this phase of salary reform, however, the lack of a systematic set of civil service position rules was a less pressing issue than the need to monetise in-kind rewards, such as free or heavily subsidised housing, health care and education, which had traditionally formed a major component of the benefits that flowed from being a state employee.

'Salarisation' was a profound change, as it altered the basis of public finance. A parallel change was the shift from relying primarily on extraction of surpluses from state enterprises to a cross-sector tax system. State employees of one kind or another comprised the great bulk of the salary income earners in the economy. But the levels of tax revenue under the evolving new system of public finance were not sufficient to provide for a state budget that would enable both the monetisation of public goods as higher salaries and their provision as 'free', universal public services.[5] Salarisation thus carried with it the overt expectation that the monetised salary would provide the individual employee with the 'ability to pay', justifying a range of new fees and charges for public services.[6]

> Government...by the end of 1992 has roughly salaried allowances for housing, health care insurance, transportation, and eradicated subsidised education (except primary education) and free of charge health care services and treatment, house granting and other high-price subsidy for public servants (Government Steering Committee 2000d:44).

While there were strong doctrinal and practical reasons to continue subsidising some public service provision, such as primary education, the practical issues raised by transition and underdevelopment precluded the possibility of a Western-style, tax-funded welfare state.[7]

Another major problem has been the perceived inadequacy of the official wage in the eyes of most public employees. The standard pay scales were set at a level that did not provide most state employees with what they considered a 'living wage', while the promotion and advancement mechanisms locked most employees into a rigid system of regular but very small increments. This state of affairs generated a myriad of interconnected problems. Among them was the widespread tendency for public employees—health workers and teachers, for example—to move partly into the private sector (while remaining on the public payroll) in order to supplement their income. The occupation of a position in many government agencies is viewed as a launching pad for a variety of private income-earning activities. Local stratagems to cope with low pay have undermined efforts to modernize the system of public administration according to the principles of the 'state ruled by law'. Most local administrative units have found ways to generate 'unofficial' funds so as to top up wages.

> Government cannot control all sources of incomes of public servants. Entities decide by themselves allowances for lunch, or additional income for public services taken from state budget or other sources of income generated by additional services (GSC 2000d:50).

Thus, while pay is supposedly uniform and set according to strict levels and categories of employment, the real situation is very different. Personnel management is highly decentralised in the state apparatus, and not regulated with a heavy hand by the central personnel agency.[8] Heads of administrative units (as with political leaders more broadly) often feel a strong obligation towards their workforce, in part a reflection of the importance of patronage in Vietnamese political life. Low pay reproduces some of the conditions under which such patrimonial rather than legal–rational norms pervade the civil service.

Thus, in the absence of sufficient resources in the national budget to make a significant impact on the adequacy of the official wage, the operations in practice of the salary system have undermined central discipline and control. Many agencies, and the workers in them, have learnt the ways of self-sufficiency only too well.

> [While]…operation of all organisations…is…run from state budget, other financial gains by the organisation are divided among and by themselves. Government completely lost control over additional incomes, although the operation is run [using] the state's assets and by state public servants (Government Steering Committee 2000d:50).

The government clearly acknowledged that the current salary system contained overt incentives to take 'unofficial' local initiatives, to which the centre was forced to turn a blind eye or even to grant its blessing. The dual problem thus emerged of reining in off-budget activities and exerting some kind of discipline over administrative agencies and service delivery units.

In a pattern familiar from the wider reform experience of *doi moi*, the centre's reforms put the official stamp on a state of affairs that had already been in existence as a result of local 'fence breaking',[9] and tried to turn them to the centre's purposes. Given budget scarcity, the very resource mobilisation capacity that led to the indiscipline was picked up as part of the solution. The chosen strategy was officially to sanction and make use of the fact that all public service delivery units were capable of generating income (including what was currently unofficial income) from their productive capacities. Such bodies in a market socialist system were engaging in a new set of social and economic relations outside the boundaries of the state, and for that reason they should neither be subject to administrative interference by line agencies, nor expect 'subsidy'. The state management principle underlying this argument was identical to the one that justified the reconstitution of state owned enterprises into autonomous business units and removal of their 'subsidies' (Painter 2003a). Thus, service delivery units should also have greater autonomy, including in matters of salary, to the extent that their revenue provided such freedom. However, if income-generating public service delivery bodies could in this manner help to solve the problems on the salary reform agenda, 'administrative' agencies, which had no major income sources other than the central budget, needed a rather different approach. For them, the solution was to seek efficiency gains through budgetary and management reform. The common element in both strategies was increased autonomy for local managers.

Thus, a new round of salarisation (this time, of income supplements derived from off-budget local revenue) was envisaged. The means to achieve this was to grant income-generating bodies much greater financial and personnel management autonomy within a more complex and transparent set of global budgeting rules, and to establish a new set of allocation rules where subsidisation was needed. These rules would serve the purpose of providing the necessary incentives both for bringing off-budget transactions into the budget, and for funding the next stage of salary reform. Vietnamese reformers arrived at a fashionable global solution— devolved budgeting, flexible pay scales and accountable management—in the course of working through some very local problems.

This strategy was worked out over a number of years. At first, the problem of low wages was dealt with simply by funding wage increases from the budget, but these rises hardly kept pace with price inflation. In 1993, the monthly basic wage was set at VND120,000 (about US$8); this was raised to VND144,000 (about US$10) in 1997, and step by step to VND210,000 (US$14) in 2001. In seeking to fund further salary increases, one option was to cut staff numbers. The government decided in October 2000 to cut overall staff numbers by 15 per cent by the end of 2002. All administrative units were instructed to submit plans showing how they would achieve the target, albeit with little concrete result. In the meantime, a high-level working group supported by experts in the Ministry of Finance framed a new set of proposals for funding a series of substantial salary increases. On 1 January 2003, the basic salary was raised to VND290,000 (about US$19), a rise of thirty eight per cent, and from October 2004 to approximately VND380,000 (about US$25). Half of these pay rises would be funded from the state budget, including savings made by local managers out of downsizing, the rest from revenue raised locally.

> For the upcoming salary reform, funds will not only come from the state budget—other avenues like allowing non-productive institutions to use part of their budgets to pay wages, and commercialising the healthcare, education and sport sectors and so forth would contribute.[10]

Separate measures applied to administrative agencies and to revenue-raising or public service delivery agencies respectively. Administrative bodies would now be funded from a lump sum allocation rather than by a funding formula based on existing levels of employment and salaries. The new 'block allocation' is effectively a one-line budget, with all the autonomy that this makes possible, and was first piloted in Ho Chi Minh City, where it led to savings and stimulated restructuring and downsizing. In December 2001, the scheme was extended to a larger number of pilots, with the clear intention to implement it across the state sector. This measure would assist both in meeting the downsizing targets and in paying the higher salary bill

> ...bearing in mind the current practices, which reveal extreme wastefulness in using funds from the State budget, giving lump sums to State administrative agencies will help promote savings, prevent wastefulness and reserve a part of the sums to improve employees' wages (Quy Hao 2003:15)

The very low level of salaries had ironically contributed to 'waste' through excessive rigidities and 'incremental creep' in staffing levels under the previous budget allocation system, with central allocation formulae based largely on the size of the workforce. Local managers sought for the most part not only to protect their employees by resisting downsizing but also to 'pad' their annual request for central budget allocations on the basis of a growing establishment. The additional cost to the official budget of taking on additional staff was very low, while the political costs of downsizing were very high.

One of the potential attractions to the centre of the kind of managerial devolution now being engineered was the expectation that a stronger set of interdependencies would be created as a consequence between local managers and the central managerial and political élite, with a concomitant weakening of the local patron–client relations that are critical to local bosses. The incentives and rewards for managers are now geared more towards taking up a more 'managerialist' stance vis-à-vis employees in pursuit of downsizing and efficiency gains, so as to provide the remaining workforce with their salary increases and supplements. As described below, the new central budget allocation and accounting processes at the same time put new instruments of potential control in the hands of the centre.

This new set of evolving relations between centre and periphery and employer and employee in the state apparatus is seen clearly in the case of public service delivery agencies. Decree 10 of December 2002 granted them extensive budgetary autonomy, allowing them to '(i) manage their own revenue accounts; (ii) adjust salary payments to reward performance; (iii) restructure their staffing to gain efficiency; (iv) set administrative spending norms that are different from those set by the government; and (v) carry forward funds unspent in the previous year' (Cuvillier and Hoan Van Hai 2002). In the course of implementing this so-called 'financial self-determination mechanism', each public service delivery agency would be classified according to their revenue generating capacities, and the amount of state budget funding (if any) would be calculated and fixed for three years (with a 'mark-up' factor to cover cost increases). At the same time as the cost of salary increases was passed down to local managers and the capacity provided to meet it from internal budgets, the discretion was granted to managers to pay above-award rates to reward efficiency-improving performance.

Thus, by a series of self-reinforcing steps, the government moved rapidly in 2001–02 towards a far more devolved system of financial and personnel management, in which local revenue-raising would play a growing role. But this was not the whole story, for the measures also forced local managers to 'open their books' and removed some (but not all) of the incentives to conceal 'off-budget' activities, in effect legitimising previously informal arrangements.[11] The aim of greater control and discipline was also to be achieved by new budget reporting and monitoring requirements.[12] Part of the 'package' of devolved accountable management everywhere is the substitution of *ex ante* input controls by *ex post* output controls, coupled with audit of financial transactions—that is, old, counter-productive systems of control are replaced by new ones, including measures to improve efficiency. The centre, however, retained a number of strict controls, limits and thresholds such that the granting of autonomy was within clear constraints. Among the latter were a set of measures to limit and monitor local fees and charges in order to retain some level of uniformity and to prevent local abuses. Despite this, a possible adverse consequence of the package did not go unnoticed by outside observers

> ...the government articulates a welcome commitment to improve the system of exemptions for education costs and the provision of free health services to poor households, (but) this may conflict with the recently-issued Decree 10...The concern here is that managers...will not be receiving the clear and consistent message that it is a high priority of government to ensure that poor people receive free primary education and curative health care (International Monetary Fund 2002:9)

OUTSIDE INFLUENCES

While clearly dealing with a set of problems that were rooted in Vietnam's historical development, the most recent salary reform measures echo themes and models that are very familiar in the global context of contemporary administrative reform, revolving around

- an increasingly decentralised system of pay and rewards, with increased management discretion
- overt reference to 'market rates' and 'ability to pay' in different employment environments
- use of differential rates of pay or 'bonuses' as an incentive mechanism to reward performance.

So what role should we attribute to the use of solutions brought in from outside Vietnam?

The overseas development aid (ODA) program has been a primary and direct source. According to the World Bank Development Indicators, annual ODA to Vietnam averaged 20 per cent of annual central government expenditures between 1994 and 1999, rising to 27 per cent in 1999. Aid has increasingly focused on 'governance', under which public administration reform is subsumed, although significant amounts of governance-focused aid only began to flow in after the adoption of the Master Program. Prior to that, Vietnam had only received some US$23 million for twelve separate projects related to public administration reform (Thang Van Phuc 2001). Among them was a series of UNDP projects beginning in 1991, the most prominent of which provided technical assistance for the conduct of the PAR Review in 2000. Since 2001, UNDP and bilateral donor programs have continued, but significant ADB and World Bank loans have also been approved, accompanied by technical assistance with central coordination of public administration reform, provision of IT infrastructure, civil service training, and reform of public finances among other projects.

The Vietnamese government, in an attempt to deal with what it perceived to be specifically local problems, set the broad outlines and objectives of the public administration reform program. The program, as such, was not 'imposed', nor was it delivered ready-made by a set of external donors or advisers under any kind of duress. One component of the public administration reform, salary reform, was not nominated by the government as a high priority for direct donor aid and technical assistance. The issue is highly sensitive politically, and goes to the core of issues of Party control, state capacity and political stability. Many donors, notably the World Bank, moreover, were perceived as having a doctrinaire and unhelpful approach to the issue based on recommendations such as radical downsizing and privatisation, presented in an ideologically insensitive manner. As we have seen, the local experts were not, as a result, inhibited from selecting from some of the same solutions, but the process of local control was vital.

The influence of donors and their advisers has been more direct in other, related parts of the public administration reform agenda. The technical experts of the Ministry of Finance who provided significant input to the salary reform issue were already involved in quite extensive dialogue with international consultants over other issues of budgetary and financial reform. Such projects were among the more popular with aid donors. A stocktake in 2001 listed eight separate aid projects and ten IMF or World Bank missions on budgeting and financial management since 1996, claiming significant results.

> Following the first Government–donor Public Expenditure Review in 2000 (PER-2000), the Government adopted in 2001 a comprehensive program to strengthen public expenditure management. The aim is to improve comprehensiveness, consistency and transparency of budgetary information as well as equity and efficiency of public spending (World Bank 2002b:30)

International consultants and local experts working directly with the Ministry of Finance in projects associated with the Public Expenditure Review have played an active role in disseminating ideas and responding to government proposals on financial reform.[13] Their role as a conduit for international 'best practice' models of public financial management cannot be dismissed. Moreover, these models are quite precise and well articulated, achieving a high level of consensus in the donor and international consultancy community (see, for example, Allen and Tommasi 2001; OECD 1998). Thus, although the government and Party wished to retain control of the agenda of problems being defined as critical, they were more than willing to be exposed to the technical detail and rationales embodied in particular solutions. Of course, experts in the Ministry of Finance hardly needed international consultants to bring the latest models of budgetary and financial management best practice to their awareness, and international textbooks could have provided the menu of contemporary thinking about devolved management, output budgeting, lump sum or one-line allocations and user charges. However, the strong involvement of World Bank, UNDP and other advisers and consultants in the budgetary reform process also directly exposed the Ministry of Finance to the global discourse of contemporary financial management.

CONCLUSION

Analysis of the wider public administration reform agenda showed the significance of themes and doctrines that related problems on the ground to wider themes of evolving Party doctrine. However, in the specific case of salary reform, both the problem definitions and the canvassing of available solutions were mainly concerned with practical dimensions of fiscal capacity and administrative control. Perhaps the strongest doctrinal influence had a somewhat perverse outcome, in that the carefully articulated doctrine of socialisation came to be coupled with more extensive use of user fees for collective goods levied on family or private income. The recourse to user fees and charges was tempered by state subsidy for basic, essential services but the overall design principles evinced a decidedly individualistic, market-driven 'capacity to pay' principle of service access. While this was carefully married with the more communitarian rhetoric of self-help or co-production, including the careful choice of the term 'socialisation', the rhetoric provided only the thinnest of veneers over what was effectively a process of commercialisation.

The adoption and adaptation of tools such as user charges and devolved budgets had very particular local implications and meanings, but also brought reformers in touch with a global reform discourse. The evidence, however, demonstrating that the proponents and purveyors of this discourse had either direct or indirect influence is mixed. On the one hand, the case of salary reform suggests that the reformers were brought to adopt these solutions by the logic of local circumstance and convenience, but overseas models and experience, particularly with financial management tools, provided at least part of the solution eventually adopted. There is, however, a two-way process in the relations with consultants and donors. Vietnamese reformers' receptivity to the concepts of modern public sector management saw adoption of particular ideas from overseas but also generated commitment among the donors funding reform implementation. The significance of this strategic aspect of reform adoption is a subject for further research, but a similar strategic relationship has been observed in other contexts, such as poverty reduction (Painter 2005). For the Vietnamese government, controlling the agenda of problem definition and the scope of the imported solutions while also tapping generous overseas aid donations, is critical.

The pattern of borrowing and transplantation that I have described has similarities with the phenomenon of 'cropping up', discussed earlier. The definition of the problems arose from a local debate about some fundamental issues of deep concern to the Party and top state officials, who were intent on achieving and maintaining control over state resources and capacities, while the internationally familiar menu of budgetary reform and devolved management offered solutions to these locally identified problems. Cropping up is both a process of reproduction or borrowing and of transformation. The use of parts of one administrative system's 'toolkit' of measures in another can be expected to produce anomalies and paradoxes. As noted earlier, the doctrine and practices of democratic centralism do not admit significant formal political devolution, although quite significant decentralisation was built into the tiered system of provincial and district administration. The unintended consequences of relaxing controls of the command economy and the attempt to build new systems of administration in the 1990s in some respects added to the power and autonomy of local units—for example, the greater reliance on local revenues put new patronage and other discretionary powers in the hands of local leaders. The new forms of devolution envisaged in the most recent salary reforms are coupled with a set of financial controls with the hope of undermining these sources of local power. In other words, paradoxically, the techniques of devolved, accountable management are being appropriated to an agenda concerned with enhancing discipline and control. Whether the design realises this objective remains to be seen, particularly in the light of the weak institutionalisation of the rules in the first place. It is just as likely to result in a new set of local unofficial stratagems and their attendant irregularities.

While the dynamics of the cropping up and the development of local hybrids suggest a Vietnamese-controlled process of reform, the longer-term implications for retaining control of the outcomes may be more uncertain. Once the 'problem' (for example, of salary reform) gets defined in terms of one set of solutions rather than another, the problem-solving and policymaking processes may become set on a course of action that carries them forward to unexpected destinations. The 'whole' that results may take on a character that each of its parts was originally disconnected from in the process of selecting pragmatically from the menu. Local actors have slipped imperceptibly and naturally into talk of 'commercialisation', when original thinking conceived of the same thing as 'socialisation', and in the process they may help transform it. Despite being adapted and transformed to suit local conditions, the borrowing of transnational administrative tools and rationales by local actors intent on furthering their own schemes has the potential to bring with it modes of thought and techniques of improvement that have new logics, and inject new resources and opportunities into the local scene, with potentially unpredictable consequences.

Thaveeporn Vasavakul (1996) and Adam Fforde (2002) have argued that the importation of external ideas drawn from the developmental experience of non-socialist states is more than just a temporary, tactical concession within an unreconstructed Communist doctrinal worldview, but part of a more fundamental rethinking by state leaders that serves to reconstruct their power on a new footing. That is, as Alexander Woodside suggests in the quotation at the head of this chapter, the results of borrowing and transplantation may be evidence less of a process of global homogenisation than of new forms of local enablement.[14] At the same time, the second and third-order consequences may yet be more profound, as digging the ground for a reformed public administration system of transplants and hybrids may have uprooted more than was intended.

ACKNOWLEDGMENTS

Research for this chapter was conducted with the support of City University of

Hong Kong Projects 7100218 and 9030995.

NOTES

[1]   The purpose is not to identify all external sources and weigh their respective influence. For example, no direct reference is made in this chapter to the lessons learnt from China. The contemporary western discourse on administrative reform is selected as a case to explore the results of interaction between local problem solving and outside ideas.

[2]   This has been the case in the administrative reform process in Vietnam. As early as 1991, a UNDP mission was providing stimulus to local debate and helping shape discussion. Since then, both bilateral donors and the international institutions have been quite active in public administration reform.

[3]   There is much overlap between these two lists. It is clearly not feasible to extract from a unified text two identifiably distinct sets of 'local' and 'foreign' proposals. These examples are chosen because they suggest strong traces and echoes from different sources.

[4]   The review was set up by government decision under the guidance of the PAR Steering Committee, which was located in the Office of Government. Five groups were established, covering different aspects of public administration reform. The groups drew on technical assistance from a small number of international consultants, provided with the help mainly of UNDP funding, and three workshops were held in May 2000 to allow national and provincial senior officials to make a contribution. Official Vietnamese and English language versions were released together in June 2000, and are available on the UNDP Vietnam Office website. The reviews formed an important input for a subsequent major announcement on public administration reform, and a new set of national programs, in September 2001.

[5]   The introduction of income and consumption taxes lagged behind 'salarisation', and their ineffective implementation accentuated the problem.

[6]   The same logic applied to rural workers who were given 'property rights' over formerly collectivised farming land. The economic proceeds of making use of those rights would provide the wherewithal for individual households to pay for those services formerly provided as one of the benefits of membership of the collective. Regulations on fee exemptions were introduced to cushion the impact on the very poor.

[7]   The current situation is that families account for about 80 per cent of the total health budget, as against the state's 20 per cent. In education, public subsidies provided respectively 61 per cent of primary, 42 per cent of lower secondary, 33 per cent of upper secondary and 46 per cent of higher and vocational education expenditure (World Bank 2001)

[8]   Oversight by the Party is another matter, albeit through a layered system of Party committees at the appropriate levels.

[9]   The importance of 'fence breaking' as a pattern of bottom-up reform is widely acknowledged in the literature on *doi moi*. Where the centre is indecisive or merely cautious, a 'blind eye' may be turned to 'illegal' local solutions and initiatives that, if effective, provide a momentum to wider reform following the granting of official blessing.

[10]   Quach Duc Phap, Director, Department of Fiscal Policy, quoted in Quy Hao (2003:15).

[11]   Additional potential side-benefits include a better set of accounting mechanisms to check fraud and corruption.

[12]   The 'modernisation' project of the public administration reform program also involves establishing effective databases and information systems pertaining to personnel and financial transactions in order to facilitate this control.

[13]   UNDP Project 96028 Phase II is located in the Ministry of Finance. Its objectives are: 'to build the capacity to conduct a public expenditure review at the central government level; to enable three provincial governments to undertake periodic public expenditure reviews, and disseminate the results and experience to other provinces; to improve the ability of the Ministry of Finance, key sector ministries and other relevant agencies to better prepare budget'. It claims the following 'results': 'improved understanding among senior government staff at all levels of the use of a PER as a tool for improving resource allocation and strengthening the budget allocation process; a core group of staff in relevant ministries and pilot provinces trained in public expenditure analysis; PER guidelines set up; PER implemented; a medium-term expenditure

framework established; recommendations for improvement of PER system'.
[14] On globalisation as an 'enabling' process, see Weiss (2003:15–19).

REFERENCES

Allen, R. and Tommasi, D., 2001. *Managing Public Expenditure: a reference book for transition countries,* Organisation for Economic Cooperation and Development, Paris.

Bennett, C.J., 1991. 'Review article: what is policy convergence and what causes it?', *British Journal of Political Science,* 21(2):215–33.

Beresford, M., 2001. 'Vietnam, the transition from central planning', in G. Rodan, K. Hewison and R. Robison (eds), *The Political Economy of South-East Asia,* Oxford University Press, Melbourne:206–30.

Brunsson, N., 1998. 'Homogeneity and heterogeneity in organization forms as the result of cropping-up processes', in N. Brunsson and J.P. Olsen (eds), *Organizing Organizations,* Fagbokforlaget, Oslo:259–78.

Christensen, T. and Laegreid, P., 2001. 'A transformative perspective on administrative reforms', in T. Christensen and P. Legreid (eds), *New Public Management: the transformation of ideas and practice,* Ashgate, Aldershot:13–42.

Cohen, M.D., March, J.G. and Olsen, J.P., 1972. 'A garbage can model of organizational choice', *Administrative Science Quarterly,* 17(1):1–25.

Common, R., 2001. *Public Management and Policy Transfer in Southeast Asia,* Ashgate, Aldershot.

Cuvillier, E. and Hoan Van Hai, 2002, 'What's going on regarding "Decree 10" implementation?', United Nations Development Programme, Hanoi. Available online at http://www.undp.org.vn/projects/vie96028/index.htm [accessed February 2003].

Do Muoi, 1995. Address of the Secretary General of the Communist Party of Vietnam to the Eighth Party Plenum of the Seventh Congress, Hanoi, 16 January.

Dolowitz, D. and Marsh, D., 1996. 'Who learns what from whom? A review of the policy transfer literature', *Policy Studies,* 44(2):342–57.

Fforde, A., 1993. 'The political economy of "reform" in Vietnam—some reflections', in B. Ljunggren (ed.), *The Challenge of Reform in Indochina,* Harvard University Press, Havard:293–322.

——, 2002. 'Light within the ASEAN gloom? Vietnam's economy since the Asian Financial Crisis', in D. Singh and A.L. Smith (eds), *Southeast Asian Affairs 2002,* Institute of Southeast Asian Studies, Singapore:357–77.

Gainsborough, M., 2003. 'Corruption and the politics of economic decentralisation in Vietnam', *Journal of Contemporary Asia,* 33(1):69–84.

Government of Vietnam, 2001, Master Programme on Public Administration Reform for the Period 2001–2010 (attachment to the Prime Minister's Decision No.136/2001/QD-TTg of 17 September 2001), Government of Vietnam, Hanoi.

Government Steering Committee for Public Administration Reform, 2000a. The

Overall Report: review of public administration reform, Government of Vietnam, Hanoi.

——, 2000b. Report of Group 1: stances and guidelines of the Party and the State of Vietnam on public administration reform, Government of Vietnam, Hanoi.

——, 2000c. Report of Group 3: review of public administration reform in the field of organizational structure of the government apparatus and state management— roles, functions, responsibilities and structure, Government of Vietnam, Hanoi.

——, 2000d. Report of Group 4: review of public administration reform in the field of human resource management and development (applicable to civil and public servants), Government of Vietnam, Hanoi.

Halligan, J., 1996. 'The diffusion of civil service reform', in H. Bekke, J. Perry and T. Toonen (eds), *Civil Service Systems in Comparative Perspective*, Indiana University Press, Bloomington:288–317.

International Monetary Fund, 2002. *Joint Staff Assessment of the Poverty Reduction Strategy*, Prepared by the staffs of the International Monetary Fund and International Development Association, International Monetary Fund, Washington, DC.

Kingdon, J., 1984. *Agendas, Alternatives and Public Policies*, Little Brown, Boston.

Larmour, P., 2002. 'Conditionality, coercion and other forms of "power": international financial institutions in the Pacific', *Public Administration and Development*, 22(3):249–60.

Organization for Economic Cooperation and Development, 1998. *User Charging for Government Services: Best Practice Guidelines and Case Studies*, PUMA Occasional Paper 22, Organization for Economic Cooperation and Development, Paris.

Painter, M., 2003. 'The politics of economic restructuring in Vietnam: the case of state-owned enterprise "reform"', *Contemporary Southeast Asia*, 25(1):20–43.

——, 2005. 'The politics of state sector reform in Vietnam: contested agendas and uncertain trajectories', *Journal of Development Studies*, 41(2):261–83.

Quy Hao, 2003. 'Easing the burden on exchequer', *Vietnam Economic Times*, February:15.

Thang Van Phuc, 2001, Promoting Public Administration Reform and Priorities for Calling Donor Assistance set out by the Government of Vietnam, Presentation by Vice-Chairman GCOP, Consultative Group Meeting, Hanoi, 7–8 December.

United Nations Development Programme, 2001. *Modernizing Governance in Vietnam*, United Nations Development Programme, Hanoi.

——, 2002. *PAR Master Programme: results and learning, 2001–2002*, Ministry of Home Affairs and UNDP Joint Paper for the Vietnam Consultative Group Meeting, United Nations Development Programme, Hanoi.

Vasavakul, T., 1996. 'Politics of the reform of state institutions in the post-socialist era', in Suiwah Leung (ed.), *Vietnam Assessment: creating a sound investment climate*, Curzon Press/Institute of Southeast Asian Studies, Singapore:42–68.

——, 2002. *Building Authority Relations: public administration reform in the era of Doi*

Moi, Asian Development Bank, Hanoi. Available online at http://www.aduki.com.au/.

Watson, A., 2001. *Society and Legal Change*, Temple University Press, Philadelphia

Weiss, L., 2003. 'Introduction: bringing domestic institutions back in', in L. Weiss (ed.), *States in the Global Economy: bringing domestic institutions back in*, Cambridge University Press, Cambridge:1–36.

Woodside, A., 1997. 'The struggle to rethink the Vietnamese state in the era of market economics', in T. Brook and Hy V. Luong, *Culture and Economy: the shaping of capitalism in Eastern Asia*, The University of Michigan Press, Ann Arbor.

World Bank, 2001. *Vietnam: managing public resources better, public expenditure review 2000*, Joint Report of the Government of Vietnam—Donor Working Group on Public Expenditure Review, World Bank, Washington, DC

——, 2002a. *Development Report 2003: Vietnam delivering on its promise*, World Bank, Hanoi.

——, 2002b. *Taking Stock: an update on Vietnam's economic reforms—progress and donor support*, Mid-year Consultative Group Meeting, Ho Chi Minh City, 23–24 May.

13

Fragmented pragmatism: the conclusion and adoption of international treaties in Vietnam

Tannetje Bryant and Brad Jessup

Although The Socialist Republic of Vietnam (hereafter 'Vietnam') has rules regarding the conclusion and adoption[1] of international treaties, they do not make clear whether international obligations entered into by Vietnam are self-executing or require the passage of national legislation to become effective domestically. The resolution to this issue is important because the mode of adoption of international treaties determines which law to apply where there is a conflict between an international treaty obligation and a domestic law. The issue also indirectly relates to how Vietnam complies with its treaty obligations.

This chapter will examine the rules with regard to the conclusion and adoption of treaties by Vietnam, questioning whether the Ordinance on the Conclusion and Implementation of International Agreements 1998 reflects an incorporation or transformation approach with respect to treaty adoption. Further evidence, specifically an analysis of the measures undertaken by Vietnam in fulfilment of its treaty obligations, the perceived application and effect of international treaties in Vietnam's socialist law regime and the treatment of treaties in domestic laws, will be relied on to conclude how treaties are adopted in Vietnam.

CONCLUSION AND ADOPTION OF INTERNATIONAL TREATIES BY THE SOCIALIST REPUBLIC OF VIETNAM

Under Article 102 of the Constitution of the Socialist Republic of Vietnam (hereafter 'Constitution'), the president is elected and capable of being removed by the National Assembly. The president is the head of state responsible for acting on behalf of Vietnam in domestic and foreign affairs,[2] and has the duty and power under Article 103(10) of the Constitution to negotiate and sign international agreements on behalf of the Socialist Republic of Vietnam with the heads of other states; to approve or join international agreements, except in cases where a decision by the National Assembly is necessary.

The National Assembly has the obligation and power, under Article 84(13) of the Constitution

to decide fundamental policies in external relations; to ratify or annul international agreements that have been signed or participated in on the proposal of the country's President.

It is the role of the Standing Committee of the National Assembly 'to carry out the National Assembly's external relations'.[3] The government—the executive arm of the National Assembly—has the duty and power under Article 112(8) of the Constitution, to conclude international treaties made in the name of the government, to undertake unified management of the external affairs of the state, and to direct the implementation of international treaties to which Vietnam has signed or acceded.

Pursuant to Articles 103 and 106[4] of the Constitution, the president promulgated the Ordinance on the Conclusion and Implementation of International Agreements 1998 (hereafter 'Ordinance'), which governs the conclusion and adoption of international treaties in Vietnam. The ordinance replaced a similar ordinance enacted in 1989 (hereafter '1989 Ordinance').

The 1989 Ordinance had many problems and deficiencies. In particular, it was passed under the 1980 Constitution, which was replaced in 1992 by a constitution that established new structures and bodies within government with which the 1989 Ordinance was inconsistent (Doan Nang 1998). For example, the former Council of Ministers was replaced by the government, the powers of the State Council were transferred to the president and the National Assembly Standing Committee was divested of its explicit power with regard to the conclusion and adoption of treaties.

There were also difficulties with the signing, approval, ratification, reservation, suspension and cancellation of treaties. In particular, the provisions in the 1989 Ordinance were not sufficiently specific and did not clearly identify the role to be played by the Supreme People's Court and the Procuracy and other government agencies in negotiating and entering into treaties (Doan Nang 1998). The 1989 Ordinance also failed to distinguish between international agreements signed by the state and those signed by other ministerial authorities. The competence of the state and other ministerial authorities to enter into treaties, and many key terms, also had to be defined. A clear explanation was needed of the effect of entering into an international agreement on domestic law and the effect of withdrawing reservations (Doan Nang 1998; Vu Thu Hanh and Jin 1997). To remedy these defects, the government passed the new Ordinance.

The Ordinance maintains many similarities with its predecessor, but rectifies provisions made inaccurate by the passage of the Constitution and seeks to clarify those provisions that were previously unclear. This is important for our discussion because the Ordinance will apply only to those treaties ratified after the enactment.[5] The 1989 Ordinance will continue to prescribe the rules for conclusion, adoption and implementation of treaties ratified between 1989 and 1998, but the new Ordinance can be used to illuminate ambiguities in the 1989 Ordinance.

THE 1998 ORDINANCE ON THE CONCLUSION AND IMPLEMENTATION OF INTERNATIONAL AGREEMENTS

Although similar to the 1989 Ordinance, the Ordinance is more expansive and overcomes some of the inadequacies of its predecessor. Notably, it sets out more clearly the rules to be applied by Vietnam in treaty negotiation, signature and ratification and the effect of treaties on domestic law. The purpose of the Ordinance is to specify the rules with regard to treaty practice in Vietnam and provide detail for the exercise of constitutional powers. The Ordinance consists of six chapters, which are further subdivided into 35 articles. The Ordinance is summarised below and in Figure 13.1.

General provisions (Articles 1–4)

Chapter 1 sets out the scope of application of the Ordinance. Article 1 details the stages of treaty conclusion, adoption and implementation that are regulated by the Ordinance and identifies the institutions that may conclude a treaty on behalf of Vietnam, namely
- the state
- the government
- the Supreme People's Court and the Supreme People's Procuracy
- the ministries and ministerial agencies.

Article 2 defines an 'international agreement' as all written arrangements concluded between Vietnam and one or many other nations, international organisations or other subjects of international law. For the purpose of this chapter, 'treaty' is used interchangeably with 'international agreement'. It also defines a number of terms used in treaty-making practice, including 'proxy', 'conclusion', 'approval', 'ratification', 'accession', 'reservation' and 'suspension', a feature absent from the 1989 Ordinance.

Article 3 sets out the principles to be applied in the conclusion of treaties, including the principle that international agreements must accord with the Constitution.[6] Article 4 classifies international agreements according to the institutions with the power to negotiate and conclude particular types of treaties.[7] The classification will depend on the character of the document and content of the treaty being entered into. Article 4(2) provides that the state may conclude treaties concerned with
- peace, security, borders, territory and national sovereignty (Article 4(2)(a))
- the rights and obligations of citizens (Article 4(2)(b))
- universal international and important regional organisations (Article 4(2)(c))
- other contents agreed upon by the signatories (Article 4(2)(d)).

Virtually all multilateral treaties fall within this category of international agreement. Most multilateral treaties lead to the loss of sovereignty of a state, as the obligations require the state either to act in a certain way or to prohibit acts. In cases where treaties do not affect the sovereignty of a nation, negotiating parties will nevertheless ordinarily demand that a treaty be concluded by the state, in its capacity as representative of all its citizens. Because the great majority of multilateral treaties fall within this classification, the discussion in this chapter focuses on this category of treaty.

Article 4(3) identifies those treaties that may be concluded by the government, including treaties made in the name of the state that are not prescribed under Article 4(2), and treaties concerning international and regional organisations beyond the scope of Article 4(2)(c).

Article 4(4) provides that the Supreme People's Court and the Supreme People's Procuracy may conclude treaties regarding international cooperation in areas within their jurisdiction.

Article 4(5) provides that the ministries and branches of the ministries may conclude treaties in the name of the state or government if the contents of the treaty fall within that ministry's or branch's field of competence and are not prescribed in Articles 4(2) and 4(3).

Conclusion of international agreements (Articles 5–22)

Article 5 sets out how treaties are to be entered into on behalf of the Vietnamese government, including their negotiation and signature. Articles 5(1) and 5(2) provide that the Ministry of Foreign Affairs, or another relevant ministry in consultation with the Ministry of Foreign Affairs, must submit all plans for the negotiation and signing of international agreements to the government.

Article 5(3) deals with preparation and negotiation of treaties. Where the treaty provisions are contrary to, or not yet stated in, any Vietnamese National Assembly or National Assembly Standing Committee legal documents,[8] they must be submitted to the National Assembly for consideration. The proposing agency is obliged to consult with the relevant ministerial bodies and seek an evaluation from the Ministry of Justice. The government then considers the ministries' opinions before reporting to the National Assembly Standing Committee, which then submits its comments to the National Assembly.

Nations with a system of treaty incorporation typically require parliamentary approval of treaties containing provisions contradictory to, or not yet stated in, existing law. Although the National Assembly is not competent to decide whether or not to commence negotiations and sign an international treaty,[9] the process of evaluation and consideration by the government and the National Assembly represents the first step in Vietnam towards such a parliamentary approval process.

The Ordinance provides for the National Assembly to receive extensive information to aid its consideration of the treaty. Article 5(4) provides that the report proposing the negotiation and signing of an international agreement must include

- the aims of the agreement, particularly its effects on Vietnam's rights and obligations
- an evaluation of the political, economic and social financial impact
- an evaluation of the observance of Article 3 of the ordinance and other provisions of law
- opinions of the Ministry of Foreign Affairs and other relevant ministries
- the title of the treaty, the name in which it is signed, and the timeframe for its implementation
- issues requiring comment.

Article 6 details which institutions are competent to decide whether Vietnam will negotiate and sign treaties after the proposals for negotiation and signature have been considered in accordance with Article 5. They are

- the president, who will do so in the name of the state
- the government, in the name of the government
- the National Assembly Standing Committee, in consultation with the government, which decides the negotiation and signing of international agreements by the Supreme People's Court and the Supreme People's Procuracy
- heads of ministries, with the permission of the prime minister, in the name of their respective ministries.

Article 7 presents the rules regarding the persons or bodies that can negotiate and sign international agreements without a proxy, stating that the president, the prime minister, the Minister for Foreign Affairs, the President of Supreme People's Court, the Chair of the Supreme People's Procuracy and heads of diplomatic missions do not require a proxy.

Article 8, to new addition in the Ordinance, deals with the authorisation for the negotiation and signature of international agreements. Under this article, delegates are permitted to negotiate and sign a treaty on behalf of the state, the government, the Supreme People's Court or Procuracy, ministries or branches, provided these bodies have authorised the delegates to do so.

The process for ratification and approval of treaties is set out in Articles 9–11.[10] Article 9 states that the agency proposing conclusion of a treaty must report to the government within 15 days of signing, providing a summary of the treaty's contents and a proposal for ratification or approval.[11]

Article 9(2) provides that the documents proposing ratification must include

- an evaluation of the agreement's impacts on Vietnam
- the necessary proposals on ratification or approval
- the opinions of the ministries concerned
- the contents of any reservation.

Article 10 states that treaties requiring ratification are those

- set out in Articles 4(2)(a) and 4(2)(b)
- that contain provisions contrary to, or are not yet provided for in, Vietnamese law

- that relate to state business
- containing provisions on ratification.

Article 10(2) goes on to provide that the president will decide whether to ratify a treaty except where there is a need for the treaty to be submitted to the National Assembly, for instance where the laws of Vietnam are either contrary to, or are silent on, the provisions of the treaty. As in Article 5(3), parliamentary approval of the treaty is required in such circumstances before it may be ratified.

Although Article 10(2) of the Ordinance purports to grant the president the power to ratify international agreements, it is unclear whether the president has this power under the Constitution. Article 84(13) of the Constitution gives the National Assembly the power to 'ratify' international agreements, though the language used regarding the president in the Constitution is different. Under Article 103(10) of the Constitution, the president has the power to 'approve or join' international agreements. The government also has the power to 'join' and 'approve' international agreements (on behalf of the government). As has already been noted, the Ordinance distinguishes between the processes of 'ratification' and 'approval'. If one were to apply the definitions in the Ordinance to the Constitution, the president would be prevented from ratifying international agreements.

Article 10(2) of the Ordinance is also inconsistent with the more authoritative Law on the Promulgation of Legal Documents (hereafter 'the Law').[12] Under Article 20(2) of the Law, the National Assembly holds the power to issue resolutions ratifying international agreements. The Law contains no similar provision giving the president the power to issue resolutions ratifying treaties. Instead, the president's power is limited to promulgating (proclaiming) the resolutions of the National Assembly, pursuant to Article 50 of the Law.

The process of ratification is set out in Article 10(3) of the Ordinance. The ministry or agency that proposed the conclusion of the treaty coordinates with the Ministry of Foreign Affairs to submit to the president a proposal for ratification. The president has 30 days to give an opinion on the submission. Once the decision to ratify has been made, the Ministry of Foreign Affairs has 15 days to put in place the diplomatic procedure required to finalise the treaty, including notifying the relevant agencies of the treaty's effects.

The process for the approval of international agreements is set out in Article 11.[13] This article provides that international agreements signed in the name of the government or a ministry and that contain provisions on approval or provisions contrary to or not yet regulated by the legal documents of the government require the approval of the government. Articles 11(3) and 11(4) detail the process of approval, which is similar to the ratification process outlined above.

Article 12 deals with accession to multilateral international agreements, describing who may seek accession of a treaty and the process involved in seeking approval or ratification according to terms of the treaty, including the documentation required and the time within which a decision is to be made.[14]

Article 13 provides that bilateral agreements must be in Vietnamese and that treaties signed in foreign languages must be translated into Vietnamese.

Article 14 provides that an international agreement concluded in the name of the state or government must be sealed by the Ministry of Foreign Affairs.

Articles 15 and 16 set out the procedures and rules with regard to reservations to international agreements.

Article 17 deals with the effect of international agreements and states that an international agreement will come into force in Vietnam according to the provisions of the agreement or under other arrangements made between the signing parties. The article also states that treaties may come into force temporarily in circumstances where full conclusion of a treaty is conditional on the occurrence of a later event under the control of the state.[15]

Promulgation and depository of international agreements (Articles 18–22)

Article 18 states that the Ministry of Foreign Affairs will manage and archive the original texts and instruments of ratification of international agreements, and Article 19 provides that the Ministry for Foreign Affairs must send duplicates of international agreements to the National Assembly, the president, the government and others.

Article 20 deals with the details of the promulgation of international agreements. It provides that all agreements must be promulgated, that is, proclaimed as a law of Vietnam, unless otherwise decided by the signing parties, the president or the government. The state must perform the promulgation of international agreements, in accordance with Article 30 of the Ordinance (see below), which is a function normally performed by the president.[16] An international agreement promulgated under Article 20 must be published in the Official Government Gazette within 15 days of the agreement taking effect.[17]

Under Articles 21 and 22, the Ministry of Foreign Affairs is required to register international agreements with the relevant international organisation and perform the function of depositary of international agreements where Vietnam is the depositary nation.

Implementation of international agreements (Articles 23-29)

Article 23 provides that Vietnam must strictly observe international agreements it has concluded. Article 24—'Ensuring the implementation of international agreements'—sets out the actions that must be undertaken for the implementation of international agreements. It provides that

- the agencies that propose the conclusion of international agreements submit to the government plans on the implementation of those agreements, clearly stating the implementation schedule, organisational, managerial and financial measures and other suggestions to ensure the implementation of the agreement.

- the concerned ministries and/or branches shall, within their functions, tasks and powers, implement the international agreements already concluded by Vietnam.
- in cases where an international agreement is breached, the agency that has proposed the conclusion of such agreement or the concerned state agency will coordinate with the Ministry for Foreign Affairs in proposing to the government measures necessary to protect the legitimate rights and interests of Vietnam.
- annually, and when requested, agencies that propose the conclusion of international agreements and relevant state agencies shall submit to the government and the president reports on the implementation of the concluded international agreements. Such reports must also be submitted to the Ministry for Foreign Affairs for monitoring.
- in cases where the implementation of an international agreement requires that legal documents of Vietnam be amended, supplemented, annulled or replaced, the agency that proposed the conclusion of the agreement and the relevant state agencies will promptly organise those changes, either directly or through another relevant state agency, in accordance with the Law on the Promulgation of Legal Documents.

Article 25 identifies the people and agencies with the authority to seek the amendment, supplement or extension of international agreements. Namely, state agencies entitled to negotiate a treaty under Article 6 are entitled to make amendments, and the institution that ratified the treaty also has the power to make amendments (Article 25(1)). These bodies must, however, first consult with, and obtain comments from, the Ministry of Foreign Affairs (Article 25(2)). Article 25(3) requires the documents that propose an amendment include

- the aim of the amendment
- the legal basis of the amendment
- the written comments from the Ministry of Foreign Affairs and others
- the contents of the amendment together with the international agreement.

Once an amendment has been decided on, the institution then coordinates with the Ministry of Foreign Affairs in completing the procedures for that amendment (Article 24(4)).

The grounds for suspension and termination of international agreements are set out in Article 26. A treaty may be suspended or terminated

- according to its own provisions
- where there is a violation of the conclusion principles prescribed in Article 3 of the ordinance
- where the international agreement is seriously violated by the other signatories.

The institution that ratified, approved or acceded to the international agreement has the competence to decide the suspension and termination of the agreement

Figure 13.1   Summary of the conclusion, adoption and implementation of international agreements under the Ordinance

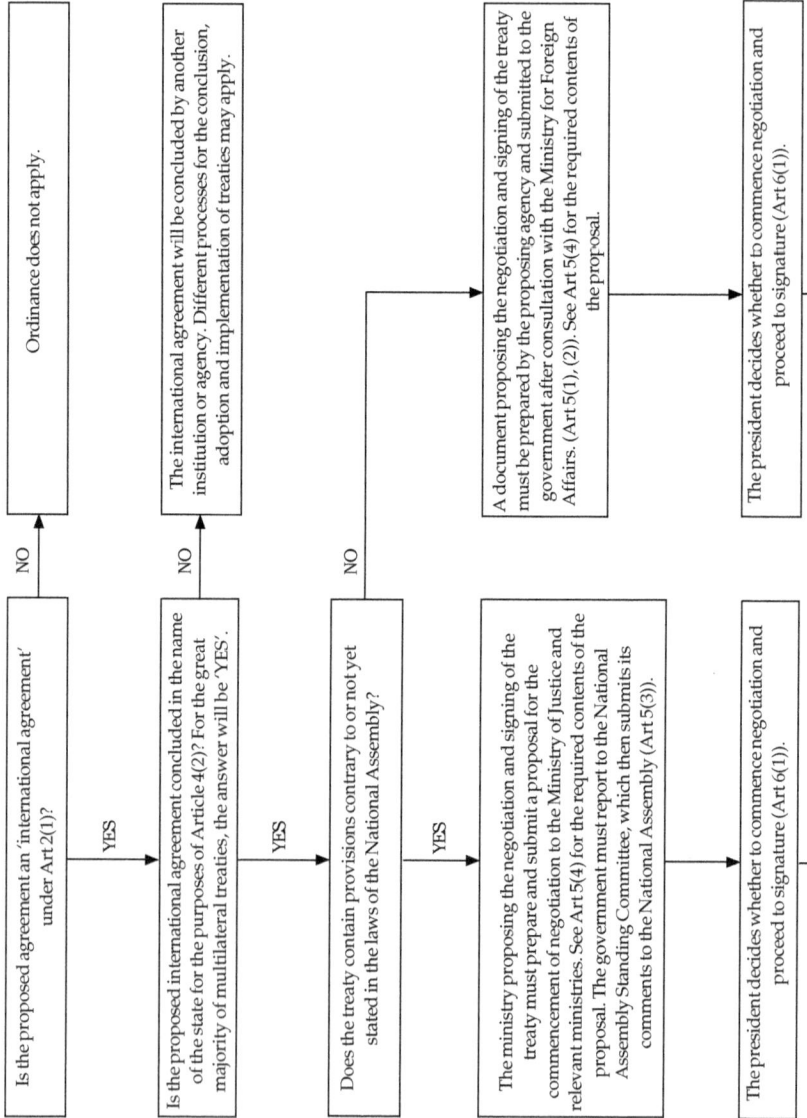

Is the proposed agreement an 'international agreement' under Art 2(1)?

NO → Ordinance does not apply.

YES ↓

Is the proposed international agreement concluded in the name of the state for the purposes of Article 4(2)? For the great majority of multilateral treaties, the answer will be 'YES'.

NO → The international agreement will be concluded by another institution or agency. Different processes for the conclusion, adoption and implementation of treaties may apply.

YES ↓

Does the treaty contain provisions contrary to or not yet stated in the laws of the National Assembly?

NO → A document proposing the negotiation and signing of the treaty must be prepared by the proposing agency and submitted to the government after consultation with the Ministry for Foreign Affairs. (Art 5(1), (2)). See Art 5(4) for the required contents of the proposal.

YES ↓

The ministry proposing the negotiation and signing of the treaty must prepare and submit a proposal for the commencement of negotiation to the Ministry of Justice and relevant ministries. See Art 5(4) for the required contents of the proposal. The government must report to the National Assembly Standing Committee, which then submits its comments to the National Assembly (Art 5(3)).

↓

The president decides whether to commence negotiation and proceed to signature (Art 6(1)).

The president decides whether to commence negotiation and proceed to signature (Art 6(1)).

Within 15 days of signature of the treaty, a document proposing ratification must be submitted to the government (Art 9). The document must include an evaluation of the impacts of the treaty and the comments of relevant agencies.

Where the treaty is one defined in Art 4(2)(a) or (b), concerns the state budget or contains a provision requiring ratification within 15 days, a document proposing ratification must be submitted to the government. It must include and evaluation of the impacts of the treaty and the comments of relevant agencies (Arts 9 and 10(1)).

National assembly ratifies treaty (Art 10(2)).

President ratifies treaty (Art 10(2)).[a]

International agreement takes effect according to its own terms (Art 17).

International agreement takes effect according to its own terms (Art 17).

Agreement promulgated by the state [ordinarily the president] (Arts 20, 30).

Agreement promulgated by the state [ordinarily the president] (Arts 20, 30).

Are the provisions of the treaty contrary to the laws of Vietnam?

NO

YES

The treaty provisions are already in conformity with the laws of Vietnam. No changes to the law are necessary.

The agency that proposed the conclusion of the treaty must seek the amendment, replacement, etc. of legal documents in accordance with the Law on the Promulgation of Legal Documents (Art 24(5)). Until such time the domestic laws will prevail over the provisions of the international agreement.

The provisions of the treaty are not yet regulated by the laws of Vietnam. There are no provisions in the Ordinance requiring the passage of legal documents incorporating the provisions of the treaty into domestic law.

The agency that proposed the conclusion of the treaty must submit plans on the implementation of the treaty to the government. The ministries and agencies implement the treaties within their own powers, and at least annually submit reports to the government and president on the treaty's implementation (Art 24).

[a] It is unclear from the Constitution and the Law on Promulgation of Legal Documents if the president has this power

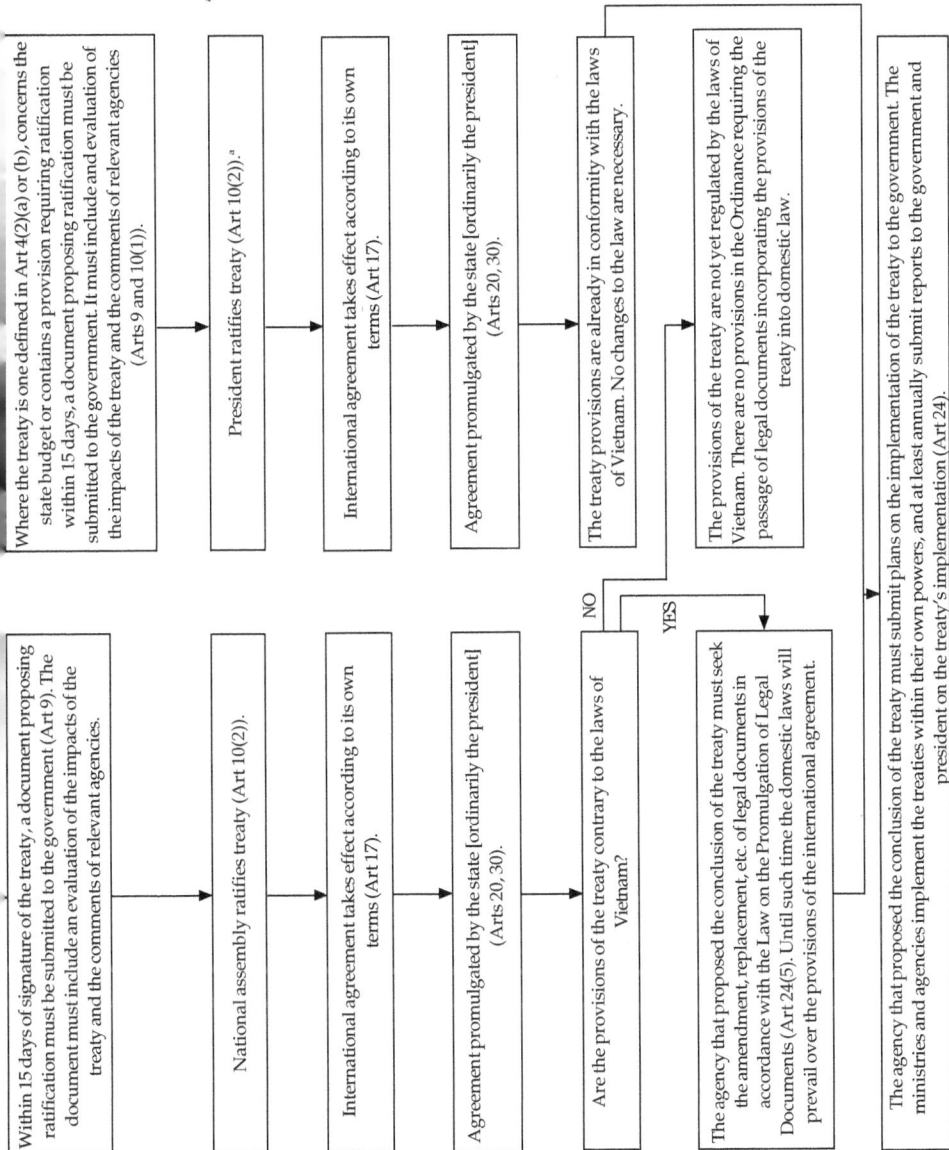

(Article 27), but a report must be provided to underpin any proposal for such an action (Article 28).

The rules regarding the interpretation of international agreements are detailed in Article 29. Generally, the contents of international agreements must be interpreted in accordance with international law. Where conflicting interpretations arise, the government must resolve the conflict.

The National Assembly Standing Committee is competent to interpret international agreements ratified by the National Assembly and international agreements that contain provisions contrary to, or not yet provided for in, legal documents promulgated by the National Assembly or the National Assembly Standing Committee. The institution in whose name the treaty was concluded is also competent to interpret the international agreement.

State management over the conclusion and implementation of international agreements (Articles 30–33)

Article 30 details the state's role in the domestic process of concluding, adopting and implementing international agreements, specifically that the state is responsible for

- promulgating legal documents on the conclusion and implementation of international agreements
- organising and ensuring the implementation of international agreements
- popularising, disseminating and guiding the implementation of legislation on the conclusion and implementation of international agreements.
- collecting state statistics on international agreements
- organising the archiving and deposit of international agreements
- supervising, inspecting, examining and handling violations of the legislation on the conclusion and implementation of international agreements
- settling complaints and denunciations related to the conclusion and implementation of international agreements.

The functions required of the state in Article 30 must be exercised by the government, assisted by the Ministry for Foreign Affairs and other ministries and agencies, according to Article 31.

Pursuant to Article 32, the National Assembly, National Assembly Standing Committee and the government must supervise the conclusion, adoption and implementation of international agreements.

Implementation provisions (Articles 34–35)

Article 34 provides that the government must issue separate regulations on the conclusion, adoption and implementation of international compacts concluded by provinces and cities that are directly under the control of the government and by other organisations.

The agency that proposed the conclusion of the treaty must submit plans on the implementation of the treaty to the government. The ministries and agencies shall implement the treaties within their own powers, and at least annually submit reports to the government and president on the implementation of the treaty (Article 24).

EVALUATION OF THE PROCESS OF IMPLEMENTING TREATIES INTO DOMESTIC LAW

Although the Ordinance provides detailed rules on the procedures concerning the conclusion, adoption and implementation of treaties in Vietnam, it does not clearly specify whether a treaty that has been ratified is self-executing or requires the enactment of legislation to incorporate the treaty obligations into Vietnamese domestic law. The question of whether the treaty-making process reflects an incorporation or transformation approach is an important one. Because Vietnam has rarely enacted laws to 'transform' the provisions of international treaties into municipal law, if the Ordinance and practice in Vietnam reflects a transformation approach, then the legal regimes established in international treaties will not displace domestic laws in Vietnam, they will not be enforceable and Vietnam would not be complying with its international obligations.

The articles in the Ordinance that provide the rules regarding the adoption of treaties are examined, to analyse the perceived application and effect of international treaties in Vietnam's socialist law regime, and to investigate state practice with respect to treaty adoption and implementation to determine whether an incorporation or transformation approach to treaty adoption prevails in Vietnam.

The competing doctrines of incorporation and transformation

The relationship between international law and domestic laws may be described by the competing theories of monism and dualism. The theory of monism posits that international law and domestic law are part of the same legal system, which may be enforced in the domestic or international arena, and international law will prevail where there is conflict. Conversely, the theory of dualism posits that international law and domestic law operate in different spheres and regulate different legal systems (Fitzmaurice 1957). Under the dualist theory, domestic laws regulate the internal activities of a state and its constituents and international law regulates the relations between states. International law must be transferred into the domestic law before creating individual rights (Balkin 1997).

With respect to the status of international treaties in domestic law, the doctrines of incorporation and transformation reflect the application of monist and dualist theories respectively.

The doctrine of incorporation, which reflects the monist theory, posits that a rule of international law becomes part of the municipal law without being expressly adopted by the legislature or the courts of the state (Shaw 1997)—its ratification results in its incorporation into a domestic legal system. The international law is said to be self-executing. With respect to treaties, a treaty ratified by the state will be incorporated into municipal law immediately on coming into effect.

By contrast, the doctrine of transformation, which reflects the dualist theory, posits that the rules of international law do not become part of municipal law until they have been expressly and deliberately enacted into domestic law by the use of the appropriate constitutional machinery, for instance, by the passage of a law through the state's legislature (Shaw 1997). Without transformation, the rights and obligations within international treaties may not be enforced in the domestic sphere; they operate only within international dispute mechanisms (Balkin 1997).

Much of the world, with the exception of a number of current and former territories of the British Empire and a collection of other nations, takes the incorporation approach to treaty-making. This is largely a result of the fundamental doctrine of *pacta sund servanda*. The principle was given the force of a treaty in the Vienna Convention on the Law of Treaties in 1969, Article 26 of which provides that 'each existing international treaty shall be binding upon all State Parties and implemented voluntarily by them' (Vu Duc Long, forthcoming).

For example, in Germany, Article 25 of the Basic Law of the Federal Republic of Germany provides that the rules of international law are incorporated into German domestic law and take precedence over domestic legislation. Similarly, Articles 93 and 94 of the Netherlands' 1983 Constitution provide an incorporation approach to treaty-making. In South Africa, ratification of a treaty is a function of the parliament (Section 231(2) of the South African constitution) and upon ratification the treaty provisions become part of the law of the republic (Shaw 1997).

In France, treaties ratified and officially published operate as laws in the domestic sphere. Article 55 of the French constitution provides that 'from their publication, duly ratified or approved treaties or agreements have a higher authority than [domestic laws] subject for each treaty or agreement, to its implementation by the other party'. A number of classes of treaties may, however, only be ratified through the enactment of legislation (Shaw 1997).[18]

Similary, Article 15(4) of the Russian constitution adopts a rule of incorporation of treaties (Shaw 1997), stating that, where there is an inconsistency between a domestic law and a treaty obligation, the treaty will prevail. This position is reiterated in Article 5 of the Federal Law of the Russian Federation in International Treaties of the Russian Federation. Article 5(1) provides that concluded treaties are an 'integral part' of the Russian legal system and Article 5(3) provides that provisions of international treaties adopted by Russia 'shall operate in the Russian Federation directly' (Butler 2002).

Although China has no constitutional provisions or specific laws dealing with the conclusion and implementation of treaties, Li Zhaojie (1993:62) concludes, based on provisions in certain laws and Chinese state practice, that China incorporates ratified treaties directly into its domestic laws. Article 142 of China's General Principles of Civil Law, for instance, states that

[i]f any international treaty concluded or acceded to by the People's Republic of China contains provisions different from those found in the civil laws of the People's Republic of China, the provisions of the international treaty shall prevail, except for the provisions to which the People's Republic of China has declared its reservations (Li Zhaojie 1993:79).

China's domestic laws relating to taxation, foreign investment, pollution, the environment and diplomatic privileges and immunities all contain provisions stating that a treaty will prevail over an inconsistent domestic law.

The Japanese process of concluding and adopting international treaties, which has been considered as reflecting an incorporation approach, is similar to that in Vietnam. In Japan, a treaty becomes a part of domestic law after the Diet has approved and the Cabinet ratified it.[19] Article 98(2) of Japan's constitution provides that treaties concluded by Japan 'shall be faithfully observed'. Shaw (1997) argues that this provision, which requires a step of parliamentary approval, reflects an incorporation approach. Interestingly, it is similar to Article 23 of Vietnam's Ordinance, which requires Vietnam to 'strictly observe' international agreements it has concluded.

The various approaches adopted in France—Vietnam's former colonial ruler— neighbouring countries such as China and Japan, and Russia—a former socialist nation—are instructive when determining Vietnam's approach to the conclusion of treaties. Some of these nations' laws do share similarities with Vietnamese laws, and each incorporates treaties into domestic law. These nations are a part of the large majority of nations who either expressly or by state practice, based on the Vienna Convention on the Law of Treaties, incorporate treaties directly into their domestic laws.

A minority of nations, led by the United Kingdom, and most nations of the Commonwealth, adopt a transformation approach to treaty provisions (Brownlie 1990).[20] In Attorney General for Canada v Attorney General for Ontario,[21] Lord Atken stated that

within the British Empire there is a well-established rule that the making of treaties is an executive act, while the performance of its obligations, if they entail alteration of the existing domestic law, requires legislative action…the stipulations of a treaty duly ratified do not within the Empire, by virtue of the treaty alone, have the force of law.

The rationale behind the adoption of the transformation approach in countries such as the United Kingdom, Australia and Canada, is that under their constitutions the executive is responsible for negotiating, signing and ratifying treaties. The institution with the power to make and amend laws, the legislature, is not involved in the treaty-making process. If treaties were automatically to become part of the law of these nations, the consequence would be that the executive could alter the laws of the state without consulting parliament (Shearer 1994; Jacobs 1987).

The same principle can be seen to operate in most of the nations where an incorporation approach to treaty provisions prevails. In nations such as France, Germany, South Africa and Japan, parliamentary approval of treaties occurs prior to, or is part of, the process of treaty ratification. In a sense, then, it could be argued that whether a nation adopts an incorporation or transformation approach to treaties will depend largely on when, if at all, parliament is involved in approving treaties.

Where the nation's parliament is involved in approving the text and obligations of the treaty before it comes into force, that nation will probably adopt an incorporation approach. Conversely, where the parliament is not involved in the treaty-making process, it will generally have a role in reviewing the treaty and deciding whether to give effect to its obligations after the treaty is in force. In such a nation the transformation approach is likely to be followed (Jacobs 1987).

The approach adopted in Vietnam

Vietnam's socialist legal regime. According to Marxist interpretations of democratic legal systems, the law is a reflection or an instrument of capitalism, used by capitalist states to maintain a privilege over other states in the international sphere and over the working classes in the domestic sphere.[22] The suspicion with which Vietnam treats democratic legal systems is expressed in its own legal system—described as being aimed at developing Vietnam in accordance with the socialist orientation, as opposed to the laws of the 'bourgeois state', which are aimed at protecting capitalism (AusAID 2001). While Vietnam's National Assembly is active, most legal controls are enacted and enforced by the administration through orders and decrees, bypassing the scrutiny of the democratic parliament (Gillespie 1997).

Since the *doi moi* reforms began in 1986, Vietnam has begun to participate in the international legal community and to ratify and accede to international treaties, principally motivated by the need to attract foreign investment to Vietnam and to integrate the Vietnamese economy into regional and international economies (AusAID 2001; Doan Nang 2002). But Vietnam has maintained its suspicion of international law, and Vietnamese bureaucrats believe that international treaties do not apply in the socialist domestic legal system—in accordance with the theory of dualism, they argue that the international and domestic legal spheres are not integrated. Doan Nang, the head of the legal group within the Ministry of Science, Technology and Environment, for instance, states that the socialist legal system dictates that national sovereignty and self-determination must be respected when entering and implementing international treaties. The mere conclusion of an international treaty does not elevate the obligations and rights in the treaty above those found in the domestic law (Doan Nang 2002). Although Doan Nang rejects the doctrine of transformation on the basis that it is impossible for states to transform international laws into domestic laws, his comments that Vietnam must and will enact laws when required in an international treaty (and that the international treaty does not automatically become the law of the state) in fact indicate that the doctrine of transformation is his understanding of Vietnam's approach to adopting international treaties (Doan Nang 2002:39). That is, that rights and obligations imposed on individuals will not become operative unless and until the rights and obligations are expressed in domestic laws.

China, which shares Vietnam's socialist ideals, appears less opposed to the incorporation of international treaties into its domestic laws. Domestic laws relating to taxation, foreign investment, pollution, the environment and diplomatic privileges and immunities all contain provisions stating that a treaty will prevail over an inconsistent domestic law, a reflection of the application of the monist international law theory and the doctrine of incorporation in China (Li Zhaojie 1993). The Chinese approach demonstrates that a socialist legal regime is capable of recognising the incorporation of international treaties, at least within specified jurisdictions. Therefore, the mere fact that Vietnam's legal system is a socialist one does not mean that an incorporation approach cannot prevail in Vietnam. Rather, the approach adopted should be determined through an analysis of Vietnam's laws, particularly the Ordinance, and state practice.

The Ordinance. It has been noted that the Ordinance does not explicitly adopt either an incorporation or transformation approach to the conclusion of treaties. The Ordinance does contain a number of articles similar to those in other 'incorporation' nations, but also has a number of articles that appear more consistent with a transformation approach.

The Ordinance (as shown in Figure 13.1) creates a different process for treaties where

1. the provisions are already prescribed in domestic law
2. the treaty provisions are not yet stated in the laws of Vietnam
3. the treaty provisions are contrary to the laws of Vietnam.

In the first class of treaty, the issue of incorporation versus transformation is irrelevant as the treaty provisions are a part of the domestic law of Vietnam before the treaty is signed and ratified. In the second and third classes, the negotiation and signing of treaties to be concluded in the name of the state must be approved by the president following consideration by the National Assembly (Articles 5(3) and 6(1)). Treaties falling into these classes must also go through a process of ratification. Although the Ordinance purports to require treaties be ratified by the president (Article 10(2)), the Constitution and the Law on the Promulgation of Legal Documents appear to reserve this power for the National Assembly. Nevertheless, according to Article 10(2), only the National Assembly may ratify treaties containing provisions contrary to, or not yet stated in, the domestic laws of Vietnam. Consequently, when the treaty enters into force it will have twice been considered by the National Assembly and approved on one occasion. Only treaties containing provisions that comply with pre-existing domestic laws may be ratified by the president. It is therefore arguable that the treaty has already been 'ratified' by the National Assembly.

This process is common to those nations that adopt an incorporation approach. Given that the National Assembly, the highest parliamentary body in Vietnam, has approved these treaties, it can be strongly argued that the moment the treaties enter into force their provisions become the law of Vietnam. The Ordinance, however, may require additional action.

Where the treaty contains provisions contrary to the domestic laws of Vietnam (class 3 above), the implementation of the international agreement requires 'legal documents of the Socialist Republic of Vietnam to be amended, supplemented, annulled or replaced…promptly in accordance with the Law on the Promulgation of Legal Documents' (Article 24(5)).

The Law sets out the types of legal documents that require promulgation and the institutions competent to promulgate them. It also specifies the rules and procedures for passing different types of legal rules into domestic law. Article 24(5) of the Ordinance means that, if an international obligation requires an amendment, supplement, annulment or replacement of a domestic law, then that change will have to go through the process required under the Law on the Promulgation of Legal Documents.

Because the Ordinance requires the alteration of domestic laws to comply with international obligations, where an international obligation entered into by Vietnam has an effect on an existing domestic law, the international obligation will prevail over the inconsistent domestic law but will first require the appropriate changes to be made to the existing domestic law. The inconsistent treaty obligation will not be self-executing but will require the passage of laws making the appropriate changes. The international obligation that conflicts with a domestic law will not take effect or form part of domestic law until the change has been made domestically. Article 24 is not clear on the process where an international agreement does not affect existing domestic law but does introduce a new obligation with domestic implications (that is, a 'class 2' treaty).

Under Article 24(1) the agency that proposed the conclusion of an international treaty is 'required to submit to the government plans on the implementation of international agreements including a schedule, organisational managerial and financial measures'. Article 24(4) requires state agencies that have concluded international agreements to submit reports on their implementation to the government and the president. These provisions, particularly given their silence on the need to enact legal documents, presuppose that the treaty provisions have already become law by the time the relevant agencies are developing plans and measures to give practical effect to the treaty's terms.

Indeed, interviews conducted with Mr Nguyen Ba Son Zang of Vietnam's Department of Foreign Affairs and Dr Dao Duc Tuan, Director of the National Office for Climate Change and Ozone Protection, have confirmed that, where treaties are not yet stated in or not inconsistent with the domestic laws of Vietnam, they will be self-executing.[23]

In summary, with regard to the issue of incorporation and transformation of concluded international agreements, the provisions of the ordinance, though not explicit, suggest that

- treaties that are contrary to the pre-existing laws of Vietnam will need to be 'transformed' into the domestic law of Vietnam. They will not be effective until the relevant laws are amended or repealed.
- treaties with provisions that are not yet stated in the laws of Vietnam will be automatically incorporated in the domestic law when the treaty comes into effect.

State practice. No specific domestic laws implementing international treaty obligations seem to have been passed. In Vietnam, treaty obligations tend to be implemented by the administration, using under-laws (typically circulars and resolutions), policies, strategies or action plans rather than specific laws passed by the National Assembly. These types of laws are more quickly and easily passed than those of the National Assembly, which meets just twice a year, and fit Vietnam's socialist legal system, in which legal control is generally exercised by administrators loyal to the government. Incorporation, because it is efficient and convenient, seems to be the approach adopted when treaty provisions are consistent with pre-existing domestic laws. If Vietnam adopted a transformation approach, whereby the rights and obligations imposed by international treaties remain in the international law sphere until given effect by the enactment of domestic laws, those obligations and rights, because of the nature of the Vietnamese socialist legal system, would be unlikely ever to be applied.

Environmental law provides some examples of situations where Vietnam has used policies and under-laws to implement international obligations without first passing legislation to transform international treaties.[24]

- Vietnam ratified the Convention on Biological Diversity in 1994. There is no comprehensive legislation implementing the convention's obligations, but a Biodiversity Action Plan 1995 is in place.
- Vietnam acceded to the World Heritage Convention in 1987, and between 1994 and 2003 two natural and three cultural heritage sites have been inscribed on the World Heritage List. There are, however, no laws in place protecting these sites from human interference.
- Vietnam ratified the Law of the Sea Convention in 1994. Various documents have identified the need for marine and coastal conservation programs and territorial sea delimitation.
- Vietnam acceded to the Convention on International Trade of Endangered Species in 1994. Article 29(5) of the Law on Environment Protection prohibits trading in precious or rare species of plants and animals, and the Council of Ministers passed the 1992 Decree Determining the List of Precious and Rare Wild Plants and Animals and Regulating Their Management and Protection.
- Vietnam acceded to the Convention on Wetlands of International Importance (Ramsar) in 1989. To date, one site has been listed as a Ramsar site—the Xuan Thuy Natural Wetland Reserve in the Red River Delta, and the Biodiversity Action Plan proposes the establishment of 64 protected wetland areas.
- Vietnam acceded to the Vienna Convention on Ozone Depletion and the Montreal Protocol in 1994, and the Vietnam Country Programme for the Phase out of Ozone Depleting Substances was formulated in 1994.

There are also domestic laws that specifically refer to international treaties and their effects. Direct reference to international agreements and their obligations is made in the Civil Code (Article 827), the Commercial Code (Article 4(1)), the Maritime Code (Article 23) and the Law on Environment Protection (Articles 24 and 25).

Article 827(2) of the Civil Code provides that, where it is in conflict with an international agreement, the international agreement prevails. Similarly, Article 4(1) of the Commercial Code states that, where a provision of the code is inconsistent with an international treaty obligation, the international obligation prevails. Article 23(1) of the Maritime Code makes reference to ships operating within Vietnamese territorial waters, stating that ships both of Vietnam and of foreign countries must observe 'the provisions of any international agreements to which Vietnam has signed or recognised'.

All three examples here seem to indicate adoption of the incorporation theory. They assume that obligations under international agreements entered by Vietnam are a part of the domestic law, but do not identify how this should be achieved.

Chapter V of the Law on the Protection of the Environment deals with 'International Relations in Respect of Protection of the Environment'. Article 45 provides that Vietnam shall implement 'all international treaties relating to the environment to which it is a signatory or participant, and shall respect all international treaties relating to protection of the environment on the basis of respect for independent sovereignty, territorial claim and mutual benefit'.

Article 48 provides that

> Where a dispute relating to protection of the environment arises in the territory of Vietnam and involves one or more foreign parties, the dispute shall be resolved by the governing laws of Vietnam and also by reference to international laws and practices. Any dispute between Vietnam and other countries in respect of the environment shall be resolved by way of negotiation, taking into account international laws and practices.

The Law on the Protection of the Environment does not detail how international treaties are to be implemented into domestic law (whether automatically upon entry into force or through the enactment of legislation), but these articles firmly state that Vietnam is obliged to fulfil the terms of any environmental treaty and supports the conclusion that obligations within treaties not inconsistent with pre-existing laws are automatically incorporated into the domestic law of Vietnam.

Although an analysis of state practice supports the assertion that treaties containing provisions not inconsistent with pre-existing domestic laws will automatically be incorporated into the domestic laws of Vietnam, it is not emphatic.

CONCLUSION

Although Vietnam has an Ordinance on the Conclusion and Implementation of International Treaties it does not clearly identify whether obligations under treaties ratified are self-executing or not. The only conclusion that is consistent with the articles of the Ordinance and current state practice, however, is that treaties that are not inconsistent with the domestic laws of Vietnam are self-executing. This view is shared by Dr Vu Duc Long (forthcoming) who concludes that ratified and concluded treaties are incorporated into Vietnam's domestic laws upon entry into force. Those treaties with obligations contrary to the pre-existing laws of Vietnam, however, will not become the law of Vietnam until the inconsistent legal document has been amended or replaced. Thereafter, the obligations under international agreements will prevail over any later domestic law.

This conclusion is not supported by other Vietnamese bureaucrats, including Doan Nang, who claims that socialist legal theory dictates that international laws are not integrated into the domestic legal system (Doan Nang 2002). Widespread acceptance of Doan Nang's claims, which are not reflected in the Ordinance, would result in a stifling of legal development in Vietnam. It would mean that the many international treaties that Vietnam has ratified or acceded to would only be binding on the state in the international legal system and would not operate to advance the livelihood of Vietnamese citizens or the protection of the environment.

It would be beneficial if Vietnam amended the Ordinance to include a provision that sets out clearly whether obligations under international agreements are incorporated into the domestic law of Vietnam upon their entry into force or whether further action is required by the state before the obligations are transformed into domestic law. The National Assembly appears to have acknowledged that benefits would flow from clarifying the relationship between Vietnamese domestic laws and treaties concluded by Vietnam, which is largely absent from the Ordinance. On 23 May 2005, the National Assembly passed the Law on Signing, Joining and Implementing International Treaties. This new law will commence on 1 January 2006 and will replace the Ordinance. All treaties concluded from 2006 will be subject to this new regime. An English language draft of the new law, dated 5 April 2005 and distributed at the National Assembly Foreign Affairs Committee workshop 'International Treaties and Roles of Legislatures', indicates the drafters' intention to include an article in the new law addressing the relationship between domestic laws and treaty obligations.

The draft law proposed a new Article 4 'International treaties and provisions of domestic law'. The final expression within this article, however, remained contentious, with various drafting options included in the draft version of the law. Generally, the options all reflected an incorporation approach to treaty adoption, supporting the conclusion reached in this chapter about the current approach in Vietnam.

It would be helpful if the new law describes how international obligations to which Vietnam is a party are to be adopted (either through transformation or incorporation) and implemented. This would be especially important where an obligation in a treaty requires the taking of specific action, for example, the passing of domestic controls or laws. As Vietnam becomes increasingly deeply connected with the rest of the world, and particularly as multinational corporations seek to invest in the country, issues of which sphere of law they are bound by—domestic or international—will grow more pressing.

NOTES

1   The authors have used the word 'adoption' to describe the process (either incorporation or transformation) of bringing international treaty obligations into a nation's domestic laws. 'Implementation' is used to refer to the process of introducing programs, policies or laws after treaty obligations have been adopted to give effect to and fulfil the obligations within the treaty.
2   Article 101, Constitution of the Socialist Republic of Vietnam.
3   Article 91(11) of the Constitution of the Socialist Republic of Vietnam. The Standing Committee of the National Assembly comprises the Chairman and Vice-Chairmen of the National Assembly and other members determined by the National Assembly. A member of the Standing Committee, however, may not also be a member of the government.
4   Article 106 provides that the president shall issue orders and decisions for the accomplishment of his duties and the exercise of his powers.
5   Article 76(1) of the Law on the Promulgation of Legal Documents states that 'only in extremely necessary cases a legal document may have a retroactive effect'.
6   A similar provision was contained in Chapter 2 of the 1989 Ordinance.
7   This is similar to Article 3 of the 1989 Ordinance.
8   That is, any laws, resolutions and ordinances. See Articles 1(1) and (2) of the *Law dated 12/11/ 1996 of the National Assembly on the Promulgation of Legal Documents*.
9   See Article 6 of the Ordinance and Article 84(13) of the Constitution.
10 The Ordinance distinguishes between acts of conclusion by the state and the government. Under Article 2, 'ratification' is a legal act undertaken by the National Assembly or President acknowledging the effect of the concluded treaty to Vietnam. 'Approval' is defined as a legal act by the government, acknowledging the effect of a concluded treaty to Vietnam.
11 A similar provision was contained in Article 7 of the 1989 Ordinance.
12 An 'ordinance' is a by-law enacted by the National Assembly Standing Committee. A 'law' is enacted by the National Assembly.
13 This was previously set out in similar terms in Article 8 of the 1989 Ordinance.
14 This was provided for in Article 9 of the 1989 Ordinance.
15 For example, the fulfilment of trade liberalisation requirements.
16 Authors' personal email communication with Ly Quoc Hung, Deputy Chief of Press, Publications and Public Information Division of the National Assembly of Vietnam, 16 July 2001 and 11 August 2001.
17 The government's Decree No. 161/1999/ND-CP, dated 18 October 1999, regulates the promulgation process in further detail.
18 Under Article 53 of the French Constitution, parliament must ratify peace treaties, commercial treaties, treaties relating to international organisations, treaties which commit the finances of the state, treaties relating to the status of persons, and those treaties involving the transfer, exchange or addition of territory.
19 Article 7 of the Japanese Constitution.
20 Some exceptions do exist. For example, treaties relating to the conduct of war or cession of territory. See Shaw (1997:112).
21 [1937] AC 326.
22 See, for example, Sampford (1989) and Keach (2003).
23 Personal communication [interview with Tannetye Bryant] with Nguyen Ba Son Zang, Department of Foreign Affairs in Vietnam, 6 November 2000. Also personal communication [interview with Tannetye Bryant] with Dao Duc Tuan, Director of the National Office for Climate Change and Ozone Protection of Vietnam, 7 November 2000.
24 See further Bryant and Jessup (2002).

REFERENCES

AusAID, 2001. *Vietnam: Legal and Judicial Development*, Working Paper 3, AusAID, Canberra.

Balkin, R., 1997. 'Chapter 5: International law and domestic law', in S. Blay, R. Piotrowicz and B.M. Tsamenyi, *Public International Law: an Australian perspective*, Oxford University Press, Melbourne:119–45.

Brownlie, I., 1990. *Principles of Public International Law*, Clarendon Press, Oxford.

Bryant, T. and Jessup, B., 2002.'The status of international environmental treaties in Vietnam', *Asia Pacific Law Review*, 10(1):117.

Butler, W.E., 2002. *The Law of Treaties in Russia and the Commonwealth of Independent States*, Cambridge University Press, Cambridge.

Doan Nang, 1998. 'Perfecting the legislation on signing and implementing international agreements', *Vietnam Law & Legal Forum*, May:18.

——, 2002. 'Right settlement of relationship between international and national laws', *Legislative Studies Magazine*, 5/6:39 (translated into English).

Fitzmaurice, G., 1957. 'The general principles of international law considered from the standpoint of the rule of law', in D.J. Harris, 1998. *Cases and Materials on International Law*, Fifth edition, Sweet & Maxwell, London:68–70.

Gillespie, J., 1997. 'Bureaucratic control of business regulation in Vietnam', in V. Taylor (ed.), *Asian Laws Through Australian Eyes*, Law Book Company, North Ryde:367–400.

Harris, D., 1998. *Cases and Materials on International Law*, Fifth edition, Sweet & Maxwell, London.

Jacobs, F., 1987. 'Introduction', in F. Jacobs and S. Roberts (eds), *The Effect of Treaties in Domestic Law*, Sweet & Maxwell, London:xxiii–xxx.

Keach, B., 2003. 'International law: illusion and reality', *International Socialist Review*, 27:n.p. Available online at http://www.isreview.org/issues/27/27.shtml.

Li Zhaojie, 1993. 'Effect of treaties in domestic law: practice of the People's Republic of China', *Dalhousie Law Journal*, 16(1):62.

Sampford, C., 1989. *The Disorder of Law: a critique of legal theory*, Basil Backwell Limited, Oxford.

Shaw, M., 1997. *International Law*, Fourth edition, Cambridge University Press, Cambridge.

Shearer, I.A., 1994. *Starke's International Law*, Eleventh edition, Butterworths, London.

Vu Duc Long, forthcoming. 'Status in the hierarchy of international treaties in Vietnam's legal system'.

Vu Thu Hanh and Alan Khee Jin, 1998. 'Country reports—Vietnam', *Asia Pacific Journal of Environmental Law*, 28:326.

14

The Vietnamese state, the Catholic Church and the law

Peter Hansen

In the village of Phuc Nhac, in the province of Ninh Binh, about 120 kilometres south of Ha Noi, stands a large whitewashed Catholic church. It is the worshipping centre of an active congregation drawn from the local population, more than 75 per cent of which is Catholic. Masses and devotional liturgies are frequent, well attended, and uninhibited.

In front of the church stands a small, somewhat neglected chapel, dedicated to the memory of St. Anna Le Thi Thanh (De), a Catholic laywoman martyred in 1841 under the emperor Thieu Tri, and canonised as a saint by the universal Catholic Church in 1988. The altar in the chapel bears the inscription

Sanguis martyrum
est Semen Christianorum

The blood of the Martyrs
is the seed of Christianity

This little tableau stands almost as an allegory of the present situation of the Catholic Church in Vietnam. Those who contend that the Vietnamese church enjoys total religious freedom justifiably point to the example of Phuc Nhac's thriving Catholic community, which goes about the articles of its faith—prayer, liturgy, sacraments, and catechesis—peacefully, unmolested and uninterrupted. The inscription in St. Anna's chapel, however, hints of another, different reality. The relationship between Catholicism and the state has through the *long duree* of almost 400 years, been fraught with conflict, mutual suspicion, antipathy, anti-Catholic persecution and martyrdom. The Vietnamese state has for centuries sought to use the law as a tool to regulate and control not only Catholicism, but other religions as well.

Many Vietnamese Catholics now see the church as suffering exactly the same persecution it endured in centuries past, its clergy imprisoned, property confiscated, and its vital functions—such education of the clergy—tightly regulated. The law, they argue, is the means by which the present Vietnamese government seeks to slowly choke life from the church. Yet, perversely, they are often keen to embrace— and perhaps even perpetuate—Catholicism's status as an embattled religion. The blood of the martyrs is, as the inscription tells us, the seed of the church.

Fundamentalist misconceptions bedevil understandings of the relationship between the church and the state. At one end of the spectrum is the view pushed by various *Viet Kieu* groups, that there is no freedom of worship at all for Vietnamese Catholics, making the practice of religion all but impossible. At the opposite end, the Communist Party of Vietnam and the Vietnamese government argue that the thriving and active church communities demonstrate the unfettered religious freedoms provided in Vietnam. The truth, as always, lies somewhere in between.

The relationship between the Catholic Church and the Vietnamese state is not governed well by the law, which remains a deeply imprecise and subjective instrument, capable of manipulation by either side. Similarly, while Marxist ideology has characterised humanity's religious/spiritual quest as illusory—famously, through the phrase 'the opiate of the masses'—this has not been the principal driver of the Party's or the state's attitude towards the Catholic Church. Although atheism remains the 'religious position' of Marxist ideology, and hence of the Communist Party of Vietnam, there is little to suggest that this ideological difference is the basis of their antagonism.

What factors, then, do govern the contemporary relationship between church and state? Historical antagonisms and earlier perceived wrongs continue to generate unease. Moreover, the Vietnamese church's desire to cast itself as a nationalist institution contradicts the state's desire to be the sole arbiter of the national history, the teller of the national story, and creator of national heroes.

But the law is an important instrument in the conduct of this historical–political conflict, capable of application and manipulation by both sides. I propose to examine certain aspects of the effects of Vietnamese law in the context of this debate and their effects on the operation of the Vietnamese Catholic Church as a religious and social institution.[1]

THE CONSTITUTIONAL CONTEXT

Article 70 of the 1992 Constitution of the Socialist Republic of Vietnam provides that

> [t]he citizen shall enjoy freedom of belief and religion; he can follow any religion or follow none. All religions are equal before the law. The places of worship of all faiths and religions are protected by the law. No one can violate freedom of belief and of religion, nor can anyone misuse beliefs and religions to contravene the law, and State policies.[2]

Provisions guaranteeing religious freedom have formed part of every constitution since Ho Chi Minh's declaration of independence in 1945.[3] Indeed, Ho declared on the first day after the promulgation of the declaration that 'the colonialists and feudal regime carried out [a] policy of division between our religious and non-religious compatriots with a view to facilitating their domination. I propose that the government declare religious freedom and unity between religious and non-religious people'.[4]

The unequivocal constitutional declaration that 'the citizen shall enjoy freedom of belief and religion' seems to support the Vietnamese government's oft-repeated claim that its legal system provides and enforces a regime of religious freedom and tolerance. Yet, dissenting voices contend that the provision is in reality a frail shield, so easily ignored, contradicted, and compromised by other provisions that it is rendered entirely hollow and meaningless. Where, then, does the truth lie?

THE CONSTITUTIONAL GUARANTEE AS EFFECTIVE

Even critics of the Vietnamese government concede that ordinary Vietnamese Catholics now enjoy reasonable freedom to attend liturgies and services at their places of worship (cf. Tran Xuan Tam 2002). Although Catholics may still face some discrimination at the local level from party or state functionaries seeking to restrict active church participation, the ordinary lay worshipper is nowadays seldom a direct victim of government restrictions. The views expressed to an *Agence-France Presse* journalist in April 2000 seem representative

> In Hanoi, the country's capital, as worshippers packed St. Joseph's Cathedral for Sunday services, Nguyen Thi Minh said how proud she was to be a Catholic. Minh, 58, said Vietnam's Catholics were free to practice their religion, but she was quick to point out that they still face discrimination. 'Although we are patriotic, Catholics have less opportunities to take important positions in society and in the armed forces. I hope this will improve in time', he said.

> Another church attendee, a 22-year old girl who asked not to be named, said plainclothes police still often monitor church services. 'All members of my family are Catholics, and I feel free to follow the Church, although I sometimes see plainclothes police walking around here at church services'.

> She added that Catholics still suffer from some stigma because of their association with the old Saigon regime, but she added that this was changing fast. 'I am happy to be Catholic, although sometimes it restricts my social relations,' she said. 'Some people are still careful about making friends with Catholics, because my father told me that during the wars, many Catholics followed and worked for enemies. But this complex is disappearing fast' (de Nerciat 2000).

Some critics of the government deride the significance of such 'superficial' liberty as nothing more than a smokescreen concealing the deprivation of any meaningful religious freedom. But such derision not only negates the government's view; it also infers that Vietnamese Catholics who feel their spiritual needs are currently being met (such as those quoted above) are deluded.

Article 70 is not entirely inconsequential. Whatever religious freedoms presently exist in Vietnam can be at least partly attributed to the constitutional protection offered by the article.

An important illustration of this constitutional protection is the tolerance granted to the local church's continued communion with the universal Catholic Church through allegiance to the Papacy. Although the connections between the Catholic Church in the Democratic Republic of Vietnam and the outside world were effectively cut between 1954–75, the Vietnamese state never required its citizens to renounce spiritual allegiance to the Vatican. In 1955, the government oversaw the establishment of an association of pro-government Catholic laity and clergy, the *Uy Ban Lien Lac Cong Giao Yeu To Quoc va Hoa Binh* [Liaison Committee of Patriotic and Peace-loving Catholics] (Denney 1990). This body became the Catholic affiliate to the *Mat Tran To Quoc* [Fatherland Front] and usurped many of the normal entitlements of the episcopal hierarchy, particularly in the realm of spokesmanship of the church. It still fulfils this role, although it has been known since 1983 as the *Uy Ban Doan Ket Cong Giao Yeu Nuoc Viet Nam* [The Solidarity Committee of Patriotic Vietnamese Catholics]. However, the association never set itself up as a church *per se*; it was always viewed by the state as an association that Vietnamese Catholics could join while remaining loyal in the spiritual realm to the established church.[5] Crucially, neither the government nor the 'Patriotic Association' made any endeavour to establish a parallel, state-controlled church, by ordaining bishops not in communion with Rome. The contention often made that the Vietnamese state claims the right to appoint bishops is incorrect.[6] Whilst they claim a veto right over Vatican appointments, and have on many occasions in the past exercised that veto in rejecting candidates proposed by the Vatican, they have never sought to ordain candidates not endorsed by the Vatican.

In this regard, the history of the Catholic Church under the Communist regime in Vietnam is radically different to that in the People's Republic of China. In 1958, the Chinese government first arranged for bishops to be validly but illicitly ordained; that is, consecrated by other validly ordained bishops, but without the approval of Rome (Tong 1993).[7] These bishops then pledged allegiance to the Chinese state and abjured allegiance to the Pope. Chinese Catholics were called on to follow this new 'Patriotic Church', with its parallel episcopacy, out of communion with the Vatican. Bishops, priests and laity who continued to profess communion with Rome—a profession deemed inconsistent with membership of the 'Patriotic Church'—were committing a punishable criminal offence and became known as the 'Underground Church' (Tong 1993).

To an outsider, these matters canvassed may appear semantic, pedantic, and inconsequential, but from a Catholic perspective, they are of the deepest significance. The Catholic Church believes that the gravest fate that can befall it is schism; that is, the division of the church. Schism threatens its universality, and thus its deepest sense of identity. Whereas religious persecution is to be endured (and perhaps even profited from), two millennia of church history provide innumerable examples of how the body of the church has been irreparably damaged by schism. In this respect, the church mirrors Vietnamese self-perceptions, whereby *mat doan ket dat nuoc* [loss of national unity], is amongst the most serious of allegations that can be levelled against history's less favoured monarchs.

What has all this to do with the Vietnamese Constitution? On one level, the original decision to permit Vietnamese Catholics' continued spiritual affiliation to Rome—almost certainly made by Ho Chi Minh himself—was a political decision, made to assuage Catholics, and to enlist their support for the post-colonial regime. Catholics have for three centuries formed a much larger and more influential segment of the Vietnamese population than in China. Moreover, Ho had successfully sought to ensure that Catholics were well represented in the broad coalition of social and political forces that comprised his government in 1945–46.[8] There is no doubt that these political considerations informed the constitutional assurance of religious freedom currently embodied in Article 70.

But the constitutional provisions also have their own efficacy. Any subsequent attempts to start a state-sponsored church—as opposed to an association of Catholic believers—and to forbid communion with Rome (as happened in China), would have been in flagrant breach of the state's own constitutional provision. In other words, the constitutional guarantee of religious freedom bolstered the Vietnamese church's capacity to preserve its most treasured asset—its membership of the universal Catholic Church. It is therefore difficult to sustain the argument that Article 70 is entirely worthless and devoid of meaning for Vietnamese Catholics.

THE CONSTITUTIONAL GUARANTEE AS INEFFECTIVE

At the same time, the contrary proposition—that Article 70 is evidence of the uncompromised nature of religious freedom in Vietnam—is similarly difficult to sustain. Its efficacy is compromised by internal inconsistencies within Article 70 itself, by inconsistencies between Article 70 and other constitutional provisions, and by inconsistencies between Article 70 and other Vietnamese laws.

Statutory interpretation of Article 70 indicates that its guarantee of religious freedom is not absolute, but qualified. The article's provision that no one can misuse beliefs and religions to contravene the law and state policies must be interpreted as derogating from an absolute guarantee. The phrase 'misuse of beliefs and religions' is indeterminate and susceptible of many interpretations. Could some ordinary religious functions, such as the Catholic engagement in social justice and advocacy for human rights, be regarded as a 'misuse of beliefs and religions'? The Catholic Church has long seen engagement in social advocacy, including support for the marginalised and opposition to structural injustice, as a fundamental role, entrusted to it by Jesus Christ as part of its emulation of his earthly mission. Yet, there is every chance that the state would interpret any endeavour by the Vietnamese church to fulfil this apostolic function as a 'misuse of beliefs and religions' under Article 70.

Article 70 provides no criteria as to what is considered a 'misuse', nor does it state who is to be the arbiter of whether a particular activity falls within the definition. Arguably, it was the constitutional drafters' intent that the determinative power rest with the Vietnamese state, with the church itself having no role to play. This potentially grants to the state the effective capacity to circumscribe what constitutes legitimate religious activity, and axiomatically, to place outside the bounds of legitimacy whatever it finds displeasing. This is not to say that the Vietnamese Party and state will always exercise this power in an arbitrary or totalitarian manner; after all, it currently tolerates a great many religious activities, which it probably wishes were not happening. Nonetheless, the connection within Article 70 between the concepts of 'misuse of religion' and 'contravening state policy', without causality, is of some concern. It suggests that religious legitimacy is contingent on congruence with the political and administrative aims of the ruling party. Taken to its logical conclusion, this renders religious activity an instrument of state policy; as, indeed, many statements from party and government spokespeople proclaim it to be. Such a view is so incompatible with the church's theological and ecclesiological self-perceptions as to render it permanently unacceptable to the church.

Reading Article 70 in the context of the constitution as a whole does little to improve the situation. Several other constitutional provisions may also be read as compromising Article 70's efficacy. As with Article 70 itself, their often benign appearance is compromised by qualifications or exceptions which render the provisions ineffective, or even retrograde, in the hands of any government with malevolent intent.

One constitutional provision often cited as an impediment to religious freedom is Article 4, which enshrines the leading role of the Communist Party of Vietnam. It states that

> [t]he Communist Party of Vietnam, the vanguard of the Vietnamese working class, the faithful representative of the rights and interests of the working class, the toiling people, and the whole nation, acting upon the Marxist-Leninist doctrine and Ho Chi Minh's thought, is the force leading the state and society. All Party organisations operate within the framework of the Constitution and the law.

This provision no doubt gives succour to anticommunist antagonists who would view the Vietnamese Constitution in an 'instrumentalist' context. Professor Mark Sidel, in his analysis of the Vietnamese Constitution, described instrumentalism thus

> [t]he instrumentalist theory is relatively clear-cut: Constitutions in Communist-Party run socialist countries have been, and remain, a means of political control by a single party, a way of expressing Communist Party political, economic and social policy in constitutional terms, a method for mobilising action, and a malleable document subject to redrafting and adoption by a compliant legislature as times and policy changed (Sidel 2002:42).[9]

The Special Rapporteur on Vietnam, Abdelfattah Amor, in his 1998 Report to the United Nations Commission on Human Rights, adopted a largely instrumentalist stance in considering the possible ramifications of Article 4 on religious freedom

> [e]ven greater concern is raised by Article 4 of the Constitution, which sets forth the principle of the Communist Party of Vietnam as the 'guiding force' of the state and of society. State policies are therefore those of the Communist Party, which has its own ideology with regard to religion, initially perceiving religion to be the opium [sic] of the people and therefore to be combated, and later evolving toward a special recognition of religion...

Whatever the ideology, the Special Rapporteur is of the opinion that, from the international law standpoint, the problems involved are similar to those of a State religion. If, for the sake of analysis, we take the Communist ideology as the 'state religion', the problems, in terms of international law, is not seen in relation to that given, but in terms of its manifestations. It is essential that that given should not be used to undermine human rights, in particular freedom of religion or belief (Amor 1998:paras 103–4).

If one takes an instrumentalist view of the Vietnamese Constitution, then its enshrinement of the Communist Party's primacy can be seen as having adverse implications for religious freedom, especially when that freedom might be used to the detriment of the Party's exercise of power.

However, 'state ideology' is not the same as 'state religion', and Amor is misguided in equating the two. To the contrary, the Party has always been emphatic in insisting that religion has no role to play in the development of state policy, nor the ideology on which it is based. There is, therefore, no theoretical inconsistency between a state political ideology, and the tolerance of religious pluralism. Ideology has never been the primary ground of contestation between the Communist Party of Vietnam and the Catholic Church. Party criticisms of the church seldom, if ever, make negative reference to Catholic theology, doctrine, or dogma. Exposition of the classical Marxist position on organised religion can nowadays only be found in obscure theoretical journals. And, as noted above, those same journals now sometimes endeavour to explain away Marx's views on religion as limited to a given historical-political context. Instead, Party/state criticism of the church concentrates on its historical antecedents, particularly its association with the French colonisation of Vietnam. While Article 4 has a considerable influence on the overall question of democratic pluralism within Vietnam, its influence on the position of the Catholic Church is largely theoretical.[10] The potentially more significant provision in terms of a constitutional threat to religious freedom is the punitive Article 13, which provides that

[t]he Vietnamese motherland is sacred and inviolable. All machinations and acts directed against the independence, sovereignty, unity and territorial integrity of the motherland, against the construction and defence of the socialist Vietnamese motherland, shall be severely punished in accordance with the law.

Although this provision refers specifically to the state—in contrast to Article 4's reference to the Party—the tight symbiosis between the contemporary Communist Party of Vietnam and the state makes it likely that threats against the Party are seen as threats also to the 'socialist Vietnamese Motherland'. Yet there is no suggestion that the practice of religion is in any way contextualised as a 'machination directed against' sovereignty. Provisions of the criminal code guarding national security have been employed against a notable Catholic dissident, Fr. Thaddeus Nguyen Van Ly, although the suggestion that his 'actions against national unity' were of a religious nature is open to question.

Another significant provision is Article 30, which covers the protection of national culture. The article concludes that 'the propagation of all reactionary and depraved thought and culture is forbidden; superstitions and harmful customs are to be eliminated'. The use of the term *me tin* ('superstition') is, again, typical of the ambiguity prevalent in Vietnamese constitutional and legislative practice. What does 'superstition' mean? How is it to be distinguished from religion? Who will judge this delineation, and what methodology will they use?

There is no suggestion that the Vietnamese government has recently used 'anti-superstition' provisions against mainstream Catholic religious practice.[11] Article 247 of the 1999 Penal Code gives some guidance as to how 'superstition' is to be viewed—'Exercise of superstitious practices: any person who practices divination, acts as a medium, or pursues other superstitious practices...'[12]

There remains a concern that legitimate religious activity may wrongly be regarded as 'superstition'. A Party statement in April 2003 declared that

> [t]he Party also recognises that there are many complicated matters in religious practices, which will create disorder and instability, and endanger national security. Many people and illegal preaching groups are taking advantage of local people's beliefs to increase superstition and disseminate hostile attitudes to erode great unity among the peoples ('Party publicises policies on religion and faith', *Vietnam News Briefs*, 25 April 2003).[13]

There is also a worrying prospect for overlap, whereby religious activities considered legitimate by the church nonetheless attract official approbation as 'superstition'. This problem most recently arose in 1998 at the 200th anniversary of the Marian apparition at La Vang. Vietnamese Catholics revere La Vang, a small village in central Quang Tri province, where in 1798, the Blessed Virgin Mary is said to have appeared to a group of poor woodcutters. Each year, on 15 August—the feast of Our Lady of La Vang—Catholics from all over Vietnam gather at the apparition site to venerate, commemorate, and celebrate these events.

Not surprisingly, the 200th anniversary celebration in 1998 saw even larger crowds than usual. The gathering of an enormous crowd not immediately under government auspices and control caused officials considerable consternation,[14] which was no doubt exacerbated by the political undertones of the La Vang apparition. The original events had occurred at a time of significant anti-Catholic persecution. The political message of the apparition—implied but unspoken in the current era—is not to lose heart in the face of state oppression, for the power of the divine remains with believers. These quasi-political implications troubled the Vietnamese government and, together with the event's tinges of superstition, prompted then Party Secretary, Le Kha Phieu, to claim that 'thrift is more important than festivals during difficult economic times' (Soloman 1998:n.p.). In other words, the La Vang anniversary did not fulfil a legitimate religious purpose.[15] A rationalist or utilitarian view can always find 'superstition' in religious ritual, and, while this has not yet occurred overtly, the provision remains a potential weapon if the Vietnamese government should decide on a more aggressively anti-Catholic stance.

No other constitutional provisions refer directly to religion, but several have a potential impact on religious freedom. For example, Article 33, which bans 'all activities in the fields of culture and information that are detrimental to national interests, and destructive of the personality, morals and fine lifeway [sic] of the Vietnamese', effectively provides a justification for limiting the church's ability to publish materials not in conformity with Party/state precepts. As will be seen in the next section, this justification is used extensively to ensure that the church—like other non-state institutions—has limited access to publishing and media.

Finally, there is a group of provisions concerning the duties of the citizen within the Vietnamese state that may also have ramifications for the practice of religion and citizens' religious rights. For example, Article 51 provides that

[t]he citizen's rights are inseparable from his duties. The State guarantees the rights of the citizen; the citizen must fulfil his duties to the State and society. The citizen's rights and duties are determined by the Constitution and the law.

Articles 76–79 provide that

76. The citizen must show loyalty to his motherland. To betray one's motherland is the most serious crime.

77. It is the sacred duty and the noble right of the citizen to defend his motherland. The citizen must fulfil his military obligation and join in the all-people national defence.

78. The citizen has the duty to respect and protect the property of the State and the public interest.

79. The citizen has the duty to obey the Constitution and the law, join in the safeguarding of national security and social order and the preserving of national secrets, and abide by the regulation of public life.

The above provisions are arguably capable of bearing a benign interpretation. Their cumulative effect, however, is to provide that the citizen's first duty is always to the state, so that where an individual's duties to church and state conflict, duty to the state must prevail.[16] This is not simply a hypothetical prioritisation. The Vietnamese state often stresses to Catholics that they are 'Vietnamese first, Catholics second'. This contradicts the Catholic Church's claims over the supreme allegiance of its adherents and thus bears potentially significant practical consequences. For instance, in the 1970s and 1980s, it was quite common for Catholics to be compelled to undertake *corvée* labour on Sundays, sometimes thereby preventing them from fulfilling their Mass obligations.[17] That the primary claim of church and state over Vietnamese Catholics focuses on notionally separate realms—the secular and the spiritual respectively—does not necessarily resolve the matter. For example, Vietnam has one of the highest abortion rates in the world, which can be at least partly attributed to the population control policies of the Vietnamese government (Haub and Phuong Thi Thu Huong 2003). How then can the church advocate its traditionally strident anti-abortion stance without contravening government policy? And on what basis should individual Vietnamese Catholic women make their personal choice?[18]

People the world over face potential conflicts between their religious and civic duties as citizens, but the cumulative effect of the constitutional provisions referred to above goes beyond this to effectively compel citizens to prioritise their duties to the state. Moreover, where the state is essentially conflated with a political party that harbours historical antagonisms and suspicion towards the church, the potential for conflict between religious and civic duties becomes all the more acute.

THE LEGISLATIVE CONTEXT

Ambiguity and resolution

The Catholic Church, well-organised and accounting for 6–10 per cent of the Vietnamese population, has always represented a significant potential challenge to the Party and the Vietnamese state.[19] The state deals with the Church not by seeking to eliminate it, but rather by regulating, circumscribing, and hence controlling it. It maintains a similar attitude to other religions. Antagonists of the current regime claim that, in so doing, the state hopes that the church will ultimately wither at the roots and die. The government, for its part, argues simply that it requires the church to follow the example of all other social institutions by submitting to the requirements of the law.

The legal regulation of religious affairs is nowadays principally embodied in Government Decree 26/1999, promulgated on 19 April 1999. It is in turn based on a directive of the Communist Party (No.37 CT/TW), issued on 2 July 1998, which directs the state to pursue a policy of regulatory control

> [t]he government will issue detailed provisions and guidance on the activities of religious orders and associations, fund-raising, financial operation, humanitarian and charitable actions, cultural and artistic activities, external relations, land use, building and repair of places of worship, training of clerics and religious dignitaries, and other activities of religions in conformity with the existing policies and laws.[20]

The Party's insistence that the state regulate religion is reflected in the preliminary provisions of the decree

> (3) Religious activities must obey the law of the State of the Socialist Republic of Vietnam.

> (4) Religious activities in the legitimate and lawful interests of the believers are assured. Religious activities in the interests of the Motherland and the people are encouraged.

> (5) All acts of violation of the freedom of belief and religion, all acts of misusing belief and religion to oppose the State of the Socialist Republic of Vietnam, prevent believers from discharging their citizens' obligations, sabotage the cause of unity of the entire people, and harm the healthy culture of the nation, and all superstitious practices, shall be dealt with according to law (Nguyen Minh Quang 2001:136).

All of the comments made above concerning the amorphous, general, and open-ended wording of constitutional provisions apply equally to these quasi-legislative provisions. How, for instance, does one define 'citizen's obligations' or 'the healthy culture of the nation'? If we were examining such legislative provisions within the context of common law systems, such as Australia's, such ambiguity could be resolved in a number of ways. First, one could look to definitional clauses that might further elaborate upon the meaning of the phrases adopted in the legislation. Second, recourse may be had to legal precedents, either binding (*ratio decidendi*) or persuasive (*obiter dicta*), indicating how the subject provisions had previously been interpreted by the courts. Or, in the absence of either of these aids, the courts can interpret the provisions, particularly to decide whether they were *ultra vires* by infringing on any express or implied constitutional guarantees or protections. None of these tools of statutory interpretation are currently used to any great extent in Vietnam.[21]

Further, the lack of a Constitutional Court, in particular, has been a matter of some recent controversy. The system provides no real means either to interpret legislative and quasi-legislative instruments or to adjudicate on their constitutionality.

In 2001, a Ho Chi Minh City newspaper carried a call from a delegate to the National Assembly 'for the establishment of a Constitutional Court [*Toa An Hien Phap*] to defend the Constitution...against the many forms of constitutional violation that at present cannot be investigated or adjudicated' (quoted in Sidel 2002:79). Legal scholar Nguyen Van Thao was even more direct in his criticism of the lack of judicial oversight

> [i]n nearly ten years of Constitutional implementation, we have never once seen the National Assembly or its Standing Committee abrogate, cancel, or suspend the implementation of a single document issued by the President, the government, or the Prime Minister. The system of monitoring is almost never exercised by the government or the Prime Minister with respect to the ministries or local authorities, despite the fact that some legal documents issued by ministries and local authorities evidently violate the Constitution or laws (quoted in Sidel 2002:71).

Such lack of resolution methods renders the laws and their interpretation more susceptible to manipulation on the part of an omnipotent state. Many would suggest that this is exactly what has occurred in relation to the Vietnamese government's regulation of religious affairs. Certainly, the specific regulatory controls imposed by the subsequent provisions of Decree 26 form the basis of many Catholic complaints about restrictions on the church's ability to operate freely as a religious institution.

The specifics of regulation

Chapter 2 of Decree 26 provides for the specific aspects and modes of state regulation of religion. Many of these provisions have drawn criticism as constituting a *de facto* impediment to true religious freedom.

Most fundamentally, all religions and religious denominations must seek the permission of the Prime Minister in order to operate legally.[22] Article 8 (5) provides that religious organisations 'which act in variance with the principles, objectives, line of worship and organizational structure permitted by the Prime Minister shall have their operations suspended'. Under Article 8(2), religious activities (for example, liturgies, prayers services, sermons, catechetical teachings) must be licensed annually or given specific permission per event under Article 8(3). Article 8 (4) provides that those undertaking religious fundraising activities must be licensed by local People's Committees. Further, according to Article 12, repairs to religious buildings, and fundraising for such repairs, can only be undertaken with state approval. Retreats and 'similar religious activities' must be in accordance with government regulations under Article 9; religious conferences must have state approval (Article 10). Finally, Article 14 provides that the printing, publication and the importation of publications and 'religious cultural articles' is to be regulated by the state.[23]

The formation, ordination, and activities of the clergy are also regulated. Persons unlicensed by the state cannot claim to be, or function as, religious clergy (Article 16). Seminaries must be licensed by the prime minister (Article 18(1)), and their activities supervised and inspected by state agencies (Article 18(3)). The bestowal of religious titles (for example, bishop, cardinal) requires the permission of the prime minister (Article 20), thus providing a *de facto* government veto over episcopal appointments. At a lower level, the appointment and transfers of clergy (to parishes, seminaries, agencies) must be approved by local People's Committees (Article 21). Clergy are obliged 'to carry out exactly their functions and roles in the domain of their religious responsibility already approved by the competent state management agency' (Article 15(2)). Religious orders must seek state permission to operate (Article 19(1)), whilst admission into monastic life must conform with the stipulations of the State Religious Affairs Committee (Article 19(2)).

The existence of religious charitable establishments and associations, while not prohibited, must 'operate under the guidance of competent state authorities' according to Article 17(2). The Vietnamese Catholic Church maintained significant welfare and educational infrastructures under pre-Communist regimes, and is now slowly re-establishing its presence in the sector through licensed activities in accordance with the article. Permission is still frequently withheld, however, and local authorities can effectively countermand permission granted by the State Religious Affairs Committee.

Given its particular connection to the Vatican, and the universal Catholic Church in general, the articles regulating foreign religious involvement are of particular importance to the Vietnamese Catholic Church. Religious organisations' international activities must comply with state policies and precepts (Article 23), and such organisations must advise the Religious Affairs Committee of any instructions received from 'foreign religious organisations', and then comply with any instructions issued by the committee (Article 22). Invitations to 'foreign religious organisations and individuals' must be approved by the Committee for Religious Affairs in accordance with Article 24. Foreigners wishing to undertake religious activities in Vietnam must register with local People's Committees (Article 25), and any aid received from foreign religious organisations must be approved by the State Religious Affairs Committee (Article 26).

Application of the decree

Whilst the situation of the Catholic Church has improved in recent years, and the overall trend has been towards greater liberalisation, these articles are not merely 'on paper' provisions. They are actively applied to control the Catholic Church and regulate its activities. The nomination of bishops, which requires prime ministerial permission under Article 20, was frequently thwarted, resulting in dioceses remaining vacant, sometimes for many years (cf. Brunnstrom 2000).[24] This situation has improved significantly over recent years, so that few Vietnamese sees now remain vacant. Local 'People's Committees' have used the decrees to refuse permission for priests to be appointed to parishes, or for churches to be built (cf. 'Vietnamese Catholics cite persecution amid success', *Fides*, 6 March 2000). Whilst the situation regarding the training of seminarians and the ordination of new priests has greatly improved recently, each of the six Catholic diocesan seminaries is restricted to only twenty students every two years. Admission of students to the seminary, and subsequent ordination, is dependent on their being vetted by the 'Religious Affairs Committee' ('An interview with Joseph Nguyen Cong Doan', *America*, 23 October 1999). This stringent requirement has led to severe shortages of clergy in some dioceses.

Restrictions on publishing are also actively enforced. For example, an attempt on the part of the 'Episcopal Conference' to publish its own permanent bulletin was quickly thwarted when permanent publishing permission was denied (Tran Cong Nghi 2001).[25]

As strident as church complaints have been concerning these particular provisions, they are in one sense all subordinate to the overarching provision that religions must be registered, and hence licensed by the state. The requirement that religious activity be approved by the state effectively limits the constitutional guarantee of religious freedom, confining it to a freedom to practice only state-sanctioned religion. In its 2000 'Report on Religious Freedom in Vietnam', the Bureau of Democracy, Human Rights and Labor of the US State Department concluded that

> [t]he government requires religious groups to register, and uses this process to control and monitor church organisations. The granting or withholding of the official recognition of religious bodies is one of the means by which the Government actively intervenes to restrict religious activities by some believers (Bureau of Democracy, Human Rights, and Labor 2000).

The Vietnamese government defends the licensing provisions, claiming that they assist in protecting religious freedom

> Virtually, 'freedom' and 'permission' in their proper sense are not contradictory. Across the globe, maybe no law-ruled state would demolish the administrative procedure of 'request for permission', which helps society differentiate between legal and illegal undertakings.

And the most important principle in this issue is that the State and law protect, guarantee and safeguard legal undertakings. 'Request for permission' is aimed to obtain permission, and permission entails the 'right to protection'. Therefore, failure to request for permission is tantamount to relinquishing a very valuable right; the right to be protected. Then, in what way is 'request for permission from the State' abnormal? (Nguyen Minh Quang 2001:117–8).

The answer to that rhetorical question lies in the falsity of the assumption that religious activity lying outside of the state purview should be regarded as illegal.

When religious figures seek to place themselves in conflict with the Vietnamese state over questions of religious freedom, however, the state does not use decrees on religion, opting instead to punish such behaviour through the criminal law. Both sides of the debate have sought to manipulate this use of the criminal law to their own advantage.

The criminal law context

Some aggrieved *Viet Kieu* observers accuse the Vietnamese Catholic Church—and especially its bishops—of being supine in the face of governmental pressure (cf. Tran Xuan Tam 2002). But there have always existed religious figures who, instead of striving for accommodation, consensus and agreement between the church and the state, challenge the *status quo,* and condemn what they perceive to be unfair treatment meted out to their religion. It is these religious dissidents that the provisions of the criminal law seek to affect.[26] It should be remembered, however, that such dissidents constitute only a small proportion of religious practitioners in Vietnam; most manage to find a way of operating under the regime, albeit sometimes an uncomfortable one.

Almost invariably, when criminal charges are laid against religious dissidents, they are made under the provisions of Chapter XI of the 1999 Criminal Code, which deals with the violation of national security. Some of the offences in Chapter XI are clearly defined and well understood in any developed legal system—treason (Article 78), espionage (Article 80), rebellion (Article 82), piracy (Article 83), and terrorism (Article 84).

Other provisions, however, are ill-defined and ambiguous, generating situations whereby actions that are currently outlawed would not necessarily be seen as criminal in other socio-political contexts. This in turn leads to allegations that these provisions are actively manipulated to achieve desired political or administrative outcomes. These amorphous provisions include 'activities aimed at overthrowing the People's power' (Article 79); 'sabotaging the infrastructure of socialism' (Article 85); 'undermining national unity' (Article 87); 'propaganda against the socialist system' (Article 88); 'endangering public security' (Article 89); and 'illegally fleeing to or staying in another country with intent to undermine the People's power' (Article 91).

The following case study, involving a well-known Catholic dissident, addresses the use of one of these provisions, namely Article 87.

THE CASE OF FR. THADDEUS NGUYEN VAN LY

Fr. Thaddeus (Tadeo) Nguyen Van Ly was born in Quang Tri Province in 1946, and ordained as a priest of the Archdiocese of Hue in 1974. He subsequently served as secretary to the Archbishop of Hue, Phillip Nguyen Kim Dien, himself an ardent critic of the Vietnamese government and campaigner for religious rights, who died in 1988. Ly had already served 10 years' incarceration; one year of *cai tao* ('re-education') from 1977 to 1978, and nine years' imprisonment (1983–92) for 'opposing the revolution, and destroying the People's unity' (see 'Archbishop calls for release of Viet priest', *Catholic Weekly (Sydney)*, 5 September 2001). Some time after being released, he was appointed to Nguyet Bieu, a small and impoverished parish of about 150 Catholics on the outskirts of Hue city.

According to the 'Free Vietnam Alliance' (not, it must be said, an impartial source), the current problems of Fr. Ly and his parishioners began in 2000, in a dispute with local authorities over confiscated land

> Soon after 1975, the Nguyet Bieu parish lost to the local agricultural commune 10,000m² of rice-growing land and 5,000m² of dry land, including 1905m² within the perimeter of the church. According to Order 297/CP, issued on November 11, 1997 by the Government, the commune must return the entire area of 1905m² of rice-growing land for compensation. In reality, however, the commune returned only 250m² of rice-growing land, and 250m² of pond surface. Not only that, it usurped an additional 200m² of land inside the church perimeter for an irrigation canal. After submitting many complaints to the local government for redress without results, the parishioners of Nguyet Bieu decided to redirect the irrigation canal around the church perimeter so that they can cultivate the lands inside of the perimeter as a source of income for the church's religious activities.

> In 16–20 November 2000, Public Security cadres arrived and prevented parishioners from removing the soil to the area to build the new canal. The people of the parish, however, continued to prepare the land beside the church perimeter for the coming growing season.

> On 4 December 2000, parishioners of Nguyet Bieu planted a large banner with the words 'We need freedom of religion' on the Church's land, in an attempt to intimidate Father Nguyen Van Ly. They uprooted the banner and threw it into the nearby pond...[27]

The scope of Fr. Ly's aggrieved response went far beyond issues pertaining to the unjust confiscation of parochial land. On 20 December 2000, he issued a statement—widely circulated by *Viet Kieu* sources—along with a subsequent letter to Pope John Paul II and other dignitaries on 11 January 2001, both of which condemned the Vietnamese government for its alleged suppression of the Catholic Church, its intolerance of religion, and its abrogation of the Vietnamese Constitution.[28] However, his most controversial and most internationally publicised criticism of the Vietnamese state came in a letter of testimony to the Commission for International Religious Freedom of the US Congress. At the time of the presentation—13 February 2001—two events of considerable political importance and sensitivity were in prospect. The first was the Ninth Party Congress, which was due to commence the following May. The second was the pending signature and ratification of a bilateral trade agreement between Vietnam and the United States. Fr. Ly, in his overall condemnation of the Vietnamese Communist Party/state, chose to address explicitly the issue of the trade arrangement

> ...The second matter that you would like me to contribute my ideas to is whether or not the US Congress will go ahead to pass the bilateral trade agreement (BTA) this Spring? How will this passing affect freedom of religion in Vietnam?

> I am only a priest, not specialising in trade and politics. I only stand on the viewpoints of a Vietnamese who loves my country enthusiastically, and is concerned about the human rights situation for my compatriots. I would like to contribute my simple ideas as follows:

> Vietnam is deeply in need of the BTA to develop its economy. In principle, I earnestly wish my country to win other nations' trust, among them the US, in order that it may soon move to prosperity, and my compatriots enjoy a civilised and developed society in all aspects.

> But if the Vietnamese communists continue to maintain a totalitarian dictatorship, do not respect the basic rights of citizens...then should the United States and other countries create more favourable conditions for Communist Vietnam to continue its dictatorial rule? It is only a minority group who will benefit from new conditions to prolong their power, and to the detriment of our miserable people, who get little from the BTA, and have to endure their fate under long-term oppression.

> (...) Therefore, if the US and other nations truly love our miserable people, are truly concerned about human rights, especially freedom of religion in our country, then the U.S. and other nations should not support the Vietnamese communists to prolong their totalitarian dictatorship. On the contrary, the U.S. and others should stop the Agreements [i.e., the BTA] that the Vietnamese communists abuse, and find ways to put hard pressures on them to bring about freedom and democracy for Vietnam (Nguyen Van Ly 2001b:n.p.).[29]

The reaction of the Vietnamese authorities to this highly provocative advocacy was swift. After receiving reports from the District People's Committee dated 14 February (the day after Fr. Ly's written congressional testimony) and the Provincial Advisory Council, the Provincial People's Committee of Thua Thien–Hue Province issued a decision on 26 February 2001, subjecting Fr. Ly to administrative detention (in effect, house arrest) pursuant to Directive 31/CP.[30] Directive 31/CP, promulgated in April 1997, authorises village-level People's Committee and Public Security officials to detain individuals without trial for between six months and two years (Human Rights Watch 1997). Article 2 of the Directive states that

> [a]dministrative detention applies to those individuals considered to have violated the laws, infringing on the national security, as defined in Chapter 1 of the Criminal Code, but [whose violation] is not serious enough to be prosecuted criminally (Human Rights Watch 1997).

There is notable concern about this article, as Human Rights Watch points out, 'because there is no criminal prosecution [under Decree 31/CP], the detainee is not brought to trial, and therefore there is no opportunity for legal defence' (Human Rights Watch 1997).

The Notice of Decision to detain Fr. Ly provided only a brief description as to why the detainment had been imposed.

> Reason for administrative detainment: Citizen Nguyen Van Ly has committed actions in violation of the laws, and harmful to the national security. However, it is considered that

Mr. Ly should be given time to be educated and favourable conditions to correct his mistakes. The administrative detention is, therefore, needed as specified by the current regulations.[31]

It seems Fr. Ly chafed at the restrictions that administrative detention placed on him, and he soon faced charges under the criminal code for breaching the terms of his administrative detainment and for having 'undermined national unity'. He was arrested in mid May 2001 and brought to trial on 19 October. After a half-day trial, he was sentenced by the People's Court of Thua Thien–Hue Province to consecutive sentences of two and thirteen years respectively, with a further five years of home detention thereafter ('Vietnam jails priest for 15 years', *Reuters*, 20 October 2001).[32] He was released into house arrest as part of the New Year amnesty of 2005. The charge that he had 'undermined national unity' was laid pursuant to Article 87 of the 1999 Vietnamese Criminal Code, which provides that

(1) Any person committing any of the following acts with intent to undermine the people's power shall be subject to a term of imprisonment of between five and fifteen years.

a. Sowing division amongst social strata, or between the people and armed forces, and the people's power and social organisations;

b. Sowing hatred, discrimination and division, and committing infringements of equal rights among the different ethnic groups in Vietnam;

c. Sowing division between religious believers and non-believers, between the former and the people's power and social organisations;

d. Undermining the implementation of the policy of international solidarity.

(2) If the offence is committed in less serious circumstances, the offender shall be subject to a term of imprisonment of between two and seven years.

Neither the court sentence nor the details obtained from the brief of the People's Procuracy gave any specific details on how Fr. Ly's actions had infringed Article 87 (Amnesty International 2003).

The imprisonment of Fr. Ly prompted condemnation of the Vietnamese state by *Viet Kieu* groups and by human rights organisations. The Free Vietnam Alliance claimed that

[w]ith world attention focused on the international fight against terror, the Vietnamese authorities quietly brought Father Nguyen Van Ly to trial in a closed-door proceeding without the presence of a defence lawyer or independent witness. Father Nguyen Van Ly had peacefully called on the Vietnamese authorities to respect religious freedom. His efforts received the support of Vietnamese and international friends...The harsh sentence against [him] is part of an escalating pattern of religious and human rights repression over the last five months (Free Vietnam Alliance 2001).

Archbishop George Pell of Sydney wrote to Vietnam's ambassador to Australia that

I formally protest Fr. Ly's arrest, and the long campaign of persecution and harassment that he and others working for religious freedom in Vietnam have suffered at the hands of the authorities ('Archbishop calls for release of Viet priest', *Catholic Weekly*, 5 September 2001:n.p.).

Unsurprisingly, the Vietnamese authorities repudiated these claims, stressing that Fr. Ly had committed non-religious crimes. A 'Voice of Vietnam' report concluded that

[i]nstead of focusing on religious activities, Nguyen Van Ly repeatedly broke the law, and was punished several times. Recently, Nguyen Van Ly conducted activities that disrupted public order, incited people to act against the administration, and undermined public order and security...He also urged his disciples to stage disruptive activities in the Truyen Nam Hamlet, and at the office of the Phu An commune People's Committee, frustrating local people and Catholic followers (Voice of Vietnam 2001:n.p.).

What lessons are to be learned from the case of Fr. Ly? First, his prosecution exemplifies how the explicit constitutional provision guaranteeing religious freedom can be made meaningless by the use of other, contrary, provisions. Some accuse the Vietnamese state of manipulating the legal process by applying national security laws to stifle religiously motivated dissent. Fr. Ly was, after all, a religious leader, who, in his antigovernment pronouncements, was conducting a campaign with a specifically religious purpose—to ensure religious freedom and tolerance for the Vietnamese Catholic community and beyond.

Such an impression is only accentuated by the vague, indeterminate and subjective nature of the national security provisions in Chapter XI of the criminal code generally, and Article 87 in particular. What does it mean to 'undermine the people's power'? What does it mean to 'sow division amongst social strata', or to 'sow division between the people's power and social organisations'? It is difficult to avoid the instrumentalist conclusion that they mean whatever suits the Party and government at any given time, convenient for silencing anyone, religious or otherwise, who would seek to speak out against those in power. Those who seek to condemn the Vietnamese government for their prosecution of Fr. Ly could argue that, in construing the provisions of Article 87, the People's Court of Thua Thien–Hue had no recourse to definitional provisions contained within the legislation or to precedents in the interpretation of the provision. In seeking a determinative outcome, the parties had no recourse to a Constitutional Court to determine whether the provisions of Article 87, as used in Fr. Ly's case, breached the guarantee of religious freedom provided in Article 70 of the Vietnamese Constitution of 1992, and was hence *ultra vires*. Such antagonists argue that the cumulative effect of these deficiencies provide for an arbitrary and manipulable application of the legal provisions, effectively negating the constitutional provision on religious freedom. This is precisely the position adopted by Amnesty International in naming Fr. Ly a prisoner of conscience (Amnesty International 2003).

But the Vietnamese government is not the only actor that can manipulate the uncertainty surrounding the provisions of the criminal code. It must be remembered that, amongst his many other actions, Fr. Ly wrote to the legislature of a foreign state (the United States), asking that they not enter into a bilateral trade agreement with his own government.

I happen to share two characteristics with Fr. Ly. First, I am a Catholic diocesan priest, and second, I am a citizen of a nation that recently negotiated a bilateral trade agreement with the United States (namely, Australia). If I were to write a widely publicised letter to the United States Congress asking that they not enter into a trade agreement with Australia, I am sure the Australian government would not take the least bit of notice. I am equally sure, however, that I would receive immediate, and possibly punitive, attention from my own diocesan authorities. The reason is that I would be seen to have strayed into areas of party-politics and public policy, which is outside my public role as a cleric, since they are not matters of a religious nature, even when that term is broadly construed.

Now, lest it be thought that I am criticising Fr. Ly for his pronouncements, or supporting the Vietnamese government for the action taken against him, I make it clear that I am doing neither. As Amnesty International stated, Fr. Ly was imprisoned solely for the peaceful expression of political beliefs (Amnesty International 2003). I do, however, suggest that there is a certain element of disingenuousness on the part of Fr. Ly's supporters in suggesting that he has been imprisoned for religious reasons, and that the action against him was part of a wider campaign to eradicate religion generally, and the Catholic Church in particular. It must be remembered that the dispute over the Nguyet Bieu lands, and his earlier letters of protest calling for religious freedom, resulted only in a house arrest. Whilst some would regard this result as iniquitous and unjust in a democratic pluralist society, it was only Fr. Ly's venture beyond religion and into party-politics that prompted the Vietnamese government to prosecute him under the criminal code. The mere fact that an act or statement comes from a religious figure does not make it *ipso facto* a religious act. Other Catholic dissidents—notably the Redemptorist priest, Fr. Chan Tin—have been no less persistent in their criticism of the government and their calls for religious freedom. Yet in recent years, none have been so harshly punished as Fr. Ly, perhaps because none have ventured so far into the political realm.

Fr. Ly's supporters are able to claim that the vagueness of the code's national security provisions enables the government to manipulate them against religion and religious figures. It is this very same vagueness that enables them to claim that he was prosecuted for his religious beliefs, when his actions were in fact not strictly religious, but political. Again, the treatment meted out to Fr. Ly would be rightly seen in any democratic pluralist society as an unacceptable restriction on political freedom. However, Fr. Ly's supporters can now portray him as a religious 'martyr'—a figure deeply symbolic and heroic to Catholics generally, and to Vietnamese Catholics in particular (see Hansen 2000). They point to his extended prison sentence as an example of religious persecution, when it is in fact the consequence of a specifically political action. This suggests that the Vietnamese Communist Party and state are not the only ones capable of manipulating the laws to obtain a desired political outcome.[33]

Furthermore, the government now seems under pressure to ensure that actions taken against religious leaders follow due process in accordance with the criminal sanctions prescribed by the law. In 1999, a Jesuit priest, Fr. Joseph Nguyen Cong Doan, imprisoned on dubious charges for many years, told the Catholic Journal *America* that

[t]he approach of the Government has softened somewhat in regard to religious figures who are accused in this way; the policy is now to try to settle the matter without a trial and incarceration. Agents of the Ministry of Public Security can no longer act with as much impunity as they did in the 1980s, arresting anyone whom they suspected and imprisoning them. Now they take much more care to follow legal procedures ('An interview with Joseph Nguyen Cong Doan', *America*, 23 October 1999).

RELIGIOUS FREEDOM—ALL OR NOTHING?

If the preceding analysis suggests that the law does not provide a complete basis for religious freedom for the Catholic Church in Vietnam, what is to be made of the competing 'fundamentalism' referred to at the start of this chapter, which argues that there is no real religious freedom in Vietnam at all? In other words, are we to conclude that these are contrasting ideas that cannot be reconciled? Or are there gradual differences between theory and practice?

In a 2002 critique of the state of religious freedom in Vietnam, a Vietnamese-American priest, Fr. Tran Xuan Tam, wrote

The VCP [Vietnamese Communist Party], using these relaxations and permissions, deceitfully causes in the mind of many superficial and inexperienced Western observers the impression that the Catholic Church in Vietnam today has a true religious freedom, though it may not be complete with respect to certain areas...However, this impression must be discarded as a false one. Religious activities cannot be mistaken for religious freedom, at least in the context of a country ruled by totalitarianism like the VCP [sic]. In this context, religious freedom for the Church must mean that she is completely independent of the Party and truly self-governing or autonomous in her own organisation, and in all her religious activities. Then religious freedom is not identical to the existence, kind and number of religious activity. Religious freedom is rather an intrinsic quality which every religious activity should have. No religious freedom can exist without religious activity, but there can be religious activities without religious freedom. Thus understood, it is obvious from my foregoing analysis that the religious freedom of the Vietnamese Catholic Church is still suppressed in essence by the Party (Tran Xuan Tam 2002).

There are several highly problematic aspects to this analysis. First, Tam concedes no credence to the legal rights granted to religious freedom and practice in Vietnam at present; even though underlying restrictions on the church remain in place, Tam contends these permitted activities do no more than create an illusion of freedom.

But drawing this radical dichotomy between religious freedom and religious activity makes no inherent sense. That Vietnamese Catholics can attend mass, receive the sacraments, read the scriptures, catechise their children, and be shepherded by bishops in union with the universal church, is no mere illusions. These activities are, for Catholics, very real and demonstrable aspects of their faith life in action. These activities demonstrate a degree of legal religious freedom that has continued to widen over recent years. To accept Tam's viewpoint is to regard the improvements in the church's situation since the late 1980s as illusory and insignificant. Yet, for Vietnamese Catholics, they are neither.

This, however, by no means suggests that religious freedom in Vietnam is complete. Insofar as religious activities remain tightly controlled by administrative law, and criminal law is applied against religious figures on spurious allegations of criminality, neither the Catholic Church nor other Vietnamese religions can be satisfied that their religious freedom is complete. But Tam's 'all or nothing' approach to religious freedom is deeply problematic. To contend simply that any restriction on religious freedom implies no freedom at all is to ignore the real improvements made in relationships between the church and the Party/state, and the increased tolerance the church has experienced over recent years. These improvements should not be overlooked, even if the Vietnamese state still seeks to control and to limit the church and its concessions are not granted out of a sense of affection and trust. If Vietnam were the 'totalitarian' state that Tam believes it is, surely even these concessions would not have been made. The description by Professor Carlyle Thayer—that 'Vietnam today is best described as an authoritarian state, not a totalitarian one'—is surely to be preferred (Thayer 2001:n.p.).

Tam's portrayal of the church as presently suffering from a crushing burden of totalitarian persecution—in effect, a sort of institutional martyrdom—must be viewed within its historical context. The Vietnamese Catholic Church's identity is deeply rooted in its suffering at the hands of persecutors over many centuries, a suffering which it believes has strengthened and sanctified it. Conversely, the historical antecedents of the Catholic Church, with their association with colonialism, party-political intriguing, and virulent anticommunism, have significantly conditioned the attitudes of the Vietnamese Communist Party/state towards it. The party–state's attitude to religion—and especially to Catholicism—is fundamentally formed by the historical experience of religion in Vietnam, and in particular by institutional religion's attitude towards nationalist and revolutionary struggles.

It is true that the doctrine of collective mastery—an inherent part of Marxist regimes—precludes alternative mass organisations, and that the Catholic Church can be seen as the mass organisation *in excelsis*. This has probably been a major factor in the Fatherland-Front endorsed Union of Patriotic Catholics' assumption of many functions—particularly in the realms of publishing and communication— that would be reserved for the church hierarchy in other societies. However, the reasons for this are not unrelated; again, the historical relationship can account for this development as much as the doctrine of collective mastery.

In most Party-sponsored analyses of Catholicism, little attention is paid to the truth or untruth of its spiritual or theological claims. What is canvassed at length is the negative historical antecedents of Catholicism in Vietnam, which led it to become (by this analysis) a tool of oppression, first in the hands of the ruling class, later in the hands of external colonial forces. In this context, Catholicism has been portrayed as the most reactionary and counter-revolutionary of all the religions practiced in Vietnam.

But some within the church can now claim that it is itself a victim of oppression, and is thus on the side of the oppressed, rather than oppressors. This is a direct challenge to the government's contextualising the merits of the Vietnamese church entirely in political and historical terms, without making allowance for either its spiritual dimension or its social contribution below the level of institutional politics.

It is therefore more than theoretically significant that, in recent years, state-sponsored journals have begun to publish articles praising the contribution of the Catholic Church to Vietnamese historical and contemporary culture and society (cf. Nguyen Hong Duong 1993; Huy Thong 2001).[34] These suggest a real acceptance of the Catholic Church's legitimacy in Vietnam, and even a concession to the church being a positive social force.[35] Such acceptance may in future be incorporated into the legal system, both in terms of legislative and quasi-legislative provisions, and the manner in which they are interpreted and applied.

The Vietnamese Catholic Church remains dissatisfied with the level of legal control exerted over it by the state, and it has reason to do so. This chapter, however, has demonstrated that recent changes have been largely positive. There are sound reasons for believing that these trends will continue if both sides can shake off the shackles of mutual historical antagonism.

NOTES

[1]   The legal situation of the Catholic Church in Vietnam, whilst distinguishable from that of other religions on some points, is sufficiently parallel to those religions that the conclusions drawn here have significant applicability to them. I have chosen to use the Catholic Church as an example of interaction between church and state, as I have a better grounding in its situation, and a greater access to sources, than with other Vietnamese faiths.

[2]   All quotations from the Vietnamese Constitution are taken from the English translation (Government of Vietnam 2001) available at http://vietforum.org/English/Documents/doc16.htm [accessed 31 March 2003]. Amendments to the constitution passed in 2001 did not directly affect Article 70.

[3]   Constitutions were promulgated in 1946, 1959, 1980, and 1992 respectively. For a brief history of the successive Vietnamese constitutions, see Sidel (2002).

[4]   Quoted in Nguyen Quang Minh (2001:110).

[5]   Indeed, it was initially Msgr. John Dooley, the Apostolic Delegate to Hanoi, rather than the Vietnamese state, who declared in 1955 that no Catholic could in good conscience belong to both the church and the 'Patriotic Association' (Denney 1990:274). Whilst this injunction is no longer in force, it is generally believed that only a minority of Vietnamese Catholics are affiliated to the Patriotic Association's successor.

[6]   For example, Associated Press reported in 2001 that 'Relations between Vietnam and the Vatican are strained because Hanoi keeps religious groups on a tight leash, and reserves the right to appoint Catholic bishops. Under Catholic canon law, the right to appoint bishops is reserved to the Pope, although the right to internal consultation is also provided to some national churches' ('Vietnam reacts coolly to naming of new Vietnamese Cardinal', 22 February).

[7]   Under the church's Canon Law (Canon 1382), any bishop ordained without the permission of Rome is illicitly ordained, and both the new bishop and the ordaining bishop are subject to excommunication (Canon Law Society of Great Britain and Ireland 1984).

[8]   In March 1946, the head of the 'Young Catholic Workers' Movement', Nguyen Manh Ha, was appointed as Minister of Economics. The Bishop of Phat Diem, Le Hu Tu, was appointed a 'senior advisor' and member of the High Council (Gheddo 1968:25).

[9]   Sidel goes on to call for a much broader frame of reference in interpreting the Vietnamese constitution than the narrow confines of instrumentalism.

[10] For a discussion of the attempts to delete or amend Article 4 at the time of the 2001 constitutional amendments, see Sidel (2002).

[11] Various charismatic sects may perhaps be less fortunate. So might charlatans, such as the group that allegedly tried to create apparitions of the Blessed Virgin Mary using laser lights ('Vietnam names three over fake religious apparitions', Reuters, 27 October 1999). Historically, the state's view of Catholic practice was less favourable. Elaborate, lengthy and costly liturgical

and devotional practices were regularly described as 'superstitious', and in some cases restricted or prohibited by local cadres. It was eventually the liturgical reforms of the Second Vatican Council, rather than government intervention, which saw these practices curtailed.

[12] All references to the 1999 Criminal Code are from Government of Vietnam (2001b). Disapproval of such practices would also accord with official Catholic doctrine, if not with Catholic folk practice.

[13] The pronouncement seems to have been made in response to unlicensed Protestant Churches working amongst ethnic minorities in the Central Highlands.

[14] Foreigners, and many of the *Viet Kieu*, were effectively prevented from attending. I applied for, and was denied, a visa to attend.

[15] Government attitudes to the event changed considerably as it reached its climax. The tone of official pronouncements became more favourable as time passed; they were, perhaps, eventually satisfied that the gathering constituted no political threat.

[16] This becomes clearer in the introductory provisions to Decree 26/1999 on Religious Activities.

[17] To the best of my knowledge, this now happens rarely if ever.

[18] Social policy questions can also bring church and state into happier alignment. The Vietnamese government has praised the Catholic Church for being in the vanguard of the campaign against 'social evils'.

[19] The Catholic proportion of the Vietnamese population is difficult to determine with precision (*Cong Giao va Dan Toc* [Catholicism and the Nation] *Magazine* 1995).

[20] All English translations of Party Directive 37 and State Decree 26 are taken from Nguyen Minh Quang (2001:125–46). The directive goes on to provide for the establishment of a government-controlled religious publishing house (2001:132).

[21] There is some recourse to legal precedent within the Vietnamese legal system, but of only very limited effect. The Vietnamese system shares this characteristic not only with legal systems in other socialist countries, but also other civil law jurisdictions, including those of most western European nations.

[22] This permission is presently provided to six churches: the Roman Catholic Church, the Confederation of Evangelical Alliances (representing Protestants), the Buddhist Church of Vietnam, and peak bodies representing the Cao Dai, Hoa Hao and Islamic faiths.

[23] Hence the reference in the Party Directive to the establishment of a state religious publishing house.

[24] Considerable progress, however, was made in this issue during 2002–3, with several important diocesan vacancies being filled.

[25] This problem does not prevent the publication of bibles, prayer books, liturgical texts and devotional works, all of which are regularly licensed. Its effect is largely to restrict publications regarding church affairs, which remain the domain of the 'Solidarity Committee of Patriotic Catholics', particularly through their weekly magazines *Nguoi Cong Giao* ['Catholics'] in Ha Noi, and *Cong Giao va Dan Toc* ['Catholicism and the People'] in Ho Chi Minh City.

[26] The spokeperson for the Vietnamese Foreign Affairs Department, Phan Thuy Thanh, employed a well-worn (and technically correct) phrase in telling foreign reporters that 'In Vietnam, no-one is detained on religious grounds, there are only law violators who are punished' ('Vietnam denies persecution of Hill Tribe People', *Deutsche Presse-Agentur*, 23 January 2003:n.p.).

[27] Untitled press release of the Free Vietnam Alliance, 6 December 2000. The Free Vietnam Alliance is a US-based organisation of overseas Vietnamese, associated with the pre-1975 republican government, who seek the overthrow of the current regime.

[28] The statement and letter are available at http://www.fva.org [accessed 15 January 2001].

[29] Fr. Ly went on to discuss, amongst other matters, the record of Ho Chi Minh, whom he came close to branding a war criminal.

[30] An English translation of the decision is available at http://www.fva.org [accessed 3 June 2001].

[31] English translation of decision at www.fva.org, last accessed 3 June 2001.

[32] The sentencing of Ly was televised nationally by the state-owned VTV ('Vietnam sentences Catholic priest', *Associated Press*, 19 October 2001).

[33] Interestingly, three strident Catholic critics of the Vietnamese government's attitude to religious freedom, writing at or after the time of Fr. Ly's case, all failed to mention him in their catalogue of complaints of religious intolerance (Tran Cong Nghi 2001; Tran Xuan Tam 2002).

[34] Previous praise of Catholicism was confined to the political role of 'patriotic Catholics' who showed their nationalist antecedents by opposing the feudalists, the colonialists (that is, the French), or the imperialists (namely, the Americans).

[35] Particularly in relation to the church's strong support for the government's 'social evils' campaign.

REFERENCES

Amnesty International, 2003. *Socialist Republic of Viet Nam - The Espionage Case Against the Nephews and Niece of Father Thadeus Nguyen Van Ly*. Available from http://web.amnesty.org/library/index/engasa410042003 [Accessed 8 April 2003].

Amor, A., 1998. *Civil and Political Rights, Including the Question of Religious Intolerance: Vietnam* (English edition), Available from http://www.vnhrnet.org/english/documents/amoren.htm [Accessed 25 March 1999].

Brunnstrom, D., 2000. 'Archbishop says Vietnam Catholics Face Problems', *Reuters*, 16 November.

Bureau of Democracy, Human Rights, and Labor, *2000 Annual Report on International Religious Freedom*, Bureau of Democracy, Human Rights, and Labor, US State Department, Washington, DC. Available online at http://www.state.gov/www/global/human_rights/irf/irf_rpt [Accessed 22 September 2000].

Canon Law Society of Great Britain and Ireland, 1984. *The Code of Canon Law in English Translation*, Collins, London.

Cong Giao van Dan Toc [Catholicism and the Nation] *Magazine* (eds), 1995. 'Cong Giao Viet Nam Sau Qua Trinh 50 Nam, 1945–1995 [Vietnamese Catholics after a process of fifty years]', *Cong Ciao va Dan Toc Magazine*.

de Nerciat, C-A., 2000. 'Vietnamese Catholics mark Easter with fervour, defiance', *Agence-France Press*, 23rd April.

Denney, S., 1990. 'The Catholic Church in Vietnam', in P. Ramet (ed.), *Catholicism and Politics in Communist Societies*, Duke University Press, Durham, North Carolina.

Free Vietnam Alliance, 2001. 'An Appeal to Oppose Communist Vietnam's Policy of Terror', Free Vietnam Alliance, Anaheim Hills, California, 19 October .

Gheddo, P., 1968. *The Cross and the Bo Tree,* Sheed & Ward, New York [tr. Charles Quinn].

Government of Vietnam, 2001. Constitution of the Socialist Republic of Vietnam, Government of the Socialist Republic of Vietnam, Hanoi (English Translation). Available from http://vietforum.org/English/Documents/doc16.htm [Accessed 31 March, 2003].

——, 2001. Bo Luat Hinh Su [Criminal Code], Government of the Socialist Republic of Vietnam, Hanoi. Available from http:// www.vietlaw.gov.vn [Accessed 8 April 2003].

Hansen, P., 2000. Making Martyrs: a study in Vietnamese church–state conflict, MA thesis, Monash University, Melbourne, unpublished.

Haub, C., and Phuong Thi Thu Huong, 2003. *An Overview of Population and Development in Vietnam*, National Committee for Population and Family Planning, Hanoi.

Human Rights Watch, 1997. *Rural Unrest in Vietnam*, Available from http://www.hrw.org/reports/1997/vietnm/Vietn97d-03.htm [Accessed 1 April 2003].

Huy Thong, 2001. 'Interrelation between Catholic and Vietnamese culture', *Social Sciences*, 82:73.

Nguyen Hong Duong, 1993. 'Integration process of Catholicism into the national culture', *Social Sciences*, 74:63.

Nguyen Minh Quang, 2001. *Religious Problems in Vietnam*, The Gioi Publishers, Hanoi.

Nguyen Van Ly, 2000. Letter to Pope John Paul II, 12 January. Available from http://www.fva.org [Accessed 15 January 2001].

——, 2001a. Letter to Various Dignitaries, 26 December. Available from http://www.fva.org [Accessed 9 January 2001].

——, 2001b. Letter of Testimony of Fr. Ly to US Congress Committee on International Religious Freedom, 13 February 2001, US Congress, Washington, DC. Available online at http://www.uscirf.gov.

Sidel, M., 2002. 'Analytical Models for Understanding Constitutions and Constitutional Dialogue in Socialist Transitional States: Re-Interpreting Constitutional Dialogue in Vietnam', *Singapore Journal of International and Comparative Law*, 6:42–98.

Soloman, A., 1998. 'Vietnam Party chief says thrift before religion', *Reuters*, 5 May.

Thayer, C., 2001. Statement to the Hearing on Religious Freedom Violations in Vietnam, US Commission on International Religious Freedom, Washington, DC, 13 February. Available from http://www.uscirf.gov [Accessed 16 February 2001].

Tong, J., 1993. 'The church from 1949 to 1990', in E. Tang and J-P. Wiest (eds), *The Catholic Church in Modern China*, Orbis Books, Maryknoll, New York:7–27.

Tran Cong Nghi, Rev. John, 2001. Letter of Testimony to the Unites States Commission on International Religious Freedom, 13 February. Available online at http://www.uscirf.gov.

Tran Xuan Tam, Rev., 2002. *An Analysis of the Vietnamese Communist Party's Suppression of the Religious Freedom of the Catholic Church*, Archdiocese of Washington, DC. Available online at htpp://vietpage.com/archive_news/politics/2002/Sep/30/0152.html [Accessed 29 September 2002].

Voice of Vietnam, 17 May 2001. 'Vietnam Arrests Catholic Priest for Defying House Arrest Order', *BBC Monitoring Service*.

Index

www.ingramcontent.com/pod-product-compliance
Lightning Source LLC
Chambersburg PA
CBHW050811270326
41926CB00062B/4583